EMERGING PERSPECTIVES
IN THE STUDY OF
FOLKLORE AND PERFORMANCE

EMERGING PERSPECTIVES IN THE STUDY OF FOLKLORE AND PERFORMANCE

EDITED BY
Solimar Otero AND
Anthony Bak Buccitelli

FOREWORD BY
Charles L. Briggs

INDIANA UNIVERSITY PRESS

This book is a publication of

Indiana University Press
Office of Scholarly Publishing
Herman B Wells Library 350
1320 East 10th Street
Bloomington, Indiana 47405 USA

iupress.org

© 2025 by Indiana University Press

All rights reserved
No part of this book may be reproduced or utilized in any form or by any means, electronic or mechanical, including photocopying and recording, or by any information storage and retrieval system, without permission in writing from the publisher.

First Printing 2025

Cataloging information is available from the Library of Congress.
ISBN 978-0-253-07273-3 (hdbk.)
ISBN 978-0-253-07274-0 (pbk.)
ISBN 978-0-253-07275-7 (web PDF)
ISBN 978-0-253-07276-4 (ebook)

*This volume is dedicated to
Alan Dundes,
our teacher and mentor. His forceful and cogent criticisms
of both performance theories and our own work helped us to
develop and clarify our own understanding of performance and
folklore. We also want to offer this work in memory of one of
our authors, Kit Danowski, whose creative and insightful work
on performance and ritual will live on to enrich scholars and
practitioners for years to come.*

CONTENTS

Foreword: Reopening Performance / CHARLES L. BRIGGS   ix

Acknowledgments   xxi

Introduction: Emerging Perspectives in the Study of Folklore and Performance / SOLIMAR OTERO AND ANTHONY BAK BUCCITELLI   *1*

I. Resituating Histories, Ideas, and Practices

1 The Weight and Lightness of Tradition: Interpreting Repetition in Folklore / ANTHONY BAK BUCCITELLI   *19*

2 Contested Ancestors: Toward a Genealogy of Everyday Life in the Postdiscipline / ERIC MAYER-GARCÍA   *37*

3 Minting Money: Queer Temporality and Performance in Ethnography / SARAH M. GORDON   *60*

4 Kenneth Burke Meets the Flop-Eared Mule: A Fiddle Tune and the Performance of Form / GREGORY HANSEN   *78*

II. Performance of Materiality, Virtuality, and the Spiritual

5 A Glitch in Time: Digital Interruptions and Spaces of Haunting / KIT DANOWSKI   *99*

6 Ancestoring: Materializing Memory, Mourning, and Resuscitation through Performance / SOLIMAR OTERO   *116*

7 Memeing Together: Performance, Competence, and Collective Creativity in Digital Folklore / SVERKER HYLTÉN-CAVALLIUS   *139*

III. Performance, Polyphony, and Embodied Knowledge

8   White Moral Feelings and National Affect in Audience Reactions to Danse du Ventre and Coochee-Coochee in the Late Nineteenth Century / PRIS NASRAT   *161*

9   Reverse, Rewrite, Reclaim Coloniality in Chicanx Flamenco at the Miss Indian World Pageant / ERICA ACEVEDO-ONTIVEROS   *179*

10   Queerly Beloved: Reflecting on Embodiments and Explorations of Gender and Pleasure through Tango Queer / CELIA MEREDITH   *194*

IV. Performing Community, Situating Dissent

11   Performing Together: Rethinking Definitions of Performance as Participatory Practice / KATHERINE BORLAND   *213*

12   A Framework for Analyzing Power and Performance: Music, Activism, and a Veterans' Anti-war Coffeehouse / LISA GILMAN   *234*

13   Spectacular Dissent / SABRA J. WEBBER   *258*

14   Performative Landscapes: An Exploration / LISA GABBERT   *279*

Index   299

FOREWORD: REOPENING PERFORMANCE

CHARLES L. BRIGGS

In folkloristics, performance perspectives became victims of their success. The notion of performance generated great intellectual excitement and sparked robust conversations across the humanities in the 1970s and 1980s. Springing from heterogeneous roots, it became a boundary-object (Star and Griesemer 1989) that provided what seemed to be a shared interpretive lens that enabled scholars in diverse disciplines working on a wide variety of subjects to be part of a shared transformative dialogue. Exchanges between an anthropologist, Victor Turner, and a theater director and scholar, Richard Schechner, were crucial in elevating performance to the status of a central organizing principle in their respective fields. Indeed, the discipline Schechner inspired is known as performance studies.

Nevertheless, what attracted each of them to performance was quite different. In folkloristics, performance emerged during an exciting period in which boundaries between anthropology, folkloristics, and linguistics were blurred as Dell Hymes forged an "ethnography of speaking" (later "of communication"). In 1975, Hymes (1981) and Richard Bauman (1977) published essays that brought diverse theoretical approaches together in presenting performance perspectives that galvanized folkloristics and linguistic anthropology. Performance also sparked excitement in media and communication studies, history, literature, and other areas. I remember being invited to keynote the annual meeting of an association dedicated to study of the Middle Ages in the 1980s. I responded that I knew very little about the period. Undaunted, I was told, "That doesn't matter—we want to learn about performance!"

In folkloristics and linguistic anthropology, what followed was a period of consolidation as these explorations became increasingly reified as the performance perspective or even performance theory. Performance became a key focus of graduate seminars and an obligatory passage point (Latour 2005) for graduate students as they moved through doctoral examinations. The concept became less a site for rethinking and transforming foundational analytics and more a formula that scholars could plug in to guide the description and interpretation of their materials. Performance became a Gibsonian affordance (Gibson 1997), rather like a stairway railing or the brace that cradles a guitar—so seemingly essential that, over time, it simply faded into the background, buried under a vast mountain of passing references. Productive critiques emerged, such as José Limón and Jane Young's (1986) call for more attention to issues of political economy, embodiment, and feminist perspectives.

Richard Bauman and I attempted to shake things up. Inspired by M. M. Bakhtin (1981) and other scholars, we tried to move discussions of poetics and performance away from a reified notion of the speech event to view performances as heterogeneous, polyphonic processes that were shot through with preceding discourses, ideologies, registers and that attempted to design futures (Bauman and Briggs 1990). We subsequently took a deep dive into genealogies of scholarly work on language and tradition to locate—and disrupt—ways that foundational concepts and practices had been reified and how they were fundamentally embedded in whiteness and social inequity (2003). However, our efforts to shake up intellectual genealogies and disciplinary canons often got framed as another orienting work for graduate reading lists and an item in citations that commonly appeared in the opening passages of theoretical introductions.

Emerging Perspectives in the Study of Folklore and Performance is, accordingly, a long-awaited kick in the pants of this process of reification. Starting with the elegant introduction by editors Solimar Otero and Anthony Bak Buccitelli, the authors use a wide range of analytics and objects of analysis to invite readers to rethink notions of performance and craft their own approaches. I see two axes as particularly valuable. One is that the contributors engage bodies of scholarship, issues, and modes of intervention that seldom entered into 1970s and 1980s formulations. They do not simply add such topics as materialities, embodiment, gender, sexuality, more-than-human perspectives, landscapes, and digital forms onto existing perspectives but use them in rethinking premises, modes of analysis, and scholarly prose. Intersectionality, critical race theory, queer theory, and spiritual and material agencies challenge assumptions about subjects and subjectivities that were often implicit in initial formulations (see Sawin 2002). A second productive axis challenges the lamentable way that foundational dialogues between discussions of performance in folkloristics and performance studies—with such notable exceptions as the work of Barbara Kirshenblatt-Gimblett (1998)—have largely given way to parallel disciplinary monologues. In performance studies, definitions of and approaches to performance have proliferated, spurred by such work as Judith Butler's (2016) and José Esteban Muñoz's (1999) powerful interventions. Beyond helping to connect conversations in folkloristics and performance studies, the essays in this volume hold the potential to spark new conversations about performance in folkloristics and catalyze valuable dialogues between folklorists and performance studies scholars.

The initial robust dialogue between the two areas was limited, in part, by the nature of the conversation between founding fathers—a term I use consciously here—Schechner and Turner. As a student at the University of Chicago in the mid- to late 1970s, my work with Turner and participation in his seminars gave me a close view of what drew him to this collaboration. Uncle Vic, as we called him, was deeply disenchanted with what he saw as the prevalence of detached ways that anthropologists related to their objects of study. He was passionate about experience (and a lot of other things). He wanted his students to focus on intense transformative experiences and feel directly engaged with them. A remarkable ethnographer, he sought to counteract the process of ethnographic reification that reduced anthropological knowledge to the consumption of ethnographic texts as detached fragments of distant worlds that did not seem to demand personal responses from readers.

This goal led Turner on a "personal voyage of discovery from traditional anthropological studies of ritual performance to a lively interest in modern theatre, particularly experimental theatre" (1982, 7). He credits Schechner for introducing him "to the workings of the experimental theatre" (15). Turner came to believe that "ethnographies, literatures, ritual and theatrical traditions of the world" could provide "the basis for a new transcultural communicative synthesis through performance" (18–19). Turner's desire for the transcendent and transformative—echoed in the deep religiosity that emerged later in his life—suggested to him that such enactments could enable people to transcend provincial cultural boundaries and appreciate "'other ways of seeing'" (18). Accordingly, Turner worked with anthropologists and actors to bring ethnographies to the stage, creating small theater-in-the-round enactments based on ethnographies. His goals were much broader: he wanted to change how anthropologists conducted fieldwork, what they studied, how they related to their interlocutors, and how they wrote and read ethnographies. I can still see his massive, bushy eyebrows dancing and hear his voice modulating symphonically as he conjured the magic of performance to instill this passion in students and colleagues.

I heard the other side of the story when I had the honor of teaching for one year in the Department of Performance Studies at New York University. There, I developed a dialogue with Schechner in which he talked about his collaboration with Turner. Given his generosity and interest in forging new possibilities, Schechner advised Turner and his collaborators on their efforts to stage works of ethnographic theater. He confessed, however, that he considered most of what emerged "bad theater." Turning an ethnography into a script and then finding actors to perform it seemed to reproduce the theatrical conventions he—as a remarkably innovative and avant-garde director and theater scholar—had challenged throughout his career. Schechner was working to disrupt "Western traditions of drama or dance" and move "beyond the idea of the performing arts as activities that take place on theater stages" (2016 [1988], 8). He sought to use performance as a means of illuminating "a broad spectrum of activities including at the very least the performing arts, rituals, healing, sports, popular entertainments, and performance in everyday life" (7). In his preface to Turner's *The Anthropology of Performance* (1988 [1987]), Schechner (1988 [1987], 7) says of Turner that "it is the mark of his generous genius that he never stepped back from thinking into a problem merely because he had no clear way out." I read this comment as expressing both admiration for his friend and a hint of ambivalence about the value of Turner's efforts to move from ritual to theater (Turner 1982) and how he endeavored to create an anthropology of performance. In a conversation in September 2023, Schechner confirmed his assessment of Turner's staging of ethnographies. Nevertheless, softening his stance somewhat, he asserted that these efforts had expanded the ways that ethnographies could be interpreted and appreciated.

As efforts by Schechner and others were transformed into performance studies, the disciplining practices enacted by its practitioners—like those of anthropologists and folklorists—have often reproduced the different directions that Turner attributes to the approaches he and Schechner brought to their years of conversation. This volume holds the potential for drawing on ways that folkloristics and performance studies have evolved and diversified, expanding the range of experiences and commitments that scholars can offer in forging new collaborations. Connecting the diverse set of perspectives and the broad range of issues advanced by the contributors to this volume presents me with a challenging task. In the interest of enticing readers by identifying some of the key insights the authors offer us, I would like to highlight two issues that might help pinpoint how they challenge received perspectives on performance.

Frantz Fanon (2008 [1952]) powerfully analyzed how language, medicine, the body, and healing are racialized. In his classic account in *Black Skin, White Masks* of being racialized as "a Negro" by a white child on a train, Fanon powerfully suggests that the voice of colonialism shapes the very nature of performance and performativity. Such racist performatives create ruptures for Black subjects through the imposition of definitions of Blackness "by the other, the white man, who had woven me out of a thousand details, anecdotes, stories" (111). Fanon articulated how it sealed him into a "crushing objecthood" in which he "found that I was an object in the midst of other objects" and burst him apart, only to have "the fragments . . . put together again by another self," a racist white one (109). He concludes that "my body was given back to me sprawled out, distorted, recolored, clad in mourning in that white winter day"—a mourning emanating from the social death imposed by white imaginations of Blackness.

We could frame Fanon's analysis of the child's speech act in J. L. Austin's (1962) terms as a primordial performative act of racialization. Nevertheless, Fanon's analysis suggests how Austin's seemingly deracialized performative acts are shaped by racial hierarchies. The racial injury that Fanon so poignantly reveals shows how performativity—when tied to racialization and racial violence—operates differently when performed by and on white subjects and persons racialized as nonwhite. In its foundational moments in folkloristics, performance perspectives often followed Austin in focusing on occasions when felicity conditions are met and performances are successful in achieving the outcomes associated with particular illocutionary forces. Like Fanon, articles in this volume are at least equally concerned with performative *failure* with the limits of performance and performativity (see Briggs 2022).

A second author who can usefully help us locate other valuable ways that these essays extend performance approaches is Julia Kristeva, particularly in her *Revolution in Poetic Language* ([1974] 1984). Kristeva distinguished between symbolic processes, which are mainly conscious and focus on signifieds organized by preexisting linguistic and other codes, and semiotic processes, which emerge from properties of signifiers, including the materiality of voices and forms of embodiment, that bring subjects into being beyond conscious control. I have used Kristeva and other psychoanalytic thinkers to argue that performances imbue dimensions of formal elaboration that unfold in performance, which Bauman and Briggs (1990) referred to as entextualization, with affective intensity and complex relations of embodiment (Briggs 2021). Poetic elaboration, including the deployment of faces, bodies, and gestures, provides an ongoing projection of internal states that, unlike referential properties of language, are more overheard by those around us. As components of semiotic processes, they provide performers and audiences with new types of awareness of how subjectivities, subject positions, and bodily entanglements are being produced. These papers offer fascinating perspectives on how affective dimensions create dynamic intensities of connection and disconnection in performance, even as they highlight dimensions of materiality and embodiment.

Eric Mayer-García draws on Fernando Ortiz's notion of transculturation and Inés María Martiatu's efforts to transform Lucumí and other Afro-Cuban perspectives into scholarly analytics in challenging Eurocentric assumptions in performance research. This move suggests the importance of changing the nature of the performances that get documented and the range of performers and audiences researched if the goal is to decolonize existing analytics. Mayer-García disrupts the universalizing tendencies in such foundational figures as Erving Goffman (1956) and M. M. Bakhtin (1981) by focusing on "conditions of displacement, duress, scarcity, precarity, and violence" (Mayer-García, 42) associated with the violence of slavery and conquest embodied in Cuban experiences of Blackness and Indigeneity. Solimar Otero's contribution similarly examines how the dynamics of race in Cuba provide productive grounds for rethinking performance. Rather than discuss how racialized histories are viewed through colonial lenses, as does Fanon, Otero traces a complex cartography of the ancestoring that takes place as Afrolatine religions turn dimensions of loss, mourning, and remembering into ways that "the body molds itself into a material source of memory" (116). These chapters extend Fanon's insights into connections among race, performance, and performativity by detailing how their entanglement fractures dominant temporalities and ontological binaries, revealing how pasts, presents, and futures and what are normally classified as humans, spirits, and objects can be copresent in the same bodies, spaces, and moments.

Sabra J. Webber pushes us to examine generally overlooked ways that performances can bring together pasts and presents of racial violence through seemingly minor variations in performance routines. She shows how performance-based interpretation can illuminate why quarterback Colin Kaepernick's act of protesting against police murders of Black people by kneeling during the national anthem at football games sparked a national controversy, white backlash, and his expulsion from the game in which he excelled. Lisa Gilman similarly pushes folklorists to document efforts to disrupt the mechanisms that sustain state violence by documenting a group of military veterans who opposed US intervention in Afghanistan and Iraq by staging a punk rock concert next to a military base. Their essays extend efforts to see how readings of poetics and performance can provide detailed critical cartographies of racial and other hierarchies and lay out alternative pasts and futures, as I attempted in my work with Spanish speakers in New Mexico (Briggs 1988). Both Webber and Gilman challenge folklorists to embrace social critique more deeply and eschew seemingly apolitical methods and analytics to contribute to efforts to counter structural racism and sexism.

Sarah M. Gordon and celia meredith draw on queer theory to question heteronormative notions of embodiment, temporality, research practices, and identities. Gordon's essay brings Fanon's discussion of failed performativity close to home—into discussions of folklore fieldwork and research trajectories, including her own. She looks at how fieldwork can require hiding queer identities and embracing linear scholarly trajectories that implicitly mirror images of heterosexual reproductive futurism. Meredith uses their own extensive dance experience to analyze how complex and intimate relations between bodies, space, sartorial materialities, movement, music, and the politics of gaze are transformed through their transposition into tango queer. She traces how dancers craft images that are both intimate and public as they are simultaneously oriented toward their partners, other dancers, and those observing. For Gordon and other contributors, the works of Judith Butler and José Esteban Muñoz provide an invaluable way of moving beyond early foundations in carving out new relations between performance studies and folkloristics.

Kristeva's analysis of how the semiotic—that is, embodied, nondiscursive, poetic modalities—and the symbolic operate both simultaneously and differentially points to important ways that these papers push performance perspectives. Gregory Hansen rethinks the work of another ancestor of performance perspectives, Kenneth Burke (1968 [1931]), whom Bauman (1977) and Hymes (1981) have acknowledged as particularly influential. Hansen keeps our focus on an instrumental fiddle tune, "Flop-Eared Mule," requiring us to listen closely to a piece in which form is everything. Hansen shifts Burke's discussion of form into a new key, reopening conversations about Burke and the place of form in performance. Buccitelli transposes the concern with form into an analytic mode, moving toward crafting new ways of thinking about performance and folkloristics. He captures how repetition, a major focus of Roman Jakobson's (1960) poetic theory, forms the semiotic core of performance in folkloristics and performance studies. Indeed, repetition—never for the first time, in Schechner's famous words—is a vital issue for performance studies and folkloristics. Buccitelli extends this discussion into affect theory, thereby challenging the aestheticizing and formalistic tendencies that have sometimes crept into performance approaches, as he analyzes how repetition shapes affective experience.

Extending conversations about affect, Kit Danowski focuses on racial spirituality in terms of how affective intensities and forms of embodiment "are not signs or signals, but the thing itself—the haunting is the shaking; it is in the body." Otero suggests that the affective intensities and material resonances that emerge in ancestoring do not simply provide means of exploring selves and connecting them with other humans but create assemblages that include objects, the dead, otherworldly realms, and musical ontologies. Pris Nasrat traces an Orientalizing trajectory that takes *danse du ventre* from its status as an ethnologized and sensationalized object to a form of popular entertainment on the streets of Coney Island to a target of legal representation and criminal adjudication in trials of "coochee-coochee" dancers. Clearly, there are shifts and conflicts between registers, which could be designated as ethnological, commercial, journalistic, juridical, moralistic, and pornographic. In keeping with the emphasis on the politics of bodies (or, as with Spillers 1987, of flesh) that centrally drives the volume, Nasrat traces affective transitions and conflicts corporeally in terms of their sartorial and fleshy dimensions and how bodies are classified in terms of race, gender, sexuality, and class. Tracing conflicts between symbolic and semiotic aspects thus requires a fleshy and political semiotics of performance.

Erica Acevedo-Ontiveros's opening description evokes a musical and corporeal dialogue between people identifying as Chicanx enacting flamenco and singers and dancers identifying as Native American as they perform jointly at the Gathering of Nations powwow and Miss Indian World pageant. This evocative description of a boundary-crossing performance suggests how semiotic dimensions complicate overt symbolic assertions of ethnic and other identities. Sverker Hyltén-Cavallius's analysis points to how representations of classical composers can be rooted in semiotic dimensions of sensuous engagement with performance practices and the training of the listener's ear. Opposing frequent emphasis on mastery of semiotic dimensions of performance and the development of heightened self-consciousness by performers, Katherine Borland draws on the remarkable work of Augusto Boal in rooting (post) theatrical performance in training persons without professional training to create ensembles through forms of bodily collaboration that "disrupt ordinary patterns of behavior and interaction" and "disable self-consciousness".

A number of the essays engage both Fanon's issues of the racialization of performance and performativity and Kristeva's analysis of the complex interpenetrations of semiotic and symbolic dimensions. Lisa Gabbert's chapter analyzes how symbolic dimensions are embodied in competing markers near the site where volunteer soldiers massacred Northwestern Shoshone in 1863. Persons who trace their genealogies through heroic narratives of settler colonialism and Shoshone descendants whose identities are shaped by stories of dispossession, violence, and trauma create competing affective landscapes that interact in precarious and shifting ways. In another example, "legend-trippers" turn the site of an abandoned convent into an "interactional landscape" (284) by using the symbolic dimensions of legends to add spine-chilling affective dimensions. Her essay might invite us to read the "no trespassing" signs posted there as attempting to regiment complex relations between competing symbolic and semiotic modes of constructing landscapes as much as to minimize material reinscriptions legally framed as vandalism.

Finally, I want to draw attention to another important way in which several chapters challenge received conventions of performance approaches in folkloristics. By and large, foundational works on performance vested creative analytic and ethnographic innovations in rather conventional academic prose that generally excluded the personal voices and experiences of scholars. In the chapters by Acevedo-Ontiveros, Danowski, meredith, and Otero, personal dimensions of the authors' deep engagement with flamenco, tango, and trance and ritual experience are not only made explicit but become part of the analytics they offer. Otero's writing challenges linear, monologic rhetorics to invite even readers who have no experience with Afrolatine ritual practices to feel the unsettling and unpredictable dynamics of the *misa*. Danowski brings the disruptive effects of the glitch into her text, shaking up academic readers' desires to follow a logical, linear rhetorical progression articulated in referential (symbolic) terms, thereby disrupting what "binary modes of thinking and being" (Danowski). They mark their movement among three voices—"the reliable narrator," "Lukumí and Palo ontologies and scholarship," and "the personal voice of the author"—by using distinct font types. Glitches become the analytic and rhetorical center of the chapter, thereby "challenging the discursive academic voice through counter-narratives that give primacy to the non-human (in this case, both spirits of nature, of the dead, and digital technologies) and the auto-ethnographic" (Danowski). Danowski accordingly models what could be more widely explored in folkloristics—explicitly experimental writing.

Beyond these particular ways of pushing the existing limits of performance approaches, one of the chief contributions of this rich collection of essays is to invite us to enter a significant reengagement with performance studies. The chapters make it clear that folkloristics and performance studies have changed significantly since Schechner and Turner's collaboration and the foundational contributions of Bauman and Hymes. These authors' efforts intersect with those of such scholars as Barbara Kirshenblatt-Gimblett and Deborah Kapchan, whose writing and teaching straddle folkoristics and performance studies, in crossing this disciplinary boundary. The contributors' positionalities and the performance studies scholars they engage demonstrate that challenging entrenched perspectives requires diverse new cadres of scholars. I hope that this volume will lead to collections whose authors are located outside North America and Europe. The book will certainly spark greater engagement with performance studies in folklore classes and will inspire students to explore the history and multiplicity of performance studies perspectives. *Emerging Perspectives in the Study of Folklore and Performance* will realize its potential if it not only draws scholars of performance studies to contemporary work in folkloristics but catalyzes new transdisciplinary dialogues that can exert transformative effects in both fields.

Bibliography

Austin, J. L. 1962. *How to Do Things with Words*. Edited by J. O. Urmson and Marina Sbisà. Cambridge, MA: Harvard University Press.

Bakhtin, M. M. 1981. *The Dialogic Imagination: Four Essays*. Trans. Caryl Emerson and Michael Holquist, ed. Michael Holquist. Austin: University of Texas Press.

Bauman, Richard. 1977. *Verbal Art as Performance*. Prospect Heights, IL: Waveland.

Bauman, Richard, and Charles L. Briggs. 1990. "Poetics and Performance as Critical Perspectives on Language and Social Life." *Annual Review of Anthropology* 19:59–88.

———. 2003. *Voices of Modernity: Language Ideologies and Social Inequality*. Cambridge, UK: Cambridge University Press.

Briggs, Charles L. 1988. *Competence in Performance: The Creativity of Tradition in Mexicano Verbal Art*. Philadelphia: University of Pennsylvania Press.

———. 2021. *Unlearning: Rethinking Poetics, Pandemics, and the Politics of Knowledge*. Logan: Utah State University Press.

———. 2022. "John Austin and Pandemic Performativity: From Cholera to COVID-19." In *Philosophy on Fieldwork: Case Studies in Anthropological Analysis*, edited by Nils Bubandt and Thomas Schwarz Wentzer, 66–83. London: Routledge.

Burke, Kenneth. (1931) 1968. *Counter-Statement*. Berkeley: University of California Press.

Butler, Judith. 2016. *Bodies That Matter: On the Discursive Limits of Sex*. New York: Routledge.

Fanon, Frantz. (1952) 2008. *Black Skin, White Masks*. Translated by Richard Philcox. New York: Grove Press.

Gibson, James J. 1997. "The Theory of Affordances." In *Perceiving, Acting, and Knowing*, edited by Robert Shaw and John Bransford, 67–82. Hillsdale, NJ: Lawrence Erlbaum.

Goffman, Erving. 1956. *The Presentation of Self in Everyday Life*. Edinburgh: University of Edinburgh Social Sciences Research Centre.

Hymes, Dell. 1981. *"In Vain I Tried to Tell You": Essays in Native America Ethnopoetics*. Philadelphia: University of Pennsylvania Press.

Jakobson, Roman. 1960. "Closing Statement: Linguistics and Poetics." In *Style in Language*, edited by Thomas A. Sebeok, 350–77. Cambridge, MA: MIT Press.

Kirshenblatt-Gimblett, Barbara. 1998. *Destination Culture: Tourism, Museums, and Heritage*. Berkeley: University of California Press.
Kristeva, Julia. (1974) 1984. *Revolution in Poetic Language*. Translated by Margaret Waller. New York: Columbia University Press.
Latour, Bruno. 2005. *Reassembling the Social: An Introduction to Actor-Network Theory*. Oxford, UK: Oxford University Press.
Limón, José E., and M. Jane Young. 1986. "Frontiers, Settlements, and Development in Folklore Studies, 1972–1985." *Annual Review of Anthropology* 15:437–60.
Muñoz, José Esteban. 1999. *Disidentifications: Queers of Color and the Performance of Politics*. Minneapolis: University of Minnesota Press.
Sawin, Patricia. 2002. "Performance at the Nexus of Gender, Power, and Desire: Reconsidering Bauman's Verbal Art from the Perspective of Gendered Subjectivity as Performance." *Journal of American Folklore* 115 (455): 28–61.
Schechner, Richard. (1987) 1988. "Victor Turner's Last Adventure." In *The Anthropology of Performance*, edited by Victor Turner, 7–20. New York: PAJ.
———. (1988) 2016. "Performance Studies: The Broad-Spectrum Approach." In *The Performance Studies Reader*, edited by Henry Bial and Sara Brady, 7–9. London: Routledge.
Spillers, Hortense. 1987. "Mama's Baby, Papa's Maybe: An American Grammar Book." *Diacritics* 17 (2): 64–81.
Star, Susan Leigh, and James R. Griesemer. 1989. "Institutional Ecology, 'Translations' and Boundary Objects: Amateurs and Professionals in Berkeley's Museum of Vertebrate Zoology, 1907–39." *Social Studies of Science* 19 (3): 387–420.
Turner, Victor. 1982. *From Ritual to Theatre: The Human Seriousness of Play*. New York: PAJ.
———. (1987) 1988. *The Anthropology of Performance*. New York: PAJ.

Charles L. Briggs is the Alan Dundes Distinguished Professor of Folklore and Distinguished Professor of Anthropology at the University of California, Berkeley. He is author most recently of *Incommunicable: Toward Communicative Justice in Health and Medicine* and *Unlearning: Rethinking Poetics, Pandemics, and the Politics of Knowledge*. He has received many awards and honors, including being elected in 2023 as a Fellow of the American Academy of Arts and Sciences.

ACKNOWLEDGMENTS

Bringing together any large project always involves the work, support, and advice of many people. First and foremost, we'd like to acknowledge the hard work and dedication of the scholars who have authored chapters in this volume. They have shown us both kindness and patience as we have worked to bring this volume forth. Second, we would also like to thank Allison Chaplin and Indiana University Press for their support of this project. Finally, we want to note that this book began out of discussions around potential panels on performance for the 2020 American Folklore Society Meeting that were followed up by a related working group session with the American Society for Theatre Research. We are especially grateful for the illuminating role Charles Briggs played as a discussant for a panel on the collection at the 2022 AFS meeting and for subsequently authoring the foreword for the volume. A special note of thanks goes to Maria Hamilton Abegunde for sharing her poetry with us for the volume. In sum, we appreciate greatly the generous input from colleagues and artists engaged with folklore studies, performance studies, and theater studies that improved this collection.

EMERGING PERSPECTIVES IN THE STUDY OF FOLKLORE AND PERFORMANCE

Introduction
Emerging Perspectives in the Study of Folklore and Performance

SOLIMAR OTERO AND ANTHONY BAK BUCCITELLI

Perry Miller, an intellectual historian of New England Puritanism and one of the foundational figures in American studies, once wrote that his graduate school mentors had cautioned him against "throwing his career away" by writing about the intellectual history of the Puritans of New England. "All that wheat had long since been winnowed," he was warned. "There was nothing but chaff remaining" (2009 [1952], viii). It is possible, we suppose, that we might be offered similar advice as we bring forth this new volume on folklore and performance now, just over half a century since a flurry of works of by folklorists such as Américo Paredes, Linda Dégh, Robert Georges, Richard Bauman, Roger Abrahams, and Barbara Kirshenblatt-Gimblett; anthropologists such as Victor Turner, Dell Hymes, and Denis Tedlock; and theater scholars such as Richard Schechner gave rise to what became known as the "performance turn" in folklore studies, as well as the contemporary field of performance studies.

Since that initial burst of activity in the 1960s and '70s, however, the diffusion of performance as both lens and key concept across a wide range of humanistic disciplines has continued steadily. Indeed, "performance and performativity have become fundamental new concepts in the humanities and social sciences" (Bachmann-Medick 2016, 77). At the same time, this diffusion has given rise, to some extent, to a much broader set of tools, approaches, and concerns as well as multifarious intellectual genealogies than were first proposed in the works of early "performance turn" folklorists, anthropologists, and theater scholars. "The buzz over performance is nearly everywhere in the Academy," D. Soyini Madison and Judith Hamera argue, which has resulted in "multiple paradigms and levels of analysis" (Madison and Hamera 2006, xiii).

Most notably, perhaps, the idea of performance itself has broadened considerably from the highly marked contexts of staged performance, ritual, or clearly framed oral narrative genre to encompass ever larger swathes of everyday human activity. "For many of us," Madison and Hamera write, "performance has evolved into ways of comprehending how human beings fundamentally make culture, affect power, and reinvent their ways of being in the world" (Madison and Hamera 2006, xii). Even half a century later, not only are new works that employ performance theories or analysis still incredibly common across the humanities and humanistic social sciences, but scholars still regularly position their work as part of a long but ongoing "performance turn."[1]

The purpose of this volume is to emphasize the ways in which performance studies and folklore studies have been developing both parallel and intersecting paths. Charles Briggs, in his foreword to the volume, reflects on this history and discusses the continued need for such work. Briggs's own work has long engaged in the critical study of how performances structure the relations of power that obtain among individuals, communities, and institutions in Latin America and the US Southwest (Briggs 2021, 60–61) as well as the workings of power that underwrite many of the core tenets and practices of scholars engaged in the study of performance. The authors in this volume follow suit by looking for bridges that cross the spaces between contemporary folklore and performance studies. For example, much of the work here is enriched by incorporating the influential work of hemispheric scholars like Diana Taylor and José Muñoz. In her overview of the field of performance studies in the US, Taylor observes that the "many uses of the performance point to the complex, seemingly contradictory, and at times mutually sustaining or complicated layers of referentiality" (2003, 3). It is in this murky yet productive context that we invited authors, scholars, and actors involved with folklore and performance studies to reconsider the ways in which performance is enacted in variegated terrains and temporalities, with special attention to issues concerning affect, the body, gesture, sexuality, materiality, and coloniality. The contributions to this volume range widely, exploring performance in the context of archives, landscapes, séances, disciplinary histories, courtrooms, football fields, dance floors, queer ethnography, old-time tunes, theater stages, pageants, coffeehouses, memes, and virtual glitches. The focus on folklore, especially the ways in which tradition, aesthetics, and creativity influence performativity, creates a throughline for thinking through the larger conversation being generated in this collection. That is, performance and folklore are coconstructed phenomena and frames that allow us to contemplate and contest history, community, and knowledge in embodied, spiritual, and virtual ways. This embeddedness offers a rationale for how the chapters that follow speak to such a diversity of forms and contexts, and to a variety of theoretical ends.

We consider how the concept of performance (or the related concept of performativity), with its stress on the processual over the textual, the "making" over or as the "thing," has contributed to reorientations in fields as disparate as gender and sexuality studies, literary studies, philosophy, economics, science studies, music, management studies, and history (Butler 2016 [1993]; Bachmann-Medick 2016, 86; Davis 2008, 1–2). As Tracy Davis observes, we might usefully speak not of one "performance turn" but of many, as "the performative turn is variously, fluidly, and playfully a turn, yes, but a turn that is ultimately a technique of dance (pirouette), leads to an unconventional routing (detour), champions social change (revolution, social or otherwise), bends for new use (deflection), proudly questions the culturally normative (deviation), like a sail propels us forward yet is obliquely positioned to the wind (tack), and though unsteady is wide open (yaw), depending upon what is apt" (Davis 2008, 2). But with this point we can also see one of the challenges that scholars with interests in performance-centered approaches have faced. On the one hand, the somewhat fractured and at times fractious pathways different disciplinary scholars have tread in pursuit of performance have given rise to a certain amount of conceptual and terminological disunity or, at times, discord (Lewis 2013, 2; Bachmann-Medick 2016, 76). At the same time, performance-focused research has often been defined by a very particular intellectual genealogy that typically runs from the ordinary language philosophy of Austin and Searle to the symbolic-structural studies of ritual pioneered by Van Gennep and Turner (as well as in a different way by Richard Schechner) to the symbolic interactionist sociology of Goffman and Bateson, through the works of Derrida, Bakhtin, and Kristeva on citationality and intertextuality and Butler's writing on performativity of identity (see, for example, Micu 2021).[2]

We should note that even though *performance* has been described as the principal keyword for American folklore studies (Bronner 2012, 23), folklorists have not always been part of interdisciplinary conversations on performance and performativity in a sustained way (with limited exceptions such as the works of Richard Bauman, Barbara Kirshenblatt-Gimblett, Charles Briggs, Deborah Kapchan, Amy Shuman, Dorothy Noyes, and Solimar Otero). Jill Terry Rudy has noted in her citational study of Bauman's *Verbal Art as Performance*, for example, that while articles in folklore journals and in *The American Ethnologist* were both likely to cite Bauman's article or book, articles in the latter were much less likely to cite works by Dan Ben-Amos, Roger Abrahams, or Robert Georges, all prominent folklorists associated with the same early performance turn in folklore studies. Instead, they tended to cite works by Bakhtin, Bourdieu, Derrida, and Turner, suggesting that "as the fields diverge from the concerns of folklorists . . . and the time from the initial publication of the article and book increases, an acknowledged association with folklore studies and the intellectual milieu of *Verbal Art* tends to decrease" (Rudy 2002, 19–20). While Rudy's observations highlight this issue with specific regard to folklore studies, the same problem seems to obtain in the interstices between other disciplinary areas engaging with performance as well. Doris Bachmann-Medick argues, for example, that "we should continue to view these clear lines of theoretical development separately because The Pioneers of the performative reorientation initially took different paths and set their own priorities. The resulting divergent generation of performance/performativity concepts in anthropology, speech act theory, theater studies and (poststructuralist) gender research, as well as in theories of ritualization and everyday stagings, did not produce a "homogeneous mélange" (2016, 76). While the production of a "homogeneous mélange" may not be desirable nor ethically possible, we take it as a central goal of this volume to reinvigorate the connection between folklore and performance studies scholars that was the hallmark of the early performance turn period. In doing so, we hope not only to reestablish the generative dialogue between performance studies and folklore that gave rise to so many fruitful ideas in the 1960s, '70s, and '80s but also to push folklorists to revisit some of the key concepts and intellectual lineages in performance studies in light of the more complex understanding of subjectivities, the body, and emotional resonances that have developed mainly outside folklore studies in the decades since the original performance turn.

In the study of performance as it has taken shape since the early confluence between folklore and other performance-focused fields, there has been a steady expansion of the contexts in which a performance lens can be applied. First, while much of the early work in performance and folklore was concerned with either forms of linguistic performance on the one hand or highly marked forms of ritual or theatrical performance on the other, there has been a gradual extension of the performance lens to more and more contexts in everyday life.[3] Second, a broader engagement with performance by scholars has produced a more varied and sophisticated understanding of the ways in which performance theories must account for contemporary concepts of subjectivity, including race, gender, sexuality, and ability.[4] Finally, the sustained attention to performance as a concept has promoted greater attention to a wide range of adjacent concepts, including practice/praxis, repetition, event, mediation, memory, mobility, materiality, enactment, affect/embodiment, ephemerality, tradition, and insurgent temporalities.

As one example of this expansion, folklorist Patricia Sawin has noted that the foundational unit of performance, the event, as it was established in early folkloristic performance studies scholarship, relies on a heightened sense of marking that distinguishes *performer* from *audience*. However, this kind of center-stage performance, she observes, has not always been available to or desirable for women. By defining its terms in this way, folkloristic performance theory implicitly favored the study of certain gendered subjects over others. She argues, for example, that "Richard Bauman's theory of performance has supported feminist work in folklore but proves incompatible with contemporary concepts of gendered subjectivity. Bauman's combination of formalist and behaviorist perspectives paradoxically de-emphasized and undertheorized audience and emotion. The threat posed by women's performance is better explained by exploring how performance constructs reciprocal positions for audience and performer, mobilizes desire, and motivates investment in gendered subject positions" (Sawin 2002, 28). As Sawin's comments suggest, recognizing contexts like gender in performance allows for a more developed analysis of the role of affect in situating the relationship between audiences and performers. In doing so, one can also ascertain the ideological formations that set the limits and possibilities of a particular performance.

In a similar way, performance-focused work in folklore has expanded from "artistic communication in small groups" (Ben-Amos 1971), a definition that stresses face-to-face engagement, to a variety of mediated contexts, most especially those enabled by or integrated with digital technologies. This expansion has prompted a rethinking of some of the key concepts in performance, including the temporal boundaries of the performance event, the ephemerality of performance, and the social boundaries of group performance (see, for example, Bock 2017; Buccitelli 2012, 2016; Lindfors 2017; Hyltén-Cavallius, (chap. 7, this volume).

As two folklorists who have engaged heavily with other disciplines, we have shaped this volume as a vehicle to stimulate the kind of reinvigorated interdisciplinary dialogue we would like to see take shape in the future. Otero trained as a folklorist at the University of California, Berkeley, and the University of Pennsylvania; teaches folklore and gender studies; works primarily on issues related to Afrolatine and Afro-Caribbean religions; and is a regular participant in the American Society for Theatre Research. Buccitelli, who also trained as a folklorist at the University of California, Berkeley, works in an American studies program and has taught and lectured regularly on issues related to the history and culture of technology, digital media, and communications. We have both written essays in the past urging folklorists to carefully reconsider established concepts and genealogies in performance studies (Buccitelli 2012, 2014, 2016; Otero 2022; Otero and Martínez-Rivera 2021), as we are both deeply committed to the idea that folklore has much to offer the conversation on performance but that there is also much for folklorists to learn through a broader engagement with the concepts, methods, genealogies, and practices that have been established in the many other disciplinary areas where performance has held sway.

In the first section of the book, "Resituating Histories, Ideas, and Practices," each of the four chapters calls for a further revaluation of key performance concepts, intellectual genealogies, or methods. In his chapter "The Weight and Lightness of Tradition: Interpreting Repetition in Folklore," for example, Anthony Bak Buccitelli discusses Søren Kierkegaard's essay "Repetition" (1843) as well as some of the ways that repetition has been construed in performance-centered works in folklore and performance studies. He argues that we should "conceive of repetition . . . not as existing in a single chain of temporal occurrences, but instead as arising from a rich social network of associations within which individuals give structure to their experience retroactively and develop a horizon of expectations for future actions" (Buccitelli). Using excerpts from a wide range of literary and philosophical sources, he observes the range of ways that repetition has been described in terms of weight/rootedness, lightness/quickness, and flavor/odor to make the case that scholars should pay attention not only to how we give retroactive shape to our experiences through repetition but also to the affective experience of repeated action. In doing so, he calls for "folklorists to consider not just the ideologies around concepts of tradition and how those are applied in everyday life, but also the rich set of factors that shape how people experience, interpret, and value repeated action in their lives" (Buccitelli).

Similarly, returning to some of the classic works that have defined both the folkloristic performance turn and performance studies as a field, Eric Mayer-García, in his chapter "Contested Ancestors: Toward a Genealogy of Everyday Life in the Postdiscipline," seeks to complicate and emend the conventional intellectual genealogy of the performance turn by placing the works of Mikhail Bakhtin and Erving Goffman, two of the theorists thought to be the most influential in contemporary scholarship on performance, into conversation with the works of Fernando Ortiz and Inés María Martiatu, Cuban scholars who have not often been included in standard historiographies. Focusing on Ortiz's 1940 articulation of a theory of "transculturation" as a revision of Redfield, Linton, and Herskovits's theory of acculturation, Mayer-García argues that "transculturation proposed a postcolonial shift in modern anthropological discourse and anticipated much of postcolonial, subaltern, and Afro Diasporic studies." He notes that Ortiz's concept cast a long shadow into the works of many later performance studies scholars, such as José Esteban Muñoz, Alberto Sandoval-Sánchez, Nancy Saporta Sternbach, Alicia Arrizón, and Diana Taylor, in helping to call attention to the workings of power relations within everyday processes such as remembering and performing. In doing so, it also calls attention to "everyday life [as] . . . an important site of renewal and resistance, a time-space where illicit practices are passed on, where life in postcolonial reality reveals the continuance of Black, Asian, and Indigenous cultures the colonial project attempts to destroy" (Mayer-García).

In relation to the works of Martiatu, Mayer-García also explores her concept of "Caribbean ritual theatre," which "straddle[s] the complex interrelation between sacred and profane," in order to demonstrate the ways in which Martiatu's theorization of these forms of performance calls into question many received categories in performance theory, including the divisions often made between special events and the everyday, the sacred and profane, the spiritual and the material, performance and ordinary action. Ultimately, Mayer-García argues, by integrating the works of these theorists into the defining canon of the performance turn, scholars will become better able to comprehend the "fluidity and immensity of communication."

Sarah Gordon's "Minting Money: Queer Temporality and Performance in Ethnography" contemplates the ways in which ethnography produces different kinds of performances and experiences of time. Effectively discussing the parameters of queer and straight time in the contexts of the fieldwork among cultural differences, postcolonial hierarchies, and discourses of sexual decadence, this chapter allows for reflection upon misperception and performance. Namely, Gordon asserts that "research, fieldwork, and ethnography: all are paradigms of performance, and we, ethnographers, assume a stage in their undertaking, performing various roles in service to the work we set out to achieve." She engages with how being queer in the field in Délı̨nę created opportunities for thinking with ethnographies by Susan Seizer and Zora Neale Hurston for their cultural reflexivity and personal reflections of liminality in transcultural encounters. Gordon also interacts with queer theorists Lee Edelman, Eve Kosofsky Sedgwick, José Muñoz, and Jack Halberstam to work through how performing ethnography as an honest and uncomfortable negotiation of power and difference may create conditions that are "queer in [their] revelation of new possibilities."

In his chapter, "Kenneth Burke Meets the Flop-Eared Mule: A Fiddle Tune and the Performance of Form," Gregory Hansen revisits the work of rhetorical theorist Kenneth Burke, often cited as a key influence in early performance theory. Using an analysis of the old-time fiddle tune "Flop-Eared Mule" as a jumping-off point, Hansen argues that Burke's writing on form "as a mode of action and as a social reality" demonstrates how "musical expression is mediated between musicians and audiences through the creation and fulfillment of expectations." Furthermore, in making a theoretical distinction between the "psychology of form" and the "psychology of information," Burkean theory offers an explanatory structure for understanding why certain expressive forms remain appealing in repeated performance and others do not. Ultimately, Hansen claims that "by grounding a formal analysis of artistry with a deep engagement in the processes of aesthetic experience, Burkean analysis gives us new ways to think about form within the wider rubric of performance theory."

The second section of this volume is entitled "Performance of Materiality, Virtuality, and the Spiritual." In this section, three authors—Kit Danowski, Solimar Otero, and Sverker Hyltén-Cavallius—use their very different studies of performances to call attention to and complicate our understanding of the binaries of the virtual and the actual, the spiritual and the material, into which reality is often divided. Collectively, this section urges readers to think about performance's role in making space for a continuum between these different axes of experience.

In his experimental chapter, "A Glitch in Time: Digital Interruptions and Spaces of Haunting," Kit Danowski reflects on the experience of glitches in digital communication, in which the "presenter's face freezes in the middle of a sentence, and the rest of us are pulled out of an affect of politely paying attention into something spontaneous," to the experience of spirit possession in Afrolatine ritual contexts. This move intends to consider "the glitch in its brief history as an art form, and trace how it mirrors and anticipates phenomenological experiences of time and identity." Ultimately, Danowski argues, by studying the role of glitches and glitching in digital communications, as well as their continuities with other forms of phenomenological experience, we are better able to push "toward a methodology for making performance that might incorporate glitch as an artistic strategy for work that embraces multiplicity and polyvocality." After all, it is through glitching that the process of sociotechnological communication itself comes back into our conscious awareness, shedding the skin of naturalness and becoming a moment when "two or more ontologies are attempting to occupy one space" or when disruptions to the ordinary flow of discourse might come to be seen as a moment of haunting, of spiritual contact.

Solimar Otero picks up on similar themes in her chapter, "Ancestoring: Materializing Memory, Mourning, and Resuscitation through Performance." Focusing on a performance of the Cuban spirit medium's song "El Congo de Guinea" and a reading of Maria Hamilton Abegund's poem "Learning to Eat the Dead: USA," Otero examines the practice of "ancestoring" in Afrolatine religions, in which the "body molds itself into material source of memory." In essence, through the cultivation of certain kinds of material forms and bodily sensations and experiences, practitioners "create sensorial conduits that produce ancestors in performance." This process, Otero argues, involves the confluence of bodies through shared subjectivities, histories, and acts of cultural creation that offer new materialities and possibilities for world-making through Black performance.

In his chapter, "Memeing Together: Performance, Competence, and Collective Creativity in Digital Folklore," Sverker Hyltén-Cavallius takes on another kind of collaborative-competitive mediated performance—what he calls "joint memeing," a term that builds on Katharine Young's concept of "joint storytelling" (Young 1987). Centering his research on r/classicalmemes, a rarefied internet subcultural space in which classical music and musicians are discussed and parodied through internet memes, Hyltén-Cavallius argues that the constant churn of discussion, creation, remixing, and remediation that occurs in that forum reflects both elements of social competition and collaboration, ultimately building a shared interpretive framework through which the meaning of musical compositions (or composers) is constantly being revised. Ultimately, the provisional frameworks of meaning that have taken shape within this online space are ambivalent. On the one hand, they often "'take down' elevated composers from a well-established canon of primarily male, European composers and make fun of them," but on the other hand, they also "evoke a rather dark image of a world of competition, from musical works to sexual attractiveness, and a dangerous intertwining of professional hierarchies and sexuality."[5]

The third section of the volume, "Performance, Polyphony, and Embodied Knowledge," continues to explore themes of multivocality, virtuality, and materiality or embodiment raised in the previous section. These chapters rely on the relationship between affect and the body to negotiate how performances mark the parameters of pleasure, racialization, and gender. In works that look at how dance encapsulates the ephemeral and material nature of performing place, of locating contexts that are fleeting yet pronounced, the authors in this portion of the volume rely on sensing specific practices in analyzing larger historical and social disruptions. Performances of the coochee-coochee, Chicanx Flamenco, and Tango Queer illuminate the ways in which the body tells stories that are polyphonic, syncopated, and deeply embedded in cultural contestations.

The lead chapter by Pris Nasrat, "White Moral Feelings and National Affect in Audience Reactions to Danse du Ventre and coochee-coochee in the Late Nineteenth Century," delves into archived performances of Orientalism in a nineteenth-century courtroom. They explore how the coochee-coochee dance represented pleasure and the policing of that pleasure for a range of audiences in Coney Island. Meticulously referring to newspaper articles of the day, Nasrat uncovers how one policeman's performance of the dance at a trial created a mediated sensation that reverberated with the public. Utilizing Xine Yao's term *unfeeling*, this piece further situates different modes of affect for minority and majority performers and public of the coochee-coochee dance. The implications of this historical review are rich and many, with Nasrat reflecting upon the ways that the dance coproduced whiteness and Asian-ness, masculinities, and what we may now call queerness in the era.

In a different kind of cocreation through dance and music, Erica Acevedo-Ontiveros considers the limits and possibilities of performing ethnic identity in "Reverse, Rewrite, Reclaim Coloniality in Chicanx Flamenco at the Miss Indian World Pageant." The chapter documents and analyzes the performance of the National Institute of Flamenco dance troupe alongside professional powwow drummers at the Gathering of Nations in Albuquerque, New Mexico, in 2018. Taking Gerald Vizenor's idea of survivance, Acevedo-Ontiveros considers how the dances offer opportunities for the body to reformat the "narrative of colonization" for both performers and audiences. The reformulated narratives produced by the creative coconstruction of dance and drumming can be understood as an intervention, one referred to in the piece as a *no sé que*, a structure of feeling left as an open framework for continued collaboration.

Celia meredith's exploration of "tango queer" in their chapter "Queerly Beloved: Reflecting on Embodiments and Explorations of Gender and Pleasure through Tango Queer" likewise delves into the potentiality of marking specific movements. In careful attention to tango choreographies and gestures, the piece offers ways to imagine nonbinary intimacies in a dance highly structured to perform gender. In researching the piece during the height of the COVID-19 pandemic, meredith's performative autoethnographic exploration of how to tango alone, through memory and video performance, offers a way to understand the pleasure of performing genre and gender that is queer and future-oriented.

The volume's last section, "Performing Community, Situating Dissent," contains chapters that put the notions of community and place in dialogue with social action and protest. Authors Katherine Borland, Lisa Gilman, Sabra J. Webber, and Lisa Gabbert take a critical look at performance's potential for cultural and material transformations. When taken as a whole, these pieces invite engagements with participatory forms of research. Their reflections reveal the embedded nature of performance in enacting both intimate and public forms of dissidence because of the symbolic power of marked action. Whether it is rethinking movement or reorienting the sense of place, communities in performance offer powerful moments of world-making that produce tangible effects in the world.

Borland's chapter, "Performing Together: Rethinking Definitions of Performance as Participatory Practice," reviews foundational texts in theater and dance alongside an ethnographic exploration of practice-based performances geared toward social justice. Working with Richard Schechner, Augusto Boal, and Liz Lerman, she illustrates how practice-based performances highlight the "operations of social inequality." In doing so, Borland demonstrates that a behavior-based approach stemming from collaborative action among students performing in the Be the Street collective created unique opportunities for actors to produce social change through targeted movement. This approach grew out of interaction with similar action-oriented theater groups, like Teatro Travieso directed by Jimmy Noriega, that illustrate the transnationality of such initiatives.

The next chapter, "A Framework for Analyzing Power and Performance: Music, Activism, and a Veterans' Anti-war Coffeehouse" by Lisa Gilman, similarly grapples with performance as a strategic tool of protest and transformation. Her analysis of what she sees as "P/power and P/performance" in both informal and official expressions is inspired by Beverly Stoeltje's work on power, ritual, and competition (1996). Looking at a Coffee Strong punk show attended by US veterans on July 4, 2009, in Lakewood, Washington, Gilman calls for socially engaged scholarship that pays attention to the entangled layers of the manifestation of power in performance. Her careful attention to the informal and formal production of punk performances and milieus at the show uncovers how social stratification can be reaffirmed and deconstructed simultaneously.

Like Gilman's chapter, Sabra J. Webber's chapter explores the complex countervalences of what happens in intense moments of protest that also leave reverberations of social challenges yet to be met. Her chapter, "Spectacular Dissent," offers an important challenge to the primacy that verbal performance has often had in performance studies undertaken by folklorists. Webber zeros in on two important moments of political protest in highly mediatized sports events: Tommie Smith and John Carlos's display of the Black Power hand gesture during the 1968 Mexico City Olympics and Colin Kaepernick's kneeling protest during the American national anthem at an NFL football game in 2016. She argues that in both cases, the athletes drew on shared traditions of expressivity but chose gestures and styles that intentionally conflicted with the noise and chaos of these mass media sports events. In this way, the "familiar practice of taking a knee," so common and commonly understood among professional athletes to signal a moment of quietude or breakage in play, is "suddenly out of place." However, as Webber rightly notes, quoting Dorothy Roberts, "silence is not just the absence of voice; silence is 'an interactive process' that responds to the conduct of other human beings." The most effective performance of protest these athletes could undertake under those expressive (and oppressive) conditions was not to shout but to remain silent in a way that spoke.

The last chapter in this collection, "Performative Landscapes: An Exploration" by Lisa Gabbert, creates an opportunity to consider place as performative on its own terms. She sees landscapes through a performative orientation borrowed from geographers but developed through the lens of folklore and performance studies. In a thoughtful review of aspects of these disciplines that inform her analysis, Gabbert identifies features like audience, framing, discursivity, and script as elements that reveal how landscapes are emergent as performances. She also opens the possibility of seeing landscapes as assemblages where "the animal, mineral, human, and nonhuman realms gather together and in which a notion of congregational or distributive agency can be applied." This expansive view of community and performance decenters the human as the sole actor in performance, a provocative notion that encapsulates the frictive and action-oriented chapters in this final section of the book.

Emerging Perspectives in the Study of Folklore and Performance is ultimately an invitation. The chapters offered in this volume illustrate that there is still much left to be discussed in terms of how folklore and performance studies inform each other as approaches, disciplines, and foci of study. The array of contexts for our explorations indicates a transnational and actively situated place for thinking and doing folklore and performance in ways that make us reconsider how we move in the world and the effects of this movement. This volume's discussion of the intersection of folklore and performance in resituating histories, materiality, virtual worlds, spiritual terrains, embodied knowledge, and social transformation will hopefully inspire similar collaborations. The connections made here and to be continued are generative, especially as performance perpetually emerges out of the intersections of scholarship, art, and practice.

Notes

1. See, for example, Larsen and Urry (2011), who are engaging with an ongoing "performance turn" in tourism studies that began in the later 1990s with works like Tim Edensor's *Tourists at the Taj: Performance and Meaning at a Symbolic Site* and his 2001 article "Staging Tourism: Tourists as Performer." See also digital media scholars Leeker, Schipper, and Beyes, who position their work as part of a "wider 'performative turn' in the cultural and social sciences'" (2017, 9).

2. It might be added, however, that a wide variety of earlier precursors to performance theories have been put forward by different scholars in different disciplinary areas. These include Walter Benjamin, Kenneth Burke, Clifford

Geertz, Milman Parry, Roman Jakobsen, and John Dewey, just to name a few. It is also notable, of course, that scholars such as D. Soyini Madison (1993), Diana Taylor (2003), E. Patrick Johnson (2006), and Thomas DeFrantz and Anita Gonzalez (2014) have been instrumental in pushing for more expansive intellectual genealogies for performance studies to more heavily include works by BIPOC, gender-diverse, and queer scholars.

3. See, for example, Conquergood (1992); Jones (1997); Buccitelli (2012); Miller (2012, 2017); Otero (2020).

4. See, for example, Muñoz (1999); Sawin (2002); Kuppers (2003); Taylor (2003); DeFrantz and Gonzalez (2014); Colbert, Jones, and Vogel (2020).

5. For a masterful, folkloristic discussion of the fundamental "ambivalence" or meaning in online environments, see Phillips and Milner (2017).

Bibliography

Bachmann-Medick, Doris. 2016. *Cultural Turns: New Orientations in the Study of Culture.* Berlin: De Gruyter.

Bauman, Richard. 1977. *Verbal Art as Performance.* Prospect Heights, IL: Waveland.

Ben-Amos, Dan. 1971. "Toward a Definition of Folklore in Context." *Journal of American Folklore* 84 (331): 3–15.

Bock, Sheila. 2017. "Ku Klux Kasserole and Strange Fruit Pies: A Shouting Match at the Border in Cyberspace." *Journal of American Folklore* 130 (516): 142–65.

Briggs, Charles L. 2021. *Unlearning: Rethinking Poetics, Pandemics, and the Politics of Knowledge.* Logan: Utah State University Press.

Bronner, Simon J. 2012. "Practice Theory in Folklore and Folklife Studies." *Folklore* 123 (1): 23–47.

Buccitelli, Anthony Bak. 2012. "Performance 2.0: Observations toward a Theory of the Digital Performance of Folklore." In *Folk Culture in the Digital Age: The Emergent Dynamics of Human Interaction*, edited by Trevor J. Blank, 60–84. Logan: Utah State University Press.

———. 2014. "Paying to Play: Digital Media, Commercialization, and the Scholarship of Alan Dundes." *Western Folklore* 73 (2/3): 235.

———. 2016. "Hybrid Tactics and Locative Legends: Re-Reading de Certeau for the Future of Folkloristics." *Cultural Analysis: An Interdisciplinary Forum on Folklore and Popular Culture* 15 (1): 78–98.

Butler, Judith. 2016 [1993]. *Bodies That Matter: On the Discursive Limits of Sex.* New York: Routledge.

Colbert, Soyica Diggs, Douglas A. Jones Jr., and Shane Vogel. 2020. *Race and Performance after Repetition.* Durham and London: Duke University Press.

Conquergood, Dwight. 1992. "Fabricating Culture: The Textile Art of Hmong Refugee Women." In *Performance, Culture, and Identity*, edited by Elizabeth C. Fine and Jean Haskell Speer, 207–48. Westport, CT: Praeger.

Davis, Tracy C., ed. 2008. *The Cambridge Companion to Performance Studies*. Cambridge, UK: Cambridge University Press.

DeFrantz, Thomas F., and Anita Gonzalez, eds. 2014. *Black Performance Theory*. Durham, NC: Duke University Press.

Edensor, Tim. 1998. *Tourists at the Taj: Performance and Meaning at a Symbolic Site*. London: Routledge.

———. 2001. "Performing Tourism, Staging Tourism: (Re)Producing Tourist Space and Practice." *Tourist Studies* 1 (1): 59–81.

Johnson, E. Patrick. 2006. "Black Performance Studies: Genealogies, Politics, Futures." In *The Sage Handbook of Performance Studies*, edited by D. Soyini Madison and Judith Hamera, 446–63. Thousand Oaks, CA: Sage.

Jones, Michael Owen. 1997. "How Can We Apply Event Analysis to 'Material Behavior,' and Why Should We?" *Western Folklore* 56 (3/4): 199–214.

Kuppers, Petra. 2003. *Disability and Contemporary Performance*. New York: Routledge.

Larsen, Jonas, and John Urry. 2011. "Gazing and Performing." *Environment and Planning D: Society and Space* 29 (6): 1110–25.

Leeker, Martina, Imanuel Schipper, and Timon Beyes. 2017. *Performing the Digital, Performativity and Performance Studies in Digital Cultures*. Berlin: Transcript.

Lewis, J. Lowell. 2013. *The Anthropology of Cultural Performance*. New York: Palgrave MacMillan.

Lindfors, Antti. 2017. "Zeroing in on Performance 2.0: From Serialization to Performative Enactments." *Folklore: Electronic Journal of Folklore* 69: 169–94.

Madison, D. Soyini. 1993. "'That Was My Occupation': Oral Narrative, Performance, and Black Feminist Thought." *Text and Performance Quarterly* 13 (3): 213–32.

Madison, D. Soyini, and Judith Hamera. 2006. "Performance Studies at the Intersections." In *The Sage Handbook of Performance Studies*, edited by D. Soyini Madison and Judith Hamera, xi–xxv. Thousand Oaks, CA: Sage.

Micu, Andreea S. 2021. *Performance Studies: The Basics*. London: Routledge.

Miller, Kiri. 2012. *Playing Along: Digital Games, YouTube, and Virtual Performance*. Oxford, UK: Oxford University Press.

———. 2017. *Playable Bodies: Dance Games and Intimate Media*. Oxford, UK: Oxford University Press.

Miller, Perry. (1952) 2009. *Errand into the Wilderness*. Cambridge, MA: Harvard University Press.

Muñoz, José Esteban. 1999. *Disidentifications: Queers of Color and the Performance of Politics*. Minneapolis and London: University of Minnesota Press.

Otero, Solimar. 2020. *Archives of Conjure: Stories of the Dead in Afrolatinx Cultures*. New York: Columbia University Press.

———. 2022. "Rekeying Latinx Performance: Gesture, Ancestors, and Community." *Journal of American Folklore* 135 (536): 230–38.

Otero, Solimar, and Mintzi Auanda Martínez-Rivera, eds. 2021. *Theorizing Folklore from the Margins: Critical and Ethical Approaches*. Bloomington: Indiana University Press.
Phillips, Whitney, and Ryan M. Milner. 2017. *The Ambivalent Internet: Mischief, Oddity, and Antagonism Online*. Cambridge, UK: Polity.
Rudy, Jill Terry. 2002. "Toward an Assessment of Verbal Art as Performance: A Cross-Disciplinary Citation Study with Rhetorical Analysis." *Journal of American Folklore* 115:5–27.
Sawin, Patricia. 2002. "Performance at the Nexus of Gender, Power, and Desire: Reconsidering Bauman's Verbal Art from the Perspective of Gendered Subjectivity." *Journal of American Folklore* 115:28–61.
Schechner, Richard. 1985. *Between Theater and Anthropology*. Electronic resource. Philadelphia: University of Pennsylvania Press.
———. 2004. *Performance Theory*. London: Routledge.
Stoeltje, Beverly. 1996. "The Snake Charmer Queen: Ritual, Competition, and Signification in American Festival." In *Beauty Queens on the Global Stage: Gender, Contests, and Power*, edited by Colleen Ballerino Cohen, Beverly Stoeltje, and Richard Wilk, 13–29. New York: Routledge.
Taylor, Diana. 2003. *The Archive and the Repertoire: Performing Cultural Memory in the Americas*. Durham, NC: Duke University Press.
Young, Katharine Galloway. 1987. *Taleworlds and Storyrealms. The Phenomenology of Narrative*. Dordrecht, The Netherlands: Nijhoff.

Solimar Otero is Professor of Folklore and Gender Studies at Indiana University Bloomington. She is author of *Archives of Conjure: Stories of the Dead in Afrolatinx Cultures*, which won the 2021 Albert J. Raboteau Prize for the Best Book in Africana Religions, and editor (with Mintzi Auanda Martínez-Rivera) of *Theorizing Folklore from the Margins: Critical and Ethical Approaches*. Her research centers on gender, sexuality, Afro-Caribbean spirituality, and Yoruba traditional religion in folklore, performance, literature, and ethnography.

Anthony Bak Buccitelli is Interim Assistant Dean for Graduate Programs, Associate Professor of American Studies and Communications, and Director of the Pennsylvania Center for Folklore at the Pennsylvania State University at Harrisburg—Capital College. His research and teaching focus on folklore theory and history, race and ethnicity, technology and culture, and space and place, among other areas.

I
RESITUATING HISTORIES, IDEAS, AND PRACTICES

1

The Weight and Lightness of Tradition
Interpreting Repetition in Folklore

ANTHONY BAK BUCCITELLI

In their important 2020 volume *Race and Performance after Repetition*, Soyica Diggs Colbert, Douglas A. Jones, and Shane Vogel call for a revisitation of repetition as a foundational notion in performance studies. They call for scholars to explore "how both 'performance' and 'race' exist in such complex temporalities that are often quickly glossed as repetition at the expense of a more nuanced temporal vocabulary" (6). Noting that performance theories have often "construed repetition as a kind of time signature, that is, a necessary temporal process in the construction of identity as well as the aesthetic formations we call theater, music, dance, ritual, pageant, and so forth," they argue that instead they intend to "demonstrate the reverse: rather than understanding race and performance as constituted through repetition, [to] deem repetition to be constituted by race and performance" (13).

Following the lead of Colbert, Jones, and Vogel, this essay will begin by considering some alternative ways of conceiving of the relationship between repetition and temporality. These include those we can read in Søren Kierkegaard's essay "Repetition" (1843), in the work of other thinkers whose ideas can be shown to overlap with Kierkegaard in important ways, and in some of the foundational but not necessarily systematically considered concepts that folklorists have long engaged with to think about the temporal relations between individual creativity and the maintenance of tradition.

From there, I will move to consider the affective dimensions of repetition. Beginning with a consideration of how the qualitative experience of repetition in the everyday has been treated in a range of literary and philosophical contexts, with only loose regard for their specific intellectual positions, the remainder of the paper will explore three different yet connected topics. First, I will consider how repeated action has often been valued in terms of its weightiness or rootedness, its lightness or quickness, or its flavor or odor. Second, I will argue for the utility of conceiving of tradition as an interpretive framework through which people engage with networks of prior associations that are experienced as repeated action. Finally, I will explore how shifts in the way people experience the value of this deemed repetition can produce both stasis and change within larger networks of tradition. Essentially, this section will call attention to the variety of ways that repetition has been characterized in affective terms in a range of literary and philosophical texts, as well as in lived contexts. These characterizations include conceiving of repetition in the form of tradition as a weighted past or as a form of renewal in the present. These examples should prompt us to ask questions about the range of values we assign to the experience of repeated action: Is it what gives weight and therefore meaning to our lives? Is it a framework for potential future acts? Or does it render us as automatons within a preordained routine?

In considering these questions, I will make the case that we can usefully nuance our thinking about repetition (and by proxy tradition) not just by paying attention to alternative modes of temporal organization within performance. Along phenomenological lines, we should also become attuned to how the affective dimensions of everyday repetition are understood as relations to the past and future.

Repetition and Temporality: Some Thoughts on Folklore and Performance

In his brief 2018 essay "On Repetition," performance studies scholar Philip Auslander discusses Kierkegaard's classic essay. Auslander neatly sums up one of the central ironies that seems to run through the concept: "One cannot repeat something that does not exist, yet the repetition is inevitably a new iteration of the existing thing." Certainly, this irony lands directly on one of the primary tensions that obtains in the study of performance: the tension between continuities with past performances and the here-and-now of in situ performance.[1]

This tension is perhaps especially relevant for folklorists like myself who have frequently defined folklore as existing between "conservatism and dynamism" (Toelken 1997) or the "individual and tradition" (Cashman, Mould, and Shukla 2011), which, since the "performance turn" of the 1970s, have been construed to refer to the relations between a current performance and past iterations (as well as the socially developed frameworks that underwrite present performances). As Simon Bronner observes of folkloristic performance theory in the United States:

> While variations exist in the use of performance, for most American folklorists applying the concept, the important principles are that: folklore is identified as aesthetically marked events (rather than textual items) situated in an observable, specific frame or stage conducive to artistic communication (usually small groups and settings set apart from ordinary life); performers take responsibility for presentation of this artistic material to an audience; performers strategically shape expressions in response to the immediate context and personal motivations, public purposes, and collateral effects; and perceptions of the meaning of the performance may vary with different segments of the audience and performers, and in different times and settings, and those perceptions are valid and discoverable in ethnographic observation (Fine 1996). (Bronner 2012, 30)

Defined in this way, something like the irony Auslander identifies may be seen as a consistent methodological stumbling block. For example, Bronner also observes that "the trouble with this poetics, as methodological critics have pointed out, is that it implies that every event is unique and operates under its own unrepeatable conditions (Fine 1988; Ben-Amos 1993; Fisher 2006)" (Bronner 2012, 29). Bronner's criticism here reflects the idea that the emergent dynamics of a performance event are irreducible, as they are construed as wholly dependent on the cluster of conditions under which a specific performance takes place. Yet, folklorists, like performance studies scholars, have actually articulated a range of ways to think about the relations between past and present performances, many of which are rooted in conceptual frameworks much older than performance studies itself.

One relevant strain of thought in folkloristics, for example, can be traced back to the distinction between langue (language as an abstract system) and parole (particular speech acts), both first defined by Swiss linguist Ferdinand de Saussure in his 1916 work *A Course in General Linguistics*. This model was later adapted to folklore studies by Russian folklore and language scholars Roman Jakobson and Petr Bogatyrev in their 1929 essay "Folklore as a Special Form of Creation." Jakobson and Bogatyrev argue, loosely speaking, that folklore should be differentiated from literature essentially at the gap between langue and parole. "Like langue," they write, "the folkloric work is extrapersonal and leads only to a potential existence; it is only a complex of particular norms and impulses, a canvas of actual tradition, to which the performers impart life through the embellishments of their individual creativity" (Jakobson and Bogatyrev 1980 [1929], 9). In other words, like language itself, folklore should be conceived of as a socially constructed abstract framework for potential future action. This framework is instantiated in particular performances, which in turn can potentially feed back into the larger system, either by reinforcing the systematic norms or by providing possible adjustments, if those come to be perceived as useful and socially acceptable rather than idiosyncratic or deviant.[2]

The communications-oriented conception of performance theory in American folkloristics has often echoed similar sentiments. For example, Richard Bauman, under the influence of the social interactionist thinking of Erving Goffman and Gregory Bateson and the ordinary language philosophy of J. L. Austin, attempted to redefine the concept of genre in folklore from a set of textual features to "an orienting framework for the production and interpretation of discourse" (Bauman 1992, 53). In the same way, then, that Jakobson and Bogatyrev saw folklore as a type of abstract system by which future folklore could be instantiated in socially acceptable ways, Bauman sees genre as a set of frames by which we organize and interpret discourse and hence produce new performances of folklore. In other words, genre is a set of rules and expectations that govern both how we express ourselves *and* how we interpret the expressions of others.[3]

These concepts should, of course, remind us of Richard Schechner's well-known conceptualization of performance as "strips of behavior" that "have a life of their own" or as "restored" or "twice-behaved" behavior in which "action and stasis" coexist. As he puts it, "Because the behavior is separate from those who are behaving, the behavior can be stored, transmitted, manipulated, transformed" (Schechner 1985, 35–36). Diana Taylor has elaborated on this idea more fully: "Performances function as vital acts of transfer, transmitting social knowledge, memory, and a sense of identity through reiterated, or what Richard Schechner has called 'twice-behaved behavior.' . . . Performances travel, challenging and influencing other performances. Yet they are, in a sense, always in situ: intelligible in the framework of the immediate environmental issues surrounding them" (Taylor 2003, 2–3). And indeed, this notion is not entirely unlike the views of practice theorists as well. Take, for example, Anthony Giddens's macroscale theory of the duality of structure, which he sees as the center of stability and change in social life. Holding the view that social life is "fundamentally recursive," Giddens argues that structure and agency form a kind of mutually constitutive feedback loop. And indeed, he applies similar thinking to his understanding of tradition. For example, he cites J. G. A. Pocock's definition of tradition as "an indefinite series of repetitions of an action, which on each occasion is performed on the assumption that it has been performed before; its performance is authorized . . . by the knowledge, or assumption of previous performance" (Giddens 1979, 200).

In this way, repetition seems to sit with an ironic smirk at the heart of the study of both performance and, in a broader sense, traditional culture or folklore. And yet, before we move forward, it might be useful to note that this tension Auslander identified in Kierkegaard's essay tells only part of the story.

Although Kierkegaard's playful essay often defies clear characterization, there are at least a few points on which he appears to be rather clear. First of all, he begins by distinguishing repetition from recollection, which he describes as "the same movement, just in opposite directions, because what is recollected has already been and is thus repeated backwards, whereas genuine repetition is recollected forwards" (Kierkegaard 2009, 3). It may be useful to compare this to John Dewey's distinction between inchoate experience and *an* experience. The former I take to refer to the phenomenology of the everyday, while the latter can be defined only retroactively when we look back upon the past and mark off specific sections as experiences we have had (Dewey 2005, 36–59).[4] In other words, we might see repetition not strictly as a set of temporal equivalencies but instead as a retroactive organization of experience into the repeated.

Moreover, with Kierkegaard, we might see repetition as a kind of mapping of this process into the future. In doing so, though, as Arne Melberg notes, "Since the movement of 'repetition' also makes it new, makes 'the new'—simultaneously with being a repeating re-duplication—'repetition' suspends the temporal order of before-after in or by that now previously called 'the instant.' The temporal dialectics of 'repetition' suspends temporal sequence: the now that is always an after comes actually before—it is the now of 'the instant,' the sudden intervention in sequential time, the caesura that defines what has been and prepares what is to become. If there is one sentence summarizing 'Repetition (in the Kierkegaardian sense of the term),' then this is that sentence" (Melberg 1990, 74). This is an important point in considering the temporality of repetition. It does not simply cite back to the past but also projects into the future. Yet, both can be seen, if we maintain this quasi-phenomenological stance, as constructions that give shape to experience rather than innate features of events. Auslander, in closing his essay with a consideration of Kierkegaard's notion that one cannot experience the same performance twice, hits on a similar kind of point: "Repetition without difference results from the audience's choosing to perceive the performance that way, not from the self-identity of the performance. Perhaps this is why Constantius was unable to experience the repetition he hoped for: he sought it in the self-identity of the occurrences around him rather than in the stance he took towards those occurrences" (Auslander 2018, 89). We also might quickly note that even the frameworks for repetition derived out of the linguistic and communications tradition described above were not always conceived of as strictly unilinear. For example, Jakobson's classic discussion of parallelism in poetry argues that orphan lines become meaningful in poetry only from within a "network of multifarious compelling affinities" (Jakobson 1966, 429; see also Tannen 2007, 100–101). In a loosely similar fashion, folklorists Linda Dégh and Andrew Vázsonyi (1975) argue that folklore is not transmitted in serial form but rather across a "multi-conduit" system—what we would now call a social network. Similarly, Africanist historian Jan Vansina locates the strength of oral traditions specifically in their networked occurrence: "Information coming from more people to more people has greater built-in redundancy than if it were to flow in one channel of communication. Multiple flow does not necessarily imply multiple distortion only, rather perhaps the reverse" (1985, 31). If we conceive of repetition, then, not as existing in a single chain of temporal occurrences but instead as arising from a rich social network of associations within which individuals give structure to their experience retroactively and develop a horizon of expectations for future actions, we might better be able to home in on the way in which affective relations play a role in the everyday experience of repetition.

Repetition, Senses, and Affective Experience: Odor, Flavor, Weight, and Lightness

Affect theorist Sara Ahmed has made precisely this point in her seminal essay "Happy Objects" (2010). Citing Nietzsche's *Will to Power* (1901), Ahmed argues that "Nietzsche helps us to loosen the bond between the object and the affect by recognizing the form of their bond. The object is not simply what causes the feeling, even if we attribute the object as its cause. The object is understood retrospectively as the cause of the feeling. . . . The retrospective causality of affect that Nietzsche describes quickly converts into what we would call an *anticipatory causality*. We can even anticipate an affect without being retrospective insofar as objects might acquire the value of proximities that are not derived from our own experience" (40). Further, Ben Highmore, following Eagleton, outlines a useful connection between affect and aesthetics, an area he calls "social aesthetics": "Aesthetics covers the terrain of both 'the vehement passions' (fear, grief, rapture, and so on) and the minor and major affects and emotions (humiliation, shame, envy, irritation, anxiety, disdain, surprise, and so forth). It is attuned to forms of perception, sensation, and attention (distraction, spectacle, concentration, absorption, for example); to the world of the senses (haptic, aural, gustatory, olfactory, and visual experience); and to the body (as gestalt and it pieces). Most importantly and most suggestively, it would be concerned with the other entanglements of all of these elements" (Highmore 2010, 121). This is exactly my point of entry to discuss the affective experience of tradition and/or repeated action. To do so, I am going to draw from a variety of ways that repetition, sometimes as a corollary of tradition, has been discussed in literature, philosophy, and popular culture. This will help us to understand the range of ways that notions of repetition or tradition have been characterized using strikingly similar language, at least more or less within the frameworks of Western modernity, as weighty, flavorful, or rooted on the one hand and light, potential, or nimble on the other. The goal here is not to show a consistent position on the weight or lightness of repetition but rather to show the range of difference in how they have been applied to temporal relations.

To begin, in the opening to the important 2016 volume *The Folkloresque: Reframing Folklore in a Popular Cultural World*, coeditor Michael Dylan Foster recounts his attempt to prepare for a 2005 lecture on the role of folklore in Miyazaki Hayao's Academy Award–winning animated film *Spirited Away* (2001).[5] Noting that while the movie seemed in every way to be referencing both Japanese and European folk narratives, there were no clear correspondences to any particular set of narratives or beliefs. "In short," Foster continues, "the film was infused with a folklore-like familiarity and seemed weighty because of folkloric roots, but at the same time it was not beholden to any single tradition" (Foster 2016, 3). Borrowing a coinage from Japanese scholar Koichi Iwabuchi, Foster argues that we might talk about instances like *Spirited Away* as emitting "an odor of folklore, as it were, which is 'strongly and affirmatively called to mind as the very appeal of the product'" (Foster 2016, 11).

Thinking about my own preparation for this essay, Foster's comments came back to me, as did a particular odor his essay itself omits: an odor of the concept that linguist and fiction writer J. R. R. Tolkien referred to as "rootedness" in creative works, which he described in two slightly different ways.[6] Speaking of the English poem *Sir Gawain and the Green Knight*, Tolkien argued that "behind our poem stalks the figures of elder myth, and through the lines are heard the echoes of ancient cults, beliefs and symbols remote from the consciousness of an educated moralist (but also a poet) of the fourteenth century. His story is not *about* those old things, but it receives part of its life, its vividness, its tension from them" (Tolkien 1997, 73). Tolkien scholar T. A. Shippey has further explained that in his writing, Tolkien strove "above all to create the sense of age, of antiquity with yet greater antiquity behind it. . . . It was his quest for 'this flavour, this atmosphere, this virtue that such rooted works have' (*Essays,* p. 72), which led Tolkien to spend so much time and effort in creating different sets of 'annals,' in different languages" (Shippey 2000, 236).[7] In other words, Tolkien's view of creative activity was organized around the idea that the vitality of storytelling is derived, at least in part, from the ability to harness a sensibility of history and tradition, a flavor of the text that stands invisibly behind it, echoes of the lived contexts of the past. Thus, in the same way that he felt he could taste the oral stories and now vanished literary texts behind *Sir Gawain and the Green Knight* from within the text itself, he set out to construct an internally consistent potential world within his own writing. To do so, he provided his world with its own vanished texts and also sought to imbue it with the flavor of a variety Northern European literary and folkloric traditions. In Tolkien's writing, folklore is a source of cultural weight, or "rootedness" as he terms it, that conveys the depth and richness of history he sought to cultivate in his imagined worlds by both creating traditions from which to draw within these worlds and giving them the odor of actual tradition.[8]

Tolkien's concept of rootedness is not unlike that of his Argentine contemporary Jorge Luis Borges, though the two have rarely been considered together. Writing of Borges in his 1985 Charles Elliot Norton lecture on "Quickness" in literature at Harvard University, Italian magical realist writer Italo Calvino described Borges's approach to writing as "to pretend that the book he wanted to write had already been written by someone else, some unknown hypothetical author—an author in a different language, of a different culture—and that his task was to describe and review this invented book." In this way, Calvino continues, "Borges has created a literature raised to the second power and, at the same time, a literature that is like the extraction of the square root of itself. It is a 'potential literature'" (Calvino 1988, 50–51). In other words, in Calvino's view, what lay behind the force of Borges's writing was the way in which it grounded itself in an internally consistent but only partially visible or actual body of previous texts. Yet, Calvino praises Borges's work not for its weightiness but for its quickness, its economy and nimbleness, which to Calvino represented a model for future literature. "I dream," Calvino writes, "of immense cosmologies, sagas, and epics all reduced to the dimensions of an epigram. In the even more congested times that await us, literature must aim at the maximum concentration of poetry and thought" (Calvino 1988, 51). In essence, for Calvino, literature, especially oral literature, has the ability to aggregate and distill the past, rendering it weightless and therefore renewing a sense of future potentiality: "Whenever humanity seems condemned to heaviness, I think I should fly like Perseus into a different space. I don't mean escaping into my dreams or into the irrational. I mean that I have to change my approach, look at the world from a different perspective, with a different logic and with fresh methods of cognition and verification" (Calvino 1988, 7). Calvino's Czech contemporary Milan Kundera captures a similar kind of ambivalence among weight, lightness, and recurrence in his classic 1984 novel *The Unbearable Lightness of Being*. Drawing on Friedrich Nietzsche's enigmatic formulation of the "myth" or "doctrine" of the "eternal return of the same," Kundera interprets Nietzsche to be imagining a situation in which all human actions and events recur eternally in exactly the same form. Formulated in this way, Kundera comments that "if every second of our lives recurs an infinite number of times . . . it is a terrifying prospect. In the world of eternal return the weight of unbearable responsibility lies heavily on every move we make." However, Kundera continues, "Is heaviness truly deplorable and lightness splendid? The heaviest of burdens crushes us, we sink beneath it, it pins us to the ground . . . [but] the heavier the burden, the closer our lives come to the earth, the more real and truthful they become" (1999 [1984], 5). Therefore, Kundera speculates, an event that does not recur is "like a shadow, without weight, dead in advance, and . . . its horror, sublimity, and beauty mean nothing" (1999 [1984], 3). Kundera's discussion is not unlike the way that American author Kurt Vonnegut Jr. would imagine a "timequake" in his 1997 novel of the same name. Vonnegut's characters are forced to relive a ten-year period exactly, watching their successes and failures as passive spectators. Ultimately, Vonnegut explores the question of whether so deeply understanding human actions in this way would be crippling or empowering.[9]

With Nietzsche, Kundera, and Vonnegut, we might consider ideologies of weight or lightness around human agency. To what extent, these figures from very different literary and philosophical traditions ask us, should we feel weighted and constrained by the past, and to what extent do we find in the past a kind of way of renewing the present? Similarly, these thinkers also ask us in different ways how we should value recurrence or repetition. Is it what gives weight and therefore meaning to our lives? Is it a framework for potential future acts? Or does it render us as automatons within a preordained routine of action?

Building on these questions about the valuation of repetition or recurrence, Michael Foster's comments call our attention not just to how folklore of the past is repurposed in the present but also to how we experience a sense of cultural weight or lightness through folklore, which can often *feel* like it connects us to the past, whether recent or distant. But this feeling exists as a set of affective relations, or social aesthetics, ranging from a constraint on individual action to a resource that deepens and enriches our experience of the present. Indeed, it is this feeling of connection in folklore, in the form of access to cultural weight, odor, or rootedness, that often gives us the sense that it is an important site and a useful tool for meaning making. Reinterpreting this kind of intertextuality, Calvino asks us to think about how this weightiness is simultaneously a kind of potential, a distillation and therefore a lightening of the past, one that renders it more useful for effective creativity in the present and future.[10]

Certainly, the discussion above is concerned with largely abstract characterizations of the experience and valuation of weight and lightness through tradition and repetition. And the authors considered are novelists and intellectuals mainly grounded in European and American literary and philosophical worlds. But folkloristic work, including Michael Dylan Foster's field-based research on the Koshiki Islands of Japan, has made strikingly similar observations. As Foster recounts, for example, when the important Toshidon festival was canceled due to weather in 2010, his acquaintances there seemed to treat the matter lightly. First surprised by this, Foster eventually comes to conclude:

> It is only through this lightness of attitude that Toshidon retains flexibility through the capriciousness of weather and unforeseen circumstances. If tradition is too heavy, tradition bearers cannot sustain it. But if they hold onto it lightly, lift it with grace and agility, the sort of delicate touch that allows for play and movement and tactical adjustment to circumstances, then there is always next year. Because, of course, as folklorists have long known, any tradition, any sense of heritage, is predicated as much on the belief in continuity with the past and the future, as it is with meaning in the present. (Foster 2007, 112)

Bodies, Practice, and the Valuation of Repetition

In light of the various ways these authors have described repetition in terms of its lived experience as weight or lightness, or in sensory terms as odorous or flavorful, it is clear that any understanding of repetition must also include an understanding of what shapes affective experience of it. We must therefore ask: What are the ideologies we have built around forms of what we understand to be tradition, and how do those shape our understood and felt experiences of the repeated in everyday life? Moreover, how do these social aesthetics shift as we retroactively give shape to experiences over time?

Here, we might begin by locating a parallel in the provocation offered by folklorists Giovanna Del Negro and Harris Berger in their 2004 essay "New Directions in the Study of Everyday Life: Expressive Culture and the Interpretation of Practice." Writing about the theory of everyday life, Del Negro and Berger observe that theorists such as Henri Lefebvre have tended to characterize the everyday as either "richly aesthetic, creative, and spontaneous" on the one hand or "alienated, bureaucratized, and, most importantly, de-aestheticized" on the other (Berger and Del Negro 2004, 6). Certainly, these valuations strongly echo the tension between weight and lightness I have just discussed.

The practice theory of Michel de Certeau contains this same tension. De Certeau certainly sees the modern world as a world of alienation in which the individual must compensate for the loss of communal relations through individual "tactics": daily actions that can aggregate into moments of personal meaning and social connection. In many ways, these tactics stand in for tradition in de Certeau's philosophical system (and I have elsewhere observed that folklore was a crucial but unrecognized area of concern in de Certeau's work; see Buccitelli 2016). He writes in his famous essay on "walking in the city" that the tactics of movement in physical spaces substitute for "local legends ... [that] permit exits, ways of going out and coming back in, and thus habitable spaces" (de Certeau 1984, 106). For de Certeau, the condition of the modern world is one in which power erases our ability to create everyday social connections. Structures of power impose themselves upon us, forcing us into set routines of labor or leisure. Yet, we might also note that in de Certeau's writing both alienation and its therapy, tactics, involve the same process: repetition or recurrence. For de Certeau, it is through the routines of tactics we create that we can open up the possibility of social and cultural connection again. By walking in certain paths through the city over and over, by replicating the "gestures, tastes, and combinations" (de Certeau, Girard, and Mayol 1998, 154) of cooks who came before us, we resist the power that is trying to control our bodies. Thus, we find within at least some versions of practice theory a similar kind of ambivalence about the repeated actions of daily life as producing either modern alienation or its reverse: rootedness in place, culture, and social relations that is specifically played out in the movement and affective experience of bodies in everyday settings.

Simon Bronner has put his finger on the very same point in his landmark essay on practice theory in folklore and folklife studies, though he approaches this point in a discussion of the split between popular and practice theory concepts of repetition. First, he notes a tendency in popular discourse to use the term *practice* to refer to the "unthinking or habitual, belying its cultural significance." Later, however, he points out that the repetition of speech, for example in the practice of repeating the word *rabbit* for good luck on the first day of a month, is a rhetorical technique for marking an utterance as significant, setting it apart from "the common, the habitual, the profane" (Bronner 2019, 17). He continues that repetition is "a revealing, symbolic practice that humans culturally frame to enact, and create, a sense of tradition" (Bronner 2019, 19)—in other words, a means for enacting a temporal connection that retroactively shapes an affective experience of weight, connection, and significance.

Later, in his discussion of a group singing tradition among the Owen-Huber family of Lancaster County, Pennsylvania, Bronner usefully points out that while most of the family had little interest in the history or traditionality of these songs, many of which came out of the well-documented British ballad tradition, the repeated act of singing together was what made the songs valued and meaningful for the family. The experience of meaning in this traditional performance was as much about the act of bringing bodies together as it was about any particular element of the performance itself or about how it was construed to connect to the past tradition. The repetitions here, we might say, were experienced as "getting together" rather than predominantly as "performing tradition" (Bronner 2019, 29).

To come back to Del Negro and Berger's essay, they argue that folklorists should treat the "everyday" as interpretive frameworks through which people come to see human action. In doing so, we can better understand the "contextual factors, ideological factors, and factors of economics and practice" that mark an event as everyday rather than as a special event. In other words, we experience things as everyday—or, conversely, as special events—based on our negotiation of a horizon of sociocultural, economic, experiential, and contextual factors that obtains at any given moment.

I also want to pick up Del Negro and Berger's notion in order to call on folklorists to undertake the same sort of inquiry in relation to the affective experience and attendant construction of repetition in tradition. And thus, I have arrived at what could perhaps be my own definition of tradition: an interpretive framework through which people retroactively construct, experience, and value repeated action within social and temporal networks, and through which they simultaneously construct horizons of expectations for future action.[11]

While this is not entirely dissimilar to the folkloristic performance concept of genre as a framework for generating future potential performances, tradition, as I define it, would seek to capture both alternative temporal modes and affective experiences and valuations more richly. Thus, we can experience certain repetitions as valued traditions that root us in our imagined pasts or as pools of potential for future action, but we can also experience them as unpleasant weights that constrain our freedom or, worse, as the kind of dehumanizing routines that American folk speech characterizes as "the grind," "the rat race," or "being on the hamster wheel."

This paper has made the case that folklorists should conceive of tradition less as a set of temporal equivalences between instances than as a rich social network of associations within which individuals give structure to their experiences retroactively and develop horizons of expectations for future actions. In doing so, it has also called attention to how the wide array of ways that the lived experience of repetition is characterized in literature, philosophy, and popular culture, even in the admittedly very limited body of works considered here, suggests that we should pay closer attention to the affective dimensions of repetition. Although weight and lightness, odor and flavor, or liberation or alienation are certainly not the only ways that the affects produced by repetition could be described, they are suggestive of the diversity of ways in which lived repetition might *feel* in experience. This calls out to folklorists to consider not just the ideologies around concepts of tradition and how those are applied in everyday life but also the rich set of factors that shape how people experience, interpret, and value repeated action in their lives.

Notes

Sections of this essay were originally delivered to "The Practice of Folklore and Folklife" lecture series at Beijing Normal University in 2020. A lightly revised version of that talk was published in translation in the Chinese journal *Folklore Studies* in 2021. The present essay has been almost entirely reconceived and rewritten but contains some seeds from that original piece.

 1. As Diana Taylor usefully notes, there is a broad spectrum of ideas on this topic. To illustrate this spectrum, Taylor contrasts the positions of Peggy Phelan, who argues for the ephemerality of performance, with Joseph Roach, who stresses the continuity between performance, memory, and history. See Taylor (2003, 5) for further discussion.

 2. Jakobson and Bogatyrev's view was generated as part of a discussion of how to distinguish between folklore and literature, though this is not always remembered. It was in some ways quite similar to Walter Benjamin's thinking in his 1936 essay "The Storyteller," in which he locates the division between folklore and literature in the ability of folklore to serve as a kind of open signifier for human experience. Whereas a work of literature occurs only once and hence produces a text and meaning specific to an individual experience, folklore, in its continual recurrence, produces an open record of human experience that can continually generate new meanings. See Benjamin (2019, 48–73), especially 48–56.

 3. It is interesting to note that disruptions to or violations of generic frameworks can be received very differently under different conditions. Certainly, this is an area where perceptions of the performer(s) play a significant role in structuring whether violations are received as reflective of mastery, deficiency, or deviance. Charles Briggs and Richard Bauman have, for example, highlighted the intertextual dimensions of genre, arguing that "the creation of intertextual relationships through genre simultaneously renders texts ordered, unified, and bounded, on the one hand, and fragmented, heterogeneous, and open-ended, on the other" (Briggs and Bauman 1992, 147). They observe the ways in which performers can exploit the intertextuality of genre to produce effects ranging from strict formal adherence to parodic play. My thanks to Solimar Otero and Charles Briggs for helping me to clarify this point.

 4. It is worth noting that French philosopher Giles Deleuze featured repetition in one of his early works, *Difference and Repetition*, originally published in 1968. In this volume, Deleuze defines repetition as "difference

without a concept" (Deleuze 1994, 16). He draws distinctions between the popular understanding of repetition as an "equivalence or resemblance of two instances separated in time" and his definition of repetition as "a synthetic *process* by which thought itself is constituted and recognizes itself" (Hughes 2009, 34, original emphasis). In this process, "we only acquire habits by synthesizing earlier members of a series in later ones. We only acquire representations in memory and language by synthesizing earlier memories that are themselves syntheses of experiences" (Williams 2013, 13). Ultimately, Deleuze's targeted understanding of repetition goes well beyond this essay's interest in the affective experience of repetition, and this larger ultimate target is not always made abundantly clear in his volume. Yet, we can at least see that Deleuze's characterization of repetition shares Kierkegaard and Dewey's sense that it is something defined retroactively through memory, though ultimately Deleuze seems to regard our everyday understanding of repetition as essentially an illusion.

5. This essay is largely concerned with Foster's account of his new coinage "folkloresque" (a kind of counterpart or even replacement for the notoriously problematic concept of "folklorism," a term first coined by German folklorist Hans Moser in his 1962 essay "Vom Folklorismus in unserer Zeit"). For useful discussions of the concept of folklorismus, see Bendix (1988, 1997); Newall (1987); Smidchens (1999). Describing his attempt to prepare for a 2005 lecture on the role of folklore in Miyazaki Hayao's Academy Award–winning animated film *Spirited Away* (2001), Foster writes, "The story feels as if it has been told before, as if the events and characters are adapted from age-old narratives and beliefs. But when I sat down to prepare my lecture, I was at a loss. Where *was* the folklore in the movie?"

6. First, Tolkien elaborates on this idea as "when plots, motives, symbols, are rehandled and pressed into the service of the changed minds of a later time, used for the expression of ideas quite different from those which produced them" (Tolkien 1997, 72). Though Tolkien was not especially connected to disciplinary folklore studies when he wrote this in 1953, this notion seems relatively consistent with contemporary folkloristic views of how both tradition and memory are reconstituted in the present.

7. Shippey is here citing the same essay, "Sir Gawain and the Green Knight" (originally delivered as a lecture at the University of Glasgow in 1953), as cited above (Tolkien 1997, 72).

8. Some scholarship has examined the ways in which Tolkien's writing simultaneously cultivated "familiarity" or "predictability" and "fear," "alienation," or "wonder." See, for example, Barkley (1981), Flieger (2017), and Walther (2020). Barkley playfully argues that Tolkien's readers are similar to hobbits: they like "books filled with things that they already (know)" (Tolkien 1967, 17, quoted in Barkley 1981, 16). She further argues that the "predictability" of his works "makes his tales recognizable as echoes of some familiar story

or undeniable truth; his predictability provides the security which allows the reader to feel part of [his] world" (16). Noting that Tolkien's fictional works are littered with contextual clues that help the reader anticipate events that take place later in the story, Barkley asks a reasonable question: Why don't readers find this boring? His "special genius," she argues, was his ability to create wonder with how events unfold, even when those events have been foretold in the text—in other words, to cultivate repetition but in a way that invokes wonder rather than boredom. Part of his ability to do this was to defamiliarize the everyday by extending or retracting time and space. By focusing in on minute details in space at certain moments, such as the tiny red tongues of birds when the Smith enters the Fairy Realm in "The Smith of Wooton Major," or Niggle's ability to "see every blade of grass distinctly" as he rides over the hill in "Leaf by Niggle," or by zooming out on time in discussions of the perception of time by Elves or Ents in *Lord of the Rings*, Tolkien, Barkley argues, creates a text that is familiar enough to feel real and comfortable to readers but vast and sublime enough to be engaging, even within his famously tightly controlled timeline and geography. In many ways, Barkley's argument echoes Tolkien's own writings about his understanding of how fantasy is constructed and what it can do. See Tolkien (1997), Shippey (2000), Zipes (2002). But she usefully also raises the issue, even if just in the context of speculative discussion, of how readers experience Tolkien's texts, and this in turn points us to the fact that his works are appealing in a way that made them hugely and unexpectedly commercially successful. Although it is well beyond the scope of this chapter, the exploration of how Tolkien cultivates affective experiences in his readers may shed light on exactly what underlies this popular embrace of these otherwise rather odd works.

9. For an excellent extended reflection and extrapolation of Nietzsche's concept, as well as a consideration of how it fits within his larger oeuvre, see Heidegger (1984 [1961]).

10. Furthermore, the kind of everywhere and nowhere of these frames of experience of folklore is brought into relief by the possibility of invoking, as Foster points out, an imagined or theoretical set of folklore of the past.

11. I use *framework* here in the singular, but not to suggest that only one definitive framework exists. As folklorists are well aware, tradition is conceived of and experienced by individuals and groups in sometimes very different ways. This definition attempts to capture a way to broadly conceive of and examine tradition, rather than to articulate a set of expectations for lived experiences or understandings.

Bibliography

Ahmed, Sara. 2010. "Happy Objects." In *The Affect Theory Reader*, edited by Melissa Gregg and Gregory J. Seigworth, 29–51. Durham, NC: Duke University Press.

Auslander, Philip. 2018. "On Repetition." *Performance Research* 23 (4/5): 88–90.
Barkley, Christine. 1981. "Predictability and Wonder: Familiarity and Recovery in Tolkien's Works." *Mythlore* 8 (1): 16–18.
Bauman, Richard. 1992. "Performance." In *Folklore, Cultural Performances, and Popular Entertainments: A Communications-Centered Handbook*, edited by Richard Bauman, 41–49. New York: Oxford University Press.
Ben-Amos, Dan. 1993. "'Context' in Context." *Western Folklore* 52 (2–4): 209–26.
Bendix, Regina. 1988. "Folklorism: The Challenge of a Concept." *International Folklore Review: Folklore Studies from Overseas* 6:5–15.
———. 1997. *In Search of Authenticity: The Formation of Folklore Studies*. Madison: University of Wisconsin Press.
Benjamin, Walter. 2019. *The Storyteller Essays*. Edited by Samuel Titan. Translated by Tess Lewis. New York: New York Review Books.
Briggs, Charles L., and Richard Bauman. 1992. "Genre, Intertextuality, and Social Power." *Journal of Linguistic Anthropology* 2 (2): 131–72.
Bronner, Simon J. 2012. "Practice Theory in Folklore and Folklife Studies." *Folklore* 123 (1): 23–47.
———. 2019. *The Practice of Folklore*. Jackson: University Press of Mississippi.
Buccitelli, Anthony Bak. 2016. "Hybrid Tactics and Locative Legends: Re-Reading de Certeau for the Future of Folkloristics." *Cultural Analysis: An Interdisciplinary Forum on Folklore and Popular Culture* 15 (1): 78–98.
Calvino, Italo. 1988. *Six Memos for the Next Millennium*. New York: Vintage.
Cashman, Ray, Tom Mould, and Pravina Shukla. 2011. *The Individual and Tradition: Folkloristic Perspectives*. Bloomington: Indiana University Press.
Colbert, Soyica Diggs, Douglas A. Jones Jr., and Shane Vogel. 2020. *Race and Performance after Repetition*. Durham: Duke University Press.
de Certeau, Michel. 1984. *The Practice of Everyday Life*. Berkeley: University of California Press.
de Certeau, Michel, Luce Girard, and Pierre Mayol. 1998. *The Practice of Everyday Life, Volume 2, Living and Cooking*. Minneapolis: University of Minnesota Press.
Dégh, Linda, and Andrew Vázsonyi. 1975. "The Hypothesis of Multi-Conduit Transmission in Folklore." In *Folklore: Performance and Communication*, edited by Dan Ben-Amos and Kenneth S. Goldstein, 207–52. The Hague, Netherlands: De Gruyter Mouton.
Deleuze, Giles. 1994. *Difference and Repetition*. Translated by Paul Patton. London: Bloomsbury Academic.
Del Negro, Giovanna P., and Harris M. Berger. 2004. "New Directions in the Study of Everyday Life: Expressive Culture and the Interpretation of Practice." In *Identity and Everyday Life: Essays in the Study of Folklore, Music, and Popular Culture*, edited by Harris M. Berger and Giovanna P. Del Negro, 3–22. Middletown, CT: Wesleyan University Press.

Dewey, John. 2005. *Art as Experience*. New York: Perigee.
Fine, Elizabeth. 1996. "Performance Approach." In *American Folklore: An Encyclopedia*, edited by Jan Harold Brunvand, New Ed edition, 554–56. New York: Routledge.
Fine, Gary Alan. 1988. "The Third Force in American Folklore: Folk Narratives and Social Structures." *Fabula* 29 (3): 342–53.
Fisher, Brock L. 2006. "Performance Approach in the Dramatic Arts." In *Encyclopedia of American Folklife*, edited by Simon J. Bronner, 950–52. Armonk, NY: M.E. Sharpe.
Flieger, Verlyn. 2017. "The Orcs and the Others: Familiarity as Estrangement in the Lord of the Rings." In *Tolkien and Alterity*, edited by Christopher Vaccaro and Yvette Kisor, 205–24. The New Middle Ages. Cham, Switzerland: Palgrave Macmillan.
Foster, Michael Dylan. 2007. "The Intangible Lightness of Heritage." *Fabula* 58 (1–2): 105–21.
———. 2016. "Introduction: The Challenge of the Folkloresque." In *The Folkloresque: Reframing Folklore in a Popular Culture World*, edited by Michael Dylan Foster and Jeffrey A. Tolbert, 3–33. Logan: Utah State University Press.
Giddens, Anthony. 1979. *Central Problems in Social Theory*. Berkeley: University of California Press.
Heidegger, Martin. (1961) 1984. *Nietzsche*. Translated by David Farrell Krell. Vol. II. San Francisco, CA: Harper & Row.
Highmore, Ben. 2010. "Bitter after Taste: Affect, Food, and Social Aesthetics." In *The Affect Theory Reader*, edited by Melissa Gregg and Gregory J. Seigworth, 118–37. Durham, NC: Duke University Press.
Hughes, Joe. 2009. *Deleuze's Difference and Repetition: A Reader's Guide*. London: Continuum.
Jakobson, Roman. 1966. "Grammatical Parallelism and Its Russian Facet." *Language* 42 (2): 399–429.
Jakobson, Roman, and Petr Bogatyrev. (1929) 1980. "Folklore as a Special Form of Creation." Translated by John M. O'Hara. *Folklore Forum* 13 (1–3): 1–21.
Kierkegaard, Søren. 2009. *Repetition* and *Philosophical Crumbs*. Translated by M. G. Piety. Oxford, UK: Oxford University Press.
Kundera, Milan. (1984) 1999. *The Unbearable Lightness of Being*. New York: Harper Perennial Modern Classics.
Melberg, Arne. 1990. "Repetition (In the Kierkegaardian Sense of the Term)." *Diacritics* 20 (3): 71–87.
Moser, Hans. 1962. "Vom Folklorismus in Unserer Zeit." *Volkskunde* 58:177–209.
Newall, Venetia J. 1987. "The Adaptation of Folklore and Tradition (Folklorismus)." *Folklore* 98 (2): 131–51.
Saussure, Ferdinand La. 1916. *Cours de Linguistique Générale*. Edited by Charles Bally and Albert Sechehaye. Paris: Payot.

Schechner, Richard. 1985. *Between Theater and Anthropology*. Philadelphia: University of Pennsylvania Press.
Shippey, T. A. 2000. *J. R. R. Tolkien: Author of the Century*. New York: HarperCollins.
Smidchens, Guntis. 1999. "Folklorism Revisited." *Journal of Folklore Research* 36:51–70.
Tannen, Deborah. 2007. *Talking Voices: Repetition, Dialogue, and Imagery in Conversational Discourse*. 2nd ed. Studies in Interactional Sociolinguistics 25. Cambridge, UK: Cambridge University Press.
Taylor, Diana. 2003. *The Archive and the Repertoire: Performing Cultural Memory in the Americas*. Durham, NC: Duke University Press.
Toelken, Barre. 1997. *Dynamics of Folklore*. Logan: Utah State University Press.
Tolkien, J. R. R. 1967. *The Fellowship of the Ring*. 2nd ed. Boston: Houghton Mifflin.
———. 1997. *The Monsters & the Critics, and Other Essays*. New York: HarperCollins.
Vonnegut, Kurt. 1998. *Timequake*. East Rutherford, NJ: Berkeley.
Walther, Bo Kampmann. 2020. "Lights behind Thick Curtains: Images of Fear and Familiarity in Tolkien." *Tolkien Studies* 17 (17): 117–36.
Williams, James. 2013. *Gilles Deleuze's Difference and Repetition: A Critical Introduction and Guide*. Edinburgh, Scotland: Edinburgh University Press.
Zipes, Jack. 2002. *Breaking the Magic Spell: Radical Theories of Folk and Fairy Tales*. Revised, Expanded, Subsequent edition. Lexington: University Press of Kentucky.

Anthony Bak Buccitelli is Interim Assistant Dean for Graduate Programs, Associate Professor of American Studies and Communications, and Director of the Pennsylvania Center for Folklore at the Pennsylvania State University at Harrisburg—Capital College. His research and teaching focus on folklore theory and history, race and ethnicity, technology and culture, and space and place, among other areas.

2

Contested Ancestors
Toward a Genealogy of Everyday Life in the Postdiscipline

ERIC MAYER-GARCÍA

Commonly known histories of performance studies date its emergence in the late twentieth century when theater makers turned to anthropology for theories to understand their practice outside the confines of traditional Western theater and drama while anthropologists turned to theater for terms and metaphors to theorize social and cultural phenomena. The collaboration between Victor Turner and Richard Schechner, or the turn toward performance by Dell Hymes, Richard Bauman, and later Charles L. Briggs, perhaps best emblematizes this narrative of performance studies' emergence. My chapter aims to complicate this narrative by giving a closer examination of several theorists who are claimed by both folklorists and performance scholars and whose inquiries point to the intermeshed nature of both fields. In this chapter, I place two theorists in common use among folklorists and performance scholars in the United States, Mikhail Bakhtin (1895–1975) and Erving Goffman (1922–82), into conversation with two theorists of folklore and performance from Cuba whose impact on these same fields in the United States has been significantly more limited—Fernando Ortiz (1881–1969) and Inés María Martiatu Terry (1942–2013). Bringing their unique perspectives into conversation with one another provides an opportunity to move the center through a reconsideration of one of performance studies' central preoccupations: everyday life.

These contested ancestors point to a longer trajectory of performance studies' emergence through its reliance on and interpenetration with the discipline of folklore. Revisiting their nonconforming, taxonomically transgressive, disciplinarily promiscuous writings in comparison to one another prompts us to rethink the pivotal role everyday life plays in performance studies and the performative turns in folklore and other disciplines. Other efforts to narrativize the origins of performance studies have adopted ancestors whose work anticipated the field and yet who had no direct role in forming it. Authors like Zora Neale Hurston, W. E. B. Du Bois, Antonin Artaud, Lydia Cabrera, J. L. Austin, Kenneth Burke, Jack Smith, Allan Kaprow, and Jane Goodall all offer distinct points of departure that create a larger, more inclusive view of what performance studies was, is, and needs to become, in addition to who belongs in the field and to whom it belongs. One of several scholars to understand the field as a "postdiscipline," folklorist Barbara Kirshenblatt-Gimblett writes, "performance [is] an organizing concept for the study of a wide range of behavior," whether that behavior belongs to humans, animals, objects, or technology ([2004] 2016, 25). Rather than organizing data into firm structures, genres, and categories, performance studies uses flexible, changeable points of reference—such as embodied practice, event, or the body—and has adapted and integrated, and continues to innovate, a myriad of analytical methods. In this way, Kirshenblatt-Gimblett defines performance studies as a "provisional coalescence on the move" and performance as a responsive concept ([2004] 2016, 25, 29). Performance studies continuously rebuilds itself midflight to respond to new problems and to follow its impetus for cultural equity, which perpetually demands a rethinking of performance in relation to multiple cultures and historical contexts ([2004] 2016, 25–26).

In adapting to new demands in time, performance studies scholars may continually rethink origins, particularly when we recognize that scholars working previously in other fields have been already using the methods or proposing the theories that our present projects call for. Below, I consider the writings of Ortiz, Bakhtin, Goffman, and Martiatu retrospectively.[1] Claimed as performance studies scholars, each in their own way exemplifies the interrelation of postdisciplinarity and responsiveness that Kirshenblatt-Gimblett illuminates in her definition of the field. I am interested in Bakhtin and Goffman because their theories are antiuniversalizing, even if others have applied their theories to universalizing claims. In fact, Bakhtin directly challenges structuralism while Goffman sidesteps totalizing truth claims through his cynicism and humor. Bakhtin and Goffman share a status as canonical thinkers, although each is emblematic of different schools of thought in US-based performance studies—Goffman to NYU's Broad Spectrum approach and Bakhtin to Northwestern University's Aesthetic Communication approach (Kirshenblatt-Gimblett [2004] 2016, 26–28).

Within US academia, scholars tend to take for granted that European and Euro-American thinkers are readily adaptable into canons as founders of a field. Too often, faculty and graduate students are uncritical in assessing what theories should be extended the status of foundational, must-read, or universal. This status is not so readily extended to scholars like Ortiz and Martiatu who write from marginalized places about performance in specific cultural contexts that decenter whiteness in Western civilization. This tendency to mark some theories as essential and others as particular or specialized speaks to the ongoing Eurocentrism that still undergirds performance studies in multiple disciplines, despite its potential to disrupt such hierarchies. Positioning Ortiz and Martiatu as ancestors of the field, my intervention aims to slightly broaden an origin narrative that is racially, culturally, linguistically, and geopolitically biased.[2]

In what follows, I begin with Ortiz and Martiatu in order to recenter performance's framing of everyday life through the Afro-Cuban cultures they wrote about. Their writings problematize marked performances as heightened or separate from the everyday. For instance, to apply Schechner's continuum of pure life to pure art to any number of performances that Martiatu describes as Caribbean ritual theater would require locating the same performance at multiple points on the continuum. Evoking Orishas in ritual contexts is both a part of everyday life and marked, just as theater inspired by Orisha myth, drumming, dance, and song is both the representation of ritual and sacred ritual action. These practices challenge the Eurocentrism of temporality that presently permeates theorizations of everyday life. Finally, I analyze an instance of Caribbean ritual theater, Eugenio Hernández's play *María Antonia* (1967), to demonstrate how performance in Caribbean contact zones complicates and problematizes Bakhtin's theorization of the utterance and the status performances of Goffman's social interaction theory.

Power and Pain in Ortician Transculturation

Although he is lesser known among folklorists and performance studies scholars in the United States, Fernando Ortiz is at the center of folklore in Cuba and one of the most important Latin American authors of the twentieth century (Moore 2018, 1–2). Trained as a lawyer and criminologist by the age of twenty-one, Ortiz's early writings like *Los negros brujos* (1906) positioned the cultures of Black people in Cuba in relation to criminal activity and delinquency. He would spend the rest of his career unlearning (Briggs 2021, 44) and, at times, failing to abandon the Eurocentric and evolutionist paradigms permeating positivism and the social sciences of the early twentieth century that put Ortiz the scholar in a thwarted relationship with his interlocutors and subjects (Birkenmaier 2016, 42).

Rafael Rojas discusses the discontinuity between the first and second Ortiz—the Ortiz of the eugenics period (1900s–1910s) and the Ortiz of the transcultural period (1940s–1950s) (2008, 44–45). The history of the emergence of the cultural relativist from the cultural evolutionist is linked to Ortiz's key theoretical contribution: transculturation, which theorizes the complex processes of transmission between cultures. Ortiz's perspective gradually changed during the 1920s and 1930s because his detailed and ongoing study of Afro-Cuban cultures outweighed or problematized his Eurocentric assumptions (Moore 2018, 8). Afro-Cuban cultures wear down Western disciplines and taxonomies. His move away from criminology and toward disciplinary eclecticism—sociology, anthropology, folklore, ethnomusicology, archaeology, philology, linguistics, history, literature, law, and politics—may be owed to the failure of any single discipline to approach analysis of the complex and holistic Afro-Cuban cultures he spent most of his time writing about. Ortiz's perspective also benefited during this period from working with Black artists and scholars as colleagues through the Society of Afro-Cuban Studies (Birkenmaier 2016, 36–37; Moore 2018, 16–19).

The various arcs of Ortiz's career intersect in his most widely read book, *Contrapunteo cubano del tabaco y el azúcar* ([1940] 1978). In it, he proposed a needed revision to one of the dominant theories in modern anthropology: acculturation. In a 1936 memorandum to the American Anthropological Association, Redfield, Linton, and Herskovits posit that wherever two cultures come into continuous contact with one another, acculturation produces "changes in the original cultural patterns of either or both groups" (1936, 149). They define acculturation universally as a process taking place under a number of contextual categories, oppression and political domination being two of the possible contexts. Although the theory includes options to consider power, Redfield, Linton, and Herskovits are blind to the power of their own gaze when outlining cultures in a hierarchy from primitive to mechanized (1936, 150–51). This culturally biased scheme categorizes through criteria favoring European and Western cultures.[3] Whereas acculturation smooths over the power relations underpinning its positivistic tenets, transculturation would be a far less significant intervention without attending to them.

Culture in Cuba—especially from Ortiz's perspective of studying the diverse, living African cultures there—disproved that acculturation was universal or comprehensive. *Contrapunteo* points out the shortcomings of the acculturation model in specific terms with numerous examples of complex innovations that continue practices of the colonized through admixture from the cultures of the colonizer. In this way, transculturation proposed a postcolonial shift in modern anthropological discourse and anticipated much of postcolonial, subaltern, and Afro-diasporic studies (Moore 2018, 2–3).

Ortiz's theory qualifies cultural loss within a history where people in the colony experience transculturation as a painful process. He emphasizes that everyone experiences this process differently based on their position in the racial hierarchy of the Spanish colonial system, which inflicted varying kinds of traumatic displacements through conquest and slavery (Ortiz [1940] 1978, 95–96). In a speech given in 1942 at Club Atenas, a Black social club in Old Havana, Ortiz represented the impact of slavery on African cultures in Cuba through the metaphor of mountainsides being slashed and burned and boatloads—no doubt an evocation of the Middle Passage—of branches, roots, flowers, and seeds, torn from their organic orientation, chaotically reordered, and jumbled together (Ortiz 1970, 17). Ortiz's theory of transculturation emphasizes partial loss, trauma, and the re-creation of new culture by marginalized groups. The process Ortiz described in his speech is undoubtedly an alternative articulation of that theory. The speech gives a sense of how Ortiz's literary style rhetorically reinforces the historical dimension of transculturation, perhaps at the cost of euphemizing the historical violence against Black people that he describes. Metaphor here also occludes the culpability of the perpetuators of anti-Black violence. Just the same, the process, as the metaphor makes clear, is violent. And yet, in the face of such violence, transculturation underscores how Black Cubans' transmission of culture defied and continues to defy centuries of systemic and ideological racism. In this light, transculturation as a process is inconceivable without attending to differentials and relations of power.

The important role of power in the theory of transculturation was not lost on performance scholars decades later when they picked up on the potential for transculturation to theorize responses of colonized groups to the violence and colonial impetus that initiates the contact zone in the first place. José Esteban Muñoz, Alberto Sandoval-Sánchez, Nancy Saporta Sternbach, Diana Taylor, Alicia Arrizón, and Lillian Manzor rely on transculturation to emphasize agency in the creation of something new out of the clash between dominant and dominated cultures (Muñoz 1999, 4–8; Sandoval-Sánchez and Sternbach 2001, 6–9; Taylor 2003, 104–5; Arrizón 2006, 5; Manzor 2023, 36–43). The artistic and everyday performances of Latine artists and communities discussed by these scholars reversed contemporary hegemonic representation by inducing cultural exchange within systems of production (Arrizón 2006, 5–6; Manzor 2023, 41). Perhaps more importantly, these same performances illuminated the transcultural nature of cultures, histories, and experiences of marginalized peoples in the Americas. For Arrizón, transculturation as an analytical lens etches "the complexity of power relations entrenched in the geopolitics of space," particularly regarding the borderlands as a contact zone in the wake of conquest, colonialism, imperialism, and ongoing militarization (2006, 5, 10–11).

Taylor drew on transculturation to correct a glaring blind spot in performance studies, which failed to address power relations of race and culture while universalizing matters of performance and memory. For instance, in Peggy Phelan's field-changing and widely disseminated critique of the politics of representation and the visible, she pinpoints ways of knowing that do not rely on mimesis, surveillance, or objectification (1993, 1–11). One of the many assertions in her argument is that the ontology of performance is its disappearance—performance becomes itself through its ephemerality (146–47). While this thesis in particular has generated lots of scholarship, including reactions against it, there are limitations to which contexts it can be applied to. Disappearance assumes a linear understanding of time and does not consider the ways Indigenous groups facing genocide for centuries have used performance to remain present and remember (Taylor 2003, 5). Examining genealogies of circum-Atlantic performance stretching back to the colonial Americas, Joseph Roach's theory of surrogation favors forgetting as part of the process of cultural transmission across racialized groups (Roach 1996, 2–3). Similarly, forgetting in the Americas would mean erasure and genocide for some and not others. Taylor responded to these debates with her theory of cultural memory, which, unlike other theories of culture as memory, attends specifically to the stakes of performance as a form of transmission for racially marginalized groups. Through cultural memory, Taylor highlights the ways transculturation, as a conscious process for performers and makers, is a tactic for remembering Indigenous knowledge through the transmission of ostensibly colonial forms (2003, 46).

Performance gives us insight into transculturation as a contemporary experience of complex transmutations that carry precolonial, colonial, and more recent history as cultural memory. Taylor emphasizes that marginalized groups make conscious choices regarding what is acculturated, what isn't, and how these elements combine with or transform retained Indigenous knowledge through the process of transculturation (2003, 104–105). Recognition of this agency centers marginalized groups in colonial and neocolonial contexts, just as it underscores the necessary consideration of power relations in Ortiz's intervention. Taylor's theory of cultural memory illuminates the stakes of performance for marginalized knowledges, memories, affiliations, and identities. Colonized and subjugated people transmit knowledge through the transculturation of form, language, practice, and meaning in response to conditions of displacement, duress, scarcity, precarity, and violence. In this context, everyday life is an important site of renewal and resistance, a timespace where illicit practices are passed on, where life in postcolonial reality reveals the continuance of Black, Asian, and Indigenous cultures the colonial project attempts to destroy.

Caribbean Ritual Theater and Everyday Life

Theater critic, folklorist, Black performance scholar, and creative writer Inés María Martiatu Terry was the most important commentator on Black theater in Cuba during the revolutionary era. In her lifetime, she accomplished much of the work of extending Ortiz's writings on Afro-Cuban ritual, music, dance, and theater to contemporary performance and performance theory more broadly. Martiatu merged discourses of folklore and ethnomusicology with theater criticism and set herself apart as one of few scholars from Cuba making interventions in international discourses of performance and cultural studies. Moving beyond her predecessors, she brought theory from Lucumí and other Afro-Cuban cultures into productive discussion with contemporary performance theory.

Martiatu's writings destabilize Eurocentric hierarchies of culture by presenting an alternative genealogy of performance through her theorization of Caribbean ritual theater. This is the work that the field of performance studies has the potential to do. Building from Ortiz's writings on the dance and theater that accompanied Afro-Cuban music in its ritual context, Martiatu positions Cuba's African cultural heritage as a performance canon alternative to Western ones. She chooses the word *theater* to describe a range of performances, sacred and profane, taking place inside and outside of conventional theater architecture. She makes this choice in part because she found Ortiz's use of the word *theater* to describe the representational practices of Vodún, Abakuá, and Bembé de Sao illuminating. As she points out, he did not add any kind of modifier to the term that defined these traditions as deficient in comparison to Western theater (Martiatu 2005, 16).

Martiatu anchors Caribbean ritual theater in practices like the divination rituals of Lucumí or Yoruba diaspora in Cuba (Martiatu 2005, 9–10). Divination is one common practice in an interconnected repertoire defining Caribbean ritual theater as a complex act of communication breaking with binaries of sacred and profane, or pure art and pure life. Possession of a medium, dancer, or actor, for instance, simultaneously communicates with the public and with deities or the dead (Martiatu 2000, 180). In fact, through this act of communication, Caribbean ritual theater facilitates a link between the world of its public and otherworldly presences evoked in altars, rhythm, dance, and song. In this regard, the creolized spiritualist practice of Espiritismo in Cuba is a clear example of the complex process of communication belonging to Caribbean ritual theater. As folklorist Solimar Otero describes the spiritualist mass, a number of spirits may present themselves to a group of mediums who collaborate in a reading of one or more of the practitioners present. The mass becomes a kind of ethnohistorical theater where the mediums use collaborative storytelling to sense and coconstruct spirits of Congo slaves, *gitanas* (Rom people of Spain), Native Americans, clergy, or spirits associated with Yoruba Orishas or Catholic saints. Encounters with spirits of the past are encounters with the imagination of Cuba's colonial history and its transculturations, which spirits and their mediums comment on through an interplay of oral genres such as personal experience narratives, jokes, legends, and prayers (Otero 2020, 75–78). Otero's account of the misa with its endless possibilities produced through a densely dialogic performance shared between the dead and practitioners exemplifies the central tenets of the continuum that Martiatu theorizes.

Whereas Martiatu draws on living practices of Espiritismo and other divination rituals for the theoretical basis of Caribbean ritual theater, she also presents a historiography for key moments when traditional Afro-Cuban cultural forms crossed over into artistic disciplines as defined in Western societies. One such moment was the period of transition immediately following the 1959 Revolution when a blossoming of events catapulted Black artists drawing on Afro-Cuban cultures to create art outside of traditional contexts. In 1959, musician and musicologist Odilio Urfé organized a folkloric festival in Old Havana that created a new kind of visibility for Afro-Cuban cultures in Revolutionary Cuba. A key figure in these efforts was a student of Ortiz, ethnomusicologist Argeliers León, who founded the Institute of Ethnology and Folklore of the Cuban Academy of Sciences and Afro-Cuban Studies at the University of Havana. In 1960, León led a folklore seminar at the National Theatre of Cuba, which was attended by a number of important Cuban artists, Black filmmaker Sara Gómez, and Martiatu herself. Headed by León, the National Theatre's Department of Folklore produced a series of performances called *Bembé, Abakuá, Yímbula* that led to the creation of the acclaimed Conjunto Folklórico Nacional. Performances like *Suite Yoruba* by choreographer Ramiro Guerra and his group Danza Moderna were also emblematic of the eruption of Afro-Cuban practices and themes in the arts during this period. Another important incubator was the 1960 playwrighting seminar led by Argentinian dramatist Osvaldo Dragún and Mexican dramatist Luisa Josefina Hernández. Black Cuban playwrights Eugenio Hernández, Tomás González, and Gerardo Fuellda León all took part. Later, the works of these playwrights became fundamental to Martiatu's criticism and formulation of Caribbean ritual theater (Martiatu 2005, 19–20; Martiatu Terry 2003, 160).

Not only do difficulties present themselves when trying to separate Afro-Cuban cultural forms into distinct disciplines of music, theater, dance, or religion, but problems also arise when distinguishing between sacred and profane contexts. Martiatu notes that:

> Art is sacred when presented in religious centers and profane in conventional or nonconventional stage spaces. Both have followed their own evolution, but they relate to and influence one another since, often, it is the same artist-believers or others influenced by these manifestations that perform in both religious centers and in professional theatre, giving continuity to a singular experience in which they navigate their responsibilities and religious experiences with their professional and artistic life. In the rituals they reclaim important sacra-magical duties that could mean life or death for followers and that are immersed in their everyday life. These rituals function as a way of having dominance over reality.[4] (Martiatu Terry 2003, 164)

As Martiatu points out, many of the artists were also devotees and practitioners of the traditions that they integrated into their art making. This greatly complicates drawing a boundary between sacred and profane contexts, especially when Santería, Palo Monte, and Espiritismo have practices that take place outside of marked ritual space. Rhythms, dances, or songs that evoke Orishas have serious stakes for believers performing them, stakes that go beyond a purely secular interest in them as aesthetic forms. Martiatu introduces the term *Caribbean ritual theater* to straddle the complex interrelation between sacred and profane contexts in the performances she includes in this category, none of which is purely sacred or purely profane. For Martiatu, the character of this theater and its role in facilitating union with the supernatural is carried out just the same in the profane theater space as it is in the Santería houses (Martiatu 2000, 181; Martiatu 2005, 18).

Everyday life as a space-time experience is not necessarily distinct from, mutually exclusive to, or opposed to ritual space-time, nor is the profane mutually exclusive from the sacred in Afro-Cuban cultures. Behavior in everyday life often carries ritual significance because, following Lucumí metaphysics, the dead or the Orishas are copresent in the lives of practitioners. By contrast, everyday life, as it is commonly conceived of in performance studies, assumes a Western understanding of temporality.

Unlearning Universalizing Paradigms of Everyday Life in Performance Studies

In this section, I would like to decenter common precepts about everyday life in performance studies by putting Goffman's and Bakhtin's theories into play with Ortiz's and Martiatu's interventions of transculturation and Caribbean ritual theater. Goffman's cynical, ironic, and at times playful approach to writing about everyday human behavior imparts a skepticism or uneasiness toward the unexamined subtext of his writing—the centrality of white maleness to the social construction of reality. In *The Presentation of Self in Everyday Life*, Goffman relies on theatrical metaphors to describe behavior in social interaction, especially as a means to express the imagined nature of social reality as a game of make believe. In Goffman's terms, interaction is limited to that which takes place in the immediate presence of others for a continuous period, and performance is "all activity of one participant on a given occasion which serves to influence in any way any of the other participants" (1956, 8). So, performance depends on a cocreated social reality among any number of participants. A *part* is something performers assume to be played on a single occasion, and a social role is a status that is accumulated through the successful performance of one or more parts on a series of occasions to the same kind of audience or to the same exact people. The performance of a social role is primarily concerned with the enactment of the rights and duties attached to its status and the privileges that the other participants extend to someone who properly performs the role (Goffman 1956, 9). Dramatization, then, is about an actor communicating their authorization, ability, and success in performing tasks associated with the social role. The emphasis in *Presentation* is on communicating authorization and proficiency, not the performance of actual tasks, rituals, or rule.

But Goffman's theorization of performance does not imply sincerity, nor does the construction of social reality imply consensus. Goffman's skepticism reveals that sincerity is almost always met with some kind of duplicity in order for performances to be able to maintain social reality, just as social reality depends on the suppression of individual feelings in order for it to be mutually agreed upon (1956, 4). His ambiguity in relation to value judgments vis-à-vis legitimate or fraudulent performances, as well as the time he spends thinking through frauds, is also telling. As Goffman points out in his discussion of misrepresentations within the realm of continuous face-to-face interaction that he defines as performance, coparticipants are less concerned with whether a performer can actually carry out the task they purport to be doing and more concerned with whether they are authorized to perform the part and therefore be extended the rights and privileges that come with its social role (Goffman 1956, 38–39). In this way, we can learn just as much about performances from frauds as we can from legitimately authorized performers. Goffman illuminates that the dramaturgy of communicating proficiency is just as necessary as the performance of the task itself in maintaining a mutually agreed upon social reality.

For Goffman, the everyday is mundane and seemingly uneventful, but it is this exact quality of the quotidian that hides in plain sight acts of performance constructing and maintaining social reality primarily through appearances. In light of Martiatu's debunking of the quotidian/ritual binary, the everyday temporality with which Goffman takes issue along with its feeling of mundaneness is a condition of Western modernity and colonial whiteness.[5] Although he is not writing from a postcolonial perspective, *Presentation* easily opens itself up to such a reading. Goffman's overtly chauvinistic tone achieved through his consistent use of masculine pronouns and stereotypes of femininity interpellate Goffman's all-male audience, just as stereotypes of Hindu castes, Blackness, and poverty center a white, classist, and Orientalist reader. When teaching Goffman, I mark his implicit biases as a convention of his time, as if to say, "I know that it bothers you. It bothers me too. But if we can just look past it, we can learn something about performance." Rather than excuse Goffman's bias for the "really important stuff," I would like to consider how white maleness is central to Goffman's understanding of the mutually-agreed-upon-ness of social reality. Seen from another light, what remains unspoken about performances of social status is that they are dependent on or at the very least qualified by the performer's positionality, something he superficially touches on in his discussion of the performer's appearance as technology of their personal front (Goffman 1956, 14–15). In this sense, there is something productive about Goffman's cynicism as well as his tendency to dwell on the play and mischief involved when the duplicity that performances require becomes exposed (35).

If Goffman's cynicism exposes the messiness covered over by the duplicitous façade of everyday performances of social status, then Mikhail Bakhtin takes it a few steps further. His antistructuralist philosophy centers the messiness of everyday life as the nexus of communication, which renews language, reshapes truth, and refashions being and becoming (Morson and Emerson 1990, 15, 51–53). The novel is Bakhtin's entry point for theorizing the communicative act and all it entails, including the enunciation of subjects and, through dialogic interaction, the negotiation and coconstruction of truth and realties. Thus, language is much more than linguistics, etymology, or a list of signs and referents. As Bakhtin writes, "language enters life through concrete utterances (which manifest language) and life enters language through concrete utterances as well" ([1986] 2010, 63). Systems cannot contain or codify this dimension of language, as language is continually reshaped by live and unrepeatable acts. Bakhtin's insistence that we cannot understand language without dealing with the complexity of the utterance is his clearest contribution to performance studies. It extends from the dialogic as a comprehensive act of communication engaged in the real world. The utterance for Bakhtin has a location, an eventness, and a historicity that imbue it with radical uniqueness while it carries traces of past utterances.

Bakhtin uses the term *heteroglossia* in place of *language* because any language is really a set of languages or heterogeneous uses in the present, complicated by uses and contexts from the past. What makes language even more heterogeneous is that it is continuously changing in an ongoing negotiation between the innovation of everyday use in multiple distinct environments and centralizing mechanisms that maintain commonly understood vocabulary and conventions, which keep any language mutually intelligible by its diverse users (Morson and Emerson 1990, 136–41; Bakhtin [1986] 2010, 60–63). Historical efforts to nationalize languages like the Académie française, for example, are important to the history of a language but ultimately are only one side of the equation of heteroglossia, which gives a more comprehensive picture of how languages continually reshape and evolve. Language, then, is a product of centralizing and decentralizing forces that make it a limitless repository of utterances.

Through the utterance, Bakhtin opens up multiple paths of questioning language through aspects of genre, style, composition, theme, sphere, epoch, and historicity, each of which plays a role in creating language (heteroglossia) as a trajectory, moving in multiple directions in an ongoing process. He conveys language as ever expansive, unwieldy, and seemingly impossible to delimit. As Bakhtin asserts, "The wealth and diversity of speech genres [or types of utterances] are boundless because the various possibilities of human activity are inexhaustible, and because each sphere of activity contains an entire repertoire of speech genres that differentiate and grow as the particular sphere develops and becomes more complex" (Bakhtin [1986] 2010, 60). Bakhtin's theorization of the utterance through performance undergirds his expansive understanding of language as heteroglossia and his theory of speech genres as fluid, diachronic, impure, and processual. As Briggs and Bauman argue in response to Bakhtin, "Genre is quintessentially intertextual. When discourse is linked to a particular genre, the process produced and received is mediated through its relationship with prior discourse" (1992, 147). They also point out that the ideology shaping previous utterances can be carried into present contexts of performance and reception through the intertextual nature of genre and that ideology also determines choices in marking or obfuscating the intertextual gap between past and present performances (147–49, 163).

Bakhtin applies his theorizations of dialogism, the utterance, and speech genres to think through communication within a single language and culture. Even though Bakhtin's view of any given language is complex and heterogeneous, his theories must be retooled in order to account for transculturation, multilingualism, and the way power operates among cultures in colonialism and its aftermath. All of these considerations greatly complicate performance and push our thinking about it further while prompting us to reevaluate universalizing tendencies in performance theory. Whereas several scholars have begun this work by applying Bakhtin's theories to performance in Cuba or referring to his theories as touchstones in their exegeses of Ortiz's writings specifically,[6] I would like to approach this productive intersection from another direction by analyzing how Caribbean contexts redirect and complicate Bakhtinian dialogism, especially as it relates to the contrasting chronotopes, or senses of time and space, of various theorizations of everyday life.

In Caribbean cultural expressions, dialogism operates between cultures in the contact zone, a space where power relations between culturally distinct and/or racialized groups mediate communicative acts. Working along similar lines as Bakhtin, Bauman and Briggs theorize how narratives or other utterances as units of discourse travel from one sphere to another, where they may carry aspects of the original context. Entextualization names the process of decontextualization and recontextualization that renders units of discourse into portable texts. It attends to the ways semiotic processes of style, genre, gesture, and so forth become the poetics that texts carry as well as the ways that poetics evolve through the semiotic processes that elaborators in new contexts introduce to them. Bauman and Briggs query the roles of power and performance in entextualization, specifically access to, value attached to, legitimacy in claims to, and legitimacy and competency in use of a text (Bauman and Briggs 1990, 73–76). Within Caribbean contact zones, utterances—along with the speech genres or ideological shaping resembling genres that frame them (Briggs and Bauman 1992, 147–48)—navigate, sustain, and challenge power relations as they move from one sphere, to borrow Bakhtin's term, to another. Following Taylor's discussions of Ortician transculturation, colonial power relations undergird the landscape of transmission across and within different cultural groups. For marginalized groups, transmission has existential stakes and works against forces of erasure. In this regard, poetics, performative contexts, and the materiality of actors' bodies and voices can operate in ways to subvert the colonial ideologies and violence of linguistic hierarchies that speech genres carry with them.

In step with Taylor, Martiatu takes up Ortician transculturation in her theorization of Caribbean ritual theater. She sets Ortiz's definition apart from articulations of transcultural performance by Patrice Pavis and Eugenio Barba dating from the 1990s, which define it as the practice of mixing forms from different cultural sources, as seen in the work of directors like Schechner, Jerzy Grotowski, and Peter Brook (Martiatu 2000, 183–84). Compared to experimentation with cultural forms of the Other taking place at one point in time, transculturation in Caribbean ritual theater concerns the historical depth of cultural knowledge practicing artists carry. The contrast Martiatu presents implies that there is more at stake than artistic expression and innovation alone. Santería, Abakuá, Palo, their accompanying performance forms, and expressive versions of those forms for broader audiences concern the continuity of African cultures in Cuba in the face of slavery, colonialism, and continued anti-Black violence. Martiatu also stresses that transculturations in Cuba are distinct from contemporary cultural experiments because they emerged over time from the Caribbean *convivencia*, or everyday coexistence of multiple cultures in the colonial contact zone (Martiatu 2000, 180). Parallel to Bakhtin's vision of the immensity of utterances and speech genres applying centrifugal force on a given language, the story of transculturation is the history of bearers of African cultures in Cuba and their countless strategic reinventions taking place in everyday life.

Case Study: *María Antonia*

Eugenio Hernández's breakthrough play, *María Antonia* (1967), dramatizes in its action and embodies in its aesthetics (and poetics) the interplay of utterances and genres across hierarchized cultures.[7] The play can serve as an example of how Caribbean ritual theater, through its transculturations, adds crucial considerations for the ways power relations of racism and heterosexism affect transmission and meaning, considerations that neither Bakhtin nor Goffman take up. Martiatu describes the play as a Caribbean version of Bizet's *Carmen*—a deadly love triangle among María Antonia, a tough, streetwise woman; Julián, a champion boxer and María Antonia's on-again, off-again lover; and Carlos, an aspiring student who falls for María Antonia and becomes violently jealous (Martiatu 1992, 938–39). The plot begins with Madrina, María Antonia's godmother, bringing María Antonia before an Ifá priest who confirms María Antonia's deadly fate. Madrina begins to tell the story of María Antonia's misfortunes, and the dramatic action flashes back to the events that began the previous day (Hernández Espinosa [1967] 1992, 945–51). On a textual level, the play is multilingual, combining Spanish with Lucumí and Efík. But the text has even greater complexity in its mixture of performance genres, merging Ifá divination, ancient Greek tragedy, Cuban vernacular theater, opera, the problem play, and Bembé rituals. Musically, the text integrates *guaguancó* rumba, *pregones* (merchant songs), and Afro-Cuban spirituals. Each of these performance genres, musical and dramatic, opens up unique chronotopes and carries a variety of speech genres that interact dialogically and reshape one another.

A number of scenes throughout the play represent aspects of Santería rituals, such as *tambores* (drumming, singing, dancing for Orishas), supplications, and offerings. The language of songs used to evoke Orishas and the dramatized speech of possessed devotees is part of the play script. As mentioned above, each of these performance genres creates its own chronotope that allows for metaphysical copresence. The play operates metaphysically on multiple levels: it dramatizes sacred copresence as artful representation while its instantiations of song and drumming simultaneously evoke otherworldly presences. Utterances in these performance genres are speech between human and nonhuman supernatural planes even as performance is one of the sites where those planes become enmeshed.

For Martiatu, the otherworldly presences in the play are not an enhanced or altered reality; rather, they are a part of what she calls Lucumí realism. Following Lucumí cosmology, the Orishas are not isolated on a metaphysical plane but rather coexist with humans and animals in the natural world. Their copresence is stored in sacralized stones and shells, and they are evoked and fed with offerings of favorite foods and washed in herbal baths specific to each Orisha (Martiatu 1984, 39–40). In the religious and artistic practices interconnected with Caribbean ritual theater—whether sacred or profane, marked or quotidian—otherworldly presences interweave themselves into our present reality through these elemental materials.

Hernández's play portrays the interconnection between these two planes by repeatedly placing them side by side. Hernández introduces copresence in the prologue when María Antonia is possessed by Cumachela, an embodiment of her ill fate and a character reminiscent of Ikú, the Orisha of death. Beyond Cumachela's frequent shadowing of María Antonia, the play dramatizes copresence through rituals and their interruption. Conventional scenes of melodramatic realism interrupt and never fully dissipate into dramatized rituals, just as the latter frames and intervenes in the former.[8] In a ritual for Oshún at the river, which is represented by dance, drumming, and song, a devotee dancing next to María Antonia gets possessed. The chorus of devotees envelopes María Antonia, who is also a daughter of Oshún, ringing a bell in her ear to call the Orisha forth. She begins to fall into a trance, but, reluctant to let Oshún possess her head, María Antonia breaks the circle of followers, interrupting the ritual. The ritual quickly dissolves into a scene where a friend, Yuyo, whom she had a one-night stand with the previous night, shows up inebriated and tries to rekindle their dalliance. She repeatedly rejects him before his wife scandalously confronts them both in front of Madrina's *ile*, or religious house. Yuyo threatens María Antonia with a knife, and, much like the ending of an earlier scene with Pitico, a man who pursues her after she insults him, she bests Yuyo in a showdown of masculinity by daring him to stab her: "¡Dale! [Do it!]" (Hernández Espinosa [1967] 1992, 985). Yuyo can't bring himself to and drops the knife.

In the play's climax, María Antonia faces down a man threatening her with a knife for a third time. The third showdown ends differently from the previous ones. In the scenes leading up to it, the veil between the human characters and otherworldly characters becomes paper thin. After María Antonia kills Julián, the drums, Abakúa spirits, and Yemayá, who possesses Madrina, respond to the violence as it takes place and before any human character witnesses it directly (Hernández Espinosa [1967] 1992, 1029–32). The different spaces of the play collapse when Madrina, still possessed by Yemayá, finds Julián dead and confronts María Antonia. The room vanishes, and the action returns to the scene from the prologue with María Antonia standing before the Ifá priest and community of Iyalochas or *santeras*. They do not offer her any ritual solutions and advise her only to become penitent in the hopes of lessening the severity of her fate. María Antonia rejects their help and asks Madrina to return home to prepare an offering for Oshún (Hernández Espinosa [1967] 1992, 1034–36). When they return, the drummers have gathered, and María Antonia leads the dancing and singing for Oshún. Carlos, whom María Antonia spent the afternoon with sharing intimate stories, hopes, and dreams, appears and interrupts the ritual. Raging with jealousy after she abandoned him for Julián, Carlos threatens to stab María Antonia. The people hold him back, but María Antonia tells them to let him go. As the dancing and drumming peak, Carlos and María Antonia are in an embrace. She dares him to stab her—"¡Dale!"—and this time the man does.[9] She holds back a scream, kisses Carlos, pushes herself away, lets out a scream, and is possessed by Oshún. María Antonia drops dead. Cumachela howls and crosses the stage (Hernández Espinosa [1967] 1992, 1037–39).

Throughout these final moments, performance genres and speech genres speaking across cultures and metaphysical planes introduce new considerations for vectors of dialogism. The play dramatizes some vectors within its fictional world and performs others to its audience. Within the world of the play, María Antonia's repeated utterance, "¡Dale!" performatively challenges Yuyo and later Carlos. She calls them cowards, directly questioning the threat of violence legitimizing their claim to dominance. The quarrel draws in witnesses around them who verbally intervene in a number of ways. Some call for blood. Some offer fighting tips and warn of María Antonia's prowess. Others question their actions or shame the adversaries for the public scandal and lack of respect for the saints. Briggs discusses how the utterer's positionality in a given context shapes a response cry—a blurting out such as "ouch!" or "eek!"

as theorized by Goffman (1981, 99–101, 121). Response cries not only project to overhearers the utterer's internal state and alignment to a situation, but they also position utterers and overhearers as particular types of subjects (Briggs 2021, 147). Within this theatrical performance, María Antonia's provocation "¡Dale!" works in a similar way. Because this utterance from her gendered and racialized positionality is incongruent to the *machista* status quo, it calls into question her direct rival's status and threatens overhearers' statuses qualified by gender, class, race, and age, positionalities shaping and limiting their behaviors and responses.

The performances taking place among the characters in this play also provide a framework to rethink Goffman's social interaction theory. "¡Dale!" points to the importance of performatives of hypermasculinity to the mutually agreed upon nature of the construction of social reality and to claiming status in this marginalized sphere. María Antonia co-opts these performatives to render herself a status of tough as or tougher than the men. Before each showdown, María Antonia repeatedly threatens gender stratification, first by insulting Pitico publicly, then through her sexual promiscuity, which, as a Black woman in this context, is a reclaiming of her body as well as an act of control and dominance over men that would use her in the same way.

However, the play does more than merely dramatize performance theory through a fictional world as the play has been performed over the decades to live audiences. To the audience watching the play, "¡Dale!" leverages another kind of performative challenge. Effectively, it points out the gap between the adversaries' performance of hypermasculinity and their more complex truth. Rather than these gendered and racialized performances being the sole truth, the gap or aperture exposes the coloniality of power (Quijano 2007, 170–72) undergirding the characters' performative behaviors and the resulting conflict. Through its repetition in the course of the play, the motif of gendered and racialized disciplining as well as María Antonia's resistance to it question the internalized racism and heterosexism the characters and their actions embody, which parallel characteristics of the Spanish colonial project—dominance by force or the threat thereof, submission, and control as well as sexual conquest, dehumanization, and objectification of Black and Indigenous bodies.

The utterances in this dramatized quotidian hypermasculine sphere intertwine with and interrupt utterances and performance genres dramatizing, evoking, and instantiating otherworldly copresence. Dialogism here works among the fictional representation of speech across metaphysical planes as divination or possession, the present reality of the actors and audience, and copresent Orishas called forth through "Song, Dance, and Drum" (Harrison

1974, 7). Copresence opens up chronotopic difference and alternative possibilities to conventional colonial time-space relationships, both within and outside of the world of the play.

Within the play, Madrina employs divination, ceremony, offerings, and supplication seemingly to interrupt María Antonia's fate. Coming to realize its inevitability late in the action, Madrina appeals to Oshún to somehow save María Antonia, and in the end something other than disaster takes place. In accepting her fate and giving her head over to the Orisha in the final moment of her life, María Antonia fulfills another predestined fate as a daughter of Oshún. As a work of art, the text performs an intervention to the reader and audience. Possessing Madrina in the penultimate scene, Yemayá laments the loss that has befallen both Julián and María Antonia, casting them as victims of a larger social malady that the play ties to their marginalized status on the one hand and the coloniality of hypermasculine imperatives on the other.

The actions in the play do refer to real-world violence against women and Black people in Cuba, including femicide in the context of the structural oppression of racialized communities. And yet, regarding spectatorship, the experience of viewing *María Antonia* is much more than experiencing Black trauma. The Orishas are not merely decorative or characteristic of a context. They shape the dramatic action, mediate the violence through their myths, and provide analysis for causality and healing. The multiple enactments of sacred embodiment, songs, dances, rituals, and copresence reaffirm the continuity of African cultures in Cuba, elevating their visibility in the public sphere. Transmission, so artfully dramatized in the play, forges that continuity and in doing so subverts dominant power relations. *María Antonia* dramatizes the places where the coloniality of power is challenged or sustained in quotidian decisions and practices. Continuous acts of transmission, whether shared among an enclosed group of practitioners or shared between a play that "recycles" cultural practices and its public (De Caro 2013, 4–6, 13), repeatedly refute the erasure the colonial project seeks to carry out.

Conclusion

As a responsive field and concept, performance continues to identify its genealogies and claim its ancestors "on the move." How we choose our ancestors determines, in part, how we define the field. As Diana Taylor reminds us, performance studies in the United States and Europe developed simultaneously in various disciplines such as visual arts, communications, anthropology, folklore, sociology, and theater. And yet, it resisted the boundaries fixed by these disciplines of origin and remains a forever emergent postdiscipline (Taylor 2016, 200). Its special power to respond, defined by Kirshenblatt-Gimblett, perhaps lies in its perpetual state of emergence. Performance studies has already responded at various turning points—the crisis of representation and the liveness debate, to name two.[10] As a postdiscipline, it has the potential to answer renewed calls to decolonize academic disciplines and to further engage with thinkers and genealogies of performance from outside of the United States and Europe. Forever imperfect, performance studies has room for growth in becoming a more globally inclusive field of inquiry by integrating perspectives from a broader range of geopolitical positions.

Within this vision of the postdiscipline is an imperative, modeled by Martiatu, to rethink performance theory from the perspective of non-Western cultures and traditions in tandem with the theories of temporality, ontology, aesthetics, and epistemology that accompany them. As an alternative genealogy and continuum of performance, Caribbean ritual theater changes what we know about the everyday with respect to dialogism, temporality, and affect. First, transmission across cultures in the Caribbean, much like elsewhere, has necessarily been transmission vis-à-vis power differentials. Performance is a critical method of knowledge transmission for marginalized groups while everyday life is a crucial site for transmission as a strategic response to forced acculturation. Issues of presence and erasure, continuity and rupture, assimilation and subversion are at stake and give meaning to cultural expressions. Such meaning remains invisible or otherwise unaccounted for without retooling performance theories like Bakhtin's or Goffman's for postcolonial contexts. To complicate matters further, we must consider that the dominant culture also changes by means of contact. So, distinguishing between cultural aspects of the colonizer and colonized, the dominant and dominated in the Caribbean is a complex matter. As we see in the performance of *María Antonia*, colonialism continues to play out in cultural processes taking place in a variety of public and not-so-public contexts.

Caribbean ritual theater presents new pathways for the utterance, further pushing our thinking on the fluidity and immensity of communication and becoming in dialogism. Race, gender, and class are crucial to understanding utterances, speech genres, response cries, and status performances as power relations shape and contextualize such everyday performances. Western conceptions of temporality break down in Caribbean ritual theater when performers speak across metaphysical planes, reaching beyond their current reality to find agency and respite. Chronotopes accompanying the performance genres discussed above interweave with the everyday. This interpenetration allows utterers to commune with otherworldly presences, to recalibrate with an alternative order that resonates with their interiority, and to sync with relationality and social structures in defiance of white supremacy and heteropatriarchy (Brown 2021, 10–11).

Notes

1. Regarding language and translation, I am reading Bakhtin in English translation and Ortiz and Martiatu in the original Spanish. I have not come across the latter's critical and theoretical writings in translation. Translation is a part of the labor required for a broader transformation of the field.

2. Folklorists in the United States have engaged with international scholars outside of Europe and have created important scholarship dealing with minoritized communities and challenging racism within the United States. For instance, Zora Neale Hurston, John W. Roberts, and Patricia Turner have written key works on African American folklore. However, the work of these folklorists tends to be omitted from histories of performance studies or discussion of performance theory.

3. In his famous essay defining folk groups, Alan Dundes makes a similar critique of definitions of the folk stemming from folklorists writing in the nineteenth century. See Dundes (1980).

4. Arte sagrado cuando se representa en los centros religiosos y profano en los espacios escénicos convencionales o no. Ambos han seguido su propia evolución, pero se relacionan e influyen entre sí, ya que muchas veces son los mismos artistas creyentes u otros influenciados por estas manifestaciones los que actúan en los centros religiosos y en el teatro profesional dando continuidad a una experiencia singular en que articulan sus responsabilidades y experiencias religiosas con su vida profesional y artística. En los ritos reivindican funciones sacro-mágicas importantes que pueden ser de vida o muerte para los creyentes y que están inmersos en su vida cotidiana. Estos ritos funcionan como un medio de dominación de la realidad.

5. Nearly all, if not all, of Goffman's diverse examples in *Presentation* come from the UK or former colonies of the British Empire.

6. Bakhtinian polyphony inspires Antonio Benítez-Rojo's reading of *Contrapunteo* through baroque fugues, where the focus is not a dialectic between tobacco and sugar but rather their relationship (Benítez-Rojo [1996] 2001, 173–75). In discussing Ortiz's metaphor that Cuba is an *ajiaco*, or stew, Rafael Rojas identifies Bakhtinian dialogism in the way each cultural element changes in the contact zone. No element remains intact. At the same time, the elements are never "totally dissolved in the abstract entity—the Spirit, the Soul, or the Identity—of the nation" (Rojas 2008, 62). For more examples of Bakhtin applied to ethnographies and analysis of performance in Cuba, see Frederik (2012) and Wirtz (2014).

7. Martiatu's analysis of the 1984 production is one of her earliest formulations of Caribbean ritual theater (Martiatu 1984).

8. My thinking on the interrupted ritual is influenced by Biodun Jeyifo's discussion of this motif in Femi Euba's plays (Jeyifo 2022, 513–14).

9. The stage directions indicate that Carlos fatally stabs María Antonia "in her sex." Whereas I do not have space in this essay to address the material, metaphysical, and symbolic meaning of this form of gendered violence, I do explore it further in my forthcoming monograph on avant-garde theater in the Americas.

10. The crisis of representation in the humanities followed poststructuralist interventions in ethnography and historiography during the 1980s. The liveness debate of the late 1990s and early 2000s generated crucial scholarship in response to interventions by media studies scholars to question long-held assumptions that defined theater and performance in terms of their ephemerality and immediacy.

Bibliography

Arrizón, Alicia. 2006. *Queering Mestizaje: Transculturation and Performance*. Ann Arbor: University of Michigan Press.

Bakhtin, M. M. (1986) 2010. *Speech Genres and Other Late Essays*. Edited by Caryl Emerson and Michael Holquist. Translated by Vern W. McGee. Austin: University of Texas Press.

Bauman, Richard, and Charles L. Briggs. 1990. "Poetics and Performance as Critical Perspectives on Language and Social Life." *Annual Review of Anthropology* 19: 59–88.

Benítez-Rojo, Antonio. (1996) 2001. *The Repeating Island: The Caribbean and the Postmodern Perspective*. 2nd ed. Translated by James E. Maraniss. Durham, NC: Duke University Press.

Birkenmaier, Anke. 2016. *The Specter of Races: Latin American Anthropology and Literature between the Wars*. Charlottesville: University of Virginia Press.

Briggs, Charles. 2021. *Unlearning: Rethinking Poetics, Pandemics, and the Politics of Knowledge*. Logan: Utah State University Press.

Briggs, Charles L., and Richard Bauman. 1992. "Genre, Intertextuality, and Social Power." *Journal of Linguistic Anthropology* 2 (2): 131–72.

Brown, Jayna. 2021. *Black Utopias: Speculative Life and the Music of Other Worlds*. Durham, NC: Duke University Press.

De Caro, Frank. 2013. *Folklore Recycled: Old Traditions in New Contexts*. Jackson: University Press of Mississippi.

Dundes, Alan. 1980. *Interpreting Folklore*. Bloomington: Indiana University Press.

Frederik, Laurie A. 2012. *Trumpets in the Mountains: Theater and the Politics of National Culture in Cuba*. Durham, NC: Duke University Press.

García-Carranza, Araceli, ed. 1970. *Bio-bibliografía de Don Fernando Ortiz*. Havana, Cuba: Instituto del Libro.

Goffman, Erving. 1956. *The Presentation of Self in Everyday Life*. Edinburgh, Scotland: University of Edinburgh Social Sciences Research Centre.

———. 1981. *Forms of Talk*. Philadelphia: University of Pennsylvania Press.

Harrison, Paul Carter. "Introduction: Black Theater in Search of a Source." In *Kuntu Drama: Plays of the African Continuum*, edited by Paul Carter Harrison, 3–29. New York: Grove Press, 1974.

Hernández Espinosa, Eugenio. (1967) 1992. "María Antonia." In *Teatro cubano contemporáneo antología*, edited by Carlos Espinosa Domínguez, 943–1039. Madrid, Spain: Centro de Documentación Teatral.

Jeyifo, Biodun. "Ritual and Theatre and the Crossroads of Poetics, Politics, and Epistemology: Femi Euba (and WS)." *Atlantic Studies* 19 (4): 513–25.

Kirshenblatt-Gimblett, Barbara. (2004) 2016. "Performance Studies." In *The Performance Studies Reader*, 3rd ed., edited by Henry Bial and Sara Brady, 25–32. London: Routledge.

Manzor, Lillian. 2023. *Marginality beyond Return: US Cuban Performances in the 1980s and 1990s*. London: Routledge.

Martiatu, Inés María. 1984. "María Antonia: Wa-ni-ile-re . . ." *Tablas* (3): 35–44.

———. 1992. "Una Carmen Caribeña." In *Teatro cubano contemporáneo antología*, edited by Carlos Espinosa Domínguez, 935–41. Madrid, Spain: Centro de Documentación Teatral.

———. 2000. *El rito como representación*. Havana, Cuba: Ediciones Unión.

———. 2005. "Teatro de dioses y hombres." In *Wanilere Teatro*, edited by Inés María Martiatu, 5–34. Havana, Cuba: Letras Cubanas.

Martiatu Terry, Inés María. 2003. "*Los bailes y el teatro de los negros en el folklore de Cuba*: La obra Orticiana en el teatro Cubano contemporáneo." In *Rito y representación: Los sistemas mágico-religiosos en la cultura cubana contemporánea*, edited by Yana Elsa Brugal and Beatriz J. Rizk, 153–66. Madrid, Spain: Iberoamericana and Frankfurt, Germany: Vervuert.

Moore, Robin D. 2018. "Introduction: Fernando Ortiz: Ideology and Praxis of the Founder of Afro-Cuban Studies." In *Fernando Ortiz on Music: Selected Writings on Afro-Cuban Culture*, edited by Robin D. Moore, 1–41. Philadelphia: Temple University Press.

Morson, Gary Saul, and Caryl Emerson. 1990. *Mikhail Bakhtin: Creation of a Prosaics*. Stanford, CA: Stanford University Press.

Muñoz, José Esteban. 1999. *Disidentifications: Queers of Color and the Performance of Politics*. Minneapolis: University of Minnesota Press.

Ortiz, Fernando. (1940) 1978. *Contrapunteo Cubano del tabaco y el azucar*. Caracas, Venezuela: Biblioteca Ayacucho.

———. 1951. *Los bailes y el teatro de los negros en el folklore de Cuba*. Havana, Cuba: Ediciones Cardenas y Cia.

———. 1970. "Discurso en Club Atenas." In *Bio-bibliografía de don Fernando Ortiz*, edited by Araceli García-Carranza, 16–19. Havana, Cuba: Instituto del Libro.

Otero, Solimar. 2020. *Archives of Conjure: Stories of the Dead in Afrolatinx Cultures*. New York: Columbia University Press.
Phelan, Peggy. 1993. *Unmarked: The Politics of Performance*. London: Routledge.
Quijano, Aníbal. 2007. "Coloniality and Modernity/Rationality." *Cultural Studies* 21 (2–3): 168–78.
Redfield, Robert, Ralph Linton, and Melville J. Herskovits. 1936. "Memorandum for the Study of Acculturation." *American Anthropologist* 38 (1): 149–52.
Roach, Joseph. 1996. *Cities of the Dead: Circum-Atlantic Performance*. New York: Columbia University Press.
Rojas, Rafael. 2008. *Essays in Cuban Intellectual History*. New York: Palgrave MacMillan.
Sandoval-Sánchez, Alberto, and Nancy Saporta Sternbach. 2001. *Stages of Life: Transcultural Performance and Identity in U.S. Latina Theater*. Tucson: University of Arizona Press.
Taylor, Diana. 2003. *The Archive and the Repertoire: Performing Cultural Memory in the Americas*. Durham, NC: Duke University Press.
———. 2016. *Performance*. Durham, NC: Duke University Press.
Wirtz, Kristina. 2014. *Performing Afro-Cuba: Image, Voice, Spectacle in the Making of Race and History*. Chicago: University of Chicago Press.

Eric Mayer-García is Assistant Professor of Theatre, Drama, and Contemporary Dance at Indiana University Bloomington. Mayer-García has published research on vanguard theatre, latinidad, and theatre historiography in *Theatre Survey; Atlantic Studies; Journal of American Folklore; Theatre History Studies*; and *Chiricú Journal: Latina/o Literatures, Arts and Cultures*, among others.

3

Minting Money
Queer Temporality and Performance in Ethnography

SARAH M. GORDON

I'm doing fieldwork.

Stare at any sentence long enough and the words fractalize through their multiplicity of meanings. What is fieldwork? We'll get to that. I'm thinking now about *doing*, its potential eroticism, whether it's possible to do some*thing* the way one might do some*one*. In fieldwork, by convention, there is the person doing and the people being done—a heteronormative patterning that reverberates through all stages of ethnography. Fieldwork organizes ethnographers into a temporal schema oriented toward the production of research outputs, compelling in many of us a queer double living. Fieldworkers organize themselves according to the norms of ethnography as queers organize ourselves according to the norms of daily life; thus, like any normatizing force, fieldwork's straight temporality reveals its own queer alternatives. This chapter draws on queer experiences—both others' and my own—to outline the performative frames of fieldwork and ethnography and the alternative queer potentials they reveal.

Central to my argument, and to my own development as a fieldworker, is Susan Seizer's 1995 article "Paradoxes of Visibility in the Field," wherein she gives a funny, insightful reflection on getting caught in flagrante with her girlfriend, Kate, near the end of their fieldwork in Tamil Nadu. The couple were beginning a three-month stint house-sitting for friends. They'd had little privacy together during their time in India, so they were thrilled by the personal space afforded them by a bungalow to themselves. Shortly after their arrival, while they were enjoying their time together, the housekeeper, Angela, rang the doorbell, but the women, not expecting her, did not hear it. When Angela came into their bedroom to mop the floors, she stumbled into an intimacy she did not expect.

Over subsequent days of tense interactions, Seizer's well-worn tools for softening cultural barriers with Tamil women failed to make any headway at breaching Angela's distrust. She explains her discovery that Kate's and her role as house sitters was not, as they had expected, to keep up with cleaning and plant watering but rather to "serve as place-markers within a hierarchy of relations" (Seizer 1995, 83). After Angela stumbled upon them, however, that hierarchy was troubled—queered, perhaps—as Seizer's "private lesbian life" (84) was rendered public and performative for an audience of one. Angela took on the role of the protector of normativity, wherein positions of authority were imbued with responsibility to behave according to acceptable paradigms. She came to the house twice daily, far more often than scheduled, staking a protective claim on the home that was her place of work and shutting down the potential for any further queer intimacies. Finally, Seizer enlisted as mediator a Tamil neighbor better acquainted with Western cultural norms. Through her, Seizer learned that Angela had not taken offense to the discovery of two women having sex—no, she was insisting that these strange women spending hours behind closed doors in the company of the homeowners' technology were surely *minting money* (91).

Seizer draws on this unexpected turn to comment on how Angela fit Kate and her into a local schema of women's affections, American imperialism, global capitalism, and racial hierarchies: "She saw our intertwined bare bodies as one among many other foreign machines in that spacious, air-conditioned bedroom, where the [German homeowner] engineer housed his big, first-generation facsimile machine, and a wireless, white, portable and rechargeable phone. . . . In the context of that bedroom, privacy made sense primarily as a property relation" (Seizer 1995, 94–95). But with all the confidence of an academic three decades and half a planet away, I read a complementary interpretation of Angela's *minting money* metaphor. Seizer mentions that Angela is Christian (85). In Dante's *Inferno*, sodomites and usurers share the third, innermost ring of the seventh circle of hell, neighbors with fraudsters who live in the eighth. *Minting money* is a metaphor for embracing gain without sacrifice, the shared punitive trait of sodomites (who enjoy sexual pleasure without the potential for reproduction) and usurers (who make money without expending labor or property). Seizer suggests that "in the blink of Angela's eye our two female bodies were transformed into machines of modern capital, a-whirr and a-glint with newly-coined values" (93), but I wonder if the opposite may also have been true: that Angela saw a *defiance* of the modern capital that informed her familiar gendered, racialized, and sexualized social order and witnessed the queer rejection of normative futurity, embracing instead the value of presence, an immediacy enjoyed in itself, for itself—a kind of sexual fraud.

Seizer did not set out to make Angela a part of her research, but the existence of an article in part about her incorporates her into "the field" anyway, and the encounter models dynamics that inform how fieldwork functions. Seizer traces the origins of the ethnographic use of the term *fieldwork* to A. C. Haddon's use of it to refer to "intensive study of limited areas" (Seizer 1995, 74). But the word itself is older than that; in excavating its layers of meaning, we can consider the concept of fieldwork as what Victor Turner calls a "root metaphor": an orienting paradigm for knowledge production (2018). Before *fieldwork* referred to site-based research, it referred to temporary military fortifications, and before that its meaning was agricultural (Oxford English Dictionary 2022). The military definition connotes conflict and a tension between opposites, and the agricultural definition connotes fecundity and extraction. The metaphor in its totality implies a kind of heteronormativity—a coming together of opposites that bears fruit in the form of data generation.

The image of ethnographic encounters as interpretable through a heteronormative or even hetero-eroticized lens is not new. George Murdock expressed his delight with a "snappy" definition of anthropology as "the science of man—embracing woman" (1952, 7). Vincent Crapanzano describes how "interpretation [through ethnography] has been understood as a phallic, a phallic-aggressive, a cruel and violent, a destructive act, and as a fertile, a fertilizing, a fruitful, and a creative one. We say a text, a culture even, is pregnant with meaning. Do the ethnographer's presentations become pregnant with meaning because of his interpretive, his phallic fertilizations?" (1986, 52). Marilyn Strathern parallels the gendered and ethnographic productions of the Other (1987), and Lila Abu-Lughod connects the construction of the non-Western anthropological Other by the Western academic Self to the de Beauvoirian female Other and male Self (1991, 139). Aisha Mahina Beliso-De Jesus describes the conventional ethnographic lens as "pornotroping" that "stimulates desires for erotic fantasies of ethnological troping mechanisms: the native savage, the hypersexed mulatta, the mystical Black sorcerer, or the forbidden access to secret spaces in protected rituals" (2016, 297).

Each of these frameworks articulates its own dimension of what Abu-Lughod, invoking Soheir Morsy, calls "the hegemony of the distinctive-other tradition": the norm that ethnographers must be different from their subjects. "The problem with studying one's own society is said to be the problem of gaining enough distance," Abu-Lughod says (1991, 141), invoking a sense of queer impossibility analogous to, in J. Jack Halberstam's (2011) terms, the threatening paradox of the butch lesbian, who embodies womanhood and masculinity at once. This distinctive-other dynamic must not just exist, but it must be intelligible to scholarly audiences and community audiences; in this respect, it requires performance, a visible articulation of a role. Seizer's usuriously queer encounter, inadvertently performed for Angela as unwilling audience, illustrates the fallout of subverting one's place in the "distinctive-other tradition" in more ways than one: by unsettling the gender dyad of sexual encounter and, simultaneously, their clear place in the "hierarchy of relations" they were tasked with sustaining. Resolution required a reaffirmation of the normative order: they shed their "treasured public dyke identity" (Seizer 1995, 99) but also, out of implicit recognition for their transgression, abdicated the master bedroom (I use this outdated descriptor intentionally, with all its racial and colonial baggage) and instead made their bed on the floor of the homeowners' son's bedroom.

For women, queers, and BIPOC (Black, Indigenous, and People of Color) folks, performance is a blurry part of everyday life. Richard Bauman has described performance as "a mode of communicative display, in which the performer signals to an audience . . . 'hey, look at me! I'm on!'" (2004, 9). But marginalized groups have long pointed out that any space becomes a stage when surrounding eyes make themselves into an audience (see, for example, Sawin 2002). Frantz Fanon points out the impossibility of asserting full Black humanity in a context wherein humanity is measured by its proximity to (or mimicry of) whiteness (1952); Langston Collin Wilkins reasserts this when he describes how white observation compels performances from Black men to manage dangerous stereotypes ascribed to them in white imaginaries (2021). Jafari S. Allen discusses how Black queer lives are flattened into performance-like hypervisibility by other people to serve their own interests (2022). Amber Jamilla Musser discusses how ethnographic pornotroping encompasses power and performance as a circuit that violently desubjectifies the bodies of Black people and other people of color (2018). Mintzi Martínez-Rivera points out that by doing research in her home community, she (and other BIPOC ethnographers) subvert the ethnographic pornotrope, transforming the *campo*/field into a decolonial and antioppressive space (2022, 181).

Quetzil Castañeda describes fieldwork as "a specific mode . . . of invisible theatre" (2006, 77). It is theater because it involves participants playing roles scripted by research goals or disciplinary expectations. It is invisible for two reasons. First, the improvisational, flexible, and transformative qualities of fieldwork introduce a "gap between the doing and the design of fieldwork such that there is always a hidden, or unknown and unknowable, element" (82). Fieldwork can't be visible when "being in fieldwork inherently and endlessly provokes the question about what is . . . doing fieldwork and when is the researcher 'doing' or not 'doing' it" (79). Seizer's story illustrates how fieldworkers are always doing *and* not-doing fieldwork. Fieldwork involves what Sara

Ahmed, describing queer alienation, calls "the concealment of labour under the sign of nature" (2014, 145); ethnographers, like queer subjects, feel "the tiredness of making corrections and departures" according to the "demands of heterosexual [or ethnographic] scripts" (147, with my insertion). Kate and Seizer sought rest from this queer tiredness in a private bedroom but found themselves reincorporated into normative pressures anyway.

Castañeda's second description of research invisibility is temporal. He says that:

> ethnographic fieldwork is governed by the teleology of the production and dissemination of ethnographic knowledge; thus, the experience and interaction of fieldwork is a potentiality that corresponds not to the right then and there but to the subsequent re-constitution of information and experience as knowledge in writing, text, and representation that circulates for other audiences of readers and viewers detached from the specific time and space of the fieldwork. (Castañeda 2006, 82)

Castañeda's formulation illustrates how fieldwork is embedded in a temporality of potentialities concealed within a normative schema that pretends to be rigid. Research temporality models itself after what Lee Edelman (2004) calls "straight time" in that it is organized teleologically toward the generation of outcomes/offspring that are understood to validate the teleological processes that created them. Queer bodies live straight time as a series of deviations, not linear causal chains but suggestions that we perform, manipulate, or sometimes hide from. Fieldwork works this way too: it is a potentiality corresponding to the eventual entextualization of knowledge, but it is also usually the outcome of earlier potentialities crafted for institutional review committees, boards of directors, funding bodies, community partners, and more.

Ethnographies beget evidence of the performance-labor of ethnographers oriented to various audience members. In *Mondays on the Dark Night of the Moon*, Kirin Narayan makes passing reference to the difficulty of putting on her "gregarious fieldwork persona" when she was exhausted from recent illness and travel (Narayan and Sood 1997, 88). In her ethnography of rural queer youth, Mary L. Gray describes how, to justify her project to her institutional ethics review board, she was compelled to pronounce stereotypes that rural youth "experienced disproportionately horrific abuse and threat their urban peers did not" even though "there are no grounds for such a claim" (Gray 2009, 191). Bronislaw Malinowski presented himself as fully embedded in and respectful of Trobriand culture, but his posthumously published journals revealed his disdain for the Trobrianders, his concealed struggles with hypochondria and sexual frustration, and his frequent sojourns to seek European company (see, for example, Hsu 1979).

Zora Neale Hurston was perhaps the first folklorist to subvert the temporal norms of ethnography by exposing their performative drive. Cynthia Ward describes how, while conducting her fieldwork for *Mules and Men*, Hurston corresponded with her mentor Franz Boas, her patron Charlotte Osgood Mason, and her friend Langston Hughes and presented a different approach and persona to each one:

> Hurston obliged each audience with what it wanted: Mason, the "little mother of the primitive world," received fawning letters "humbly and sincerely" wishing her good health and encouraging her to feel assured that "her" material was for her eyes only.... At the same time, though, Hurston surreptitiously sent copies of her material to both Boas and Hughes.... Hurston conveyed contradictory descriptions of her methodology to her different audiences. Six months before assuring Boas that she was trying "to be as exact as possible. Keeping the exact dialect as closely as I could ... so that I shall not let myself creep in unconsciously." ... Hurston had confided to Hughes that she had to "rewrite a lot ... not only ... to present the material with all the life and color of my people, [but] to leave no loopholes for the scientific crowd to rend and tear us." (Ward 2012, 301–2)

Hurston's letters to "little mother" Mason directly allude to the reproductive metaphor that informs research processes. Her letters to Boas suggest a respect for the distinctive-other tradition. But to Hughes, she articulates a desire to embed within this hetero-reproductive ideal a celebration of her community enabled by queer proximity.

Hurston's research interlocutors formed yet another audience for whom Hurston had to perform. The labor of this performance appears in her autobiography, where she describes improving research outcomes by discarding "Bernardese" English in favor of speaking in the local style. Another example of such performative adaptation appears in *Mules and Men*, where she describes telling a fib to explain away the alienating effect of her expensive clothing:

> I mentally cursed the $12.74 dress from Macy's that I had on among all the $1.98 mail-order dresses.... I did look different and resolved to fix all that no later than the next morning.
>
> "Oh, I ain't got doodley squat," I countered. "Mah man bought me dis dress de las' time he went to Jacksonville. We wuz sellin' plenty stuff den and makin' good money. Wisht Ah had dat money now." (Hurston 1990, 63–64)

Hurston subjugates one heteronormativity—the distinctive-other tradition—under another more traditional one. But by referencing this directly in the text, Hurston draws attention simultaneously to the performative demands inspired by these normativities and to the queer alternative of laying them bare. Aisha Beliso-De Jesús points out that Hurston "created a temporal shift in her writing" (2016, 299). Academia is "unrithmic," relying on the "between beat"; Hurston "provides the 'beat between' and thinks up devices to fill in those remaining spaces but allows for neither an indulgence of a liberal quest for self nor a devolution into exoticized romanticism" (Beliso-De Jesus 2016, 298).

The heteronormativity of research manifests in reproductive futurism, a term coined by Lee Edelman to describe the logic that the "child remains the perpetual horizon of every acknowledged politics, the fantasmatic beneficiary of every political intervention" (Edelman 2004, 3); in other words, to argue that one's position stands to benefit "the children" is generally to assert that one's motivation transcends the political even if one's argument, orientation, or behavior does not. Edelman calls this a Ponzi scheme (4) that claims to benefit future generations while in fact profiting at their expense, and queerness, in its complex rejection of the fetishizing of future generations, becomes symbolic of the "death drive" of social order. It is easy to make a cynical argument that ethnography has, at its worst, been a Ponzi scheme of a similar structure, with "the Child" replaced by the document due to be created at the end of an ethnographic encounter. Like farmers, our fieldwork orients itself toward its harvest; like soldiers, we hope it will keep us (metaphorically, professionally) alive.

Edelman suggests that to queer the temporal orientation of reproductive futurism is to exist in resistance of the broader symbolic system—widely accepted as an immutable truth, not a symbolic system but a reality—that it informs. José Esteban Muñoz (2009) offers a loving critique of Edelman for his cynicism in suggesting that queerness demands a retreat from futurism to take refuge in a present that, Muñoz points out, can be as toxic to queer people as reproductive futurism can be. Muñoz (2009, 1) says that "queerness exists for us as an ideality that can be distilled from the past and used to imagine a future"; queerness orients us toward the edge of the possible, it invites imagination, and it insists on "something better, something dawning" (189). Queer anthropologist Margot Weiss invokes Black queer anthropologist Shaka McGlotten in suggesting queer anthropology is "wanting to know, to know more—'a commitment to a wondering curiosity' rather than 'disciplinary certainty'" (Weiss 2016, 635; quoting McGlotten 2012, 3). If we face the source of our queer exhaustion, if we confront the heteronormativities that compel research performance, we must be able to imagine queer alternative modes.

Cree scholar Shawn Wilson articulates his Indigenous research paradigm in terms of ceremony. He is speaking specifically about research by and about Indigenous people, and his book queers (my term, not his) normative research temporalities and teleologies. In his words:

> *Something that has become apparent to me is that for Indigenous people, research is a ceremony.* In our cultures an integral part of any ceremony is setting the stage properly. When ceremonies take place, everyone who is participating needs to be ready to step beyond the everyday and to accept a raised state of consciousness. You could say that the specific rituals that make up the ceremony are designed to get the participants into a state of mind that will allow for the extraordinary to take place. As one Elder explained it to me: if it is possible to get every single person in a room thinking about the exact same thing for only two seconds, then a miracle will happen. It is fitting that we view research in the same way—as a means of raising our consciousness. (Wilson 2008, 69, emphasis in the original)

Wilson's framework emphasizes the performative dimension of research and suggests a temporal orientation that centers the moment of contact and mutual alignment in search of shared goals. Wilson's "extraordinary" echoes temporal ideas suggested by Muñoz (2009, 25), who argues that queerness is "a potentiality" and "the thing-that-is-not-yet-imagined." Wilson's orientation toward research as a framework for establishing human connections powerful enough to elucidate new potentialities suggests Muñoz's concept of queer ecstatic time: ecstasy, a moment "marked by both self-consciousness an obliviousness, possesses a potentially transformative charge" (24) with queerness as a utopian "horizon" wherein "the temporal stranglehold I describe as straight time is interrupted or stepped out of" (32). Beyond that temporal stranglehold lies the potential for knowledge production that is more adaptable, more relevant, and less burdened with performative perfectionisms. Halberstam (2011, 6) explains that "queer time is a term for those specific models of temporality that emerge ... once one leaves the temporal frames of bourgeois reproduction and family, longevity, risk/safety, and inheritance"—all concepts that act as clear metaphor for the driving impetus of research time.

Eve Sedgwick, in querying the ways that knowledge is performative, engages with the concept of paranoid theorizing, contending that critical practice is often built on a central methodology of intellectual defensiveness. Sedgwick (2002, 126) describes how paranoia is, in Leo Bersani's terms, "an inescapable interpretive doubling of presence" wherein our epistemologies create and are created by the objects of our paranoia that we desire to overcome through critical engagement. She then points out that according to Freud and other psychoanalysts, paranoia is rooted in repression of same-sex desire. The repression, of course, is not caused by the desire but by the social vilification of it; the paranoia reveals Muñoz's queer horizon. Paranoid theorizing is tied up in the fear of humiliation: the negative affect that emerges from the surprise of not-knowing. Sedgwick encourages reparative reading as a counterproject to the paranoid: rather than orienting itself around paranoia's rigid temporality wherein everything always-already-was, all surprises are bad, and mistakes are humiliating, reparation orients itself toward growth, toward the enlistment of possibilities—in a word, toward love. This reparative orientation is grounded in the embracing of error since the fear of humiliation surrounding mistakes is so often what causes us to fear those mistakes in the first place (2002, 145).

Halberstam (2011, 12) draws a direct connection between the "queer art of failure" and effective ethnographic encounters, suggesting that a fear of failure lends itself to the predetermination of outcomes assessed as "mastery" rather than open-minded engagement considered as "conversation"—because there is more risk in conversation, more potential to be wrong, more potential to lose when we expected to win. David Todd Lawrence takes this up in reflection on his work with Elaine Lawless in Pinhook, Missouri, where they set out with community-driven goals but had to accept, in the end, that the work they created was theirs only. "[Pinhookians] were already telling their own story. . . . So, what was it we were really offering to them? Unable to answer this question through the passing years, Elaine and I came to see ourselves as having failed the people of Pinhook," Lawrence says (2022, 134). Implicit in Lawrence's reflection is the question of what success might have looked like—and whether ethnography in any form could have achieved it in this context. There are implicit questions of privilege, of structural inequities that both define success and determine its relative accessibility. Patricia Sawin, reflecting on Richard Bauman's canonical definition of performance ("the assumption of responsibility to an audience for a display of communicative competence" [Bauman 1977, 4]), asks: "If that is performance, do women perform?" (Sawin 2002, 31). If "success" in ethnography is a book and peer-reviewed articles, could ethnography ever "succeed"—which is to say, benefit—the mostly Black displaced and dispossessed people of Pinhook? Ethnographic success is not built for Pinhookians, and in realizing this, Lawrence, inspired by Halberstam, embraces failure: "The 'successful' project is always a failure and . . . ethnography is always a failure, and . . . because of, not despite this fact, we should continue to pursue it, dwelling in the failure, being vulnerable, accepting what it means to fail to understand, perceive, transcend, connect. . . . Maybe there is something wonderful to be found in not knowing, being confused, being lost, striking out and failing miserably" (Lawrence 2022, 145). The fear of failure inspires a paranoid foreclosing of the visibility of our mistakes, but by taking queer delight in leaning into failure, leaning *into* mistakes, we can unveil new, less-paranoid ways of knowing. Quoting personal communication with Joseph Litvak, Sedgwick says, "Doesn't reading queer mean learning, among other things, that mistakes can be good rather than bad surprises?" (Sedgwick 2002, 145).

What I love so deeply about "Paradoxes of Visibility in the Field" is its anticipation of Sedgwick's argument by reorienting the queer from the paranoid to the reparative. I can think of little more humiliating than the idea of being caught midcoitus in the field, but humiliation is intentionally absent from Seizer's account ("one laughs at these misunderstandings so as not to cry," she says [1995, 74]). In a rejection of paranoid temporality and reproductive futurity, Seizer orients toward reparation. In Shawn Wilson's terms, there were two seconds in which everyone in that room was thinking exactly the same thing, and even though that thing may have been a curse word, those two seconds made possible the extraordinary. They encountered Muñoz's ecstatic time: at once self-conscious and oblivious, possessing transformative charge. The encounter was not a seed of mortification at having transgressed, at having failed at the performance of appropriate roles, but a door opening to the possibility of transcending the roles that might have generated that mortification in the first place.

Ruth Behar (1996) points out that ethnographic knowledge, like theater, is illusory: it's a "tragedy" to try to resuscitate something of the ethnographic experience from scattered fieldnotes and a "theater of farce" when ethnographers assert ourselves as authorities about people and cultures among whom we are helpless and adrift in direct social encounter. Behar calls for ethnographic vulnerability: "We anthropologists . . . leave behind our own trail of longing, desires, and unfulfilled expectation in those upon whom we descend. About that vulnerability we are still barely able to speak," she says (25). Inspired by Behar's call to vulnerability and Seizer's exercise of it, I close this chapter with a reread of my own field experience, a theater of layered heteronormativities reimagined now through the lens of queer potential.

This is a story of my own fieldwork performance as it was shaped by my queer paranoia and its associated doubling of presence. I spent a total of about thirteen months between 2009 and 2011 in Délı̨nę, in the Sahtu region in Canada's Northwest Territories, where I supported local archive digitization and knowledge documentation initiatives while developing my doctoral project. I have published very little from this work. I have said in other forums that the work I did was for the community above all other audiences, and I remain steadfast in that assertion, but I remain burdened with a dogged sense of failure for it—a sense of failure that takes the form of impostor syndrome and managing the urge to apologize or rationalize my decision. I reread that research performance now through the lens of reparation, querying that failure (*my* failure) in terms of the possibility it suggests "more creative, more cooperative, more surprising ways of being in the world" (Halberstam 2011, 2–3).

I arrived in Délı̨nę under invitation from a senior scholar who had been recruiting graduate students to support local endeavors in cultural documentation and digitizing of the local archive; I had a letter of support from the Chief and I felt well set up to develop the relationships that I hoped would enable the development of a community-driven doctoral research topic. But while I wanted to do community-driven work, I didn't actually know how, and the environment I arrived in was different from what I had expected. Despite the letter of support, the Chief did not understand my motive for being in Délı̨nę, and while I was met with kindness from every new acquaintance, that kindness was paired with the mistrust common to over-researched and under-resourced colonized people. Before I could do research, I had to develop trust. So I built relationships oriented toward that futurity: how could I help people trust me enough to let me do the work (and create the products) I wanted to do? With academic arrogance, I imagined my work as a solitary project that would generate its value from the contribution of my scholarly expertise. I intended to work reciprocally, but still, the idea of developing a project so collaborative it would decenter me challenged what I thought I knew about how ethnography was performed.

The need for outcomes produced in a fixed time frame tied to my funding and my degree trajectory informed the way I presented myself. In particular, it took a very long time before I let anyone know I was gay. When I was teased about my love life—whether I had one or whether I should develop one in Délı̨nę—I did my best to avoid lying outright, but I did not correct assumptions that my hypothetical partners were male.

This was a performance gendered, contextual, and professional. Unlike Seizer's situation in early 1990s Madras, 2009 Délı̨nę had hundreds of satellite TV channels, (limited) high-speed internet, and social media, so local frameworks for understanding urban settler lesbian identities required none of Angela's metaphors. There were no out gay women there, but I befriended a few gay men in town, two of whom confirmed my impression that the concept of Two-Spiritedness, often erroneously treated as a pan-Indigenous phenomenon in North America, was not relevant there. Those gay male friends were well loved and well connected in the community, but they had grown up there. I was a stranger, and while the idea of being out did not feel more physically dangerous there than it did in my then-home of Indiana, I feared the outcomes for my work if lived openly and wound up being ostracized. I had too much money and time committed to the project to be able to change my plans without jeopardizing my ability to complete my degree. So, for the first time in many years, I donned heteronormativity like an invisibility cloak.

This wasn't the only way that I sought to smooth any of my surfaces that I feared others might find jagged. Every time I left my house, I performed the least offensive version of myself: one who was infinitely patient and unjudgmental and always had time for anyone who asked for it. I didn't hate this version of me (I learned a lot from her!), but she was exhausting to maintain; I have never before or since so keenly felt Ahmed's sense of queer tiredness (2014, 146).

Perhaps that was why, in the middle of my first summer in Délı̨nę, I cut my hair. I took a weekend away with another graduate student to get a change of scenery and help her, a geographer, with a bird study she was conducting in a nearby community. Like Seizer, we stayed in a borrowed home, and in its kitchen my friend sheared my shoulder-length curls to barely an inch off my scalp. When we returned to Délı̨nę the following day, we wandered up to a cook-out in front of a friend's house. We had both been living with Morris and Bernice Neyelle, a couple in their late fifties who often housed visiting researchers. Bernice was a tiny woman of outsized personality and effervescent kindness. Morris was a philosopher; my fondest memories of that summer are of sitting at his kitchen table into the small hours of the morning, mesmerized by his storytelling. Morris and Bernice were at this cook-out, and as we mingled over sodas and supper grilled over an open flame, Morris jostled me with his elbow: "When I first saw you just now, I thought, *Who's that boy walking over this way?*"

We laughed. "I wanted a change," I said. "Do you like it?"

"Sure." It wasn't convincing, but he was kind.

Nobody else commented. The haircut was, I imagine, folded into my white, urban, academic familiar strangeness. But it was, to me, the first step of many in embracing a more masculine queer performance, one that intertwined rather than subjugated my own sense of femininity, increasingly confident in its rebellion against neoliberal reproductive futurity.

My hair was still short when I returned to Délı̨nę a year later. Anticipating a nine-month stay, I arranged housing with a local deacon. Délı̨nę is mostly Catholic, and the local church owned a small bungalow where the priest would stay when he visited the community for a couple of days every month or two. The house sat empty the rest of the time, but it had to be heated all winter, so I lived there, covering the expenses of maintaining it, on the condition that I would absent myself whenever the priest came. It was a comfortable setup in every respect but one. There were two posters on the wall near the front door, one a picture of a baby held in cupped hands that proclaimed the sanctity of fetal life, and the other a picture of a bride looking coyly up at the camera from the arms of her groom, promoting the use of the rhythm method for contraception. It is a testament to the depth of my research performance that I lived there for nine months and left those posters up.

In the time between my first and second trips to Délı̨nę, I fell in love, and unlike Seizer, it wasn't with someone who would be near me in the field. Huddled on a sofa safely out of view of those disapproving posters, I spoke to her on the phone, nurturing the wonderful thing we'd quickly built before I'd left. When I went out, I couldn't talk about her. In the house, my brain overcompensated, struggling to think about anything else. I lived half in a constant future: when I would be home, when this would be done. And I lived half in an impossible present: in Délı̨nę, but not—or at least not entirely, not fully. I reentered the house, and the walls oriented me toward the future, the Child, productivity and reproductivity, and then I telephoned the woman who, to no fault of her own, stood in their way.

For months, exhausted and divided, I made no measurable progress on the doctoral research that was the reason I was putting myself through this. I remembered the mistrust I had encountered on arrival and oriented myself toward its resolution; I made friends; I attended community parties, I volunteered, I served food to Elders at holiday feasts. And, divided and exhausted as I was, I loved this. I loved calling numbers at Bingo night, I loved judging the Halloween costume contest (the most incredible costume contest I have ever attended); I loved showing up at community events with an open schedule and empty hands and an offer: *How can I help?*

Above all, I loved connecting people with archive recordings. People would visit our office at the back of the government building to ask if we had recordings from one Elder or another, and if we did, I would burn CDs for them to take home. I made CDs for other purposes, too: for use at the annual Spiritual Gathering and for use on the local radio station. Word traveled, and people would approach me around town and ask me, Do you have anything from my ʔehtsée [Elder, grandparent]? From this illustrious Chief? From that revered prophet? I invited them to visit my office so I could check. The stories were discussed not as relics from the past but as still-living voices of passed-on people: "My children just love Rosie," one mother told me, even though Rosie had passed away before her children were born. In this one statement, linear temporality collapsed, the present a palimpsest of the before and the after.

A senior scholar working with me suggested I was putting too much time into burning CDs and not enough time into my research. But in the moment, connecting people with these recordings felt invaluable: nobody else was doing it. Months passed, and I did not conduct a single interview. The particular presence of my life in Délı̨nę, being and building relations most of all, did not lend itself well to the instrumentality of an interview. I reencountered my queerness through, in Seizer's (1995, 98) terms, the ways I "fit in and stuck out differently in ... other systems of differences." I was infinitely and indefinitely present, my focus on the immediate, and interviews involved a reorientation toward futurity, toward outcomes that felt hard to imagine now. In failing to progress, I encountered new ways of being, new ways of creating.

And yet I knew: I had a doctorate to finish, and every passing week was time that pressed me toward the point where I would have to succeed or fail, measured by the evaluation of a document I would create. I wanted to succeed, to earn the respect of my own committee of elders, but the person I performed felt incapable. Time became my only rudder, but it was irreconcilable to itself; I was living twice, all versions conflicting. It had to end.

One of my gay Dene friends had an affectionate tendency to double my name, calling me "Sarah Gordon Sarah Gordon," and in retrospect it felt like he was naming both dimensions of me: the one he encountered every day and the one I kept at home. He began to joke about hooking me up with one of his female friends. I had never told him I was gay, but he might have read meaning into my androgynous appearance, so I couldn't tell how serious he was about it. Feeling like my twinning of myself was splitting me in half, I finally asked him as we walked down the gravel road one sunny day.

"Did you know I was gay?"

He blinked at me, and then he laughed. "No."

And then we changed the subject, and nothing much changed between us.

After him, I cautiously told a few other people: friends who cared for me, the folks who checked in on me if I went too long without visiting. Nobody seemed affected, and I was confronted by how much of my personal and professional paranoia I seemed to have hauled north with me from Indiana.

The pieces of myself slid into each other, my shadow reattaching itself to my body at the feet.

Then, the interviews started.

The project I had set out to do, the one I had put in all my proposals, felt grounded in some other time. I abandoned it. I hired an experienced interpreter named Dennis Kenny who quickly became frustrated by my interviews' lack of direction; I had lost the ability to think forward, toward quantifiable knowledge production. When my questions stalled, Dennis would sometimes jump in with questions of his own to move things forward, subverting our established and expected roles.

But still the outcomes delighted him, and me, and often the people on the other end of the microphone. They shared narratives of every genre, stories of their lives, stories of their world, stories of the cosmos. On the microphone, an Elder chatted with a Raven—a sacred bird—outside her kitchen window.

Reflecting on this now, I consider how Mintzi Martínez-Rivera (2022) describes how reimagining the field outside of heteropatriarchal, colonial, and racialized dualities, particularly in the Latinx world, co-occurs with a reimagination of the field outside of physical space into transnational or even transdimensional potentials. I don't pretend that I, a white settler academic interviewing Indigenous Elders, could ever eliminate the colonial dynamics of my work or my relationships any more than I can say that my own experiences mirror those of the many Person of Color scholars I have cited in this chapter. But in both respects, I can recognize myself as an ethnographic other: one who has been observed in the role that I play and invited to experience the potential of performing differently.

I deposited the interviews in the local archive. They were beautiful and chaotic, and when I eventually went home to Indiana, I had to make sense of them. I had to write; the normative temporality dictated that the project didn't matter unless it bore scholarly fruit. So I wrote something. It took longer than I hoped, and to this day I'm not convinced it was very good. But it satisfied the requirement; it tied off its temporal agenda. I deposited a copy of the thesis in the Délı̨nę archive and provided additional copies to community leaders. I don't think anybody read them. I tried to gain support from community leaders to transition the project to a book, but that conversation never gained traction, and so those outcomes remained in my dissertation and in the hands of the Délı̨nę Go'tı̨nę Government, and that's all.

A failure, perhaps.

And yet, in the spring of 2022, I spoke to a Dene friend with whom I was developing a new project. Morris Neyelle, the kind philosopher and storyteller who hosted me during my first summer in Délı̨nę, had passed away just a week earlier from colon cancer, and the intense grief that knotted my stomach—that sucker-punches me now, as I think of him—was a fraction of the grief reverberating through Délı̨nę.

"It's been a real trauma for the community," my friend said.

"I interviewed him twice," I told her. "The recordings are in the archive, but I'll bring more copies when I come up."

She paused for a moment. "Sarah," she said. "Do you know what a gift those will be?"

I am not the only one to have interviewed Morris; there must be dozens of other visiting academics who have done it. But each one folds time, an emergence of the impossible—something extraordinary happening, in Shawn Wilson's terms. Morris's voice now; his presence outliving him. "My children just love Morris," a mother might one day say about those recordings that have my voice on them, too.

Legendary queer folklorist Kay Turner (2021) imagined a *deep lez* folkloristics, one that embraces the pleasure in the pain of decolonizing a discipline. "Folklore provides endless resources for understanding the human love and fear of queer beings dwelling down below, or in cracks, or in shadows, or in the blinding start of snowstorms" (26), she said and only now, in this reflection, do I realize that I was the one in the cracks, filling gaps, somewhere between hiding and creating my own space. As part of their resolution with Angela, Seizer and her girlfriend relocated from the master bedroom in their borrowed bungalow to the floor of the child's room, accepting Angela's authority in some spheres while asserting their own in spaces where authority does not normally reside. Something new emerged, different and queer in its revelation of new possibilities. I think of my voice appended to Morris's on those tapes: not the point of the recording but there, trying to stay out of the way, camped out on the floor of an ancillary bedroom. I try to be the stage, not the performer, but I'm part of the show just the same. I commit usury, benefiting from my proximity to him, sacrificing nothing for what I gain. I mint money, but the value is real.

Notes

I extend the warmest gratitude to my wife, Annie Corrigan, who was the girl on the other end of the phone all those years ago. To Susan Seizer for her kind words when I showed her an earlier version of this chapter and told her that her work had inspired me to write it. To Solimar Otero, Anthony Buccitelli, and two anonymous reviewers for their feedback that helped make the chapter better. And to Morris Neyelle, whose sudden passing was a tragedy and a devastating ode to Northern health care inequity, and whose memory inspires me every day.

Bibliography

Abu-Lughod, Lila. 1991. "Writing against Culture." In *Recapturing Anthropology: Working in the Present*, edited by Richard Gabriel Fox, 139–62. Santa Fe, NM: School of American Research Press.

Ahmed, Sara. 2014. *The Cultural Politics of Emotion*. 2nd ed. Edinburgh, Scotland: Edinburgh University Press.

Allen, Jafari S. 2022. *There's a Disco Ball between Us: A Theory of Black Gay Life*. Durham, NC: Duke University Press.

Bauman, Richard. 1977. *Verbal Art as Performance*. Long Grove, IL: Waveland.

———. 2004. *A World of Others' Words: Cross-Cultural Perspectives on Intertextuality*. Oxford, UK: Blackwell.

Behar, Ruth. 1996. *The Vulnerable Observer: Anthropology That Breaks Your Heart*. Boston: Beacon.

Beliso-De Jesus, Aisha Mahina. 2016. "A Hieroglyphics of Zora Neale Hurston." *Journal of Africana Religions* 4 (2): 290–303. https://doi.org/10.5325/jafrireli.4.2.0290.

Butler, Judith. 1988. "Performative Acts and Gender Constitution: An Essay in Phenomenology and Feminist Theory." *Theatre Journal* 40 (4): 519. https://doi.org/10.2307/3207893.

Castañeda, Quetzil E. 2006. "The Invisible Theatre of Ethnography: Performative Principles of Fieldwork." *Anthropological Quarterly* 79 (1): 75–104.

Crapanzano, Vincent. 1986. "Hermes' Dilemma: The Masking of Subversion in Ethnographic Description." In *Writing Culture: The Poetics and Politics of Ethnography*, edited by James Clifford and George E. Marcus, 25th anniversary, 51–76. Berkeley: University of California Press.

Edelman, Lee. 2004. *No Future: Queer Theory and the Death Drive*. Durham, NC: Duke University Press.

Fanon, Frantz. 1952. *Peau Noire, Masques Blancs*. Paris: Éditions du Seuil.

Goffman, Erving. 1975. *Frame Analysis*. Harmondsworth, UK: Penguin.

Gray, Mary L. 2009. *Out in the Country: Youth, Media, and Queer Visibility in Rural America*. New York: New York University Press.

Halberstam, J. Jack. 2011. *The Queer Art of Failure*. Durham, NC: Duke University Press.

Hsu, Francis L. K. 1979. "The Cultural Problem of the Cultural Anthropologist." *American Anthropologist* 81 (3): 517–32.

Hurston, Zora Neale. 1990. *Mules and Men*. New York: Harper Perennial.

Lawrence, David Todd. 2022. "When We Blew It: Vulnerability, Trying, and Failure in Ethnographic Fieldwork." *Journal of Folklore Research* 59 (3): 129–47.

Martínez-Rivera, Mintzi Auanda. 2022. "Doing Research of/from/at Home: Fieldwork Research Ethics in Latinx Contexts." *Journal of American Folklore* 135 (536): 180–89.

McGlotten, Shaka. 2012. "Always Toward a Black Queer Anthropology." *Transforming Anthropology* 20 (1): 3–4. https://doi.org/10.1111/j.1548-7466.2011.01140.x.

Muñoz, José Esteban. 2009. *Cruising Utopia: The Then and There of Queer Futurity*. New York: New York University Press.

Murdock, George P. 1952. "Anthropology and Its Contribution to Public Health." *American Journal of Public Health* 42:7–11.

Musser, Amber Jamilla. 2018. *Sensual Excess: Queer Femininity and Brown Jouissance. Sensual Excess*. New York: New York University Press. https://doi.org/10.18574/nyu/9781479807031.001.0001.

Narayan, Kirin, and Urmila Devi Sood. 1997. *Mondays on the Dark Night of the Moon*. New York: Oxford University Press.

Oxford English Dictionary. 2022. "Fieldwork, n." In *Oxford English Dictionary Online*. Oxford, UK: Oxford University Press. http://www.oed.com/view/Entry/69952.

Sawin, Patricia E. 2002. "Performance at the Nexus of Gender, Power, and Desire: Reconsidering Bauman's Verbal Art from the Perspective of Gendered Subjectivity as Performance." *Journal of American Folklore* 115 (455): 28–61. https://doi.org/10.2307/542078.

Sedgwick, Eve Kosofsky. 2002. *Touching Feeling: Affect, Pedagogy, Performativity*. Durham, NC: Duke University Press.

Seizer, Susan. 1995. "Paradoxes of Visibility in the Field: Rites of Queer Passage in Anthropology." *Public Culture* 8:73–100.

Strathern, Marilyn. 1987. "An Awkward Relationship: The Case of Feminism and Anthropology." *Signs* 12 (2): 276–92.

Turner, Kay. 2021. "Deep Folklore/Queer Folkloristics." In *Advancing Folkloristics*, edited by Jesse A. Fivecoate, Kristina Downs, and Meredith A. E. McGriff, 9–34. Bloomington: Indiana University Press.

Turner, Victor. 2018. *Dramas, Fields, and Metaphors: Symbolic Action in Human Society*. Ithaca: Cornell University Press.

Ward, Cynthia. 2012. "Truths, Lies, Mules and Men: Through the 'Spy-Glass of Anthropology' and What Zora Saw There." *Western Journal of Black Studies* 36 (4): 301–13.

Weiss, Margot. 2016. "Always After: Desiring Queerness, Desiring Anthropology." *Cultural Anthropology* 31 (4): 627–38. https://doi.org/10.14506/ca31.4.11.

Wilkins, Langston Collin. 2021. "Black Folk, White Gaze: Folklore and Black Male Precarity." *Journal of Folklore Research* 58 (3): 77–98.

Wilson, Shawn. 2008. *Research Is Ceremony: Indigenous Research Methods*. Halifax, Nova Scotia, Canada: Fernwood Publishing.

Sarah M. Gordon is Associate Professor of Folklore at Memorial University. Dr. Gordon studies the intersection of folklore and power, both internally to the field's academic history and elsewhere in digital and anti-colonial spaces. Her work has appeared in *Journal of American Folklore, Journal of Folklore Research*, and *Western Folklore*.

4

Kenneth Burke Meets the Flop-Eared Mule
A Fiddle Tune and the Performance of Form

GREGORY HANSEN

Performance theory provides resources for analyzing and interpreting folklore within living social contexts. Theorists draw heavily from anthropological linguistics, speech communication, literary approaches, and other disciplines to complete studies of verbal artistry within communicative events. Common interests include consideration of ways that narratives emerge within interaction between storytellers and audience members as displays of communicative competence that are expressed and subjected to evaluation (Bauman 1975, 293). The emphasis often is on emergent qualities of storytelling and other genres of oral literature. A living context of performance generally is central to these studies. Although some performance scholarship has provided deep insights into performances entextualized in earlier events, performance theorists tend to blend their own fieldwork with their cultural interpretation. A performance-centered study of music, for example, is apt to focus on an event in which a ballad is sung, gospel music is presented, or blues music emerges in a local jam session (Glassie 1982, 247; Hinson 1991; Ferris 2016). The in situ emphasis has yielded important insights into creativity, but performance theory also has wider applications that deserve more consideration. Applying ideas resonant with performance theory to existing texts, in this case transcriptions of instrumental music, revives what first may appear to be a lifeless representation of a past rendition of a tune. Special emphasis on artistic form can reveal nuanced elements of the performative qualities of expressive culture, elements of creative expression that may first appear moribund on the printed page. Latent aesthetic qualities may become unleashed by recognizing how specific elements of form are encapsulated within a musical transcription. Alan Jabbour's meticulous transcription of a wonderful fiddle tune provides a case in point. An in-depth consideration of the formal qualities in the tune can revitalize elements of the musical artistry that Jabbour recorded well over half a century ago (Jabbour 2008).

Instrumental Music and Performance Theory

As folklorists initiated a shift into contextualism during the 1960s, they focused primarily on in situ performances of verbal arts and musical expression. Performance theorists framed folklore in terms of events. Roger Abrahams's influential assertion that "folklore is folklore only when performed" remains a central concept when considering how traditional expressive culture is negotiated and emergent within social contexts (Abrahams 1972, 28). By the 1970s, folklorists employed performance-centered approaches to study a wide variety of musical and verbal art in foundational studies of ballads, blues, gospel, performed sermons, and other genres (Davis [1985] 2017; Ferris 2016; Hinson 1991; Riddle 1970). The emphasis on vocal music in these kinds of studies is an important legacy of performance theory, and folklorists interested in music continue to use performance theory as a central research paradigm. Their work has typically explored lyrical qualities associated with sung texts. Folklorists have found performance theory useful for studying musical expression in their exploration of musical repertoire, self-presentation with diverse social contexts, variations of song lyrics within different performance situations, and other topics. As Burt Feintuch noted, there were relatively few studies of instrumental music by folklorists prior to the 1970s (Feintuch 1975). His studies of Earl "Pop" Hafler's fiddling are some of the first to use performance theory for studying instrumental folk music; today, in-depth musical analysis often is the providence of ethnomusicologists.

In the half century that has followed Feintuch's initial interest in using performance theory to study instrumental music, scholarship on fiddling has blossomed. Researchers explore a range of topics including histories of musical styles within regions and ethnic groups, life histories of individual musicians, stylistics analyses, historical-geographic elucidation of the life histories of various tunes, analyses of historical tunebooks, inquiries into the dynamics of festivals and contests, and an array of interests relevant to the music's social history and its contemporary manifestations (Beisswenger 2002; Cauthen 1989; Goertzen 2011; Marshall 2006; Perlman 2015; Titon 2001). Within this wealth of scholarship, often there is a bifurcation between ethnomusicological transcription and analysis versus performance-centered interpretation of expressive culture. Living tunes are transcribed as texts, and researchers may also explore older written variants preserved in the pages of tunebooks and other older written representations (Goertzen 2017). Consequently, the tune may be cast somewhat as a static artifact, thereby obscuring performative qualities of the music at its most basic level. This tendency to turn live music into entextualized artifacts may be amplified through the legacy of musicological approaches that contribute to contemporary scholarship. This tendency to view a tune as a somewhat static text may also be influenced by folklorists' relegation of instrumental music to ethnomusicologists. Bringing some of the foundational concepts of performance theory back into studies of written transcriptions of tunes, however, has the potential to enliven our understanding of musical creativity.

One important resource for reanimating written transcriptions of instrumental music is renewed consideration of performative qualities of musical form—an important component of musicological analysis. Researchers directly identify formal patterns using broad cover terms such as *verse* and *chorus*, but they also identify form in music through alphabetical or numerical systems as exemplified in Alan Jabbour's extensive scholarship on fiddling. These conventional approaches to determining how form is integral to music-making provide important resources for understanding musical creativity, and they provide a strong basis for revitalizing how form is a dynamic aspect of per*form*ance. This shift from form as a component to structure to form as a creative action yields a more vibrant approach to reading musical transcriptions.

Not only does Kenneth Burke's rhetorical theory offer vibrant ways to explore form as an artistic resource, but his work also is an important precursor to performance theory. His treatment of form needs to be integrated into a wider perspective on language that he termed *dramatism* (Burke 1967). Burke's approach to language as a form of symbolic action provided a strong influence on writers such as Dell Hymes and Richard Bauman and their contributions to performance theory (Hymes 1981b, 239; Bauman 1975, 295). Burke's writing on the psychology of audience has also influenced rhetorical approaches to folklore, especially through his articulation of the role of form within literary expression (Burke 1968b, 29; Davis [1985] 2017; Rosenberg 1970). How might Burke's delineation of aspects of literary form be applied to the analysis of instrumental music? Burke's treatment of form in his classic articles "Psychology and Form" and "Lexicon Rhetoricæ" provides resources for connecting patterns of literary form to musical analysis (Burke 1968a, 1968b). Burke's own music criticism tended to focus on classical music and jazz, but his writing on form is especially valuable for examining formal patterns in folk music. This chapter analyzes the performance of form within traditional fiddle tunes to demonstrate how Burke's larger theory of the psychology of audience can enhance more conventional approaches to musical transcription, such as those used by Alan Jabbour. Burke's writing on the psychology of audience provides a valuable schema to enhance our understanding of the place of form within performance studies.

I was unable to find any evidence that the rhetorical theorist Kenneth Burke ever encountered the "Flop-Eared Mule." Burke was an accomplished pianist and insightful music critic in the 1920s and '30s for *The Dial*, but he mainly wrote about classical music, and his tastes were predominantly highbrow (Overall 2013, 1). It is known that he greatly appreciated the artistry of his grandson, Harry Chapin, but he would have preferred violin caprices to old-time fiddle tunes. Nevertheless, aspects of his rhetorical theory provide valuable resources for the study of fiddle tunes, which are especially useful resources to explore through Burke's writing as they display prominent formal patterns that relate to their overall structure as well as more nuanced elements of how a fiddler uses smaller formal patterns as creative resources. Delineating elements of musical form via Burke's "Lexicon Rhetoricæ" provides insight into musical semiotics in terms of the appeal of the musical notes themselves, and Burke's rhetorical theory also enhances our understanding of musical performances.

Burke's voluminous writing is complex and often arcane. In regard to specific applications, his writing also is frequently straightforward and brilliantly lucid. His treatment of form is a particularly relevant case in point. Form can be a nebulous idea. Folklorists may sometimes too loosely equate form with genre, and researchers of a formalist bent may define form as both the overall shape and the individual patterns that are present in written texts and transcriptions. Burke gives us a way of thinking about form less as an abstract idea and more as a mode of action. Burke writes, "A work has form in so far as one part of it leads a reader to anticipate another part, to be gratified by the sequence" (Burke 1968a, 124). He draws connections between literary form and musical form by conceptualizing form as "an arousing and fulfillment of desires" (Burke 1968a, 124). In this perspective, Burke enfolds a consideration of form within his overall treatment of language as a mode of action.

Despite the challenges of defining form in musical expression, folklorists and ethnomusicologists who study fiddling offer a great deal of attention to musical form. They may elucidate formal patterns when completing transcriptions of contemporary performances as well as explore the form of older representations of tunes within a range of established collections. An excellent case in point is Alan Jabbour's transcriptions of tunes within the American Folklife Center's "Fiddle Tunes of the Old Frontier: The Henry Reed Collection" within the Library of Congress (American Folklife Center; Jabbour 2008). His notes on his mentor Henry Reed's performance of the well-known hoedown "Flop-Eared Mule" provide a model for considering different approaches to formal analysis of tunes. The ostensibly simple tune actually contains a wealth of creative resources that show the value of using fiddle tunes to understand how formal qualities of music are essential resources for artistic performance. Jabbour's analysis of the tune is an excellent model for understanding conventional treatments of musical form. To understand salient elements of his musicological transcription and analysis, it is essential to consider this specific tune within the wider context of old-time fiddling.

What Is Old-time Fiddling?

The origins of American fiddling are difficult to pinpoint exactly, but the instrument is present during colonial times and shows a variety of European precedents. Scottish, Scots-Irish, and British influences predominate, although studies of tunes demonstrate influences from a range of European nations. Furthermore, an entire generation of fiddle scholars has demonstrated influences from Black musicians that have been evident for at least three hundred years (Cauthen 1989, 4). Alan Jabbour, Joyce Cauthen, and other writers argue that distinctively American styles emerged by the early nineteenth century. These styles are characterized by African American influences, unique instrumentation that includes the pairing of fiddles with banjos, surprisingly diverse multiethnic contributions, and the development of uniquely American fiddle tunes (Jabbour 2008, 10). Music associated with the instrument during this era likely was simply referred to as *fiddling*. It definitely comprised a wide variety of genres and styles, including marches, reels, jigs, hornpipes, and other dance forms. By the twentieth century, the term *old-time* can be seen in print. It came to describe approaches to playing that instrument that is in inherent contrast to high-style violin playing as well as more modern forms of music such as jazz and, eventually, bluegrass and country and western styles (Beisswenger 2002, xi). *Old-time* now is somewhat ambiguous. Depending on the region and the musical communities, it can refer to only the tunes that remain vibrant from an oral/aural tradition to any tune that is simply seen as time honored. Despite the vagaries of definition, it is useful to consider how the term often is used to make distinctions between a style of fiddling associated with bluegrass that emerged on the commercial airwaves in the 1940s and '50s and ways of playing the instrument for old-time dances and old-time jam sessions that feature fiddling that musicians may somewhat tautologically define as *old-time*.

The term is artificial, but it remains valuable to consider specific attributes of fiddling that are constructed as old-time. These attributes index distinctive features of various tunes as well as some of the characteristic musical patterns that researchers find interesting. As we will see, they all help to define salient aspects of "Flop-Eared Mule" that are pertinent to Burke's treatment of form. Terms such as *bluegrass* and *country* are also haunted by definitional demons, but many folklorists and ethnomusicologists do find it useful to place old-time fiddling in contrast to these major styles. *Old-time string band* often refers to music that predates commercial country music and bluegrass. It does encompass original and contemporary tunes that are composed in a style that reflects both old and new musical traditions. But musicians and aficionados generally share community aesthetic values about what constitutes old-time music. Consider how Jay Ungar and Molly Mason's 1982 tune "Ashokan Farewell" not only is too easily characterized as a traditional fiddle tune but is also accepted as an old-time waltz by contemporary players. There is a feel to playing these kinds of waltzes that makes the category "country waltz" a resonant genre of the music. Another attribute associated with old-time music is the focus on oral and aural musical traditions. Fiddle researchers recognize that many of these tunes appear in tunebooks (Goertzen 2017, 79–84). They note that an old-time tune may have anonymous origins that predate its inscription in print, and researchers also recognize that composed tunes often enter aural traditions through secondary orality. However, there are distinctive attributes of style that depend heavily on aurality, and mastering a wide range of techniques and textures is essential for performing in a style that others accept as old-time. Beginning violinists studying through the Suzuki method learn tunes like "Liza Jane," but it is unlikely that most fiddlers would accept their renditions as old-time hoedowns. Specific elements of style can be identified through an analysis of form, but the feel of the music is grounded in shared and negotiated aural traditions that sound different from violin playing, country fiddling, and the hot licks of bluegrass music.

Characteristic genres and styles of playing do emerge when listening to tunes that are classified as old-time. Here, typical genres that often are subsumed include reels, jigs, hornpipes, schottisches, strathspeys, polkas, mazurkas, waltzes, and other genres whose origins predate the establishment of commercial media. Other genres with origins more connected to the music industry may also be represented as old-time as some fiddlers will play blues music, ragtime, sentimental parlor tunes, gospel hymns, and a variety of pop tunes as old-time music. Occasionally, Disney show tunes like "It's a Small World (After All)," for example, may show up in song circles, but their reception will vary depending on the tastes and modes of fellow musicians. The music is heavily grounded in performance contexts. Jam sessions are hotbeds for fiddling. Fiddle contests may also codify old-time as a distinctive style and perhaps further constrain what can be performed by creating distinctions between Old-Time and Open so that older styles are preserved and honored as evident within the Official Florida State Fiddle Contest (Florida State Fiddlers' Association 2022). There is a performance context that underlies and perhaps unifies these other two contexts. Namely, old-time fiddling is seen as dance music. Fiddlers recognize how old-time is strongly associated with hoedown tunes used for square and step dancing and that this style is grounded in the formal qualities of reels, hornpipes, and European dance tunes. Old-time fiddling can also include couple dances as fiddlers may master waltzes, schottisches, polkas, and a range of styles that the community considers to be old-time. The specific formal qualities of dance tunes are clearly evident through the use of Burke's rhetorical theory. Understanding connections between Burke's writing and fiddling requires some background on folklorists and ethnomusicologists' documentation of the tune itself.

"Flop-Eared Mule"

Some of the challenges and ambiguities evident in attempts to define old-time fiddling become resolved when focusing on specific tunes. An analysis of "Flop-Eared Mule" reveals characteristic patterns of old-time fiddle tunes. Its history and place within cultural contexts further demonstrates its value to scholarship on fiddling traditions. Comparisons of tunebook versions, recordings, and field transcriptions allow researchers to identify its numerous variants. Drew Beisswenger notes that "Flop-Eared Mule" has a number of names and that it is commonly performed throughout the United States (Beisswenger and McCann 2008, 196). Some call it "Lop-Eared Mule," "Big-Eared Mule," or "Long-Eared Mule," and it also has been called "Karo" and "Asheville." Other names also emerge that provide researchers with more clues about its formal properties and origin. Jeff Todd Titon documented the tune as "The Old Schottische" in Kentucky, and the tune also has been called "College Schottische" (Titon 2001, 147, 152). Beisswenger and McCann suggest that the earliest version may be "Detroit Schottische," a tune credited to Adam Couse, who taught dance in Detroit and published the tune in 1854. This version includes four parts, each played in a different key: D, A, G, and C (Beisswenger and McCann 2008, 163). It is unlikely that Couse created this composition out of whole cloth as versions of the tune include melodic lines common to dance music, and composer credit during this era could be assigned to those who simply wrote transcriptions or reworkings of existing tunes (Goertzen 2017, 66).

The written version of the tune entered oral tradition in intriguing ways. First, fiddlers dropped two of the different parts as the tune became condensed down to the typical binary structure of many tunes. We will see how specific formal features are integral to defining both the A part and the B part. Another interesting musicological element is that the tune retained a change of key as it shifted into this second strain. Fiddlers typically kick off the tune in the key of G and then shift into D. These key changes are not particularly common, but G and D are commonly used by fiddlers. The tune's early publication and variant names also reveal some interesting layers to its history. "Flop-Eared Mule" likely originated as a schottische before it shifted into a new genre to become a hoedown tune. Schottisches are played in 4/4 or 2/4 time and are popular dance tunes in various regions of the United States. But "Flop-Eared Mule" is often associated with fiddling in the South, where schottisches are rare. Schottisches can refer to either a musical genre or a dance style that features couples who complete skipping and hopping steps as they work around a circle on the dance floor. When the "Detroit Schottische" transformed into a hoedown, it began to resemble the reels that form the infrastructure of square dances played at hoedowns. This dancing style influenced how the fiddlers played "Flop-Eared Mule" as reels tend to be faster than schottisches, and hoedown fiddlers tend to play hard, with strong down-bows and a different feel to what constitutes a sense of *bounce* that is definitive of both the musical and dance genres that are identified as hoedowns.

Fiddle scholars are intrigued by the dynamic elements of old-time music and its place within oral and aural traditions. Whereas researchers may explore the rich musical expression that is part of genres not seen as old-time, they take a different focus when they explore bluegrass or other styles connected more to commercial genres, which simply are not as influenced by the long history of square and step dancing that is integral to old-time fiddling. Folklorists who began documenting and analyzing instrumental folk music discovered the need to explore fiddling within its long and vibrant context of dance and informal jam sessions. They focused on what has become a wide but definite corpus of tunes and genres, and much of their interest follows the significant scholarly interests of early folklore in a tune's origins, diffusion, and distribution. These interests and more research questions have drawn generations of folklorists and ethnomusicologists to focus on tunes that are well integrated into local repertoires as well as characteristic of genres and styles seen as old-time.

Henry Reed's Version of the Tune as Transcribed by Alan Jabbour

Alan Jabbour's fieldwork with numerous fiddlers in Appalachia is foundational to contemporary research on old-time music. His research is now curated by the Library of Congress's American Folklife Center as "Fiddle Tunes of the Old Frontier: The Henry Reed Collection" (American Folklife Center). As Jabbour expanded his interest in violin playing to focus on Appalachian and southeastern United States fiddling, he found a mentor in Henry Reed, forming a model relationship between folklorist and folk performer that remains a vibrant approach for learning about music today (Carter 1991, 73). Reed's rendition of "Flop-Eared Mule" provides a model for considering Jabbour and other researchers' well-established approaches to formal analyses of tunes. He recorded this version on June 18, 1966, in Glen Lyn, Virginia, during a field session that he completed with Karen Jabbour, his wife and research partner. Notes from his fieldwork show the characteristic ways that form is represented in musicology.

>Meter: 4/4
>Strains: 2 (high-low, 4–4)
>Phrase structure: ABAC QRQS (abcd abce qrst qrsu)
>Compass: 12
>Key: G/D
>Rendition: 1r-2r-1r-2r-1r-2r-1r-2r-1
>Stylistic features: Slurs predominate in bowing. It is interesting how many times through he played this (4½ times through, which is more than his usual). His playing is also clean, as if he had a moment unhampered by physical impediments so kept going.
>*Handwritten*: Played 4 times thru plus 1st str. once at end. Transcription from 2nd time thru (1st run of each str.). The style is lilting, w. the 1st of each pair of 16th notes longer than the 2nd.

Jabbour's fifty-year-old transcription of a fiddle tune provides an excellent text that can be read through Burke's approach to form. The specific features in Jabbour's analysis of Reed's playing become clearer when considering the tune's actual score.[1] At this point, however, consider how he characterizes form as patterns within a musical system. The 4/4 meter is common within the hoedown genre and represents how the formal rhythmic pattern is established through sets of four beats to each measure. The strains refer to how the tune is composed of two distinct parts, somewhat analogous to a verse and a chorus. Within each strain are specific musical phrases that establish set formal patterns and their variations. A compass of twelve means that the notes of the tune range over an octave and a half, or twelve notes of the scale. Note how the tune's form includes a key change as it modulates from the key of G to D. The notes on "rendition" refer to the field recording as Jabbour notes how Reed arranged the strains within this specific performance. Each strain is number 1, 2, and so on, with the letter *r* representing that the strain is repeated. This notation shows that Reed played the first strain twice and the second strain twice and that he then repeated the whole tune three more times before ending it with one rendition of the first phrase. Jabbour's discussion of stylistic features includes formal elements that include how Reed ornamented the basic formal structure, and Jabbour further describes Reed's style of playing in his handwritten notes.

Burke Meets the "Flop-Eared Mule"

Further consideration of Jabbour's treatment of form is essential for connecting Burke's rhetorical treatment of form to "Flop-Eared Mule." Jabbour analyzes form to reach various conclusions. He notes that this widely played instrumental tune was found in nineteenth-century compilations and analyzes Henry Reed's version to show its relationship to cognate versions and antecedents that include the "Detroit Schottische." Formal analysis is essential for placing the tune within a specific genre, as Jabbour recognizes that it is commonly played as a breakdown within dances and jam sessions. Jabbour provides a detailed transcription and notes on the tune. Its formal qualities include the 4/4 meter, the delineation of the entire tune's phrase structure, and a key change between the A part and the B part. Jabbour also considers the place of form within performance when he notes that Reed played the tune four and a half times through a cycle that could conceptually consist of complete repetitions. Jabbour notes that when Reed cut the overall formal pattern of a strain into half, this variant became a crooked tune—a tune that breaks up the typical formal patterns that are characteristic of a larger corpus of dance tunes. Along with the analysis of overall formal patterns, it is important to recognize that Jabbour also writes about the stylistic features of Reed's playing by noting the predominance of slurs in his mentor's bowing and the clean and lilting style of play. These stylistic elements also are manifestations of formal patterns and relevant for exploring connections among form, texture, and ornamentation in music.

Jabbour's written analysis gives us a way to look at form as a tangible attribute of the tune itself. Burke's approach to form includes this perspective, but his theory opens the topic up a bit more widely. When he notes that the tune likely shifted from being played as a schottische to become a breakdown, he provides an exemplary instance of what Burke terms "conventional form." Here, the aesthetic qualities of the tune involve its appeal to "form *as* form" (Burke 1968a, 126). Fiddlers, listeners, and dancers experience this manifestation of form when they recognize the music as belonging to the hoedown genre. Minor or incidental elements of form, such as the formal qualities of bowing, and specific stylistic qualities allow musicians to consummate this shift from the schottische to the hoedown. This shift in genre requires mastering the specific minor formal qualities that are key elements of the new genre. Burke's perspective is helpful here as it emphasizes the performative elements of form. It is a mode of action that allows for a creative transformation of genre that Dell Hymes identifies as metaphrasis (Hymes 1981a, 87). Genre shifts are common within old-time fiddling as hornpipes, marches, parlor tunes, and other genres can serve as the melodic basis for what will become a hoedown. These transformations through metaphrasis are most recognizable through live performances, for they can be difficult to represent fully thorough written transcription. It is notable that these creative shifts in form are evident in other musical genres. Reggae, for example, has been bluegrassized by melodic banjo pickers, and a wide range of creative expressions have been reintegrated into various canons of country music. Dolly Parton explains that she takes music that she likes and adapts it to her own style, and the song becomes *Dolly-ized.*

Shifting from a text-centered approach to form to the idea of form as a mode of action provides wider ways to explore how people experience music. Burke's treatment is resonant with phenomenological perspectives that adapt rhetorical theory to studies of music. The charter document is his essay "Lexicon Rhetoricæ," in which Burke delineates a wide spectrum of ways that people use formal features of language that also are evident in musical expression. Burkean analysis reveals why it does not take long for those who are new to fiddling to recognize a common formal quality to these tunes. On the broadest level, most fiddle tunes have a binary structure of the A part and the B part. Burke's theory characterizes this kind of feature as conventional form (Burke 1968a, 126), evident both in the physical identification of this binary structure and in the way that a musician must master formal conventions required for performing a tune. Conventional form can precipitate an appeal to form as form, and it is a dynamic process. Most fiddle tunes consist of two parts, but the formal qualities of the tune also provide resources for creating tunes with three, four, or more strains. There is also a recursive process that can emerge in the mastery of this conventional form, for the A part is generally played two times before the musician moves to the B part, which also is played twice. The fiddler will then return to the A part and complement this strain with another rendering of the B part. Consequently, the length of the tune is dictated not by the written musical text but by the desires of the audience and performer(s).

A conventional form may be as encompassing as the complete structure of the tune, but there are also smaller conventions that are characteristic and often indexical of the genre itself. Burke terms these "minor or incidental forms" (Burke [1931] 1968a, 127). The initial triplet in the first strain of "Flop-Eared Mule" is a quintessential example of minor form. Its formal qualities define it as a kickoff, and recognition of the three notes serves an indexical function. It keys in those familiar with Reed's version that they may be about to hear the full tune. The same process may also show up through a few beats of shuffle bowing that musicians sometimes refer to as *putting in the potatoes*. These kinds of introductions build anticipation and create the desire to hear a full tune through the presence of both indexical and iconic elements of fiddling. Freud termed this process of anticipating an aesthetic experience as *forepleasure* (Freud 1993, 208–12). He and Burke recognized that part of this artistic experience involves the arousing of desire and the anticipation of its fulfillment. The use of minor forms to spark forepleasure is not necessarily incidental to its appeal. Consider, for example, how audiences break out into applause when they hear the double-shuffle, or hokum bowing, section characteristic of the "Orange Blossom Special." Here, the recognition of the appeal of a minor form as form explains why they clap—even when the technique really is not that difficult for fiddlers to master.

A fiddle tune has its own syntax. The notes flow logically into each other in various phrases, and—outside of new genres such as jamgrass—few fiddle tunes are atonal. If we were to think of this process in rhetorical terms, Burke's delineation of a syllogistic progression as an element of form works well to describe the movement of melody within a fiddle tune's strains. Jabbour's analysis of the specific formal aspects of "Flop-Eared Mule" demonstrates a rational form within its artistic structure that is built on establishing, repeating, and creating variations on various syntagma. After the initial triplet, the tune's melody progresses down the key of G in the first measure, climbs back up in the second measure, and then reestablishes the initial run in the fourth measure. The specific qualities that define the tune are central to how listeners will evaluate the quality of the fiddler's performance. As Burke writes, mastery of form is not a window-dressing applied over artistic expression; rather, it's integral to the process of creative expression. Burke's orientation here reveals his modernist impulse to merge rational qualities of creative expression with artistic impulses.

The repetition of melody lines helps to define the tune. Burke identifies repetitive form as an important aspect of aesthetic appeal. When listeners and performers recognize the patterns that emerge through repetition, they are experiencing this aspect of form, a process that also is highly useful for fiddlers who are initially learning the tune. Excessive repetition, however, is artistically boring, and Burke includes variation on a theme within the general guise of repetitive form. Thus variation, and the logical progression to its fulfillment, is evident here in measure four as the phrase ends with the double-stopped G and B played either as dotted eighth notes or as quarter notes. These variations are noted in Jabbour's transcription, and they help to create the crooked-tune quality of Reed's variant. As Burke explains, these types of variations lead to a sharpened awareness of the essential characteristics of the artistic expression.

I remain unconvinced that music works entirely through syllogistic progressions of form. Neither would Burke. He offers a counterpart to logical progression through what he terms "qualitative progression" (Burke 1968a, 124). This appeal to form involves the forward movement of syntagmatic relationships, but Burke notes the subtle qualities of this creative resource. Qualitative progression emerges when one element prepares listeners for another element of the work of art. As listeners internalize the formal characteristics of the A part, they may build up expectations for listening to themes and variations that are apt to emerge in the B part. The formal qualities that unfold through this process establish the definitive elements of qualitative progression. In "Flop-Eared Mule," the anticipation is enhanced by the change from G into the key of D. Even without doing a note-by-note analysis of the transcription, it is still clear that there are formal similarities between the four measures of the A part and the four measures of the B part. There are syntagmatic differences between parts A and B, but the main difference is the paradigmatic shift into the new key. Listeners will recognize variations in the melody lines, but the key change is a predominant feature separating the two strains. The paradigmatic relationship here is clearly established because it is impossible to play in both the key of G and the key of D at the same time. The shift from one key to another is artistically set up through the last little run in measure four and then realized when the fiddler moves to the second strain. Note that repetitive form also is central to the appeal of the B part and that there is an alternative melody line present in measure four. In this section, the sequence of sixteenth notes that flow D, F♯, G, and A sets up the change back to the key of G just as the same notes in the A part index this shift into the key of D.

Burke's "Lexicon Rhetoricæ" includes discussion of both the interrelation of forms and the conflict of forms. Various formal properties are intertwined in the fiddle tune as the drones and double stops interanimate each other, and these musical forms serve to ornament the tune. Conflicting forms are subtly evident in various performances of "Flop-Eared Mule" and in numerous other fiddle tunes. Conflicting form is evident most directly when Henry Reed would add an extra beat at the end of the second repetition of each strain to call attention to the modulation in key by breaking time and playing with the quality of "Flop-Eared Mule" as a crooked tune. These kinds of subtle interconnections with form are also evident when various musical phrases serve as mirror images of each other. A prominent example is evident in the runs that move up the scale rather than down the scale in the fourth measures of each of the two strains. These combinations can be heard as manifestations of the conflict of form as well as a more encompassing qualitative progression of form.

Significant form is another important entry in Burke's "Lexicon Rhetoricæ." The rhetorician makes a wordplay here, as the significance can refer both to a highly resonant use of form but also to the use of formal devices to create a strong presence of a theme's content. Burke rejected "a quasi-mystical attempt to explain all formal quality as 'onomatopoeia,'" but "Flop-Eared Mule" has elements that emphasize how formal techniques can create iconic and symbolic resonance (Burke 1968a, 135). The fiddle's tone color works well to convey the braying of a mule through musical mimicry. The fiddle may bray an iconic hee-haw / hee-haw that often is most evident in the first four notes of the B part. It also lurks under the surface as a semiotic resource in various phrases in the first strain. Musical onomatopoeia shows up in quite a few fiddle tunes. The mule's witty braying demonstrates not only that form conveys content but that form also can be content. An especially apt use of a symbolic representation of content may become what Burke terms a "symbolic charge" when the content evoked through the artistic expression becomes vividly resonant through the audience's shared experience of form (Burke 1968a, 164). Recognizing and experiencing these charges is central to the appeal of symbolic expression, and Burke describes the vibrancy of this effect as "vigor" (181). If we pushed the argument a bit, perhaps the presence of significant form makes "Flop-Eared Mule" a tone poem. Perhaps not. Nevertheless, coaxing the fiddle to hee-haw like a mule adds to the tune's delight.

As a rhetorician and literary critic, Burke includes rhythm and rhyme within his lexicon (Burke 1968a, 130). When a fiddler such as Henry Reed played at a house party, rhythm would likely be the most important formal property. A hoedown is a dance tune. The formal patterns expressed as rhythm provide the dance's core appeal. Dance fiddlers could make mistakes in playing a melody line, miss full accuracy in their intonation, mess up ornamentation, and err in other ways, but a fiddler who could not keep time was apt to have a short career playing for dances. Some were even replaced by dance participants who could simply tap out dance rhythms on the floor with broom handles (Hansen 2007, 48). Even in-depth descriptions of the rhythmic complexity of players like Henry Reed and Alan Jabbour do little to fully convey the appeal of experiencing the mastery of rhythmic form within live performance. The richness of a full-scale experience of the power of rhythmic expression is a prime example of Burke's articulation of a "formal charge" (Burke 1968a, 164).

These masterful and vital expressions of form are central to Burke's views on aesthetics. When formal charges merge with symbolic charges, the result is vibrant artistic expression.

All good tunes must come to an end. Just as a conventional form kicks off the tune, a conventional form brings the tune's performance to its close. Jabbour did not include the specific phrase that Reed used to end the tune, but he likely heard a version of the "shave-and-a-haircut / two-bits" tag to close out the tune. When this conventional ending is bookended with the triplet that kicks off the tune, we can see how incidental form frames the tune as a tune or, as in Bauman's discussion, keys a performance (Bauman 1975, 295–97). This keying metaphor displays a clever rhetorical ambiguity. It can refer to how a key may initiate a performance just as turning a key starts a car's engine. This indexical function, however, can shift into a metacommunication. Keying may also create a frame, somewhat analogous to a musical key, that provides listeners with a reference point for interpreting what is performed.

As this consideration of a fiddle tune using Burke's writing on form suggests, there is a rich potential for using rhetorical approaches when analyzing musical form. His focus on form as a mode of action and as a social reality provides fruitful ways to explore how musical expression is mediated between musicians and audiences. He also provides fresh and vivid ways to explore how listeners internalize formal elements of music. Form becomes individuated, Burke writes, when its qualities become engrained into our psychology, especially when it is subsumed within the unconscious mind. The tune's qualities literally become part of ourselves and can constitute significant elements of our sonic identities (Overall 2017, 233). The iconic and symbolic expressions that emerge through the masterful use of form can also become individuated. After we experience characteristic patterns of form, the wide range of formal features in a tune like "Flop-Eared Mule" finds its place in our psyche—waiting to emerge through the formal qualities of music that are made manifest in performance.

What does a consideration of Burkean rhetoric bring to an understanding of the performance of form within musical expression? Burke's writing on form and rhetorical theory is most useful when we move beyond simply delineating formal patterns for the sake of analyzing form. Instead, his "Lexicon Rhetoricæ" is most useful when placed in relationship to his articulation of a larger psychology of form. In foundational publications written during the 1930s, Burke provided new insights into communication by focusing on what people do with words and symbols. He grounded these interests in relations between the social use of rhetoric and individual psychology. To understand his interest in specific formal devices within the lexicon, it is key to ground these perspectives in a larger rubric subsumed as the "psychology of audience" and demarcated by a division that he makes between the "psychology of information" and the "psychology of form" (Burke 1968b, 30–32). Both terministic screens, he asserts, need to be defined in terms of each other. The psychology of information refers to how individuals process communication in terms of garnering new information whereas the psychology of form relates to how we process the management of new information. If we were to think of "Flop-Eared Mule" in terms of its appeal to the psychology of information, the result might be your engagement with this chapter that you are now reading. If we were to think of the fiddle tune in terms of its appeal to the psychology of form, its appeal would be your reaction to hearing a performance of the tune. His emphasis on considering the psychology of form is essential to Burke's wider views on aesthetics. His work reminds us that artistry cannot be reduced to the acquisition of new information. Rather, form and its management are central to aesthetics and the power of art. One of Burke's most important statements of the relationship between the two modes of responding to communication is this oft-cited proposition: "The hypertrophy of the psychology of information is accompanied by the corresponding atrophy of the psychology of form" (Burke 1968b, 33). Throughout his rhetorical theory, Burke asserts the value of aesthetic dimensions of symbolic communication, often with references to music. One reason why musical expression can stand up to repetition, he writes, is that its primary appeal is to the psychology of form rather than to sheer information (Burke 1968b, 36). "Flop-Eared Mule" is appealing with repeated listening because this relatively simple tune is created through a mastery of musical form. By grounding scholarly formal analysis in artistry with a deep engagement in aesthetic experience, Burkean analysis gives us new ways to think about form within the wider rubric of performance theory.[2]

Conclusion

Returning to our central consideration, we gain a greater appreciation for Burke's writing on the psychology of audience. Namely, his approach recasts form more as an artistic action than as an arcane attribute of musical transcription and analysis. Burke's rhetorical theory enlivens the ostensively static qualities of musical notation. It allows us to enter into the creative space of the performer's mind, and it illustrates patterns of creative expression that allow audience members to experience aesthetic elements of performance on a visceral level. This kind of amplified emphasis on form has applications to analysis of other musical offerings as well as a wider array of genres of expressive culture.

Notes

1. "Flop-Eared Mule." The tune includes a triplet that picks up the first strain of four complete measures in the A part. It changes key from G to D in the B part, which also consists of four complete measures. Extra measures are added as each strain is repeated, thereby making the tune crooked.

2. This chapter is an expanded version of an earlier conference paper presented at the 37th Annual International Country Music Conference, Nashville, Tennessee, June 4, 2021 (online).

Bibliography

Abrahams, Roger D. 1971. "Personal Power and Social Restraint in the Definition of Folklore. In *Toward New Perspectives in Folklore*." Special issue, *Journal of American Folklore* 84 (331): 16–30.

American Folklife Center. n.d. Fiddle Tunes of the Old Frontier: The Henry Reed Collection Online Presentation (AFC 1999/016), American Folklife Center, Library of Congress. Compiled from fieldwork of Alan and Karen Jabbour. https://www.loc.gov/collections/henry-reed-fiddle-tunes.

Bauman, Richard. 1975. "Verbal Art as Performance." New Series, *American Anthropologist* 77 (2): 290–311.

Beisswenger, Drew. 2002. *Fiddling Way Out Yonder: The Life and Music of Melvin Wine*. American Made Music Series. Jackson: University of Mississippi Press.

Beisswenger, Drew, and Gordon McCann. 2008. *Ozark Fiddle Music: 308 Tunes Featuring 30 Legendary Fiddlers with Selections from 50 Other Great Ozark Fiddlers*. Pacific, MO: Mel Bay.

Burke, Kenneth. 1967. "Dramatism." In *Communication Concepts and Perspectives*, edited by Lee Thayer, 327–60. Washington, DC: Spartan Books.

———. (1931) 1968a. "Lexicon Rhetoricæ." In *Counter-Statement*, edited by K. Burke, 123–82. Berkeley: University of California Press.

———. (1931) 1968b. "Psychology and Form." In *Counter-Statement*, edited by K. Burke, 29–44. Berkeley: University of California Press.

Carter, Tom. 1991. "Looking for Henry Reed: Confessions of a Revivalist." In *Sounds of the South*, edited by Daniel W. Patterson, 73–89. Occasional Papers, No. 1. Chapel Hill: Southern Folklife Collection at the University of North Carolina.

Cauthen, Joyce H. 1989. *With Fiddle and Well-Rosined Bow: A History of Old-Time Fiddling in Alabama*. Tuscaloosa: University of Alabama Press.

Davis, Gerald L. (1985) 2017. *I Got the Word in Me and Can Sing It, You Know: A Study of the Performed African-American Sermon*. University of Pennsylvania Press Anniversary Collection. Philadelphia: University of Pennsylvania Press.

Feintuch, Burt Howard. 1975. "Pop Ziegler, Fiddler: A Study of Folkloric Performance." PhD diss., University of Pennsylvania.

Ferris, William. 2016. *Give My Poor Heart Ease: Voices of Mississippi Blues*. H. Eugene and Lillian Youngs Lehman Series. Chapel Hill: University of North Carolina Press.

Florida State Fiddlers' Association. 2022. Official Florida State Fiddle Contest. https://flafiddlers.wordpress.com/fiddle-contest.

Freud, Sigmund. (1905) 1993. *Wit and Its Relation to the Unconscious*. Translated by A. A. Brill. New York: Dover.

Glassie, Henry. 1982. *Passing the Time in Ballymenone: Culture and History of an Ulster Community*. Philadelphia: University of Pennsylvania Press.

Goertzen, Chris. 2011. *Southern Fiddlers and Fiddle Contests*. American Music Series, edited by David Evans. Jackson: University of Mississippi.

———. 2017. *George P. Knauff's Virginia Reels and the History of American Fiddling*. American Made Music Series, edited by David Evans. Jackson: University of Mississippi Press.

Hansen, Gregory. 2007. *Florida Fiddler: The Life and Times of Richard Seaman*. Tuscaloosa: University of Alabama Press.

Hinson, Glen. 1991. *Fire in My Bones: Transcendence and the Holy Spirit in African American Gospel*. Contemporary Ethnography Series, edited by Dan Rose and Paul Stoller. Philadelphia: University of Pennsylvania Press.

Hymes, Dell. 1981a. "Breakthrough into Performance." In *"In Vain I Tried to Tell You": Essays in Native American Ethnopoetics*, edited by Dell Hymes, 79–141. Philadelphia: University of Pennsylvania Press.

———. 1981b. "Breakthrough into Performance Revisited." In *"In Vain I Tried to Tell You": Essays in Native American Ethnopoetics*, edited by Dell Hymes, 200–259. Philadelphia: University of Pennsylvania Press.

Jabbour, Alan. 2008. "Fiddle Tunes of the Old Frontier." In *Driving the Bow*. Fiddle and Dance Studies from around the North Atlantic, Volume 2 within series, edited by Ian Russell and Mary Anne Alburger, 4–13. Aberdeen, Scotland: Elphinstone Institute, University of Aberdeen.

Marshall, Erynn. 2006. *Music in the Air Somewhere: The Shifting Borders of West Virginia's Fiddle and Song Traditions*. Morgantown: West Virginia University Press.

Overall, Joel Lane. 2013. "Kenneth Burke, Music, and Rhetoric." PhD diss., Texas Christian University.

———. 2017. "Kenneth Burke and the Problem of Sonic Identification." *Rhetoric Review* 36 (3): 232–43.

Perlman, Ken. 2015. *Couldn't Have a Wedding without the Fiddler: The Story of Traditional Fiddling on Prince Edward Island*. Charles K. Wolfe Music Series, edited by Ted Olson. Knoxville: University of Tennessee Press.

Riddle, Almeda. 1970. *A Singer and Her Songs: Almeda Riddle's Book of Ballads*. Edited by Roger Abrahams. Baton Rouge: Louisiana University Press.

Rosenberg, Bruce A. 1970. *The Art of the American Folk Preacher*. New York: Oxford University Press.
Titon, Jeff Todd. 2001. *Old-Time Kentucky Fiddle Tunes*. Lexington: University of Kentucky Press.

Gregory Hansen is Professor of Folklore and English at Arkansas State University. He is author of *A Florida Fiddler: The Life and Times of Richard Seaman* and editor (with Shihan de Silva Jayasuriya and Mariana Pinto Leitão Pereira) of *Sustaining Support for Intangible Cultural Heritage*. His research specializes in public folklore and the folklife of America's South. In addition to his research on fiddle tunes, bluegrass, and blues music, Hansen has completed research on public presentations of heritage. He is also a Folklore Fellow of the American Folklore Society.

II
PERFORMANCE OF MATERIALITY, VIRTUALITY, AND THE SPIRITUAL

5

A Glitch in Time
Digital Interruptions and Spaces of Haunting

KIT DANOWSKI

INTRO

This is a chapter about glitches.

This is a chapter that glitches.

A chapter about glitches that glitches.

"The connections between Afrolatinx spirituality"

The glitches in thought in this chapter are reflections of the time in which they were forming.[1] Glitches are part of the collective consciousness for those who spend part of their time on Zoom, when lags from time zones and connections and bandwidth cause all kinds of digital scrambling. This is definitely a reflection of the pandemic, with a collective moving further into a digital world (**I have not seen my kid in nearly two years**). Social life, at least for a portion of the pandemic, has recently involved a mass learning curve for how to construct ourselves online. We have had ample preparation through decades of moving toward a mode of being that is hybrid cyborg. Through a more intensive immersion into digital mediums, our experience of the glitch is more commonplace. It is a familiar experience where we log in to a meeting, our face in a square of other faces, or blank screens, and someone is presenting a talk about something. The presenter's face freezes in the middle of a sentence, and the rest of us are pulled out of an affect of politely paying attention into something spontaneous, like we were momentarily disconnected from the borg. Accompanying this is the understanding that this will also happen to us, or has already happened to us, that we have been the face that freezes. No one is in control of their representation in the digital space, and this glitching happens to everyone.

This subjective experience of glitching was familiar to me. . . . It reminded me of the moments just before trance possession. **Writing from the perspective of someone who has been possessed, who has the experience of being taken over by another, in ritual situations, I wonder if this is not unique. I wonder if others experience spirit possession as a kind of glitch, like breaks in the software, or like two tracks interrupting each other, working out a resolution.**

I consider the glitch in its brief history as an art form and trace how it mirrors and anticipates phenomenological experiences of time and identity. I will also consider how, in Afrolatine ritual contexts, there are already entanglements that are already very much like glitching. This is hinting toward a methodology for making performance that might incorporate glitch as an artistic strategy for work that embraces multiplicity and polyvocality.

Confession: I should not complain about this academic life. But in collaborations and conversations where we are writing or planning presentations centered on otherness and difference, we start with questioning the modes of inquiry and underlying structures and agree to challenge these in the paper, presentation, or lecture. Then I find myself observing how, as the deadline approaches, the alternative structures are left behind, how otherness and difference are ultimately edited out of the final draft. There is an assumption that the object cannot also be the plaque that explains the object. There is an assumption that there needs to be a plaque.

In that spirit, then, of the glitch, and the multiple, there will be several voices that run through this chapter, indicated through different fonts. As you might already notice. These fonts are (in order of appearance):

TIMES NEW ROMAN: This voice here, which is the "reliable narrator" and the thread that tries to capture all of this as well as the general argument about the glitch; the point of view of the academic.

ROCKWELL: Discourse that refers specifically to Lukumí and Palo ontologies and scholarship (or writes consciously from inside these ontologies) is in this font; the point of view of the ritual practitioner.

AVENIR: The personal, or more confessional, or most deeply subjective, is this one.

The writing will glitch as a means of challenging the discursive academic voice through counternarratives that give primacy to the nonhuman (in this case, both spirits of nature, of the dead, and digital technologies) and the auto-ethnographic. There is also a subtle nod to Karen Barad's diffraction theory, looking at entanglements and reading through difference. Privileging the nonhuman, auto-ethnography, and diffraction make up a methodology to consider the glitch in relation to the phenomenologies of digital glitching and trance possession. Looking at the glitch this way might point toward how the digital glitch interrupts and makes visible a way of seeing the world that is much older than the technology that produces it. There are other technologies that precede the glitch that might, in effect, offer similar phenomenological experiences. These older technologies exist in modes of being that come from worldviews where communication with the dead is not unusual and, here specifically, ontologies of Afrolatine ritual experience.

Simply put: When a practitioner is getting possessed, or ridden, or mounted, by Orisha or Egun (drawing from mostly witnessed and sometimes-experienced possessions), there is often a fight. The practitioner is struggling against something, which sometimes presents as violent shaking, sometimes softer, where it looks like the practitioner and the possessing subject are simultaneously trying to take control of the practitioner's body.

From my experience with this: At this point, we become more than one (or, better, more aware of our multiplicity). I am the one who walked into the room an hour ago, and I am the one who is trying to walk into the head of the one who walked into the room an hour ago, and we both have pasts and futures we carry with us, and all of those flicker through consciousness at once, and it's very, very much like watching a glitch on the screen. There is a binary between self and spirit in this relationship; the binary is better understood if it is understood that it is not binary. It is slippery, like gender can be slippery.

I find myself googling things like, "How can you tell if you're not nonbinary?"

HISTORY OF THE GLITCH

The term *glitch* probably comes from the Yiddish *glitsch*, which means "to slip," and started to come into use in reference to technology with radio in the 1940s. It came into more public use in 1962, when astronaut John Glenn used the word in his book *Into Orbit*: "Another term we adopted to describe some of our problems was 'glitch.' Literally, a glitch . . . is such a minute change in voltage that no fuse could protect against it" (Siner 2013). The term becomes more ubiquitous when electronic technologies become more ubiquitous. Now, it is generally recognized that a glitch is "a transient error in an electronic system . . . a misbehaviour, and in particular a misbehaviour that you can replicate, and then play around with, modify" (School of the Art Institute of Chicago 2016). More phenomenologically, a glitch can refer to the user's experience of "a moment when you're snapped out of a moment that you're participating in" (School of the Art Institute of Chicago 2016).

Glitching worked its way into quotidian experience with the internet and digital video technologies, and underground artists started to work with intentional glitching in the 1970s, but it has come into its own since the 1990s. As an artistic strategy, glitch art can be purely aesthetic, although there are often (arguably usually) political applications. Glitch in this sense is an intentional or accidental means of momentarily undoing usual modes of discourse. The moment of glitch holds the potential for opening up spaces for nonlinear experiences of time. It can be used as a critique of capitalism, as a demonstration that technology is failing; the ghost in the machine is sleeping. The glitch is also a potential for blurring or erasing boundaries, borders, and binaries. Legacy Russell brings glitch up to the contemporary moment, reinvigorating the term with applications to gender theory with her manifesto *Glitch Feminism*, where she writes, "The glitch is a passage through which the body traverses toward liberation, a tear in the fabric of the digital" (2020, 19). Glitching queers both time and space, or reveals them as such.

The viewer's subjective experience of watching glitch art, which allows for a kind of daydreamy attention that occasionally gets pulled into focus when associations suddenly congeal, is very similar to the experience of the kinds of stuttering, freezing, and crashing that happen on Zoom. The necessary presence for having a conversation with another human being is interrupted, and space opens up for both reflection and anxiety on past and future. Glitch is not the accidental temporary disruption that gets smoothed over through the force of the rest of the weave of the cloth; it is a disruption in binary modes of thinking and being that require new ways of weaving. It points to both fixed ways of knowing and alternate ways of knowing and being. It serves as one means of interruption, "to critique the nature of (white) meaning itself, to challenge through a literal critique of the sign the meaning of meaning" (Gates 1988, 47). This requires a revision of "the received sign" (Gates 1988, 47). If "the Greek word for 'sign,' semi, is also the word for 'grave'" (McFarland 2019, 410), then glitch is the one who knocks on the grave and asks the dead to wake up for a conversation over coffee.

The connections between Afrolatine spirituality and queer realness

There is a history of technology incorporating haunting very soon after its invention and mass appeal. Photography's early years saw the development of new techniques for interfering with development that led to spirit photography. The appeal of the phonograph went beyond the reproduction of recordings, but the possibility of saving the voices of the dead, with recordings of "his master's voice" that might speak to us from beyond the grave. Not to mention the experiments with uncanny machine voices, produced through recordings or metallic squeaks (Dolar 2006), that carried strong uncanny connections to the supernatural. There were stories of the dead speaking through Morse code that helped move along the development of tapping as a means of communicating with the dead in Spiritist circles. This is consistent throughout the twentieth century as well. For example, the TV play *The Stone Tape* from 1972 (UK) has researchers studying the paranormal (looking for a new medium for recording the dead!) all having visions of a woman falling to her death; finally, it is revealed that the memories were not recorded in the equipment but in the stones in the house. The idea of a stone carrying memory is for another more initiated crowd reminiscent of how memories are stored in quartz, leading all the way up to the ghosts coming through the TV in *Poltergeist* (McMullan 2019). This tendency for technology to incorporate haunting also works its way into the glitch, where the moment of glitch can be seen as a sign of supernatural communication: the phone that sends a text from someone who died (Kopsky 2017), the authority figure who is suddenly stuck in a cat avatar (Victor 2021), or the whispery sounds of the dead interrupting a Zoom meeting (UTIA 2020).

TRANCE AND COPRESENCE

I find myself googling things like, "How can you tell if you're not nonbinary?"

Trance experience is one of glitching, where two or more ontologies are attempting to occupy one space at the same time. In Lukumí practices, the possessing subjects are known as Orisha (very broadly speaking, a pantheon of deities or presences that are related to elements of nature). In Palo they are called *mpungo*, or *kimpungo*, or *muertos* (which translates as "the dead" and again, very broadly speaking, can represent very specific personalities that may have once been in human form, or may be a congruence of personalities that comprise a spirit related to nature). **It's a little more complicated than that, but you do you.** There are practices of mediumship that draw from these traditions as well as from spiritism as introduced to Latin America via French medium Alan Kardec, morphing over time and eventually becoming what is called Espiritismo. In *espiritista* ceremonies, or *misas*, the spirits possessing are, generally speaking, the dead either from along the ancestral lineage or from a kind of archetypal pantheon from folk tradition. **Pantheon is not really right, but lots of practitioners do use that word (for lack of a better), and it works for them, so. . . .** Trance possession has many names and is referred to as being mounted (Daniel 2005, 9), being ridden (like a horse), *recibir una inspiración* (get an inspiration), *caer en trance* (fall into trance) (Cabrera 1986, 2), being touched, hit, and so forth. The spirits can come down or rise up to the head of the initiate, signifying the cosmic realms above (*ile l'orun*, kind of like heaven) or from the bottom of the ocean below (Daniel 2005, 22). The experience of trance possession is something like glitching. It is a misbehavior that you can replicate. In a Lukumí or Palo drum, there are particular rhythms that, if played in a particular order, with careful attention to the dancers, can be manipulated to invoke possession.

It's March 2020, and I am starting to cough. I moved to England in 2018, on the southeastern coast in a place called Portsmouth. Everyone is indoors now. The citizens of Italy were quarantined a couple of months ago. A couple of months ago here, everyone said they could not imagine that happening here. Now here we are, here is like everywhere else. Like everyone else, I'm learning how to use Zoom. Every couple of days, I am talking to my godsister, a child of Oshun, in NYC. She has a cough too. We stay in even closer contact than usual over the next ten days, sharing stories about symptoms: shaking and sweating, fevers and chills, and the cough, that strange cough that feels like fiberglass exploding in the chest. This might not be what I think it is, but it might be, and the news is reporting that some people with the symptoms are going to sleep and not waking up again. Time moves very slowly. Or not necessarily slowly but differently. Time is different now. When we talk, we are getting used to the lags, learning how to live with the glitches as part of what this is like. This is what time feels like anyway. There are moments that freeze and moments when lags correct themselves and we know we missed something and we try to fill in the gaps even more than usual. There are missing pieces to everything, and we have to fill in the blanks by paying attention to the verbal and facial cues on the screen, by remembering what it was like to be outside, in crowds, in public spaces.

For those of us who talk to the dead on the regular, that's also different. There are more dead, more shadows, more sounds at night. My godsister and I have the symptoms of whatever this is, and that feels like another kind of spirit, a kind of cohabitation by something, and as we talk we start to talk about the thing we're thinking about but didn't know how to put into words before we started talking, and we are talking about how this feels like there is something around all of us, like a cloud, and in some of us, and that the dead have never been closer. She is in a place where bodies will start to overfill the morgues, and I am in a place that has seen lots of plagues before, including the Plague. The dead are around, and we sometimes feel them moving through us.

"The connections between Afrolatine spirituality and queer realness is clearly located in a sensibility of transformation"

These are states that are distinguishable as copresence and trance possession, although they are not clean binaries. There are no clean binaries from colonialism, just wounds that are infected and cannot be cleanly healed; you will always see the fissures, like the space where the plants were grafted together. Here I am borrowing the idea of copresence from Beliso-de Jesús as a means of describing this state of consciousness where the dead and the spirits are active. The state of consciousness is not particularly unique, but it is everyday, less mystical and more ontological. *Copresences* is a term that is used:

to reference the complex multiplicity of racial spiritual embodied affectivity that the term las *presencias* indicates. Copresences are sensed through chills, shivers, tingles, premonitions, and possessions in and through different transnational Santería bodies and spaces. They are active spiritual and religious subjectivities intimately tied to practitioners' forms of movement, travel, and sensual body registers. Dead African slaves, Yoruba diaspora Orisha, and other racialised entities form part in a reconfiguration of practitioners' body-worlds. (Beliso-de Jesús 2015, 7)

It's 2015, and I'm somewhere in Los Angeles, in the backyard of a house whose front is flanked by seven marble statues of a Greek god—at least that is how I remember it. I'm one of seven santer@s—the minimum you need for this initiation ceremony. It's morning, and we are tearing herbs into plastic basins, singing the songs that accompany this work. As time goes on, time starts to bend and stretch out in front of me. I am looking down into my own basin, a little daydreamy. The smell of these wet herbs always sends me elsewhere. I begin to notice that I have been seeing others here for quite some time. These others are not the same as the ones, like me, doing the tearing and the singing. I start to notice that I have been noticing without attention that it feels like there are other hands on my hands. The present has become slippery, and the past is working through our present hands, working toward some collective future. I don't know the term "copresence" yet, but this is that. Ontologies glitch each other, and I'm struggling to reconcile them because I mistakenly assume that they demand reconciliation, as if multiple spaces have to resolve into one instead of existing in multiplicities.

Palo experience can also manifest as this experience of copresence. It is very specific embodied knowledge, and it takes some time before the practitioner starts:

> Realising that a twinge of suspicion, a chill, and the turns of the stomach that accompany astonishment were the dead was crucial to understand the ubiquity of the dead in Palo and thus Palo's importance overall. (Ochoa 2010b, 32)

These physical manifestations are not signs or signals but the thing itself—the haunting is the shaking; it is in the body. Recognizing these is a beginning of this knowing, which develops over time through relationship with the dead, until one recognizes that:

> In the force of her baseness, in the blood and lush mass of feathers that covered her, in the soaking aspirations of cane rum I delivered as her supplicant, in the cloud of cigar smoke that enveloped her, and in the prone body of her keeper at her feet, she crossed into modes of feeling, and of matter, that are called "Palo." (Ochoa 2010a, 410)

This living archive that is coconstituted with the dead is what Otero calls an archive of conjure, where:

> Spirit guides borrow the body and voice of mediums in ways that confound singular understandings of their origins and leave residual transcripts on bodies, memories, and places that constitute a living archive of conjure. (Otero 2020, 126)

I have a *prenda* for Zarabanda, my *muerto* that I received in Palo initiations. This particular prenda is an iron pot that contains things. Because of the secrecy and the oaths to secrecy, I won't say what things. But they include things of the world, like dirt, like sticks, like herbs, and things that were once alive. The prenda is as Robert Farris Thompson describes: "the Kongo cosmos in miniature" (1984, 121). Through the prenda, the initiate has access to the world of the dead, so the prenda is a kind of medium:

> In the praising of the dead, in the ritual field of activation that moves spirits to compose with their surrounds, the prendas-ngangas-enquisos act as intercessors. Intercessors are not simply mediators. Their practice is not simply to enter into the middle, but to be the middle, the middling force that alters everything with which it comes into contact. (Manning 2015, 63)

I was scratched just a couple of weeks ago to Zarabanda, and now we are having a misa before I make Ocha. This is not unique to how these things go: often, when someone is marked for initiation in Lukumí, if they also have a Palo connection, they will do the *rayamiento* (scratching) ceremony in Palo. This is because the Ocha ceremony in Lukumí is "the last word." So I am recently scratched and preparing to be initiated to Obatala in Lukumí.

This misa is in the *mesa blanca* tradition in Espiritísmo (which might be considered supplemental to these other traditions), and it draws on both Afrolatine and European-descended spiritism practices of working with the dead. This is called an investigation misa, where members of my spiritual family collectively contact the dead, to hear and see what they might hear and see, and to bring in advice ahead of my initiation. In misas, the dead sometimes, or even often, communicate with the living through trance possession. Up until this moment, I have seen others in states of trance but never experienced it myself. But at some point in the misa, I remember the smell of Florida water was strong, and the white candles got brighter, and suddenly I was being surrounded and spun, like a dog, being spun around confused, like a dog. I remember seeing my Padrino's face, and he gave me a nod to "go with it," and I trust him, so I go with it. The world of the white cloth and candles and a world of deep sea and barnacles and old bones are jutting against each other. I think they're fighting each other, but that's just me. They're existing at the same time, bleeding into each other, and then a voice that isn't mine starts laughing in the back of my throat.

I find myself googling things you can replicate.

PAST AND PRESENT

Talking to my godsister in March 2020 about time, and as we are talking we are not aware that the seasons are changing and a year has gone by and then the seasons are changing again and we are talking about time, how during this pandemic, consciousness of time is going different.

Rasheedah Phillips, in her articulation of Black Quantum Futurism, describes "time as cyclical, spiral, revolving, and usually anything but linear" (2014). Cristina Sharpe describes the experience of time in the wake, where "the past that is not past reappears, always to rupture the present" (2016, 9).

In Palo cosmology, the conception of the universe is circular and repetitive: a circle divided into quarters, with each quarter representing a moment in time. Half the moments are in the land of the living, and the other half are in the land of the dead. They are separate, but they are porous and fluid and influence each other.

I find myself googling things like, "How can you tell if you're not nonbinary?"

> "The connections between Afrolatinx spirituality and queer realness is clearly located in a sensibility of transformation—transformations shared at historical, cultural, and spiritual crossroads"

As Solimar Otero describes, when Madre de Agua mounts in misa contexts, the past and present blend, which "creates a temporal palimpsest that allows for the perception of different kinds of time" (Otero 2020, 123). Nina Angela Mercer calls this sacred temporality "palimpsestic time" and refers to dead time, cosmic time, and ecstatic time, that "through ecstatic time, we access dead time in line with Kongo cosmic time, which is always a time of transformation, where new bodies of knowledge are produced in communication with the ancestors" (2021, 14).

In both Palo and Lukumí cosmology, temporality moves outside of the strict linearity of Newtonian physics, incorporating that forward movement with the time of the dead as well as deep time. Deep time is a concept from geology (the irony—and the connection to iron—here might not be lost on the more initiated readers) as a conceptual framework for thinking about history on a massive scale, not in terms of human events in history but geological eras. This way of thinking comes from the Enlightenment . . . unless you wonder if that's not a colonial way of thinking—and I wonder about that, too. **Especially because there are Indigenous ontologies that have this concept in mind, and for much longer; for example, the concept of the Irunmole in Yoruba cosmology. The Irunmole are the Orishas who were there at the very beginning, witnessing the beginning of the universe.**

The phenomenon of brain fog, perhaps compounded from isolation and excessive screen time, is common at the moment of writing this. We are thinking about our thinking and how it doesn't work like it used to. A very dear friend went from lucidity to dementia during the pandemic, saying he had come unstuck in time, like Billy Pilgrim in *Slaughterhouse-Five*. I spend days like everyone, looking from screen to window to wall, and notice that the afterimages are sometimes like ghosts. And all of these things stack together, moments of glitches that stack together, and we become a little more aware of the trick of linearity. Or the trickster opening the door where time and space intersect, where the Newtonian conceptions of cause and effect, past and present, start to come undone. In Lukumí practice, the trickster is Eleggua, derived from the Yoruba Esu:

> The most fundamental aspect of the Yoruba is that there exist, simultaneously, three stages of existence: the past, the present, and the unborn. Esu represents these stages, and makes their simultaneous existence possible, "without any contradiction," precisely because he is the principle of discourse both as messenger and as the god of communication. (Gates 1988, 37)

It is not surprising, then, that Eleggua is in charge of these shifts in time. This is an embodied experience, that sense of ritual presence when the moment feels loaded, with multiple ontologies communicating at once. The moment that slows starts to feel like one is entering deep time, the time of the Irunmole:

> When an entire repertoire of physically habituated motor responses and ways of responding, such as religious dance and ceremonial spirit possession, are modelled on and perpetuate an earlier African tradition, the effect of calling them up is, among other things, to recreate the past and participate in it. (Brandon 1997, 148)

THE GLITCHENING: WHERE ONTOLOGIES MEET (DISCRETELY)

The glitch is nonbinary.

My path of Obatala in the Lukumí tradition is Alagemma, the Chameleon. For some paths, Obatala is male, some are female, and others androgynous. There is considerable variation and disagreement about these variations. I met with a godsister, a daughter of Oshun, sometime late in the first pandemic year, one of the moments when the lockdown restrictions were lifted. We met on a marsh near her flat in London, and she told me that Alagemma is in some circles considered to be one of the patrons of trans people. I wonder why this keeps coming up, this connection with my path and gender binaries, and how lots of elders told me to be proud of who I am no matter what. There is no plaque for this.

There is a story from Yorubaland where Obatala, as the creator Orisha, is making the people to populate the earth. Obatala is making human beings, forming them with the hands, and sipping on palm wine while making people. Obatala gets drunk and does not realize it. In the morning, coming to, Obatala sees albinos, hunchbacks, little people, and many others who do not fit the mold. From that point on, anyone with any "marks of

difference" is held as sacred to Obatala, as a reminder of the original moments of creation.

I find myself googling things like, "How can you tell if you're nonbinary?"

In this way, difference and otherness are not the mistakes in the weave but become part of a continuous narrative. The glitch is there in the beginning, and part of the structure of the universe, interlacing "algorithmic uncertainty with subjectivity" (Shabbar 2018, 197). To return to the pandemic time, then, and the glitch. I had thought that there would be a renaissance in glitch art, and maybe that is still to come, or maybe it is so ubiquitous that I just cannot see it from here. Glitch art has been used as a means of queering, and as protest, like in Andie Shabbar's *Queer-Alt-Delete* (2018), and through processes of scrambling and deconstructing, perform Muñoz's disidentification, where:

> Disidentification is about recycling and rethinking encoded meaning. The process of disidentification scrambles and reconstructs the encoded message of a cultural text in a fashion that both exposes the encoded message's universalizing and exclusionary machinations and recircuits its workings to account for, include, and empower minority identities and identifications. Thus, disidentification is a step further than cracking open the code of the majority; it proceeds to use this code as raw material for representing a disempowered politics or positionality that has been rendered unthinkable by the dominant culture. (Muñoz 1999, 31)

It would be naively optimistic to think that the integration of our digital selves throughout these times has produced a new sense of self, of becoming, leaving the old shells behind.

As glitch feminists, we want to ghost the binary body (Russell 2020, 50).

It would be naive to think that we have arrived, when we are "not yet here.... Put another way, we are not yet queer, but we can feel it as the warm illumination of a horizon imbued with potentiality" (Muñoz 2019, 1) and my aim is not to articulate another utopia. But. The past and present that are together also include the future, and time is just not what it used to be. We can't go back to that Newtonian experience of linear time, because the binary between present and past (or present and future, or past and future) is not as solid as it used to be. This slippage, this fluidity:

> requires us to claim our continuous range of multitudinous selves. As we fail to assimilate into a binary culture, we do so by asserting all components of ourselves—the masculine, the feminine, and everything in-between— as

being part of a continuous narrative, rather than existing as polar points. (Russell 2020, 51)

Every ceremony starts with honoring the ancestors and propitiating Eleggua. Eleggua is the trickster Orisha, the Orisha of the crossroads, the one who controls and can cause chaos. There's a famous story where there is a town where everything is peaceful and calm. To stir things up, Eleggua comes through the town wearing a hat that is red on one side, and black on the other. One person said to another, "Did you see that little boy just now, the one with the red hat?" The other one said, "I saw the boy, but he was wearing a black hat." They started arguing, and soon the town was in chaos. Eleggua likes to stir things up, in order to keep things fresh, but also to teach that a singular point of view, or that things can only be binary, red or black, is missing a bigger picture. Eleggua possesses qualities of "individuality, satire, parody, irony, magic, indeterminacy, open-endedness, ambiguity, chance, uncertainty . . . the classic figure of mediation and of the unity of opposed forces" (Gates 1988, 6).

It is 1993, and I am in my first Ocha house. My godmother is getting ready to do a *diloggun* reading for someone, and instead of the usual twenty-one shells, there are only twenty. She tells me that this is 100 percent Eleggua; that sometimes her sacred objects disappear for a while, that they travel in between worlds and usually come back.

It's 2003, and I am thinking about changing houses. I have Elekes and a pocket Esu from my first house. I've been carrying him with me everywhere for years. I keep him in a little bowl where he gets regular offerings of honey, palm oil, pennies, rum, and cigars. This is Arizona, so for most of the year the palm oil is runny, and Esu is soaking in these things. But now it's winter, and the palm oil has hardened around him, keeping him pretty firmly in place. Whenever I go anywhere, I have to dig him out of the palm oil. I am getting ready to visit my potentially new godfather, a child of Oshun, and I go to collect my Esu. Except I see that he is gone (a god-size hole where Eshu used to be); there is an outline of his silhouette in palm oil, like an Ana Mendieta *silhueta*. I have no idea where he went. He never did come back. (I changed houses.)

If "glitch *art* interlaces algorithmic uncertainty with subjectivity in ways that facilitate an experimentation with new political becomings" (Shabbar 2018, 197), then does it follow (can it follow) that when it crosses into life that the same becomings are . . . you know, becoming? In the way of alternating between discordant tones until something else becomes perceptible, that difference in tone that Gavilán Rayna Russom talks about (Russom 2022), binary does not have to be oppositional. Binary might be a reference to abstract set terms within an algorithm that is always already programmed for difference.

> Trans people, by transitioning, don't force one body into a second shape. They let the only body they have grow into itself until it's whole. Transition isn't a corruption of gender. It's a fulfilment. (Geffen 2020, 217)

Nonbinary is a misbehavior that you can replicate.

> The connections between Afrolatinx spirituality and queer realness is clearly located in a sensibility of transformation—transformations shared at historical, cultural, and spiritual crossroads that dare to envision bonds, imagine pasts, and forge a futurity of compassion and hope. (Otero 2021, 98)

Notes

1. Editors' note: the use of different fonts and spacing in this piece is a structural part of the author's argument. Likewise, the presentation of quoted material and citations as poetic verse is intentional. The author's history as a performance artist and playwright is reflected in this chapter.

Bibliography

Beliso-De Jesús, Aisha M. 2015. *Electric Santería: Racial and Sexual Assemblages of Transnational Religion*. New York: Columbia.
Brandon, George. 1997. *Santería: From Africa to the New World: The Dead Sell Memories*. Bloomington: Indiana University Press.
Cabrera, Lydia. 1986. *Reglas de Congo: Palo Monte, Mayombe*. Miami: Universal.
Daniel, Yvonne. 2005. *Dancing Wisdom: Embodied Knowledge in Haitian Vodou, Cuban Yoruba, and Bahian Candomblé*. Cambridge, UK: Cambridge University Press.
Dolar, Mladen. 2006. *A Voice and Nothing More*. Cambridge, MA: MIT Press.
Gates, Henry Louis. 1988. *The Signifying Monkey: A Theory of African-American Literary Criticism*. Oxford, UK: Oxford University Press.
Geffen, Sasha. 2020. *Glitter Up the Dark: How Pop Music Broke the Binary*. Austin: University of Texas Press.
Kopsky, Anna. 2017. "18 Real Messages from the Dead That'll Make Your Blood Turn Cold." *BuzzFeed*, August 8, 2017. https://www.buzzfeed.com/annakopsky/messages-from-the-dead.

Manning, Erin. 2015. "In the Rhythm of Another Relation." In *prendas—ngangas—enquisos—machines {each part welcomes the other without saying}*, edited by Elke Marhöfer, 63–68. Berlin: Archive.

McFarland, Robert. 2019. *Underland: A Deep Time Journey*. London: Hamish Hamilton.

McMullan, Thomas. 2019. "Ghosts in the Machine: Dead Ringers: How the Smartphone Can Connect Everyone—The Living and the Dead . . ." *The Face*, October 31, 2019. https://theface.com/life/ghosts-paranormal-activity-technology-smartphones.

Mercer, Nina Angela. 2021. "In the Fugitivity of Becoming: The Ringshout as a Tactical Choreographic and Improvised Technology of Intimacy and Activism." Unpublished paper delivered at the American Society for Theater Research conference, San Diego, CA.

Muñoz, José Esteban. 1999. *Disidentifications: Queers of Color and the Performance of Politics*. Minneapolis: University of Minnesota Press.

———. 2019. *Cruising Utopia: The Then and There of Queer Futurity (10th Anniversary Edition)*. New York: New York University Press.

Ochoa, Todd Ramón. 2010a. "PRENDAS-NGANGAS-ENQUISOS: Turbulence and the Influence of the Dead in Cuban-Kongo Material Culture." *Cultural Anthropology* 25 (3): 387–420.

———. 2010b. *Society of the Dead: Quita Manaquita and Palo Praise in Cuba*. Berkeley: University of California Press.

Otero, Solimar. 2020. *Archives of Conjure: Stories of the Dead in Afrolatinx Cultures*. New York: Columbia.

———. 2021. "Afrolatinx Folklore and Representation: Interstices and Anti-authenticity." In *Theorizing Folklore from the Margins: Critical and Ethical Approaches*, edited by Solimar Otero and Mintzi Auanda Martínez-Rivera, 83–102. Bloomington: Indiana University Press.

Phillips, Rasheedah. 2014. "Afrofuturism: Black Presence in Sci-Fi Worlds of Technology, Magic, Fantasy." *BLERDS*. August 12, 2014. https://blerds.atlantablackstar.com/2014/08/12/afrofuturism-black-presence-in-sci-fi-worlds-of-technology-magic-fantasy/.

Russell, Legacy. 2020. *Glitch Feminism: A Manifesto*. New York: Verso.

Russom, Gavilán Rayna. 2022. "Trans Feminist Symphonic Music." ithinkibetterfollowyouaround.com, February 17, 2022. https://ithinkibetterfollowyouaround.com/2022/02/17/gavilan-rayna-russom-trans-feminist-symphonic-music.

School of the Art Institute of Chicago. 2016. "GLITCH: A Brief History of Unstable Media Arts at SAIC." https://youtube.com/UKrlv6D1Tx0.

Shabbar, Andie. 2018. "Queer–Alt–Delete: Glitch Art as Protest against the Surveillance Cis-tem." *Women's Studies Quarterly* 46 (3/4): 195–212.

Sharpe, Christina. 2016. *In the Wake: On Blackness and Being*. Durham, NC: Duke University Press.

Siner, Emily. 2013. "What's a 'Glitch,' Anyway? A Brief Linguistic History." *NPR*, October 24, 2013. https://www.npr.org/sections/alltechconsidered/2013/10/24/239788307/whats-a-glitch-anyway-a-brief-linguistic-history-meaning-definition.

Thompson, Robert Farris. 1984. *Flash of the Spirit: Afro & Afro-American Art & Philosophy*. New York: Knopf Doubleday.

UTIA. 2020. "The Ghost of Zoom." https://www.youtube.com/watch?v=WGZikDqUCJU.

Victor, Daniel. 2021. "'I'm Not a Cat,' Says Lawyer Having Zoom Difficulties." https://www.nytimes.com/2021/02/09/style/cat-lawyer-zoom.html.

Kit Danowski is Senior Lecturer in Performance at the University of Portsmouth. They are author of *Performing with the Dead: Trances and Traces.*

6

Ancestoring
Materializing Memory, Mourning, and Resuscitation through Performance

SOLIMAR OTERO

At the start of a séance in Havana, Cuba, in 2019, I remember Susy, my *ojubona*,[1] holding out a glass of water from the spirits' table (*bóveda*) to me and saying, "Esto es ahora tú perfume [This is now your perfume]."[2] As a new Santería priestess, I could not wear cosmetics nor apply synthetics to my skin. During the year of strict observance of religious rules, my *iyaboraje*, the water of the bóveda served as a "safe" element that I could apply to my person. The water placed on my skin threaded together the contiguous traditions of Espiritismo, Santería, and Palo through its material contact with the dead. An important Afro-Cuban proverb is often reiterated to establish these connections by practitioners: "Ikú bi ocha [The dead give birth to the gods]" (see fig. 6.1). Water and the cartography of the bóveda allow us access to the terrain of the dead and their movements, qualities, and methods for bringing distinct religious traditions together (see Wirtz 2021).

This chapter situates ritual work done on the bóveda alongside the performance of the Cuban spirit mediums' song "El Congo de Guinea" and a reading of Maria Hamilton Abegunde's poem "Learning to Eat the Dead: USA" to flesh out how sounding Blackness resuscitates the dead as a form of archiving. Here, *sounding Blackness* refers to the ways that race is constructed through sound creatively and politically to a diversity of effects (see Sinitiere 2018). The bóveda, song, and poetry rely on Afro Diasporic understandings of metaphysical dispersals and arrivals of the departed as fluid and directed. Performances and objects that are passed along in Afrolatine religions contain elements of mourning, loss, and remembering that are associated with slave and Indigenous pasts of ancestors and practitioners.[3] They constitute a type of ancestoring where the body molds itself into a material source of memory. Ancestoring extends the temporal and spatial dimensions of who and what

Figure 6.1 Altar for Ancestors and Olokún and Yemayá. Construction by Martin Tsang and Alexander Fernandez. Commissioned by the Latino Studies Program, Indiana University, Bloomington, September 7, 2023. *Photo by Charles Exdell. In the author's private collection.*

perform race and religiosity. In addition, the artifacts of transcriptions of songs, poetry, associated sacred objects, and images provide a unique repository with which to consider the continuum between enactment, presence, and remains.[4]

The bóveda is a table assembled by spirit mediums for communication with the dead in private and public rituals (see fig. 6.2, Otero 2020b). It contains glasses of water and objects like rosaries, flowers, candles, perfume, and tobacco. The bóveda is a multifaceted body that holds and projects multiple subjectivities, geographies, and histories. This is an important element to keep in mind as the songs and poetry I will be discussing in this chapter also create opportunities for fleshing Black and brown ancestors through assemblage and performance.

When I speak of *Black and brown* in this piece, I mean the emergent and contested manifestations of Afrolatinidad regarding phenotype, bodily sanctification, and national identity that operate within Espiritismo's transnational networks (see also Beliso-De Jesús 2015). In terms of entities, I emphasize their Black and brown natures as ways of illustrating how the racial and ethnic

Figure 6.2 Bóveda. Havana, Cuba 2013. Photo by Hector Delgado. In the author's private collection.

dynamics of a spirit's biography and necrography are interconnected elements of how they are recognized by the community as having certain histories (Panagiotopoulos and Espírito Santo 2019). The space between Blackness and brownness is fluid, and there is movement in the community and among spirit guides between these racial and ethnic locations that are also affectively accessed. Thus, when the transmigration of entities merges with the mediums through the sensorial invocations brought upon through water, scent of perfume, tobacco smoke, color of flowers, and the sting of sprayed *agua ardiente* (cane liquor) onto bodies during ceremonies, we are also witnessing racial crossings.

The placement of objects is crucial to the spiritual cartography of the bóveda. Historically, we can see that by 1902, Hilario Mustilier Garzón, an *espiritista* from Santiago de Cuba, kept a spirits table that included Catholic elements: on "a large table . . . were a wooden cross adorned with flowers and several images depicting Christ's and Mary's Sacred Hearts, the Mystery of the Trinity, and the Crucifixion" (Román 2007, 41). Mustilier also healed using Afro-Cuban guides and techniques alongside his vernacular interpretations of Catholicism, which got him into trouble with the law due to the policing of Black religious cultures on the island (Román 2007, 41). Thus bóvedas, through their form, display a history of strife and pain felt by Afro-Caribbean practitioner ancestors. The glasses of water, flowers, and photos of the dead illustrate a continuation of an innovation that flew in the face of multiple kinds of religious and racial orthodoxy. As Fred Moten has observed about Black aesthetics and the denial of Black subjectivity in the Americas, "The history of blackness is a testament to the fact that objects can and do resist" (2003, 1).

Black spirits do a lot of the heavy lifting in the practice of Espiritismo (Wirtz 2014, 166–69, 248–53). This is a key division of labor to consider when situating the multiracial and multicultural composition of transnational Afrolatine spiritual families involved with the practices of spirit mediumship. Various scholars have commented on how the racialization of spirits also informs the categorization of ethnic forms of Blackness into different forms of spiritual practice (Palmié 2014; Wirtz 2014; Viarnés 2007; Beliso-De Jesús 2015; Pérez 2016). Though it is usually frowned on to mix Santería and Palo ritual practices, for example, in Espiritismo *cruzado*,[5] cross-pollination vigorously occurs. This re-rendering and blending of different kinds of Blackness is enacted in song, prayer, embodiment, and the objects produced and utilized at misas. Espiritistas also commonly add the presence of European, Asian, Indigenous, Middle Eastern, and Rom spirit guides to their personal and communal resources for ritual work (Wirtz 2014; Otero 2016; Mason 2002, 95).

An obvious manifestation of these racially and ethnically marked spirits appears as representations on bóvedas. A good case in point would be the Native American imagery often displayed on spirit tables and in altars.[6] Thus, though Black spirits are at the heart of most of the ancestors recognized in Espiritismo, *all* spirits are racially and ethnically marked. Decidedly, then, the history of racial inequality and ethnic difference in sites like Cuba, Puerto Rico, and the United States frames some of the most pressing social negotiations taking place in the realm of spiritual praxis and religious authority among espiritistas today. Placement and display of spiritual objects on personal bóvedas provide clear visions of these tensions and of coexistence.

A bóveda holds objects that remember, heal, witness, and resist being forgotten. This allows for mediums to have visceral experiences of ancestors privately and in communion that also generate new actions and relationships through conjure (Otero 2020a, 25–26). Conjure in Espiritismo's context constitutes acts of becoming, ontological negotiations between ancestors and mediums' bodies, mediated often through the material culture of the bóveda, that make material memories of race, ethnicity, pain, and migration.[7] Fred Moten's work on Black performance is insightful as he explains that sounding Blackness occurs in the scream of the objectified that signals an "ani*mater*iality" that is "painfully and hiddenly disclosed always and everywhere in the tracks of black performance" (2003, 18, emphasis in original). Here, Moten illustrates how matter and sound can move through each other through the metaphor of the mother, the *mater*, to birth both memory and intergenerational trauma of slavery through Black performance.

The ways that mediums and ancestors share bodies, voices, movements, and subjectivities line up with how ani*mater*iality can be understood in the bóveda's particular Black performative context. Memory objects passed along in Afrolatine religions contain elements of mourning, loss, and remembering associated with slave and indigenous pasts of ancestors and practitioners. These inherited objects are thus also raced and marked within a space-time performative, a chronotope, of colonial Blackness that helps to produce Cuban expressions of spirit mediumship (Wirtz 2014, 9–10).[8] Attending to the ways that material culture can be racialized through religious practice is central to understanding the complicated and contentious process of making persons, deities, and ancestors. As Diana Espírito Santo observes in Afro-Cuban traditions of work with the dead, "the self is more than just itself. It leaves traces and can become ontologically associated with objects" (2018, 68).[9]

Locating the discursive and experienced locations of Black embodiment, Harvey Young asks us to think about how "the black body continually doubles real bodies" (2010, 23). In mitigating the multiplicities of Black subjectivities with the experience of collective projections of Blackness onto bodies that create violent consequences in the world, he provides an exploration of how embodying Blackness resides in repositories of experiences that are deployed through critical memory. This is the kind of re-membering[10] that helps us think through how the bóveda offers a disambiguated set of subjectivities of the dead that are reconstituted through ritual performances. These performances story the memory of the lives of guardian spirits, often Black and former slaves, in ways that are doubled in "real" bodies through mediums (Otero 2020a, 85–87). The spirits are called on to appear, as we will see in my analysis of "Congo de Guinea," and their presences are accessed through a critical and imaginative performative that also recalls sociohistorical legacies of violence and subjugation.[11] Spiritual sojourning, maroonage, and Black fugitivity are thus transformative strategies for constituting corporeality through shared memories that are also temporarily embodied within these choreographed frames (ife 2021).

Rituals that bring out the dead, like misas, narrate their strategies for resistance and agency in another life. These lessons to mediums often include descriptions of conjure to be reactivated by the living in a kind of magical pedagogy for fighting against personal and systematic injustice. The creation of material culture and use of organic materials are central in most cleansings and protection spells prescribed by ancestor spirits. For example, mediums and other kinds of practitioners can be told to make spirit dolls, cleanse with herbs, and perform other acts of commemoration with and for Afrolatine spirit guides (Espírito Santo 2015; Otero 2020a). These enactments and the objects that are produced from them clearly emerge from a Black ani*mater*iality that is also creolized and holds the very tensions found in the historical realities and cultural crossings of Caribbean coloniality (Moten 2003, 18, emphasis in original).

Spiritual objects emerging from this context illustrate the necessity for adopting an ontological approach that Sabine Marschall describes as "treating meaning and thing as an identity" (2019, 4).[12] In this manner, material culture like glasses on a bóveda, as containers of the dead, spark the physical transformation of a medium into an ancestor whose body aches from injuries acquired in a past life from slavery, other kinds of servitude, and/or maroonage (Otero 2020a, 85–86; Ochoa 2010, 48–49; Warden 2007, 106). Spirit guides in Espiritismo continue their toil, albeit for the advancement of a larger spiritual good that includes working with human subjects that are embroiled in the consequences of the history of slavery, colonialism, and disenfranchisement in places like Cuba, Puerto Rico, and the United States. As a refrain from the traditional song "Congo de Guinea" relates:

> Congo de Guinea soy, buenas noches criollos, Congo de Guinea soy, buenas noches criollos, yo deja [sic] mi hueso allá, yo vine a hacer caridad, yo deja mi hueso allá, yo vine hacer caridad.[13]
> [I am a Congo from Guinea, good evening creoles, I am a Congo from Guinea, good evening creoles, I left my bone over there, I came to perform charity, I left my bone over there, I came to perform charity.]

"Congo de Guinea" is a popular song that mediums perform around the bóveda at the start of a misa to invite spirit guides to gather (Moore 2025, 106–08).[14] The mediums sing the part of the African Congo, greeting the Cuban *criollos* assembled at the séance, asserting his desire to perform good works. The perspective in the song illustrates an identification with El Congo, especially with his subjectivity as an African mobile spirit subject. The materiality of his former existence is not lost on the community—"yo deja mi hueso allá [I left my bone over there]," and the recognition of the sacrifice made by this African ancestor in life as a slave, and in death as a spirit guide, is the blood that binds this kinship. It is no accident that a single bone is mentioned in the refrain as practitioners of Palo, who also work with the dead, utilize objects like bones in their spiritual cauldrons known as *ngangas*, which also house the dead (Palmié 2023; Ochoa 2010; Cabrera 1979). The ideas of spiritual flight and material remanifestation expressed in the lyrics come from both the belief of a return to Africa by slaves upon their death and the belief in the transmigration of souls found in nineteenth-century French spiritism. Thus, the song plays with the layers of African, Criollo, and European identity that shaped and contested each other in the colonial Americas.

The refrain quoted in "Congo de Guinea" brings this visceral and embodied history toward a vision of the present that suggests presence and action. As El Congo says, "Yo vine a hacer caridad [I came to do charity]." His declaration reinforces the belief in good works that serves as a foundational principle in Espiritismo. It is significant to note that the spirit's promise of charity is channeled multiple times through the mediums' bodies as the refrain is repeated during the ritual. Therefore, the performance of the song acts as a shared oath to make manifest material acts in this world that are inspired by the spirit world. The collapsing of voice and intention performs the relationship of material and spiritual copresences among spirit guides and mediums. Songs in a misa produce a reality where subjects, intentions, and embodied acts are shared artistically.[15] Through such activities, a religious community can engage in healing, testimony, and witnessing with and for their ancestors.

An analysis of the remaining verses is useful for situating the multiple subjectivities of Afrolatinidad being produced in the performance of the song.

The following excerpt of "Congo de Guinea" is performed by Los Nani in their album *Espiritistas ¡A Cantar!* (1997):[16]

Del mundo de los misterios	From mysterious worlds
Yo voy en busca de un ser	I come in search of someone
Kiako, Kiako,[17] bajo a la tierra.	Quietly, quietly, I descend on earth *Kiako*,
Kiako, a cumplir misión	Quietly, Quietly, I complete my mission
Ay yo vengo de *ina, ina*[18]	Oh, I come from the fire, flame
Pero yo vengo de Oludumare	But I come from Oludumare [God in heaven]
Cuando un Congo es de belleza	When a Congo is beautiful
Yo saludo a sus collares	I salute your necklaces
¡Vamos a comer! ¡Vamos a hacer dulces!	Let's eat! Let's make sweets!
Coro: Tapa la cazuela, que sabroso está el dulce.	Chorus: Cover the pot, what a delicious sweet!
¡Eh, Congo va a comer!	Hey, Congo is going to eat!
¡Muerto va hacer dulce!	The dead will make sweets!
Coro: Tapa la cazuela, que sabroso está el dulce.	Chorus: Cover the pot, what a delicious sweet!
¡Eh, eh, Ta José va comer, Ta José come dulce!	Hey, hey, Ta José will eat, Ta José eats sweets!
Coro: Tapa la cazuela, que sabroso está el dulce.	Chorus: Cover the pot, what a delicious sweet!
Ta José y su cazuela	Ta José and his pot
Coro: que sabroso está el dulce	Chorus: What a delicious sweet!
Francisca y su cazuela	Francisca and her pot
Coro: que sabroso está el dulce	Chorus: What a delicious sweet!
Ay come, come, que come tu dulce	Oh, eat, eat, now eat your sweets *Coro:*
come, come, que come tu dulce	Chorus: Eat, eat, now eat your sweets
La mala rabia, Francisca,	*La mala rabia,*[19] Francisca
come, come, que come su dulce	eat, eat, now eat your sweet!
El dulce de coco, ay Ta José, come dulce	*El dulce de coco,*[20] oh Ta José, eat sweets
Coro: come, come, que come tu dulce.	Chorus: Eat, eat, now eat your sweets
Ae, Salamale Malekunsala	*Ae, Salamale Malekunsala*[21]
Coro: Ae, Salamale Malekunsala.	Chorus: *Ae, Salamale Malekunsala*

Like many songs for the dead in Cuba, this performance of "El Congo de Guinea" is antiphonal[22] and uses half-*coros* to accelerate the calling of the specific entities associated with Congo spirits, like Ta José[23] and Francisca (Warden 2007, 92–93; Carpentier 1988, 267, 270–74). The song starts out slowly as a salute to both the mediums and the Congo spirits. It quickly picks up into a rumba-style rhythm when we get to the phrase "¡Vamos a comer! ¡Vamos a hacer dulces! [Let's eat! Let's make sweets!]." The action in the lyrics mirror the kinetic movement of a spirit enjoying a borrowed body, a delicious sweet made to affectively please their senses. The leader and coro urge the many different Congo spirits, like Ta José and Francisca, to "come, come, que come tu dulce," eat up the sweets being offered in gratitude for their journey and labor with the community of mediums. There is a desire for an active sign of presence, through the sense of taste in this instance, that illustrates the importance of ancestoring through the body. From the very start of "El Congo de Guinea" there is a blurring of subjectivities that serves to make materiality more malleable as voice, touch, and thoughts are shared and coconstructed.

Jayna Brown provides a metaphysical methodology that is useful to listening to "El Congo de Guinea." As she writes, "I am thinking of practices, real and imagined, through which we access other realms," planes that "are always with us and around us, like electricity of sound waves" (2021, 9). Brown explicitly locates sound waves and vibrations from Black music as modes to accessing otherworldly realms of becoming through a pliable materiality, through the kind of performative ancestoring I am suggesting: "Music . . . is a form of travel through which our material bodies transfigure past time and the human form from other worlds" (10). El Congo de Guinea is voicing this kind of journeying as he moves from mysterious worlds ("el mundo de los misterios") to the séance in search of someone to work for and with. El Congo, through song, is made into flesh, and his journey of transmigration reflects a transfiguration for all of those singing for, with, and through him. Further, the communication between El Congo, the lead vocal, and the chorus illustrates the building of a shared narrative of arrival that is experienced through an interorality that is common to Cuban rituals with the dead (Otero 2015; Wirtz 2014; Beliso-De Jesús 2015; Espírito Santo 2018).

El Congo's travels resonate with the Black Utopias suggested by Afrofuturist aesthetics and performance (Brown 2021; Keeling 2019). Again, he descends from "the world of mysteries" onto the earth to complete his mission ("Kiako, Kiaco, a cumplir misión"). El Congo becomes a celestial astronaut, a time traveler who traverses universes that tie Black histories to Black presents and Black futures in song.[24] Thus, mysterious terrains can be accessed to create new worlds through sound. The ways that El Congo emphasizes mystery in the song is powerful in that they provide a framework for lives beyond the now that offer elements of hope and continuity. This mirrors both José Muñoz's notion of singular identities in the brown commons and Ana-Maurine Lara resuscitation of the ancestor Shee in her poems in *Kohnjehr Woman* (Muñoz 2020, 1–7; Lara 2017b). In the former, El Congo is a singularity, a presence, who helps create a community of praxis that is both fleeting and reproduceable through performances in the brown commons that is the misa spiritual. In the case of the latter, El Congo, like Lara's conjure woman Shee, tells of his movement and power through a Caribbean terrain where his servitude is retooled for revolt, efficacious labor, and community making through sensorial communion (Lara 2017a, 1–3, 12).

Following our senses, then, a different kind of sight is an important element that Congo spirits bring to rituals that call on them: "¡Vititi, vititi! [Sight, sight!]," cries El Espíritu de La Conga Portuguesa as she takes a lit candle and passes the hot wax over Susy's eyes.[25] This Conga spirit visits with us during a misa in 2018 at Tomasa's house, where we are gathered along with Riguito, an elder Tata Nkisi (Palo priest) who is participating in the activity. The entity is new to our community, and Riguito is speaking with her, translating her speech, which mixes Portuguese, Spanish, Kikongo, and Lucumí. La Conga is *looking* for us, after us, in ways that we can't see.[26] She urges us to be careful in our workplaces, to not let strangers in our homes, to never drink from a cup left unattended anytime, anywhere. This advice is wise, and we believe in its potency because we belong to the brown commons that is invested in creating a better world through practices rooted in Black pasts and Black futures. Our mixed identities in terms of race, ethnicity, and national origin only reinforce the importance of doing this work from the perspective and guidance of La Conga Portuguesa. She's been there, she's here now, and she sees.

The layered ethnic identity of La Conga Portuguesa reflects the reality of Afro-Atlantic creolization that has created complicated subjects since the sixteenth century (Heywood and Thornton 2007; Landers 2011). Portuguese Catholicism, Islam, and Indigenous religions coexisted in central Africa, and enslaved people coming to Cuba from this region brought their religious admixtures with them. The mixture of Portuguese, Kikongo, Lucumí, and Spanish spoken by La Conga Portuguesa reflects linguistically the ancestoring I am referring to in this chapter. Her pronouncements serve as embodied residuals of past subjectivities that are sensed and performed into being. It is important to note that Kristina Wirtz's studies of Afro-Cuban speech during rituals illustrate how some linguistic performances of Black speech like *bozal* can reinscribe colonial representations that flatten rather than flesh out Black subjectivities (2007, 2014). With this caveat in mind, my own understanding of La Conga Portuguesa and El Congo de Guinea as doing the work of fleshing out spirit is contingent on the context of the communities that are enacting the communion with these beings.

The multilayering of ethnic markers through speech is echoed in "El Congo de Guinea." This is common in many Afro-Cuban folkloric expressions of music and ritual due to a historical depth of religious mixing (Ortiz [1950] 2001; Cabrera 1979; Wirtz 2014; Miller 2009). The song brings in elements of Kikongo with phrases like "kiako, kiako [quietly, quietly]" being interspersed with Lucumí descriptors like "ina, ina [fire, flame]." El Congo can be referring to the light of the physical flame on candles used in rituals, the spiritual realm of light, or the phrase "¡luz! [light!]" that confirms visions received during a misa. The many valences that the voice of El Congo produces in the song allows for a depth of meaning that becomes interconnected through the unpacking of the sound done through detailed listening and participation in Afro-Cuban musics (Vazquez 2013).

The following verse, "But I come from Oludumare," orients the listener to El Congo's benevolence since he is approaching the mediums from a Yoruba heavenly realm. Yet, El Congo moves swiftly onto the material plane, entreating other dead, like Ta José and Francisca, to eat their sweets. The voice of the lead and the coro interchange subjectivities with the Congo dead in singing and sounding out the rumba rhythm that concludes the song. The last verses repeated, "Salamale Malekunsala," echo the ritual greeting commonly used for Congo ancestors in Cuban Palo and Espiritismo. This adds yet another layer of religious intermingling that demonstrates a density of Blackness and brownness, a space where multiple commons intersect and physically connect. The handshake that accompanies our voices as we say "Salamale Malekunsala" in touching the Congo as he materializes fleshes out this connection.

In "Congo de Guinea," Kikongo, Yoruba, and Muslim afterlives are situated next to each other to create an expansive map of futures in the hereafter that also reflect the sociopolitical realities of performing Blackness and brownness through religion in postrevolutionary Cuba (Moore 2004; Warden 2007; Ayorinde 2004; Bodenheimer 2015; Wirtz 2014; Abreu 2019). Conflict over religious affiliation, ethnicity, racial identification, sexuality, and gender make up part of the landscape in contemporary Cuban spiritual circles (Beliso-De Jesús 2015; Strongman 2019; Thorne 2020; Meadows 2021). Over and again, social performances centering on religious authority, authenticity, and efficacy in relation to these tensions lace ritual contexts. "Congo de Guinea" addresses these issues through religious and linguistic code-switching that suggests a frame of reference of mutual respect. The verse "Cuando un Congo es de belleza / Yo saludo a sus collares [When a Congo is beautiful / I salute your necklaces]" illustrates an example of religious recognition rooted in acceptance. The Congo, in saluting the Yoruba *ilekes*, necklaces that signal devotion to the Orishas, counters contentions between Lukumí and Palo practitioners that are often overplayed, especially in Havana, since many of individuals practice both traditions, albeit in ritually separated settings (Ochoa 2020; Bodenheimer 2015; Beliso-De Jesús 2015). The song illustrates how Espiritismo cruzado, an open form of spiritist worship that allows for ethnic, racial, and cultural crossings, situates its spirit messengers as instruments of communication, travelers that carry a multiplicity of skills (Otero 2020a; Espírito Santo 2018). The Congo spirit in the song is diplomatic, polyvocal, and efficacious in works of conjure.[27] He is cosmopolitan in many respects, and his religious and linguistic mutability allows for the religious community to recognize the traversal of boundaries as a marker of power and potentiality.

A final consideration of the song "El Congo de Guinea" acts as a bridge to discussing Maria Hamilton Abegunde's poem "Learning to Eat the Dead: USA." The importance of the cycle of eating by and for the dead is essential to working through materiality and resuscitation through the care of remains. El Congo is invited to eat sweets from *la cazuela* (pot) that are prepared specifically for him and his fellow spirits, Ta José and Francisca. The performers sing the verses "Eh, Congo va a comer! / ¡Muerto va hacer dulce! / *Coro:* Tapa la cazuela, que sabroso está el dulce [Hey, Congo is going to eat! / The dead will make sweets! / Chorus: Cover the pot, what a delicious sweet!]" This rumba is an invitation to cocreate bodies that taste, eat, are fleshed. Specific desserts that spirits enjoy, like el dulce de coco and la mala rabia, are invoked alongside the dead to entice their arrival. Taste is a vital component of establishing lasting relationships with entities. Often discerning in their palates, both the dead and Orisha require foods be prepared in meticulous ways (Pérez 2016, 2023). In the song, El Congo, Ta José, and Francisca are called so that they can experience the deliciousness of the dessert while also paying attention to how the sweets are cooking in the pot.[28] The command—"¡Tapa la cazuela!"—conjures multiple scenes that point to the heat of the pot and its contents. The active hot pot creates a layered reference to the dead in Palo traditions who are housed in *ngangas* (iron pots) (Cabrera 1979; Ochoa 2020). Ngangas are sites of feeding, communication, and labor with the dead that are often "heated" up with rum, gunpowder, or other substances. Thus, the song creates a bridge between Palo and Espiritismo through Congo spirits' own sensorium and dwelling places where heat becomes a vehicle for vivification. In this manner, the dead are intimately connected to the ways that matter and essence are transformed through a kind of cooking that also suggests that eating by and for the dead performs presence.

"Learning to Eat the Dead: USA" (Abegunde 2018)[29] is a poem that connects an attention to remains to the eating, digesting, mourning, and healing of Black bodies and souls. As Abegunde writes:

"Learning to Eat the Dead: USA"[30]
for Diamond Reynolds

When they invite you to dinner, say yes.
Arrive early, choose the chair closest to the door.
Pay attention to who sits where.
Pay attention to who drinks what.

When they lay your lover's body face down,
Do not vomit when your host saws off his head.
Do not cry when the guests crack his fingers and elbows.
Look as they turn him over to lick the back of his neck.

When they ask if you'd like to try some, politely refuse.
Instead, pour your glass of water over his feet.
Wash between his toes. Massage what remains of his heels.
Do not look at his knees which someone has started to suck.

When the hosts walk towards you with a slice of cranium,
Insists that you taste its peculiar pungency, and says
I have eaten Black man brains a million times, but never like this . . .
Decline, sit still, breathe, pray, pray. Pray.

Pay attention to who stops eating when you do this.
Pay attention to who whispers to whom.
Pay attention to who picks up the wine bottles.
Pay attention to who slips the steak knives into their laps.

When a guest offers you more water, ignore her.
Pour olive oil over his feet. Kiss them gently.
Place your cheek against his soles. Listen to the lesson on how
To be awake even while sleeping.

Only when they bring you his heart do you accept.
Demand to hold the whole organ.
Place it on your plate.
Do nothing as they wait for you to eat.

Pick up his heart. Rub it against your face. Rub it against your neck.
Feel its weight on your shoulders.
Take your knife and cut a small chunk from the center.
Rest it against your chest. Let it dissolve into your own.

Put what you have cut into your mouth.
Caress the shards of metal with your tongue.

If you chew, your anger will poison you.
Swallow nothing, not even a piece of skin.

Abegunde dedicates the poem to Diamond Reynolds, the girlfriend of Philando Castile, a Black man who was killed by Minneapolis police at a traffic stop in 2016. Reynolds live streamed the murder in a visceral and necessary act of witnessing and accounting of the ongoing terror enacted upon African Americans in the United States. The poem takes the shape of a dinner party where the partner of a deceased Black man is asked to sit and partake of his body: "When they invite you to dinner, say yes. / Arrive early, choose the chair closest to the door." Abegunde similarly invites the reader to witness a macabre but necessary scene of reckoning: "When the hosts walk towards you with a slice of cranium / Insists that you taste its peculiar pungency, and says / I have eaten Black man brains a million times, but never like this . . . / Decline, sit still, breathe, pray, pray. Pray." However, Abegunde turns this cannibalistic consumption on its head: "Pick up his heart. Rub it against your face. Rub it against your neck. / Feel its weight on your shoulders. / Take your knife and cut a small chunk from the center. / Rest it against your chest. Let it dissolve into your own. / Put what you have cut into your mouth. / Caress the shards of metal with your tongue. / If you chew, your anger will poison you. / Swallow nothing, not even a piece of skin." The poem instructs, challenges, and leads the reader through a sensorium of the grotesque that depicts the horror experienced by Black communities in the face of white supremacy.[31] Eating the dead in the poem then takes on multiple and deliberate meanings, some that decidedly suggest a framework for recuperation through consumption.

Ingestion is an important mode of ancestoring that allows the body to incorporate elements of presence through taste as traces of essence.[32] Indeed, the absence created by the dead can be understood as a kind of pronounced presence (Wirtz 2022; Otero and Wirtz 2023). One can see elements of Christianity's transubstantiation in the poem's framing of a feast of a tortured and mutilated body. In doing so, Abegunde points to the ritual significance of the sacrifice of Black bodies to the foundational ideology of white supremacy in the United States, which has at its heart evangelical Christianity (see Cone 2013; Allen [1999] 2021; Mathews 2008; Bailey and Snedker 2011; Belew 2019). Coupling imagery from the Bible with the lessons of vigilance learned from state-sanctioned violence, Abegunde writes, "Pour olive oil over his feet. Kiss them gently. / Place your cheek against his soles. / Listen to the lesson on how / To be awake even while sleeping." The anointing of Christ's feet is alluded to here while the reality of "being awake even while sleeping" speaks to the intergenerational trauma and strategies of survival passed on in Black communities.

Yet, Abegunde's poem layers these elements of the Christian Last Supper with Africana ways of knowing, carrying, and making the dead through the very materiality of the body-as-feast constructed in the poem.

"Learning to Eat the Dead: USA" mirrors the ways that spirits materialize through taste and mourning in the song "El Congo de Guinea." In a continuum of re-membering, materiality is produced through performances that voice the sense of taste and touch. Death is then transformed into the substance of an African Diasporic expressive culture that weaves together memory and words into presence. The poem and the song take the effects of "archives of Black woundedness" and create an opportunity for witnessing that sensually brings the dead into the space for one to mourn yet also touch (Musser 2018, 96; see also Spillers 1987). The vivification that occurs sonically illustrates what Kevin Quashie calls Black aliveness, a state of being that centers world-making without negating the reality of violence and loss (2021, 3). Quashie's understanding of Black aliveness grows out of listening to poetry and understanding Black expressive cultures as sites for healing as trauma is witnessed. Congo spirits, the bóveda, and the dead lover in Abegunde's poem offer opportunities for Black aliveness in embodying the dead through song, glasses of water, and words. These elements, which range from sound to material culture to a combination of both (a poem is read and heard), create sensorial conduits that produce ancestors in performance.

There are metaphysical logics at play in how eating and death are connected in Black and brown manifestations of Orisha worship that enrich our understanding of ancestoring in the poem, material culture, and performances being discussed in this chapter. *Ibú Kolé* is a road of the deity Ochún that is symbolized by the vulture and associated with witches (Otero 2020a, 14; Murphy 2001, 41; Flores-Peña 2001, 117; Brown 2022, 295–96).[33] "Learning to Eat the Dead: USA" borrows from Ochún Ibú Kolé's necessary work of consuming carrion as a cyclical element of nourishment that connects life and death.[34] Abegunde's status as a priestess of Yoruba traditional religion resonates with this reading of the poem. Likewise, in misas, participants are conjuring the dead through their senses and offering their bodies to be shared with them. In both of these instances, the transformation of the dead into a kind of aliveness is coproduced through cohabitation and absorption. As Abegunde writes, "Pick up his heart. Rub it against your face. Rub it against your neck. . . . / Rest it against your chest. Let it dissolve into your own." This verse provides a poetic example of how African Diasporic and Afrolatine commemoration with the dead provide "a window into a specific kind of self, subject to disassembly and reconstruction" (Espírito Santo 2018, 74). Thus, the elements of "re-manifestation" I have been considering here in material culture, ritual, song, and poetry illustrate that death and aliveness are coproductions that are collectively experienced with specific purposes in mind. Namely, the performance of a kind of spiritual activism where Black and brown ancestors work alongside community members to assemble themselves as a body that resignifies violence and trauma. As noted, the proximities of Afrolatinidad encompass a continuum of Blackness and brownness that situates a shared and complicated history of spiritual and political struggle, invention, and cohabitation.[35]

The ways that the dead can be resuscitated in the performance of ritual, the creation of material culture, and the reading of poetry lead me to how bodies are constructed through shared subjectivities, histories, sexualities, and Blackness in Africana religions. The performances of constructing a bóveda at a misa, singing "El Congo de Guinea," and witnessing[36] "Learning to Eat the Dead: USA" illustrate how materiality and spirituality constantly turn into each other in a regenerative cycle. The bodies, objects, presences, and senses shared in the performances studied here are situated in the very voices that pronounce how prayers, lyrics, melody, and meter unfold in the latter. These commemorative practices that interweave subjects and texts illustrate how spiritual activism with ancestors provides road maps to future actions that heal, fight, and create (Beliso-De Jesús 2015; Otero 2020a; Matory 2018). Through breath, sweat, taste, and tears, ancestors are coconstructed in multifaceted bodies that perform pasts, presents, and futures that offer deep connections and emerging worlds.

Notes

1. An ojubona is a second godmother who tends to new priests during their initiation. I am grateful to the ritual specialists in Mantilla, Cuba, for their generous support and guidance of this work. I am also indebted to Maria Hamilton Abegunde for sharing the powerful poetry that appears in this chapter.

2. All translations from Spanish, Lukumí, and Cuban Kikongo to English are mine. In some instances, I have opted for figurative rather than literal translations to preserve the spirit of the lyrics and phrases analyzed in the chapter.

3. I am asking for the work of mourning to be reconceptualized in Indigenous ways that move the scope and temporality of this work beyond a single instance of mortality. This recontextualization considers institutional frameworks that interrupt and intersect with mourning. See Briggs and Briggs (2016).

4. For more on presence in Hemispheric performance perspective, see Taylor (2020).

5. Espiritismo *cruzado* is a form of spiritism that combines elements from African, European, Indigenous, and Hemispheric religious practices in Cuba (see Warden 2007; Moore 2025; Otero 2020a; Espírito Santo 2015; Pérez 2016).

6. For a good reflection on Native American spirits in Afro-Atlantic spiritual practices, see Wehmeyer (2007).

7. For more on the aesthetics of bóvedas as artistic creations, see Flores-Peña (2004).

8. Fanon's articulation of the reproduction of Blackness as Other through the phrase "Look! A Negro!" illustrates another kind of performative that races subjects (2008, 89–91).

9. Espírito Santo sees subjectivities in Espiritismo as "synchronicities" that produce "assemblages" rather than "essences" that are negotiated through lenience and plasticity (2018, 67, 69). She proposes that elasticity acts as "a vital component to successfully working with the dead in Congo-inspired religions in Cuba" (69).

10. *Re-membering* is used to here to address both memory and materialization of the dead.

11. Tracy Hucks makes a powerful intervention in insisting that acts of torture forced upon Black bodies in colonial Trinidad and Tobago constituted a type of white civic religion (2022, 97).

12. For presence, affect, and objects, see also Armstrong (1981).

13. Transcript from a *misa de coronación* collected by the author, Havana, Cuba, 2013. See https://www.youtube.com/watch?v=AUwLpFNsTeU for a recorded version of "Congo de Guinea" by Los Nani, from the album *Espiritistas ¡A Cantar!* (1997), accessed September 13, 2024. For an alternate version of this refrain, see Castro Ramírez (2010, 63).

14. There is a cycle of songs dedicated to Congo spirits in Cuban rituals for the dead, especially as they are called upon in a ceremony known as *cajón pa' los Muertos* (see Warden 2007, 91–107, 144).

15. Robin Moore's recent work on the *violín espiritual* illustrates how elements of sonic and ritual transformation in violin performances stem from songs performed at misas (2025).

16. Warden notes that this album by Los Nani is the first recording "featuring the music of cajón ceremonies" and also "the only one that has been in Cuba" as of 2007 (2007, 108).

17. *Kiako* can be translated into the command "quiet, be still" in an Afro-Cuban Palo Mayombe context (Megenney n.d., 56, 61).

18. *Ina* is fire in Yoruba.

19. *La mala rabia* is a Cuban dessert made from sweet potato and brown sugar from the province of Pinar del Río.

20. *Dulce de coco* is a popular Cuban dessert made from coconuts.

21. The use of "Salamale Malekunsala" in the song refers to the Muslim greeting "Salamalekun" and response "Malekunsala" that is reserved for

saluting the dead upon arrival at a misa or a cajón drum ceremony (see Warden 2007, 62–63).

22. Indicating a call and response performance.

23. *Ta José* refers to a common spirit whose popularity exploded in the 1950s through devotion by a Havana-based medium, Leocadia Pérez Herrero, leading to what was called the José Movement (Warden 2007, 28; Morales 2001).

24. We can connect this expression of Black futures with how Black Power movements and Afrocubanismo intersected in Cuba to create a shared idea of racial consciousness between the US and Cuba (see Abreu 2019; Brock and Casteñada Fuertes 1998).

25. For more on divination and sight as expressed in songs for Congo spirits, see Cabrera (1979, 159).

26. Wirtz discusses the relevance of visual acuity in terms of altars and divination in relation to a cosmogenic relationality between espiritistas and the spirits they keep (2021).

27. In a related observation, J. Lorand Matory suggests that Congo spirits represent "the power, the competence, and the efficacy of the slave, which regularly exceed those of the master" in Afro-Atlantic religions (2022, 421).

28. The trope of cooking is important to the study of Afro-Cuban religions regarding authenticity, historicity, and innovation (see Palmié 2013, 2014, 2023).

29. "Learning to Eat the Dead: USA" by Maria Abegunde, *Tupelo Quarterly*, accessed September 13, 2024, https://www.tupeloquarterly.com/editors-selections/learning-to-eat-the-dead-usa-by-maria-abegunde/.

30. Poem used by permission, courtesy of Maria Hamilton Abegunde.

31. The poem's setting resembles that of Jordan Peele's film *Get Out*, where the danger to Black bodies in white domestic spaces is made palpable (2017).

32. This is related to how Elizabeth Pérez explores the importance of "gut knowledge" and food preparation in her work on Africana sacred foodways (2023).

33. In a patakín, or sacred narrative told by Lukumí practitioners, Ochún saves humanity by turning into a vulture and flying to Oludumare's heavenly kingdom (see Murphy 2001).

34. David H. Brown documents how the Ifa divination verse of Baba Eyiogbe is associated with the refrain "here, the vulture descends upon corpses" (2022, 175).

35. I must note the important presence of Asian Caribbean ritual and aesthetic histories and practices in the racial and ethnic continuums found in Afro-Atlantic religions. Please see Martin Tsang on "yellow blindness" in the study of Afro-Cuban religions (2023).

36. Erving Goffman illustrates how audiences are coparticipants in performances (1959, 8). This coparticipation extends to readership and reception of texts (Otero 2007; Bakhtin 1981).

Bibliography

Abegunde, Maria Hamilton. 2018. "Learning to Eat the Dead: USA." *Tupelo Quarterly*, November 14, 2018, Editors' Selections.

———. 2020. "Keeper of My Mothers' Dreams." *Fire!!!* 6 (2): 6–35.

Abreu, Alberto. 2019. "Cuba: Una encrucijada entra las viejas y las nuevas epistemologías raciales." *Cuban Studies* 48:56–70.

Allen, James, ed. (1999) 2021. *Without Sanctuary: Lynching Photography in America*. Foreword by John Lewis. Santa Fe, NM: Twin Palms.

Armstrong, Robert Plant. 1981. *Wellspring: On the Myth and Source of Culture*. Berkeley: University of California Press.

Ayorinde, Christina. 2004. *Afro-Cuban Religiosity, Revolution and National Identity*. Tampa: University Press of Florida.

Bailey, Amy Kate, and Karen A. Snedker. 2011. "Practicing What They Preach? Lynching and Religion in the American South, 1890–1929." *National Library of Medicine, AJS* 117 (3). https://www.journals.uchicago.edu/doi/10.1086/661985.

Bakhtin, M. M. 1981. *The Dialogic Imagination: Four Essays*. Edited and translated by Michael Holquist and Carl Emerson. Austin: University of Texas Press.

Belew, Kathleen. 2019. *Bring the War Home: The White Power Movement and Paramilitary America*. Cambridge, MA: Harvard University Press.

Beliso-De Jesús, Aisha M. 2015. *Electric Santería: Racial and Sexual Assemblages of Transnational Religion*. New York: Columbia University Press.

Bodenheimer, Rebecca M. 2015. *Geographies of Cubanidad: Place, Race, and Musical Performance in Contemporary Cuba*. Jackson: University Press of Mississippi.

Briggs, Charles L., and Clara Mantini-Briggs. 2016. *Tell Me Why My Children Died: Rabies, Indigenous Knowledge, and Communicative Justice*. Durham, NC: Duke University Press.

Brock, Lisa, and Digna Casteñada Fuertes, eds. 1998. *Between Race and Empire: African-Americans and Cubans before the Cuban Revolution*. Philadelphia, PA: Temple University Press.

Brown, David H. 1996. "Towards an Ethnoaesthetics of Santería Ritual Arts: The Practice of Altar Making and Gift Exchange." In *Santería Aesthetics in Contemporary Latin American Art*, edited by Arturo Lindsay, 77–146. Washington, DC: Smithsonian Institution Press.

———. 2003. *Santería Enthroned: Art, Ritual, and Innovation in Afro-Cuban Religion*. Chicago: University of Chicago Press.

———. 2022. *Patakín: Orisha Stories from the Odu of Ifá*. Ocean, NJ: AshéExpress.

Brown, Jayna. 2021. *Black Utopias: Speculative Life and the Music of Other Worlds*. Durham, NC: Duke University Press.

Cabrera, Lydia. 1979. *Reglas de Congo*. Miami, FL: Colección de Chichereku en El Exilio.

Carpentier, Alejo. 1988. *La Música en Cuba*. La Habana, Cuba: Letras Cubanas.
Castro Ramírez, Luis Carlos. 2010. *Narrativas sobre el cuerpo en el trance y la posesión: una mirada desde la santería cubana y el espiritismo en Bogotá*. Bogotá, Colombia: Universidad de los Andes, Ediciones Uniandes.
Cone, James H. 2013. *The Cross and the Lynching Tree*. Ossining, NY: Orbis.
Espírito Santo, Diana. 2015. *Developing the Dead: Mediumship and Selfhood in Cuban Espiritismo*. Gainesville: University Press of Florida.
———. 2018. "Assemblage Making, Materiality, and Self in Cuban Palo Monte." *Social Analysis* 62 (3): 67–87.
Fanon, Frantz. 2008. *Black Skin, White Masks*. Translated by Richard Philcox. New York: Grove.
Fernández, Alexander. 2017. "Odú in Motion: Embodiment, Autoethnography, and the [Un]Texting of a Living Religious Practice." *Chiricú: Latina/o Literatures, Arts, and Cultures* 2 (1): 101–17.
Flores-Peña, Ysamur. 2001. "Overflowing with Beauty: The Ochún Altar in Lucumí Aesthetic Tradition." In *`Oṣun Across the Waters: A Yoruba Goddess in Africa and the Americas*, edited by Joseph Murphy and Mei Mei Sandford, 113–27. Bloomington: Indiana University Press.
———. 2004. "'Candles, Flowers, and Perfume': Puerto Rican Spiritism on the Move." In *Botánica Los Angeles: Latino Popular Religious Arts in the City of Angels*, edited by Patrick Arthur Polk, 88–97. Los Angeles, CA: UCLA Fowler Museum.
Goffman, Erving. 1959. *The Presentation of Self in Everyday Life*. New York: Bantam Doubleday.
Heywood, Linda M., and John K. Thornton. 2007. *Central Africans, Atlantic Creoles, and the Foundation of the Americas, 1585–1660*. Cambridge, UK: Cambridge University Press.
Hucks, Tracey. 2022. *Obeah, Orisa, and Religious Identity in Trinidad: The White Colonial Imagination, Vol. I*. Durham, NC: Duke University Press.
ife, fahima. 2021. *Maroon Choreography*. Durham, NC: Duke University Press.
Keeling, Kara. 2019. *Queer Times, Black Futures*. New York: New York University Press.
Landers, Jane G. 2011. *Atlantic Creoles in the Age of Revolutions*. Cambridge, MA: Harvard University Press.
Lara, Ana-Maurine. 2017a. "I Wanted to Be More of a Person: Conjuring [Afro] [Latinx] [Queer] Futures." *Bilingual Review/La Revista Belingüe* 33 (4): 1–14.
———. 2017b. *Kohnjehr Woman*. Boston: RedBone.
Los Nani. 1997. "Congo de Guinea." In *Espiritistas ¡A Cantar!* New York: Legacy Recordings.
Marschall, Sabine. 2019. "'Memory Objects': Material Objects and Memories of Home in the Context of Intra-African Mobility." *Journal of Material Culture* 24 (3): 253–69.

Mason, Michael Atwood. 2002. *Living Santería: Rituals and Experiences in Afro-Cuban Religion*. Washington, DC: Smithsonian Institution.

Mathews, Donald G. 2008. "The Southern Rite of Human Sacrifice: Lynching in the American South." *Mississippi Quarterly* 61 (1/2): 27–70.

Matory, J. Lorand. 2018. *The Fetish Revisited: Marx, Freud, and the Gods Black People Make*. Durham, NC: Duke University Press.

———. 2022. "Slavery in the Heart of Freedom: Race, Religion, and Politics through the Lens of BDSM." Unpublished manuscript.

Meadows, Ruthie. 2021. "*Tradicionalismo africano* in Cuba: Women, Consecrated *Bata* and the Polemics of 'Re-Yorubization' in Cuban Ritual Music." *Ethnomusicology* 65 (1): 86–111.

Megenney, William W. n.d. "Bantu Survival in the Cuban Lengua de Mayombe." *Islas*, 51–63. https://rbb85.wordpress.com/wp-content/uploads/2011/09/bantu-survival-in-the-cuban-lengua-de-mayombe.pdf. Last accessed September 13, 2024.

Miller, Ivor. 2009. *Voice of the Leopard: African Secret Societies in Cuba*. Jackson: University Press of Mississippi.

Moore, Robin. 2004. "Revolution and Religion: Yoruba Sacred Music in Socialist Cuba." In *The Yoruba Diaspora in the Atlantic World*, edited by Toyin Falola and Matt D. Childs, 260–90. Bloomington: Indiana University Press.

———. 2025. *Violín: Mediating Musical Style and Devotional Practice in 21st-Century Cuba*. Cambridge, UK: Cambridge University Press.

Morales, María Isabel. 2001. "The José Movement: A Phenomenon in Cuban Spiritualism." Master's thesis, Florida International University.

Moten, Fred. 2003. *In the Break: The Aesthetics of the Black Radical Tradition*. Minneapolis: University of Minnesota Press.

Muñoz, José. 2020. *The Sense of Brown*. Durham, NC: Duke University Press.

Murphy, Joseph M. 2001. "A River of Many Turns: The Polysemy of Ochún in Afro-Cuban Tradition." In *Ọsun across the Waters: A Yoruba Goddess in Africa and the Americas*, edited by Joseph Murphy and Mei Mei Sandford, 34–45. Bloomington: Indiana University Press.

Musser, Amber J. 2018. *Sexual Excess: Queer Femininity and Brown Jouissance*. New York: New York University Press.

Ochoa, Todd Ramón. 2010. *Society of the Dead: Quita Manaquita and Palo Praise in Cuba*. Berkeley: University of California Press.

———. 2020. *A Party for Lazarus: Six Generations of Ancestral Devotion in a Cuban Town*. Berkeley: University of California Press.

Ortiz, Fernando. (1950) 2001. *La africanía de la música folklórica cubana*. La Habana, Cuba: Letras Cubanas.

Otero, Solimar. 2007. "Spirit Possession, Havana, and the Night: Listening and Ritual in Cuban Fiction." *Western Folklore* 66 (1/2): 45–74.

———. 2015. "Entre las aguas / Between the Waters: Interorality in Cuban Vernacular Religious Storytelling." *Journal of American Folklore* 128 (508): 195–221.

———. 2016. "Crossing Spirits, Negotiating Cultures: Transmigration, Transculturation, and Interorality in Cuban Espiritismo." In *The Caribbean Oral Tradition*, edited by Hanetha Veté Congolo, 85–107. New York: Palgrave MacMillan.

———. 2020a. *Archives of Conjure: Stories of the Dead in Afrolatinx Cultures*. New York: Columbia University Press.

———. 2020b. "Stories of Our Lives: Material Culture, Memory, and Narrative on the Bóveda." *Louisiana Folklore Miscellany* 30:39–54.

Otero, Solimar, and Kristina Wirtz. 2023. "Subversive Spirits and Ostentatious Materials: An African Diasporic Necropolitics of Agitation." *American Religion* 5 (1): 11–32.

Palmié, Stephan. 2013. *The Cooking of History: How Not to Study Afro-Cuban Religion*. Chicago: University of Chicago Press.

———. 2014. "Historicist Knowledge and Its Conditions of Impossibility." In *The Social Life of Spirits*, edited by Ruy Blanes and Diana Espírito Santo, 218–40. Chicago: University of Chicago Press.

———. 2023. *Thinking with Ngangas: What Afro-Cuban Ritual Can Tell Us about Science and Vice Versa*. Chicago: University of Chicago Press.

Panagiotopoulos, Anastasios, and Diana Espírito Santo. 2019. "Introduction." In *Articulate Necrographies: Comparative Perspectives on the Voices and Silences of the Dead*, edited by Anastasios Panagiotopoulos and Diana Espírito Santo, 1–14. New York: Berghahn.

Peele, Jordan, dir. 2017. *Get Out*. United States, 114 minutes, English, Color. New York: Universal Pictures.

Pérez, Elizabeth. 2011. "Spiritist Mediumship as Historical Mediation: African-American Pasts, Black Ancestral Presence, and Afro-Cuban Religions." *Journal of Religion in Africa* 41 (4): 330–65.

———. 2016. *Religion in the Kitchen: Cooking, Talking, and the Making of Black Atlantic Traditions*. New York: New York University Press.

———. 2023. *The Gut: A Black Atlantic Alimentary Tract*. Cambridge, UK: Cambridge University Press.

Quashie, Kevin. 2021. *Black Aliveness, or a Poetics of Being*. Durham, NC: Duke University Press.

Román, Reinaldo M. 2007. *Governing Spirits: Religion, Miracles, and Spectacles in Cuba and Puerto Rico, 1898–1956*. Chapel Hill: University of North Carolina Press.

Sinitiere, Phillip Luke. 2018. "'Most Pleasant to the Ear': W. E. B. Du Bois's Itinerant Intellectual Soundscapes." *Sounding Out!* Blog, August 13, 2018. https://soundstudiesblog.com/2018/08/13/most-pleasant-to-the-ear-w-e-b-du-boiss-itinerant-intellectual-soundscapes.

Spillers, Hortense J. 1987. "Mama's Baby, Papa's Maybe: An American Grammar Book." *Diacritics* 17 (2): 64–81.

Strongman, Roberto. 2019. *Queering Black Atlantic Religions: Transcorporeality in Candomblé, Santería, and Vodou*. Durham, NC: Duke University Press.

Taylor, Diana. 2020. ¡Presente! *The Politics of Presence*. Durham, NC: Duke University Press.

Thorne, Cory W. 2020. "'Man Created Homophobia, God Created Transformistas': Saluting the Oríchá in a Cuban Gay Bar." In *Queering the Field: Sounding Out Ethnomusicology*, edited by Gregory Barz and William Cheng, 364–79. New York: Oxford University Press.

Tsang, Martin A. 2021. "Write into Being: The Production of the Self and Circulation of Ritual Knowledge in Afro-Cuban Religious Libretas." *Material Religion* 18 (2): 228–61.

———. 2023. "Ingesting Indenture: Lydia Cabrera, Yellow Blindness, Chinese Bodies, and the Generation of Afro-Chinese Religious Knowledge." *History and Anthropology* 23 (3): 1–17.

Vazquez, Alexandra T. 2013. *Listening in Detail: Performances of Cuban Music*. Durham, NC: Duke University Press.

Viarnés, Carrie. 2007. "Cultural Memory in Afro-Cuban Possession: Problematizing Spiritual Categories, Resurfacing 'Other' Histories." *Western Folklore* 66 (1/2): 127–60.

Warden, Nolan. 2007. *Afro-Cuban Traditional Music and Transculturation: The Emergence of Cajón pa' los Muertos*. Saarbrucken, Germany: VDM Verlag Dr. Muller.

Wehmeyer, Stephen C. 2007. "'Indians at the Door:' Power and Placement on New Orleans Spiritual Church Altars." *Western Folklore* 66 (1/2): 15–44.

Wirtz, Kristina. 2007. *Ritual, Discourse, and Community in Santería; Speaking a Sacred World*. Gainesville: University Press of Florida.

———. 2014. *Performing Afro-Cuba: Image, Voice, Spectacle in the Making of Race and History*. Chicago: University of Chicago Press.

———. 2021. "Scopic Regimentation of Cuban Popular Religious Altars." *Semiotic Review* 9 (April). https://www.semioticreview.com/ojs/index.php/sr/article/view/70.

———. 2022. "The Politics of Presence and Absence in Semiotic Perspective." Paper delivered for the *Society for Linguistic Anthropology* conference, April 8, Boulder, CO.

Young, Harvey. 2010. *Embodying Black Experience: Stillness, Critical Memory, and the Black Body*. Ann Arbor: University of Michigan Press.

Solimar Otero is Professor of Folklore and Gender Studies at Indiana University Bloomington. She is author of *Archives of Conjure: Stories of the Dead in Afrolatinx Cultures*, which won the 2021 Albert J. Raboteau Prize for the Best Book in Africana Religions, and editor (with Mintzi Auanda Martínez-Rivera) of *Theorizing Folklore from the Margins: Critical and Ethical Approaches* (IUP, 2021). Her research centers on gender, sexuality, Afro-Caribbean spirituality, and Yoruba traditional religion in folklore, performance, literature, and ethnography.

7

Memeing Together
Performance, Competence, and Collective Creativity in Digital Folklore

SVERKER HYLTÉN-CAVALLIUS

Introduction

Over the last two decades or so, internet memes—or, more and more often, just *memes*—have become a staple of online interaction.[1] The concept of memes was originally invented to describe a cultural counterpart to biological genes, traceable as a multitude of meaning-carrying cultural building blocks, but in its everyday use it has come to signify shared and altered digital content, usually in the form of combinations of texts and images or film snippets.[2] Scholars from a range of disciplines have approached memes as, for example, political discourse and protest (Denisova 2019; Shifman 2014), as play (Seiffert-Brockmann, Diehl, and Dobusch 2018), and as participatory conversations (Milner 2016). The production, use, and sharing of memes are also prime examples of a participatory culture in which users as prosumers take part in both production and consumption of content (Jenkins 1992, 2006). At a more general level, meme studies tend to look at the almost innumerable variations that indeed are important to understand memes, which is not surprising, since memes are fundamentally variations of variations of variations. But with the joy of indulging in the abundancy of links in a memetic chain—just as tracing all variants of, for example, a folk song—comes a risk of seeing too much *langue* and too little *parole*.[3] However, here I want to draw attention to memes in their concrete usage, how memeing as a process is constituted by sometimes extensive collaborative performances.

In this article, I will suggest that memes in their concrete usage can fruitfully be understood as a kind of collaborative performance that I will refer to as *joint memeings*.[4] I want to make clear that such joint memeings in no way presuppose a sense of shared project or goal among the performers, but in the cases described here they carry out a common work of chiseling out meanings and associations, joking, and suggesting new memes. Applying the concept of joint memeings, inspired by Katharine Young's (1987) discussion of joint storytelling, to the interplay between memetic images and comments, I suggest that interaction among interlocutors is an integral part of memeing as performance. When I look at memeing in terms of performance, I set out from Schechner's suggestion that we study performance as "not only art but as a means of understanding historical, social and cultural processes" ([1998] 2016, 9). In this sense, performances are as much to be found on the physical stages of concert venues, opera houses, parliaments, or comedy clubs as in the situational and temporary stages of small-scale interaction among friends or family. The performance perspective in folklore studies was developed in the early 1970s in a more general turn from text to context and language in use, from—as Richard Bauman phrases it—folklore as "item" to folklore as "event" (Bauman 2012, 98, quoting Bauman 1972, v), from structural and comparative text analysis to pragmatics and linguistic anthropology, but was also inspired by the same theoretical concerns that spurred the formation of performance studies, such as Goffman's dramaturgical approach to social interaction and Turner's ritual theory (Goffman 1959, 1974; Turner 1969, 1974). The folkloristic take on performance initially came to focus on performances of verbal *art* in a way similar to the focus on staged events in theater studies that performance studies departed from. The emergence of performance studies and the turn to performance in folklore studies were thus at the same time, in a paradoxical way, each other's opposite: one looking for performances in everyday, ritualized, and offstage contexts, the other emphasizing artistic dimensions to communication. Since then, however, folklorists have explored not only artful masters of verbal art (Bauman 1986) but also, for example, "broken narratives" among victims of HIV (Drakos 2005) or the complex movement in and out of different phenomenological realms during oral narrative performances (Young 1987), contributing in different ways to a nuanced understanding of performances as intricate and multivocal collaborations.

Performance 2.0: From Memes to Memeing

Memeing, along with digital folklore in general, requires us to rethink and rephrase some of the fundamental notions of performance based on face-to-face interaction. As Anthony Bak Buccitelli proposes, the specific aspects of "performance 2.0" are, more fruitfully, not seen as deviations from face-to-face performances but as worthy of attention in themselves (Buccitelli 2012).

Buccitelli exemplifies such aspects as temporal extension, permanence (in relation to the ephemeral character of face-to-face performance), audience mixing (as opposed to a clearly demarcated set of interlocutors), and serialization (that all interaction, also simultaneous or overlapping, is arranged in series). These aspects are perhaps best thought of in relative terms: many of the individual memes I have looked at are, for example, permanent only in the sense of remaining accessible but in reality attract little to no interaction after a short peak comprising at most a few weeks after posting. But in light of these aspects, Bauman's definition of spoken verbal performance as the "assumption of responsibility to an audience for a display of communicative competence" becomes difficult to translate to digital performance, since both responsibility and audience are elusive (Bauman 1975, 293). Digital performances have also highlighted the seamless flow of cultural expressions between mass-mediated popular culture and vernacular creativity, a centuries-old dynamic that has intensified in an age of seemingly unlimited digital accessibility (cf., e.g., Martín-Barbero 1993). Altogether, aspects such as these place the collective performance of memes somewhere on a continuum between what Schechner terms the broad-spectrum approach ([1998] 2016, 8) and the more delimited forms of aesthetically marked communication that have engaged folkloristic studies of performance (Bauman 2012; Klein 2021). In that sense, directing our attention to joint memeings as collaborative performances allows us to also reflect on the theoretical intersection of performance studies and folkloristics.

I will first provide a brief introduction to some of the concepts I use to describe the performance. I will refer to the presentation and caption of a meme (in this article, images) in a context (in this article, the subreddit) as a *performance opening* (cf. Schegloff and Sacks 1973; Young 1987, 31f). From another perspective, the meme itself could be seen as the primary text, but here we will look at memeing as process—that is, the performance of memes. I will refer to the user posting the meme as *primary meme performer* and the other contributors (e.g., in comments, evaluations, and repostings) as *secondary meme performers*. This is not to say that the primary meme performer is most important in the entire performance, just that their contribution is necessary for all that is to come. With this perspective, performance openings function as initiators of a collaborative performance. As previously stated, joint memeing alludes to Katharine Young's notion of joint storytelling. Young refers to "the contribution by different persons of the narrative clauses which carry forward the plot. In this instance, hearer becomes teller" (1987, 176). Joint memeing—at least in the examples discussed here—does not involve supplying narrative clauses in a common plot but contributing to the performance. Finally, the concept of meme requires a comment. It is commonly used on at least three levels, of which I mainly will be applying two: in Dawkins's sense, referring to meaning-carrying building blocks of culture that evolve and mutate over time in a way similar to genes, in the sense of a variant (a meme / Internet meme) of a genre of digital folklore (memes), and in the sense of individual examples of that meme (Dawkins 1976; McNeill 2017).

It is by no means self-evident where the performance of a given meme starts or ends. One could argue that some of the image macros featuring Ludwig van Beethoven that I have come across originate in 1819, when Joseph Karl Stieler painted a portrait of his friend the composer, or with the rise of image macros in the 2000s. And is the reposting and further sharing of a meme in another group or on another platform a continuation of the same performance or a new one? To analyze memes in terms of performances is to circumscribe an instance in a performance that might have begun long before and might still be going on somewhere else. Not least in relation to the memes discussed in this article, it is also relevant to ask to what extent memes carry connotations from one performance context to another. Clearly memes, in common with other expressive forms, carry *some* significance between contexts. However, as a well-known example, when Pepe the Frog went from being a hijacked alt-right mascot to becoming a symbol of the progressive forces for democracy in Hong Kong, Pepe *also* became something else and in this new context had no right-wing connotations (Victor 2019). "It just looks funny and captures the hearts of so many youngsters," as one protester put it (Victor 2019). As I will try to demonstrate in this article, meme formats can travel far and wide, and as much as we might recognize their origins, it is also crucial to understand them in their concrete instance of usage.

Performances of classical music memes require a number of competences—not only the *performative* competences of genre (e.g., composition of images, texts, and audio), timing, captioning, commenting, and evaluation but also *technical and historical subject* competence (cf. Briggs 1988, 357ff). While some classical music memes use canonized and widely known composers such as Bach, Beethoven, or Mozart as stock characters in image macros that will be intelligible to people with little or no music knowledge at all, others require more specialized knowledge (e.g., of medieval church modes), music literacy, or some experience of playing music instruments. As I will show, this competence also constitutes a border between the community I discuss and other groups of highly specialized memes; the performative competences seem to unite them with many other contexts of meme performance and, on a general level, also with offline performances in other genres.

Into the Classical Music Memescape

Over the last years, I have been researching memes as a way that classical music takes shape in social media. The study is part of a larger interdisciplinary research project on how classical music, with its connotations to high culture, to elevated historical and hierarchical status and power, is represented and negotiated in contemporary popular culture.[5] Early on, I realized that the online groups and constellations I followed were to a large extent dependent on memes, often shared from other accounts, for their daily subsistence. This led me into the birthplaces of these memes—often other Facebook groups and accounts, subreddits, and Instagram accounts more or less centered around classical music meme production and sharing. Within the larger frame of the project as a whole, including studies of uses of classical music in, for example, contemporary action movies (Ethnersson Pontara 2021) and orchestra advertising (Bergman 2021), these classical music memes stood out as a preeminently folk discourse on both canon and everyday experiences, poaching (de Certeau [1984] 2002) mediated popular culture. There is, of course, a lot to be said about classical music memes on a more general level. They are shared among platforms and built on a set of shared competences that set classical music people apart from others. Central to classical music memes is a widely accepted canon of Western, predominantly European, male composers that in some cases are known also to people outside the smaller circles, and much of the humor relies on the effect of placing canonized, historical figures in a current meme or in relation to current popular culture—a comic inversion of value that is already rapidly restored in captions or comments. Memeings of classical music are complex collaborative acts that make both sense and nonsense[6] of canonized composers, workplace environments, and embodied musical experience and indulge in a highly intertextual play with references. Thus, memeings both provide insights into how classical music is understood, represented, and negotiated among participants in these online contexts and allow us to approach questions of online performances in a more general sense.

At the center of this article stands the subreddit r/classicalmemes ("classical music memes"), which, as of today, has around twenty-five thousand subscribers.[7] On Reddit, one of the world's largest sites, with more monthly users than more widely known sites such as Instagram, Twitter, or Amazon, twenty-five thousand subscribers is a relatively small number. However, subreddits function as interest groups, so these can, of course, be a lot more niche than classical music memes. A 2021 article on Reddit statistics gathered externally describes the site's users as around two-thirds male, predominantly white, from around 50 percent US IP addresses, with higher education, and politically slightly to the left (Sattelberg 2021). In the subreddit, which currently hosts three to four posts a day, I will focus on performances of Virgin vs. Chad memes.

r/classicalmemes was created in 2012 as an offshoot of r/classicalmusic as a subreddit entirely devoted to classical music memes. In line with classical music memes in general, posts require at least an interest in classical music but vary greatly in terms of necessary knowledge. Some posts are film snippets with music, such as a footage from a DJ booth in front of a massive audience carefully synchronized to intensely rhythmic music composed by Béla Bartók, where the humorous effect arises from the clash between the classical orchestral piece and the dancing and partying DJ and crowd. A meme requiring more competence is based on two pictures of composer Caroline Shaw. In the first one she seems to be thinking about something, with the text "Looking for details and patterns in movements"; in the second one, she is laughing, along with the text "The detail of the pattern is movement."[8] This meme is aptly posted with the caption "Memes for 8 Voices," referring to her piece "Partita for 8 Voices." These two examples might both give a sense of the stylistic and thematic span of memes shared in the subreddit and tell us something about the devotion to classical music required.

From Lisa Simpson to Chad Liszt

Our first example begins with a Lisa Simpson presentation meme that appeared on Reddit in 2018 and originally contained an image of Lisa Simpson on stage lecturing about bullying.[9] The image in the meme was taken from an episode of the TV show *The Simpsons* that first aired in 2001. The meme has been used in a number of ways in different contexts but usually in order to make a statement about something. The image itself has also been altered over and over, from just changing the text on the screen behind Lisa to swapping Lisa and/or the audience for other characters; however, it always retains enough elements to keep within the same meme format.[10] Often the meme has been used to stir debate by throwing out a potentially controversial statement. The image in this meme is also symbolically interesting in that it stages a lecturing position—that is, it constitutes not only a reference to a character in a scene in a TV series but also a discursive position for the primary meme performer as someone who is explaining how it is. This is also how this first example of memeing starts off.

r/classicalmemes user u/chickenchicken12 posted the Lisa Simpson presentation meme on March 5, 2019, with the caption "just speaking the truth." The text on Lisa's screen said "Liszt is just show-offy Chopin." The combination of a statement within the meme and further underlining it in the caption demonstrates that the user has a good knowledge of how to use this specific meme. This variant of the meme also displays performative competence on behalf of this user. They expose knowledge of group norms and conventions and conform to an agreement that memes that juxtapose pros and cons of different composers or musicians are appropriate in this context. And, not least, they make use of a prevalent current meme format addressing in-group topics. They also demonstrate some of the historical or technical competence valued within the group. For example, comparing the Romantic composer Liszt to Chopin (as opposed to, say, Khachaturian or Riley) acknowledges historical genre commonalities and, not least, a widely held canon of classical music.

The memetic image starts off a conversation in the comments, just as was likely intended. The first comment demonstrates awareness of this: "Let's see how this will turn out." This kind of opening comment is abundant in social media when it comes to any kind of controversial posts with potential to stir debate, and they tend to come early since they have played out their role as soon as a discussion starts; however, they can also appear in connection to comments further down in threads that can ignite discussion or conflict. The exact form they take varies, from allusions to other performance situations (preparing popcorn or movie theater references) to the more neutral kind in this case. Essentially, they function as both audience evaluations of the quality of the post and to "prepare the floor" for a continued performance. As is often the case in this subreddit, many comments form part of a discussion on aesthetics and canon.[11] The performance opening here opens up for demonstrations of musical and historical knowledge.

The performance takes a new turn when u/werberd comes in: "Lizst was way more important than Chopin lol, somebody should get on a virgin Chopin vs. chad Lizst meme." At first this sets off an exchange on the pros and cons of the two composers, measuring the "importance" and quality of their orchestral and piano works against each other. But then comes an actual try at the suggested virgin vs. Chad meme. It reads as a textual meme, using the opposition of virgin and Chad qualities typical of the meme but without the pictures associated with the meme format.

Originating on 4chan board /r9k/ in 2017, the virgin vs. Chad meme peaked on this subreddit in 2018 and 2019, usually juxtaposing different composers from the canon of classical music.[12] The meme had originally begun as a depiction of "the virgin walk" in contrast to the stride of the physically, economically, and sexually superior Chads (eventually with the added surname Thundercock). The meme carried more than a streak of feelings of both failure and inferiority mixed with both admiration and contempt for Chads and

Figure 7.1 Meme: Virgin Chopin vs. Chad Liszt

especially the women allegedly attracted to them (cf. Ging 2019). But the meme soon found its way into quite different contexts. A key to the success of a meme is its plasticity, its capacity to convey strikingly different messages in different contexts. This means that a meme originating in what can be described as an incel environment could transform into portraying anything from the generational differences of Zoomer vs. Boomer to Chad trans man vs. virgin cis man, or even meta-memes comparing "virgin" brrr-memes to "Chad" virgin-Chad memes. There is also a subreddit entirely devoted to virgin vs. Chad memes (with a population of almost 175,000 "chads"). In short, the virgin vs. Chad meme, in common with other popular meme formats, appears across a wide range of online contexts, ideologically ranging from manosphere misogyny to queer and trans awareness, from fantasy nerds to fans of classical music. In its abstract, textual form, the meme comes forth as a humorous account of the pros and cons of the two composers:

> CHOPIN:
>
>> Hated public performance
>> Always sick
>> Died at thirty-nine
>> All his students died
>> Shit orchestrator
>> Way too many pieces with the annoying ABA form
>> Rarely wrote anything larger than an octave
>> Big nose
>
> LISZT:
>
>> Incredible confidence
>> Brilliant showman
>> Literally the first rock star

Lived to seventy-four
Good orchestrator
Many successful students
Made great strides toward Debussy
Tenths everywhere!
Sexy AF

This combination of comparisons of the composers' musical qualities and relative historical importance, as well as their character traits, appearances, and physical health are typical of the classical music memescape. As I have discussed elsewhere, many memes take down elevated composers from a well-established canon of primarily male, European composers and make fun of them, only to rapidly restore their status through references to their importance in relation to the canon and their key works (Hyltén-Cavallius 2021b). If we look at the layout of these pros and cons, they also follow the style of other virgin vs. Chad memes. Chad Liszt is full of confidence, sexy, physically fit (lives to seventy-four!), and in every way a great composer whereas the virgin Chopin dies at thirty-seven and hates public performance. Given the importance of canon and historical impact in memeings in this subreddit, students and importance in relation to subsequent generations of composers are mentioned, as are characteristics of the musical styles of the two composers. On the one hand, this sometimes drastic way of combining musical and historical aspects and sex appeal or bodily features is common and likely a key aspect of what makes classical music memes funny within the subreddit. On the other hand, it combines notions of masculine sexual successfulness with the idea of the male genius central to the canon of Western music. This combination evokes a rather dark image of a world of competition, from musical works to sexual attractiveness, and a dangerous intertwining of professional hierarchies and sexuality (Citron 1993, Pettersson 2004, Scharff 2018).

In her discussion of sexism and racism in online gaming, Nakamura shows how even if the games, especially over the 2010s, came to open up a wider spectrum of characters, gaming is still home to systemic racism and sometimes violent misogyny, something that has been defended by many as central and inevitable to gaming culture (Nakamura 2019). As Phillips and Milner put it, the internet and its problems are at the same time admittedly global and dominated by a US way of looking at and formulating issues (Phillips and Milner 2021, 14). The use of meme formats originating in highly misogynist environments to stage battles between the strengths and weaknesses of male composers, which also points to their heterosexual successfulness in relation to objectified women (both anonymous and recognized composers, as we shall see shortly), could be interpreted as a result of the meme format carrying with it pollution from its specific origins (cf. Phillips and Milner 2021). However, as much of contemporary scholarly debate on classical music reveals and also criticizes, centuries-old gender and race-biased histories and institutions combine with strict internal hierarchies and classical music's position as high culture superior to other genres to create a world that is hostile to not only women but also people of color, members of the LGBT community, and underprivileged groups (Bull and Scharff 2021; Ross 2020; Scharff 2018). With this in mind, the meme format might rather be seen as instrumental in sustaining a historically persistent view of classical music as consisting of male, predominantly white, European geniuses sometimes surrounded by female muses.

Joint memeing is a collaborative performance: an initial meme is collectively explored in short comments, followed by the suggestion of a new meme for the same two composers, which is then performed in a textual form and in turn evaluated and further commented on. Reddit has a function for anonymously "upvoting" or "downvoting" posts and comments, similar to the reaction emoji of other social media. These constitute a rudimentary form of evaluation that is also tied to a kind of moral system used by Reddit called karma—the sum of a user's upvotes and downvotes, intended to reflect on users' contributions to the community. Along with comments, these could further add momentum to an ongoing meme performance, even if it is hard to know how many upvotes or downvotes came between different comments. For example, as of the moment I write this—three years after the initial posting—the suggestion to make a meme has twenty-three votes, which, if they'd come in fast, could have spurred the user behind the textual meme (which in turn got forty-eight votes).

Memeing is then carried on with both serious and more humorous evaluations now turning to the details of the textual memes. "omf it's not Chopin's fault he got TB imao" earned the following comment: "He wouldn't have gotten it if he were a CHAD." A recurring trait in such short comments that both elaborate on and hold up individual segments of the textual meme is the movement between serious (commenting on the content of the meme as if it were a serious statement) and more humorous levels, frequently (but not in this case) leading to reminders from users that it is *just a meme*. Other comments turn rather to bodily experiences of performing music by the composers such as this comment on the body needed for music: "grows 4 feet long fingers so that I can play la Campanella" (u/Agobmir). Again, such comic comments on the body in relation to the demands of notated music have been the source of other memes and can be understood as works of both contextualizing and invoking a certain memetic intertext.

What is really at stake in this joint memeing? Is it a performance of classical music canon, a playful conversation on aesthetic differences and music history? Or are canonized composers used as characters in a preset narrative, kind of like superheroes combatting each other with their different superpowers? Joint memeing is a collaborative work of chiseling out possible lines along which one can elaborate different aspects of a meme. It is a work of associating, comparing, contextualizing (e.g., through relating to other memes) and not least prolonging and extending a meme into a collaborative creative and interpretive effort. Here, joint memeing constitutes what Jenkins, following de Certeau, terms textual poaching—acts through which readers of popular culture "fragment texts and reassemble the broken shards according to their own blueprints," creating their own meanings outside of official interpretive practice (Jenkins 1992, 26). In that sense, it can be about all of these: a sometimes jocular, sometimes serious discourse on classical music and aesthetics, a subtle (and not so subtle) way of celebrating male geniuses and their sexual success, and a use of historical figures as interchangeable characters in a clash of titans.

Memes of Competition

This textual version of the virgin-Chad meme began with the request that "somebody should get on a virgin Chopin vs. Chad Lizst meme." The meme has appeared on r/classicalmemes now and then, in the form of battles between composers (Shostakovich vs. Mahler, Brahms vs. Wagner, Salieri vs. Mozart), between different kinds of listeners (the Virgin Mahler Fanboy vs. the Chad Mahlerite), between characters in operas and between kinds of music.

Battles between composers are, of course, not a new phenomenon in a classical music context. Apart from animosity and actual feuds or even physical fighting between contemporaries, concert programs have been composed from this angle, popular representations of classical music have built on it (such as Peter Shaffer's 1979 play *Amadeus* and Milos Forman's film adaptation from 1984), and it has also been a recurring trope in classical music historiography and music criticism. It is not new to the subreddit either; in fact, historic conflicts have appeared now and again in the subreddit's history. Rather, the suggestion that somebody should get on a certain meme comes forth as a way to seize an opportunity to mold a well-established way of conceptualizing the classical canon in an up-to-date meme format.

Reverse Memeing: A Case of Retelling the Canon

Another meme with the purely descriptive caption "the virgin Brahms vs the chad Wagner" was posted by a now deleted redditor on April 10, 2018, and again focuses musical importance, sexual success, and physical appearance. The two, portrayed by the images typical of the meme but with faces

Figure 7.2 Meme: The Virgin Brahms vs. the Chad Wagner

looking like the two composers, are juxtaposed in the following way (clockwise from top):

the virgin Brahms	the Chad Wagner
takes 14 years to write first symphony	writes the music of the future
basically kills Hans Rott	grows the beard of the future
bad with ladies	takes 2 years to write Tristan
falls for friend's wife; never makes a move	enjoys royal patronage
Beethoven wannabe	sires many children
plays piano for hookers	encourages new talent
overweight	bangs friend's wife; he knows but doesn't intervene
doesn't have kids	political and social activist
writes conservative music	

The traits in comparison are not arranged symmetrically, even if some are clearly specific comparisons (the children, sexual success, work tempo, and innovativeness). After a few initial comments about Robert Schumann and Wagner's neckbeard (neckbeard is contemporary slang for *nerd*), a user says "lol @ 'political and social activist,'" likely referring to Wagner's outspoken antisemitism, and this is soon commented on by u/LNhart: "tbf proto Nazism is chad af." About an hour later, another user returns to this: "Wagner was a proto-nazi shithead, this meme should be reversed." Four hours later, u/LNhart adds a reverse textual meme:

> VIRGIN WAGNER:
>
> > actual neckbeard
> > hated Jews for subverting culture but heavily inspired Jewish composers like Mahler and Schoenberg to completely transform the Western musical canon

settled for the Hans von Bulow's ex
tips beret

CHAD BRAHMS:

facial hair full of spirit and vigor
Academic Festival Overture basically a drinking song
legendary status cemented as one of the Three Bs, knocking Berlioz off
Able to seduce MILFs the world over using his Lullaby[13]

One can note how the neckbeard, introduced in the original meme as—probably with tongue in cheek—something innovative and ahead of its time, now returns as a symbol of failure. The reverse meme also addresses Wagner's antisemitic views and points to his importance for two likewise canonized twentieth-century Jewish composers and their impact on musical canon. Irony and ambivalence are central to many exchanges going on in this subreddit, and the comments on Wagner's political and racist ideas in the original meme are not necessarily to be taken literally. The comment about Wagner's proto Nazism being "Chad as fuck" can both be a sarcastic way of saying the composer was ahead of his time and a way of pointing to Chad's ambivalent character: Chad—both idolized and despised—has it all. Just as in the Chopin vs. Liszt meme, canon plays a central part—every name, every story (just think of the implicit stories behind the comments on their sexual success), every comparison presupposes a universally acknowledged canon. In the performance of classical music memes, canons—what Marcia Citron defines as "specified bodies of work in a given field [that] exert tremendous power" (Citron 1993, 15)—come forth rather as sets of both ridiculed and elevated fictional characters that can be arranged in competitions or battles of the kind that constitute both these examples. Comparison stays within the limits of canon, like when Berlioz gets kicked out of the "three B's" by Brahms. The combination of musical aspects, looks, and the composers' sexual success creates humor and at the same time reinforces canon in what seems to be a predominantly homosocial interaction. In line with the origins of the virgin vs. Chad meme, women appear only as ways to stage masculine success—Cosima Wagner is referred to as a "friend's wife," and the reverse meme refers to Clara Schumann, a highly respected composer in her own right, as "Hans von Bulow's ex"; other references are made to "hookers," "ladies," and, in the reverse meme, "MILFs." Again, the use of the virgin vs. Chad meme comes forth as a contemporary way to formulate an androcentric classical canon, one that refers to women only in their capacity to stage male success and sexuality.

The reverse meme reads as a comment to both the original meme and, again, the comment about the need for a reverse meme. One user suggests the meme; another carries it out. Just as in the previous example, users collaborate in performing the meme. It seems that here it is the ironic comment about "political and social activist" that sets off the reverse meme, and it is also the comment with most upvotes (forty-three) while the actual suggestion to make the meme gets only ten. Interestingly, the suggestion gets a comment—"true"— that is in effect an evaluation, followed by the reverse meme, which, apart from upvotes, gets two separate evaluations ("much better" and "big if true"). Parallel to this, another user comments on the meme: "That's the high quality meme I'm here for." After a final individual comment outside the reverse meme thread—"ripperoni Hans Rott #neverforget"[14]—the memeing ends.

Performing Memes: Contest and Collaboration

Competition is a central component in memeing. Israeli communication scholar Limor Shifman includes competition in her very definition of memes (Shifman 2014, 18–23) while others have noted that "like online video games, people engage in the act of altering and sharing memes via social media, simply because they emerge in a playful process of collaborative interaction and play" (Seiffert-Brockmann, Diehl, and Dobusch 2018, 2865). The act of participating in the meme performances discussed here, then, constitutes usually playful contests that are both competitive and collaborative. From the large-scale competition that propels the spread of a meme across different social media platforms and groups to the minute competition in isolated memeings such as the ones discussed here, meme performances seem to take the form of contests. But the memes discussed here are also centrally *about* contests: which composer wins in terms of attractiveness, musical legacy, and sexual success? The joint memeings sometimes come forth as arguments or quarrels where the composition and posting of a meme function as artful and jocular ways of initiating a collaborative performance that is simultaneously play, contest, debate, and joke.

In her discussion on joint storytelling, Katharine Young asks whether joint storytelling is to be understood as collaborative narration and concludes that it might as well be competitive (1987, 182). The same can be said of joint memeings. The virgin vs. Chad memes already in their composition stage competition, both between the two characters and between the performers. However, this competition also propels the performance onward in a collaborative fashion. Joint memeings such as the ones described display a variety of ways of engaging with and continuing a performance. I have shown how different kinds of evaluations, from comments that both evaluate memes and prepare the floor for a continued performance to the technical functions of upvotes or downvotes, potentially can function as momentum in the collaborative effort and are built into Reddit's explicit moral and status system of karma. Another form of collaboration is what could vaguely be called spin-offs—comments that take details from a meme or a comment and explore them in different ways. In the Lisa Simpson meme, one comment focuses on the concepts of "important" vs. "better" through examples showing that the two are not the same. In the Brahms vs. Wagner meme, Wagner's "beard of the future" is commented on with "Wagner had a literal fucking neckbeard," referring to "neckbeard" as a current synonym of nerds and nerd culture. The most striking similarity, though, in these two joint memeings is how variations on the original memes are suggested and then carried out in textual form—the first in the form of another meme format, the latter in the form of a reverse meme where the Chad becomes virgin and vice versa.

Returning to the relationship between performance studies and the perspective on performance in folkloristics addressed in the introduction, joint memeing suggests that there are both important continuities and significant differences between face-to-face performances and online performances. While joint memeing clearly constitutes performance in Schechner's broad-spectrum sense—both entertaining and community-strengthening and with a distinct character of play, "showing doing" with a clear awareness among performers of what they are doing (Schechner [2002] 2020, 4ff)—it is perhaps less evidently so from a folkloristic performance perspective, where it is unclear in terms of both responsibility and audience. With inspiration from Buccitelli's formulation of a performance 2.0, I have regarded joint memeing as a collaborative and competitive performance in which the specific members and circumstances of a small subreddit contribute to evolutions of memes in their comments.

Notes

1. I will not delve further into the background and emergence of the internet meme here; please see Milner (2016, 16f) for a brief history of internet memes.

2. Wiggins and Bowers (2015) comment that the vernacular use of the term has been hijacked to denote something quite different from what Dawkins intended: instead of memes surviving through their own adaption and living through people's largely unreflected reproduction of them, the current term denotes cultural material most intentionally shaped and transformed by individuals.

3. This is not meant as a critique, just as a reminder that memes are simultaneously intertextual, pragmatic, and contextual (cf. Blank 2018, 6).

4. Cf. Bock's (2017) discussion of (a more wide-reaching) collective performance.

5. The project, *Classical Music for a Mediatized World: Visual and Audio-Visual Representations of Western Art Music in Contemporary Media and Society*, is funded by the Swedish Research Council and headed by musicologist professor Tobias Pontara at Gothenburg University.

6. Cf. Stewart (1979) on nonsense in folklore.

7. r/classicalmemes became a private community in June 2023 as part of the massive protest against the increasing costs of the Reddit API in relation to third-party applications (Porter 2023). This has complicated updating information about the subreddit in this article.

8. Memes that use combinations of text and faces or heads with different expressions comparing knowledge or states of mind are so abundant that they might be described as a meta-meme format; examples include Kombucha Girl, Blinking White Guy, and Expanding Brain/Galaxy Brain.

9. Know your meme. "Lisa Simpson's presentation." https://knowyourmeme.com/memes/lisa-simpsons-presentation, accessed June 23, 2022.

10. Please note that I say "meme format" to stress the basic formal characteristics of the meme in question. This parallels the emic concept of "meme template," but whereas the latter seems to imply the iterability of the *same* image(s) (and fonts, or film snippets, etc.), for example through the use of meme generators, the former allows for more comprehensive changes.

11. An interesting example of this was a user who commented in r/classicalmemes that this was a place for serious discussion, as compared to classical music subreddits.

12. Know your meme. "Virgin vs. Chad." https://knowyourmeme.com/memes/virgin-vs-chad, accessed June 23, 2022.

13. This refers to the Wiegenlied, one of the world's most popular lullabies, composed by Brahms.

14. This refers to Hans Rott, an Austrian composer whose first symphony Brahms apparently did not approve of. Possibly this comment adds to the list of virgin Brahms' drawbacks.

Bibliography

Bauman, Richard. 1972. "Introduction." In *"And Other Neighborly Names": Social Image and Cultural Process in Texas Folklore*, edited by Richard Bauman and Roger D. Abrahams, v–ix. Austin: University of Texas Press.

———. 1975. "Verbal Art as Performance." *American Anthropologist* 77 (2): 290–311.

———. 1986. *Story, Performance and Event. Contextual Studies of Oral Narrative*. Cambridge, UK: Cambridge University Press.

———. 2012. "Performance." In *A Companion to Folklore*, edited by Regina F. Bendix and Galit Hasan-Rokem, 94–118. Chichester, UK: Wiley-Blackwell.

Bergman, Åsa. 2021. "'Wherever You Are Whenever You Want': Captivating and Encouraging Music Experiences when Symphony Orchestra Performances Are Provided Online." *Open Library of Humanities Special issue Representing Classical Music in the 21st Century* 7 (2). https://doi.org/10.16995/olh.4679.

Bial, Henry. 2014. "Performance Studies 3.0." In *Performance Studies in Motion. International Perspectives and Practices in the Twenty-First Century*, edited by Atay Citron, Sharon Aronsson-Lehavi, and David Zerbib, 30–41. London: Bloomsbury.

Blank, Trevor J. 2018. "Folklore and the Internet: The Challenge of an Ephemeral Landscape." *Humanities* 7 (2): 50. https://doi.org/10.3390/h7020050.

Bock, Sheila. 2017. "Ku Klux Kasserole and Strange Fruit Pies: A Shouting Match at the Border in Cyberspace." *Journal of American Folklore* 130 (516): 142–65.

Briggs, Charles L. 1988. *Competence in Performance: The Creativity of Tradition in Mexicano Verbal Art*. Philadelphia: University of Pennsylvania Press.

Buccitelli, Anthony Bak. 2012. "Performance 2.0: Observations toward a Theory of the Digital Performance of Folklore." In *Folk Culture in the Digital Age: The Emergent Dynamics of Human Interaction*, edited by Trevor J. Blank, 60–84. Logan: Utah State University Press.

Bull, Anna, and Christina Scharff. 2021. "Classical Music as Genre: Hierarchies of Value within Freelance Classical Musicians' Discourses." *European Journal of Cultural Studies* 24 (3): 673–89. http://doi.org/10.1177/13675494211006094.

Citron, Marcia J. 1993. *Gender and the Musical Canon*. Cambridge, UK: Cambridge University Press.

Dawkins, Richard. 1976. *The Selfish Gene*. Oxford, UK: Oxford University Press.

de Certeau, Michel. (1984) 2002. *The Practice of Everyday Life*. Berkeley: University of California Press.

Denisova, Anastasia. 2019. *Internet Memes and Society. Social, Cultural, and Political Contexts*. London: Routledge.

Drakos, Georg. 2005. *Berättelsen i sjukdomens värld: att leva med hiv/aids som anhörig i Sverige och Grekland*. Eslöv: Symposion.

Ethnersson Pontara, Johanna. 2021. "The Phenomenal Side of Operatic Performance: The Implications of Promotion Strategies on Cinematic Representations of the 21st Century." *Open Library of the Humanities Special Collection: Representing Classical Music in the Twenty-First Century* 7 (2): 1–24. https://doi.org/10.16995/olh.4676.

Evans, Timothy H. 2018. "The Bowling Green Massacre." *Journal of American Folklore* 131 (522): 460–70.

Ging, Debbie. 2019. "Alphas, Betas and Incels. Theorizing the Masculinities of the Manosphere." *Men and Masculinities* 22 (4): 638–57.

Goffman, Erving. 1959. *The Presentation of Self in Everyday Life*. New York: Anchor.
———. 1974. *Frame Analysis. An Essay on the Organization of Experience*. Boston: Northeastern University Press.
Hyltén-Cavallius, Sverker. 2021a. "Classical Music Goes Viral: Memeings and Meanings of Classical Music in the Wake of Coronavirus." *Open Library of Humanities Special Collection Representing Classical Music in the Twenty-First Century* 7 (2): 1–23. https://doi.org/10.16995/olh.4678.
———. 2021b. "Memeing Music: Canon, Play and Competence in Digital Folklore on Classical Music." *Ethnologia Scandinavica: A Journal for Nordic Ethnology* 51:102–18.
Jenkins, Henry. 1992. *Textual Poachers: Television Fans & Participatory Culture*. New York: Routledge.
———. 2006. *Convergence Culture: Where Old and New Media Collide*. New York: New York University Press.
Klein, Barbro. 2021. *I tosaforornas värld. Gustav berättar*. Stockholm: Carlssons.
Martín-Barbero, Jesús. 1993. *Communication, Culture and Hegemony: From the Media to Mediations*. London: Sage.
McNeill, Lynne S. 2017. "Lol and the World Lols with You: Memes as Modern Folklore." *Phi Kappa Phi Forum* 97 (4): 18–21. https://www.phikappaphiforum-digital.org/phikappaphiforum/winter_2017/MobilePagedArticle.action?articleId=1234339#articleId1234339.
Milner, Ryan M. 2016. *The World Made Meme: Public Conversations and Participatory Media*. Cambridge, MA: MIT Press.
Nakamura, Lisa. 2019. "Gender and Race in the Gaming World." In *Society and the Internet: How Networks of Information and Communication Are Changing Our Lives*, edited by Mark Graham, William H. Dutton, and Manuel Castells, 127–45. Oxford, UK: Oxford University Press.
Pettersson, Tobias. 2004. "De bildade männens Beethoven: musikhistorisk kunskap och social formering i Sverige mellan 1850 och 1940." PhD Diss., Göteborg: University of Gothenburg.
Phillips, Whitney, and Ryan M. Milner. 2021. *You Are Here. A Field Guide for Navigating Polarized Speech, Conspiracy Theories, and Our Polluted Media Landscape*. Cambridge, MA: MIT Press.
Porter, Jon. 2023. "Major Reddit Communities Will Go Dark to Protest Threat to Third-Party Apps." *The Verge*, June 5, 2023. https://www.theverge.com/2023/6/5/23749188/reddit-subreddit-private-protest-api-changes-apollo-charges.
Ross, Alex. 2020. "Black Scholars Confront White Supremacy in Classical Music." *The New Yorker*, September 21, 2020. https://www.newyorker.com/magazine/2020/09/21/black-scholars-confront-white-supremacy-in-classical-music.

Sattelberg, William. 2021. "The Demographics of Reddit: Who Uses the Site?" Alphr, April 6, 2021. https://www.alphr.com/demographics-reddit/.

Scharff, Christina. 2018. *Gender, Subjectivity and Cultural Work. The Classical Music Profession*. London: Routledge.

Schechner, Richard. (1988) 2016. "Performance Studies: The Broad-Spectrum Approach." In *The Performance Studies Reader*, edited by Henry Bial and Sara Brady, 7–9. London: Routledge.

———. (2002) 2020. *Performance Studies: An Introduction*. 4th ed. Abingdon, UK: Routledge.

Schegloff, Emanuel and Harvey Sacks. 1973. "Opening up closings." *Semiotica* 8: 289–327.

Seiffert-Brockmann, Jens, Trevor Diehl, and Leonard Dobusch. 2018. "Memes as Games: The Evolution of a Digital Discourse Online." *New Media & Society* 20 (8): 2862–79.

Shifman, Limor. 2014. *Memes in Digital Culture*. Cambridge, MA: MIT Press.

Stewart, Susan. 1979. *Nonsense: Aspects of Intertextuality in Folklore and Literature*. Baltimore, MD: Johns Hopkins University Press.

Turner, Victor. 1969. *The Ritual Process. Structure and Antistructure*. London: Routledge.

———. 1974. *Dramas, Fields and Metaphors. Symbolic Action in Human Society*. Ithaca, NY: Cornell University Press.

Victor, Daniel. 2019. "Hong Kong Protesters Love Pepe the Frog. No, They're Not Alt-Right." *New York Times*, August 19, 2019.

Wiggins, Bradley E., and G. Bret Bowers. 2015. "Memes as Genre: A Structurational Analysis of the Memescape." *New Media & Society* 17 (11): 1886–1906.

Young, Katharine Galloway. 1987. *Taleworlds and Storyrealms. The Phenomenology of Narrative*. Dordrecht, Netherlands: Nijhoff.

Sverker Hyltén-Cavallius is Associate Professor of Ethnology at Stockholm University, a research archivist, and research coordinator at the Swedish Performing Arts Agency. He is editor of *Creative Shifts: Musical Flows in 1960s and 70s Sweden*. His areas of interest include popular music and collective memory, digital folklore and ethnography, oral narrative, and popular representations of natural history.

III
PERFORMANCE, POLYPHONY, AND EMBODIED KNOWLEDGE

8

White Moral Feelings and National Affect in Audience Reactions to Danse du Ventre and Coochee-Coochee in the Late Nineteenth Century

PRIS NASRAT

On August 7, 1896, Detective Anthony Vachris took the stand in a crowded Coney Island courthouse. Vachris, dubbed by the *New York Journal* as "the guardian of Coney Island's morality" (1896), testified as an arresting officer against coochee-coochee dancers charged with indecent conduct. When the judge asked him to describe the dance, Vachris replied, "It is very hard to describe" (*Brooklyn Daily Eagle* 1896c). Given the lack of verbal evidence, Judge Nostrand enquired if Vachris could perform the dance. The detective said he could, so the judge instructed Vachris to "show it to the jury" (*Brooklyn Daily Eagle* 1896c). Pulling up his coattails, Vachris danced. The detective's performance interrupted courtroom norms, and audience reactions ranged from disgust to raucous laughter. The courtroom spectacle of a dancing policeman raises numerous questions. What do the emotional responses to Vachris's performance do in the context of racialized moral policing in the late nineteenth century?

Here, I examine the white moral feelings that surround three performances of the dance that Detective Vachris performed. First danse du ventre, translated as belly dance, at the 1893 World's Columbian Exposition, Chicago. Second, performances staged at Grand Central Palace, New York City, following the exposition's closure. Finally, the dance colloquially known as the coochee-coochee, staged as a popular amusement on Coney Island.

My examination of these performances, from the World's Fair to the moral policing of it at Coney Island, is in service of a more extensive set of questions about white moral feelings as seen in the policing of performance. Rather than consider morality to be a code of ethics or a set of rules about the state, I draw on scholarship on emotion and consider morality felt. Audience feelings are as present in what might be called folk performance as they are in popular performance. Here, I explore what performance does affectively to demonstrate how emotions are vital to understanding white morality.

In thinking about white moral feelings, I consider whiteness as a power relation that is spatialized, positional, and relative. Whiteness can be aligned with and moved closer to. Sara Ahmed offers the idea of affective economies that consider alignment through feelings. In her conception of affective economies, Ahmed explains, "Emotions do things, and they align individuals with communities—or bodily space with social space" (Ahmed 2004, 119). In other words, white moral feelings act to configure racialized and gendered difference. José Esteban Muñoz's conception of whiteness as national affect complements Ahmed's theorization. For Muñoz, "whiteness is a cultural logic that can be understood as an affective code that positions itself as the law" (2020, 10). He argues that whiteness is "an affective gauge that helps us understand some modes of emotional countenance and comportment as good or bad" (Muñoz 2006, 680). The combination of positioning and positive and negative affects that Muñoz points to show how white morality circulates through emotion. I consider these performances of white moral feelings a reaction to perceived excess. As Lauren Berlant writes, "'excess' points to an intensity that, encountered in relation to an action or an atmosphere, is irrational, outside of ratio" (2015, 195). As Jillian Hernandez argues, "aesthetics of excess are the classed/racialized/gendered by-products of transcolonial conquest" (2020, 57). The white gaze is what labels aesthetics of excess, and thus the audience's affective reaction to the dance provides insight into white national affect. Excess, as projected by the white gaze onto racialized dancers, works closely in conversation with another theorization offered by José Esteban Muñoz: disidentification. Muñoz explains that disidentification is a "third mode of dealing with the dominant ideology, one that neither opts to assimilate within such a structure nor strictly opposes it" (1999, 108). Disidentification allows us to think about the affective position of performers themselves as they find themselves under the white gaze. It also complicates our understanding of Adjie Costello, a racialized Mexican performer arrested by Vachris in her performance of Oriental dance.

Danse du Ventre Staged at the World's Columbian Exposition

The World's Columbian Exposition, also known as the World's Fair, holds the first stages where I consider performances of danse du ventre. The exposition ran from May to October 1893, celebrating the four hundredth anniversary of

Columbus's arrival in the United States and white American progress in the arts, sciences, and industry. The lengthy subtitle of Hubert Bancroft's *Book of the Fair* frames the exposition as a "congress of nations, of human achievement in material form" that was designed to show the "progress of mankind in all the departments of civilized life" (Bancroft 1893). The fair served as a transnational stage, with human exhibits including performance designed into the exposition. Paige Raibmon argues that the fair was the "first time human exhibits were part of a North American fair" (2005, 35). In a retrospective published after the exposition closed, folklorist Stewart Culin lamented that it was "a matter of the deepest regret that the many opportunities at the exposition for systematic study in folk-lore as well as other branches of anthropology has passed away without more direct and permanent contributions having been made to science" (1894, 59). As a meeting point of folk and popular performance, the exposition acted as a stage where a range of white moral feelings about danse du ventre could be witnessed.

Danse du ventre was one form of performances at the World's Fair that Culin might say folklorists missed. Songwriter Sol Bloom, who had been placed in charge of the development of the Midway Plaisance, recounts in his autobiography that "when the public learned that the literal translation was 'belly dance,' they delightedly concluded that it must be salacious and immoral," and this desire for the immoral made the dance a "gold mine" (1948, 135). The dance was staged at the Street in Cairo exhibit roughly midway on the Midway Plaisance, as well as at the Turkish and Algerian Villages. Hubert Howe Bancroft's *Book of the Fair* describes the Midway as a "spacious thoroughfare, a mile in length and 600 feet in width" and that it "was crowded with sight-seers" through night and day (1893, 835).[1] From the start of the fair, the Street in Cairo exhibit was incredibly popular. A *Chicago Tribune* front page following the opening of the exhibit declared that it "was as busy as State Street during holiday shopping time" (*Chicago Daily Tribune* 1893). The September 1893 edition of *Cosmopolitan* included a guide by Julian Hawthorne to "Foreign Folk at the Fair." Hawthorne addressed potential visitors, saying, "You have never spent ten cents to better purpose" than to gain admission to the Street in Cairo. By the close of the fair, of all the exhibits on the Midway, "Cairo Street led in popularity, with the admissions exceeding 2,250,000," and the total revenue from concessions on the Midway Plaisance was over $4 million (Bancroft 1893, 881). Charles A. Kennedy made a modern-day comparison between the villages on the Midway Plaisance and Disney World (Kennedy 2014).

The millions of visitors who visited the Midway Plaisance were exposed to white supremacist and settler colonial ideas of cultural progression. Sarah

Gualtieri argues that the fair was "a place of imperialist racialized fantasies run amok" for those cultures who were included (2009, 7). Notably, Black Americans were excluded from exhibiting at the exposition, as highlighted in the pamphlet "The Reason Why the Colored American Is Not in the World's Columbian Exposition," edited by Ida B. Wells (Wells 1893). Many scholars have rightly pointed out that this idea of "progress of mankind" was a racialized ideology that could be seen in the spatial organization of the Midway Plaisance itself. Paige Raibmon points out the doubled meaning of "progress" at the 1893 World's Columbian Exposition as both "evolutionary and industrial" (2005, 35). As for the Midway itself, Robert Rydell argues that it was considered important due to the "vivid illustrations of evolutionary principles provided by ethnological villages" (1984, 64). Further, Robert Allen describes how the midway's cultural villages portrayed a social Darwinist progression from "primitive," then a Street in Cairo halfway along. At the progressive end were German and Irish villages that sat adjacent to the White City exhibit building that housed occidental art and industrial exhibits (Allen 1991). The layout of the Midway Plaisance provided an immersive stage where the audience traveled toward white modernity, which spatially manifested the idea of racialized progress.

The dances at the fair garnered a range of white moral feelings that can be seen through the moral debates about the dance in the press. The *Brooklyn Daily Eagle* article "Those Egyptian Dancers," published on August 5, 1893, shows that antivice politician Anthony Comstock, known for the Comstock Act, and a women's committee made efforts to stop performances of the dance. The article opens by stating that "perhaps the oriental dance on the Midway Plaisance will be stopped, and perhaps not" (*Brooklyn Daily Eagle* 1893b). This "perhaps" or "perhaps not" shows the tension between American audiences' mixed and ambivalent feelings for danse du ventre. Amira Jarmakani describes this ambivalence toward dancers at the fair as a "sort of simultaneous attraction and repulsion" (Jarmakani 2008, 67). Attraction and repulsion are not an oppositional binary but were felt together by white American audiences of the dance, and Jarmakani argues that these mixed feelings reflect broader American anxieties around modernity. Orientalism aligns individuals and communities through feelings in its configuration of difference through white moral feeling. These Orientalist affective alignments are not singular with white feelings such as desire and disgust that produce knowledge about the dance's morality while others have detached feelings through positioning the dance outside of morality by understanding it as traditional.

The contradictory feelings and understanding of the dance between traditional folk dance and popular performance readily fit the analytic of folkloresque, as proposed by Michael Dylan Foster and Jeffrey A. Tolbert (Foster and Tolbert 2015). The moral judgments about the dance and how it is stigmatized are also connected to the idea of a stigmatized vernacular. In their 2016 edited volume, Diane Goldstein and Amy Shuman argue that folklorists are well positioned for "analysis of the performance of stigma, the process of stigmatization, and the political representation of stigmatized populations" (Goldstein and Shuman 2016, 4). My analysis of the moral discourses surrounding these dances reveals how white American morality can be understood through racialized feelings. Racialized affect extends our understanding of folkloresque performances—that is, performances in the space between tradition and popular, through the type of attention to stigma that Goldstein and Shuman point to, thereby expanding on how we understand the workings of morality through vernacularized stigma as an affective process.

Desire and disgust are two of the most evident feelings that circulate through the performances of stigma that surround the morality of danse du ventre at the World's Fair. Despite the racialized fantasies, studying performances of danse du ventre reveals much. In *Imagining Arab Womanhood*, Amira Jarmakani argues there is "much to be discovered in the interplay between dominant and resistant representations of the 'Orient' at the fair" (Jarmakani 2008, 100). Edward Said's framework of Orientalism is a fundamental theoretical starting point for studying the white moral feelings in reaction to the dance. Said describes Orientalism as a "Western style for dominating, restructuring, and having authority over the Orient" (Said 1994, 3). While in *Orientalism* Said focuses on European Orientalism, Amira Jarmakani rightly points to critiques of Orientalism for reification of the Orient/Occident binary that "obscures the heterologic nature of each category" (Jarmakani 2008, 21). Following Jarmakani, I am less interested in the identification of Orientalist framings and more interesting in exploring the question of what the Orientalization of these performances does. I consider what Orientalism does here through feelings that surround the dance to better understand white morality as including a range of affective responses. As Tim Dean points out, scholars engaging with *History of Sexuality: Volume One* have overlooked the pleasure in the formation power-knowledge-pleasure, generally using either power-knowledge or biopolitics (Dean 2012). In doing so, I also recognize Riley Snorton's compelling critique that "Foucault overlooks how race functions as a necessary prefix to the particulates of his compound term ('power-knowledge')" (2017, 39). I extend Foucault's power-knowledge-pleasure formulation to think with power-knowledge-affect in understanding Orientalist white moralizing reactions to the dance as that creates and maintains understandings of national affect.

Rather than the idea that the dance is immoral, a *Brooklyn Daily Eagle* journalist argues that the dance undesirable and disgusting due to its coming from a non-Western tradition. In other words, the dance is seen as an excess, lying outside white American national affect. The article asserts that danse du ventre dancers do not "satisfy the occidental notion of grace or beauty" (*Brooklyn Daily Eagle* 1893b). Specifically, "to the eye of" the journalist, the dancers appear "personally lacking in refinement and soap" (*Brooklyn Daily Eagle* 1893b). One reading of the article might suggest that danse du ventre is a traditional dance and, therefore, moral. However, I argue that he states that both beauty and morality require whiteness. Desire cannot be felt due to tradition. The journalist's mention of soap is meaningful. Anne McClintock argues that nineteenth-century soap advertising offered "an allegory of imperial progress as spectacle" (McClintock 1995, 214). This advertising led to soap becoming understood as having a power that "could convert other cultures to 'civilization'" (223). In coupling refinement and soap together here, I argue the journalist is not passing comment on observed cleanliness but rather reflecting the American Orientalist knowledge of "progress" and "civilization." The commodity racism that McClintock identifies emphasizes how moral feelings and a sense of national affect are reproduced through commercial representation or popular entertainment.

Feelings of disgust at danse du ventre as a Middle Eastern folk dance are held within the racialized progressivism of American Orientalism. The article compares "civilized dancing" to "barbaric dancing" through gesture, the feelings the performance evokes in audiences, and how the dance is participated in, stating that "civilized dancing is done with the legs. Barbarians dance with their bodies and arms. Civilized dancing is pleasing, sometimes, and barbaric dancing is tedious. Civilized people share in the dance. The oriental has his dancing done for him and smokes on a divan as he watches it" (*Brooklyn Daily Eagle* 1893b).

This claim about the undesirability of the dancers as they are "barbaric" not only produces disgust but also produces other affective positions in the form of interest and desire for knowledge. The journalist writes that "there is a theory that old men are not led astray by such exhibitions as theirs [the dancers] because when lewd action is set forth by a person of disagreeable personality, it becomes disgusting" (*Brooklyn Daily Eagle* 1893b). The dance is disgusting as it does not align with national affect and thus falls outside morality. The journalist claims this means that "it becomes a question if it is not a duty that the student owes to ethnology to see the dancing" (*Brooklyn Daily Eagle* 1893b). Disgust produces a Foucauldian pleasure and ethnological knowledge. The journalist argues that those who felt immorality and disgust had attended the performances with "the intention of being offended" (*Brooklyn Daily Eagle* 1893b). Those watching with the expectation of entertainment felt amusement. Feelings of disgust coexist with pleasure, and these feelings are relational and vary with participant and observer.

The journalist concludes, "The result of the contest is awaited dispassionately," however a different desire motivates the article. This is not an erotic desire toward the dancers but a desire in the totalizing Orientalist will to know. Michel Foucault set out the relationship between power-knowledge and pleasure in *History of Sexuality: Volume One*. This pleasure in the truth is one part of what Foucault describes as being "the pleasure of knowing that truth, of discovering and exposing it, the fascination of seeing it and telling it, of captivating and capturing others by it, of confiding it in secret, of luring it out in the open-the specific pleasure of the true discourse on pleasure" (1990, 71). The pleasure of knowing produces an imperative to witness the dance to understand "the orient" and know the dance's morality. Despite the journalist's claim of dispassion in his analysis, the writing pleasures in his knowledge of how to understand the dance as moral or not. American Orientalism, in this case, takes pleasure in knowing the West through widespread knowledge of ethnological tradition as a discourse of racial progress and the binding of morality to modern white subjects. For the journalist, morality is considered only in relation to white subjects, whether American erotic dancers or in a spectator's intent. This contradicts Sol Bloom's recollection that at the fair the "danse du ventre, while sensuous and exciting, was a masterpiece of rhythm and beauty; it was choreographic perfection, and it was so recognized by even the most untutored spectators. Whatever they had hoped to see, they were enchanted by the entertainment placed before them" (1948, 135). The feelings on display in "These Egyptian Dancers" reveal how the popular understanding of danse du ventre as traditional is still grounded within racialized concepts of progress. The white feelings that circulate the debate about the dance's morality are a mix of desire, repulsion, and unexpected emotion. These emotions align spectators against perceived excesses of the performers and the dance, which makes the popular understanding.

Desire and disgust are not the only affective responses to danse du ventre; the article points out that there were "those who go to sleep while it is going on" (*Brooklyn Daily Eagle* 1893b). Tediousness to the point of sleep is a surprising audience reaction to the danse du ventre. While the bored tolerance of the dance could indicate disinterest, Anne Pellegrini reminds us that "tolerance works to affirm existing social hierarchies by establishing an us-them relationship between a dominant center and those on the margins" (2007, 920). Even feelings of bored tolerance or academic curiosity work to reproduce the binarism of American Orientalism that American spectators understood the dance through. In contrast, dancers seen as belonging to American modernity can cause feelings about morality; tradition allows the journalist and others to position the dance outside of morality and modernity, or apart from national affect, through the ideology of racial progress.

The World's Fair was ostensibly about anthropology, although it was treated as entertainment. The fair was very much a United States imperialist project that reinforced conceptions of race, gender, and sexuality. The dancers were positioned within a white supremacist system of racial progression. This positioning generated a range of white moral feelings, clearly present in my reading of the "Those Egyptian Dancers" article. While "in the New York dive the purpose of the dancers is to demoralize," at the fair the danse du ventre was "traditional" and considered beautiful by its own people (if not by the reporter). For audiences, the article points out the contradiction that Comstock attended with "the intention of being offended" versus those who went with the expectation of entertainment. Despite the debate, at the fair the dancers seemed somewhat protected from moral critique by the anthropological and cultural grounding, a protection that became weaker as the performers started to work in New York.

Danse du Ventre Staged in New York City

After the Chicago World's Fair closed in October 1893, elements of the Midway including danse du ventre, quickly appeared in New York City. On November 30, 1893, a "miniature World's Fair" (*New York Times* 1893) opened in New York at Grand Central Palace, then in spring 1894 a more fully replicated exhibition opened at Madison Square Garden (*New York Times* 1894). The ambivalence seen at the World's Fair continued to be present. One article on the Grand Central miniature fair emphasizes the blend of fine art, with "over $250,000" worth of artwork, but notes that the "Midway Plaisance features" stole the show. In contrast, a review of the Madison Square Garden midway exhibition declares that "the representations and scenes from the Occidental world are not the least interesting."

By 1895, popular concessions of variations of the dance had appeared at Coney Island. As it spread, danse du ventre came to have many names—muscle dance, coochee-coochee, hootchie-kootchie. There is some confusion regarding the evolution of the name coochee-coochee, but as Gertrude Scott importantly notes, during the fair's run "the term Hootchie-Kootchie was not then applied to the danse-du-ventre. No writer, in either the daily press or the histories and memorial volumes published shortly after the Fair, called the

Middle Eastern dances by this name" (1991, 211). Along with changing names and venues, the moral debate turned into moral policing accompanied by arrests and trials. This section examines two New York trials of the morality of the dance, the first with danse du ventre performers who had performed at the World's Fair and the second of dancers of the popularized form called the coochee-coochee on Coney Island.

The December 6, 1893, issue of the *Brooklyn Daily Eagle* ran a front-page article titled "The Midway Dancers Fined" (1893a). This article is one of several across a range of newspapers that sensationally report on the arrest and trial of three Algerian dancers.[2] The public's desire to know the dance is immediately evident in the article. The courtroom was "besieged by persons who wanted to get good seats" as rumor had spread that the dancers were to appear in costume and were going to dance. The packed audience at the trial included "many women" who seemed to want to see the dance. Disgust is also readily apparent in the article. Captain Berghold, the arresting officer, called the dance "vile and indecent"; another policeman testified that upon seeing the "wicked" dance, women in the audience "ran from the room with their hands to their eyes" (*Brooklyn Daily Eagle* 1893a).

Performance was used to give evidence. Officer McMahon both gave oral testimony and attempted to imitate danse du ventre. As with Vachris's later courtroom performance, the spectators "burst into laughter" (*Brooklyn Daily Eagle* 1893a) as McMahon tried to show how specific moves of the dance were indecent. One of the arresting officers, Officer McMahon, described how the dancers had "'extorted' their stomachs, moving and distending them" (*Brooklyn Daily Eagle* 1893a). McMahon tried to imitate one move and was parodied by the defense lawyer: "The two men held up their arms, threw back their bodies and glanced archly at each other" (*Brooklyn Daily Eagle* 1893a). The same gestures were performed by the prosecution witness and by the counsel for the dancers in attempts to sway the jury's feelings. Race and gender determined who was allowed to give evidence through the body. When one of the dancers, Zora, was asked to show the court the movements she had been doing before her arrest, when the police had observed her, she "made a movement as if to throw off her tunic," causing the audience to rise in a rush to stop her (*Brooklyn Daily Eagle* 1893a). The courtroom temporarily became a "tableau worthy of reproduction on canvas" (*Brooklyn Daily Eagle* 1893a). The description of the courtroom as a tableau highlights the dramatic staging of the trial.

The use of tradition to argue the dance's morality is amplified by appeals to the quality of past audiences of the dance. The *Brooklyn Daily Eagle* journalist reported that danse du ventre had been performed and well received by society women and international nobility at the World's Fair in Chicago.

The defense lawyer argued that "this dance had the sanction of Uncle Sam at the World's Fair. . . . You wouldn't accuse Uncle Sam of immorality, would [you]?" (*Brooklyn Daily Eagle* 1893a). The article details how George Hastings, a reporter and theater critic at the *Herald*, gave evidence based on his previous viewings of danse du ventre in Paris and London. Hastings testified the dance was one of "poetic motion" and was then questioned in the following exchange.

"Where in London was it performed?" asked Judge Koch.

"In the Gaiety theater," answered Mr. Hastings.

"Is that a reputable playhouse?" continued the judge.

"Oh, most certainly," answered the witness with a smile of pity for the judge's ignorance. "It is patronized by the elite, the Prince of Wales, and the royal family." (*Brooklyn Daily Eagle* 1893a)

The invocations of past virtuous audiences—society women, Uncle Sam, and the Prince of Wales—can be understood as appealing to national affect. Spectators aligned with national affect could gaze upon the excessive Oriental dance and their emotional reactions through the power and knowledge relationship they perceived themselves to hold. In other words, the discourses about the morality of the dance—whether arguing that the dance is cultural art or the moral policing of the performance as disgusting—create feelings that align whiteness and distance excessive racialized affects of the dancers. This is further demonstrated when policing of the performance intensifies as the dance is performed by dancers of other races on Coney Island.

Coochee-Coochee at Coney Island

The move from the more ethnographic and art-focused stages of the World's Fair, Grand Central Palace, and Madison Square Garden to Coney Island marked more than just a location shift. Coney Island makes no pretense at being anything more than an entertainment center. To many in the United States, Coney Island needs no lengthy introduction; it is a beachfront neighborhood in the south of Brooklyn that has entered the American psyche as a site of popular entertainment and amusement parks. In his memoir, Sol Bloom reminisces that when danse du ventre became "imitated in amusement parks over the country," such as Coney Island, "it became debased and vulgarized, it began to acquire the reputation that survives today" (1948, 135).

Having set out the varied feelings regarding discourse about danse du ventre's morality, I return to the Coney Island trial where Detective Vachris danced. Adjie Costello and Dora Denton were two of five dancers arrested by Vachris.[3] As detailed in the *Brooklyn Daily Eagle* article "The Midway in Court," the dancers appeared before Judge Nostrand on Friday, July 10, 1896, following their arrest the night before. The headline's invocation of the Midway Plaisance shows that three years after the World's Fair, the connection between Orientalized dance and the exposition remained. The subsequent hearings and trial of these dancers were widely reported in the press, including the *Brooklyn Eagle*, the *Sun*, the *New York Times*, and the *Herald*, culminating with the hearing where Detective Vachris danced. Not only was the policing of performances at Coney Island at that time a personal moral issue, but it also formed a key strategy of a larger moral reform movement including laws such as the Raines law, which prohibited Sunday sales of alcohol. To understand what Vachris's dance was doing, I consider the circulations of power-knowledge-affect that surrounded the performance through feelings between the dancing policeman, the onlookers, and the arrested women.

Newspaper reports focus primarily on Costello's arrest, adjournments, arraignments, and jury selection, ending with the jury trial, where Vachris danced, between early July and late August 1896. The dancers' repeated appearances in court created a temporal genre of anticipation among the hetero-Orientalist onlookers. The audience anticipated Costello's second court appearance. Before Judge Nostrand arrived, "the courtroom was crowded in anticipation of some spicy development in connection with the recent raids on the 'Coochee-Coochee' dancers at the Island" (*Brooklyn Daily Eagle* 1896a). The anticipation for Costello was not just for the trial as entertainment; the crowds anticipated her performing the coochee-coochee. Her defense lawyer, John Shorter, fueled this anticipation by proposing the idea of Costello performing for the jury. In court, he said, "We want the jury to attend the Streets of Cairo, and we want Detective Vachris to go with them. Adjie will then repeat the dance for which she was arrested, and her trial can then go on." At the trial, when the lawyer repeated his proposal for Adjie to dance for the jury on the Streets of Cairo, they "smiled in anticipation." However, their desires were interrupted by Judge Nostrand, who insisted "the jury cannot leave this court for this purpose" (*The Sun [New York]* 1896). Although Costello might have been able to perform in the courtroom, like Zora, her version of the dance was never seen, causing a never-filled, lingering anticipation.

"The Majesty of the Law Was Buried in Mirth"[4]

While Vachris struggled to describe the coochee-coochee dance, the journalist's description of Vachris's courtroom performance is rich with evocative and sensationalist language. The *Times* article recounts that

> Vachris bounded to his feet. He gazed languidly about the stuffy courtroom and rolled his eyes in wonderful simulation of a bacchante getting inspiration

for a revel. Then, daintily clutching the skirts of his uniform coat, he began the first lazy movements of the dance.

Backward he bent, and forward. Now he stood on one foot, and now a mighty policeman's boot went toward the ceiling. Now he swayed to the right, now to the left, and in a trice he was almost on the floor, wriggling and twisting until he was red in the face, down which all the humidity in the courtroom seemed to be precipitated. (*New York Times* 1896)

The Sun further spotlights the desirability of Vachris, emphasizing how "the muscles under his shirt rippled" and that "a sweet and alluring smile bedecked his countenance" throughout his performance (*The Sun [New York]* 1896). The description of Vachris's dance is multisensory, and time is taken to describe his costuming and movement and the visceral audience experiences. The courtroom stage's cross-cultural encounter was full of gender inversion, performance, and affective audience responses. The article goes on to reveal the audience's reactions.

Judge Nostrand leaned with breathless intent over the rail. The crowd in the courtroom was a half-smothered, laughing unit. The majesty of the law was buried in mirth, and Vachris worked tirelessly on. (*New York Times* 1896)

Court time has been interrupted by both Vachris's performance and the laughter. While Costello was found innocent by the jury, the judge felt differently about the coochee-coochee and, "in spite of the verdict, said it was immoral" (*The Sun [New York]* 1896).

The ten minutes of courtroom laughter in response to Vachris's performance can be understood through the carnivalesque. Historian of Coney Island John E. Kasson argues that commentators frequently used the idea of carnival to understand the appeal of Coney Island in the late nineteenth century, "against the values of thrift, sobriety, industry, and ambition," or as an excessive counter to national affect (Kasson 1978, 150). Like the folkloresque, the carnivalesque is not strictly carnival but a carnival sensibility in the popular realm. Carnival laughter for Bakhtin is a serious matter, and it is "the laughter of all the people," "universal," directed at everyone. He further argues that carnival "laughter is ambivalent: it is gay, triumphant, and at the same time mocking, deriding. It asserts and denies, it buries and revives" (Bakhtin 1984, 11–12). The courtroom laughter was ambivalent. The smothering carnivalesque laughter that Vachris's performance evoked perhaps ultimately led to the jury acquitting Costello after "exactly half a minute" of deliberating (*New York Times* 1896). The jury could perhaps see no immorality in coochee-coochee as danced by a white man.

Through laughter, this suspension of time and law is further mediated through the newspaper reports. The *Times* takes the carnivalesque interruption of court time and speculates a radically different future for Vachris. The article includes a bordered mock billboard with "great letters" that "flame out," which broke the column.

```
+----------------------------------+
| ONLY LIVING MALE COOCHEE-COOCHEE |
| DANCER IN THE WORLD              |
+----------------------------------+
```

Vachris worked for one of Coney Island's "purveyors of pleasure," complete with billboards and barkers, who would draw crowds from far and near (*New York Times* 1896). The *Times* article further speculates that two jurors would be moved to write about the performance with "pens dipped in fire" (*New York Times* 1896). In this imagined future, Vachris transcends reality—the article explains how he would attract "Sunday school Superintendents and providers of parlor entertainments" who "would trample each other in haste to secure the lissome, agile, graceful, wonderful Vachris" (*New York Times* 1896). The *Times* created a carnivalesque tale that granted this fantasy Vachris appeal that was desirable and attractive to pleasure seekers and moral citizens. As a white man, Vachris was allowed to put on the excessive affect of the coochee-coochee for a moment through the carnivalesque.

I argue that while there may be transgressive resistance through the carnivalesque laughter that the dancing detective invokes, it is not liberatory. In his cultural history of burlesque, Robert Allen problematizes Bakhtin's universal carnival and argues that antiauthoritarian and transgressive cultural production can be diffused "into a discourse of resubordination" (Allen 1991, 35). Allen points to Terry Eagleton's argument that carnival needs to be understood "not as a rupturing of social control but as an instrument of social control" (36). The carnivalesque operates within the fields of power-knowledge-affect, not outside it, and the carnivalesque spectacle of the Oriental dance is racialized in excess of white national affect.

While the discourses surrounding coochee-coochee dancers focus on morality and indecency, the Orientalist gaze found in the journalistic accounts of the dance and when describing racialized dancers works toward the production of knowledge about heterosexuality. This is seen in how Costello's arrest is described solely from her court appearance. The journalist wrote, "Last Tuesday, Detective Antonio Vachris stepped into the Streets of Cairo, as the show is called, and saw a dark-eyed, swarthy-faced, black-haired young woman doing a dance. He was shocked, and he arrested her" (*Brooklyn Daily Eagle* 1896a). Reporting on the case across numerous publications illustrates the Orientalist gaze on Costello. The *Sun* article "Couchee Dance in Court" describes Costello as veiled, with "midnight hair" and "sleeves four yards in circumference." The descriptions of Costello during the trial emphasize the desires of the jury. The *New York Times* recounts how the "jury smiled at each other, glanced shyly at the dancer, and unanimously declared that they had no prejudice and would give the fair Adjie as impartial a trial as possible" (*New York Times* 1896). The *Sun* describes how "Adjie cast a languishing glance at the Jury, who mopped their brows and declared fervidly that they had no prejudice on earth against the lady" (*The Sun [New York]* 1896). These desiring gazes can be understood through what Eng-Beng Lim terms hetero-Orientalism and homo-Orientalism (Lim 2013). Lim uses these to examine cross-cultural Asian performance in sites of colonial encounters. Whether coy or sweating profusely, I argue, the jurors held a hetero-Orientalist desire for Costello.

In comparison to Costello, the reporting on Dora Denton shows a different racialized proximity to morality through whiteness. In "Adjie to Dance for the Jury," Denton is heralded as "a girl of quite another caliber" compared to Costello. The reporter goes on to note that Denton, "with her sedate dress, a rather pretty face, and a pair of eyeglasses . . . looked more like a Sunday school teacher than an exponent of the forbidden dance" (*Brooklyn Daily Eagle* 1896a). The language describing Denton appears free from the Orientalizing gaze that had been directed at Costello. As Denton was unmarked and not described using Orientalizing language, I argue we can read her as a white woman through the journalist's eye. Denton's moral superiority is further evident in how she supposedly resembled a Sunday school teacher, a description that echoes that of Vachris and his potential future attraction to "Sunday school Superintendents." Her entire journey through the courts is less commented on, and when she was discharged, the newspapers only briefly mentioned it. As with the debates about performers at the World's Fair, the descriptions of Denton and Vachris show how morality is proximate to white national affect and the Oriental other is seen as excessive.

One complication in understanding how race and morality work together arises from Costello's testimony: she identified as Indigenous Mexican. When on the stand, she exclaimed, "I'm no Turk . . . but I'm a Mexican, a true-blooded Indian." Costello disavowed that she was performing the coochee-coochee but instead performed "a purely Spanish dance" (*Brooklyn Daily Eagle* 1896a). Jayna Brown argues that Black performers of *Salome* "dancing in the guise of other colonized women was a form in which African women could simultaneously celebrate their own sensual bare footedness and claim their bodies as modern" (Brown 2008, 188). While the specificness of Brown's argument to Black women should not be lost, Costello's performance of the coochee-coochee in the guise of an Orientalized woman shows a disidentificatory strategy. Building from Brown, I argue that rather than Orientalized drag, Costello was performing and testifying by using disidentification from her position as an Indigenous Mexican. In *Disidentifications*, Muñoz uses "queer of color" to describe performers and cultural makers whose "different identity components occupy adjacent spaces and are not comfortably situated in any one discourse of minority subjectivity" (Muñoz 1999, 32). Given the racial diversity of the performers, I follow Muñoz's suggestion to "move beyond notions of ethnicity as fixed (something that people are) and instead understand it as performative (what people do), providing a reinvigorated and nuanced understanding of ethnicity" (Muñoz 2020, 12) when examining the folk performance of danse du ventre and coochee-coochee.

This theory of adjacency in queer of color performance that Muñoz identifies is further developed in his later writing. In *The Sense of Brown*, Muñoz offers the idea of brownness and the brown commons, arguing that "we know that some humans are brown in that they feel differently, that things are brown in that they radiate a different kind of affect," and that "brownness is about contact and is nothing like continuousness. Brownness is a being with, being alongside" (Muñoz 2020, 2). As a Mexican, Costello appeared excessive to the national affect, and rather than an analytic of appropriation, or what Katrin Sieg terms ethnic drag, there is an alignment between her brownness and that of Oriental performers that Muñoz and Brown allow us to see.

Costello's testimony shows her placing herself beside other arrested dancers. These dancers include others who are racialized, such as Lou Mattin, whom the article identifies as Black, and who was arrested with Costello in 1896. The morning after Costello was arrested and first put before the judge, the courtroom crowd included "all the other couchee-couchees as well as the other occupants of the Streets of Cairo, the Midway and other such classic resorts at[t]ended to show their sympathy" (*Brooklyn Daily Eagle* 1896b). Evidence of the solidarity of dancers in the face of policing is revealed in Costello's testimony. At a pretrial arraignment, Costello described how she had been arrested the previous year for the same offense and said, "I had to pay $25. More than that, I had to go down into my stockings, where I had $250 saved and help to pay for other girls as well" (*Brooklyn Daily Eagle* 1896a). For comparison, the Street in Cairo performers at the World's Fair were paid $500 for six months' work (Jacobs 2015, 318). Sarah Gualtieri draws on the work of Mae Ngai to argue that Arab performers were not just objects of Orientalist gaze "but active subjects in an entrepreneurial undertaking" (Gualtieri 2009, 36). Costello's financial aid to cover the other performers' fines shows her entrepreneurship, her ability to make money working as a dances[5], and how she considered herself within a performance community. I argue that Costello shows she was acting through mutual aid by covering the fines of other arrested performers. Disidentification and affective alignment away from whiteness allow the complexity of Costello dancing coochee-coochee not as an Egyptian, Algerian, or Turkish woman but as a woman still subjected to the Orientalizing gaze.

From the outset as danse du ventre at the World's Columbian Exposition in Chicago to its popularization as the coochee-coochee dance on Coney Island, feelings circulated around the performance and performers. These feelings worked to uphold a racialized understanding that drew on the language of tradition and folk performance. Through the stage of the Coney Island courtroom, multiple contested discourses around the coochee-coochee performance were revealed. Audience anticipation of coochee-coochee's morality shifted with the perceived race of women performers such as Costello and Denton. Despite the interruptions of morally and racially policing the everyday lives of minoritized performers, we can see solidarity through mutual aid and performers showing up in court together. For performance that sits between traditional and popular, a queer person of color can use excess and national affect to think about Orientalism and white morality.

Notes

1. For a detailed account of the Midway's layout, see Scott (1991).
2. For further reading on nineteenth-century women and sensational news, see Lisa Duggan's *Sapphic Slashers*.
3. The other three dancers—Lou Mattin, Fatima Siema, and May Asher—were discharged at an arraignment on July 21 ("Got a Jury for the Dancers").
4. "Vachris Danced In Court" (*Brooklyn Daily Eagle* 1896c).
5. For other work on womanhood and labor in the period, see the work of Kathy Peiss's *Cheap Amusements*, Nan Enstad's *Ladies of Labor*, and Linda Jacobs's article "Playing East."

Bibliography

Ahmed, Sara. 2004. "Affective Economies." *Social Text* 22 (2): 117–39.
Allen, Robert C. 1991. *Horrible Prettiness: Burlesque and American Culture*. Chapel Hill: University of North Carolina Press.
Bakhtin, M. M. 1984. *Rabelais and His World*. Bloomington: Indiana University Press.
Bancroft, Hubert Howe. 1893. *The Book of the Fair*. Vol 1. Chicago: Bounty.
Berlant, Lauren. 2015. "Structures of Unfeeling: Mysterious Skin." *International Journal of Politics, Culture, and Society* 28 (3): 191–213.
Bloom, Sol. 1948. *The Autobiography of Sol Bloom*. New York: G. P. Putnam's Sons.
Brooklyn Daily Eagle. 1893a. "The Midway Dancers Fined," December 6, 1893, 1.

---. 1893b. "Those Egyptian Dancers," August 5, 1893, 4.
---. 1896a. "Adjie to Dance for the Jury," July 10, 1896, 16.
---. 1896b. "The Midway in Court," July 8, 1896, 16.
---.1896c. "Vachris Danced in Court," August 7, 1896, 12.
Brown, Jayna. 2008. *Babylon Girls: Black Women Performers and the Shaping of the Modern*. Durham: Duke University Press.
Chicago Daily Tribune. 1893. "Cairo Street Open," May 28, 1893, 1–2.
Culin, Stewart. 1894. "Retrospect of the Folk-Lore of the Columbian Exposition." *Journal of American Folklore* 7 (24): 51–59.
Dean, Tim. 2012. "The Biopolitics of Pleasure." *South Atlantic Quarterly* 111 (3): 477–96.
Foster, Michael Dylan, and Jeffrey A. Tolbert. 2015. *The Folkloresque*. Logan: University Press of Colorado.
Foucault, Michel. 1990. *The History of Sexuality: An Introduction*. New York: Vintage.
Goldstein, Diane E., and Amy Shuman, eds. 2016. *The Stigmatized Vernacular*. Bloomington: Indiana University Press.
Gualtieri, Sarah. 2009. *Between Arab and White: Race and Ethnicity in the Early Syrian American Diaspora*. Berkeley: University of California Press.
Hernandez, Jillian. 2020. *Aesthetics of Excess: The Art and Politics of Black and Latina Embodiment*. Durham: Duke University Press.
Jacobs, Linda K. 2015. *Strangers in the West: The Syrian Colony of New York City, 1880–1900*. New York: Kalimah.
Jarmakani, Amira. 2008. *Imagining Arab Womanhood: The Cultural Mythology of Veils, Harems, and Belly Dancers in the U.S.* New York: Palgrave Macmillan US.
Kasson, John F. 1978. *Amusing the Million: Coney Island at the Turn of the Century*. New York: Farrar, Straus and Giroux.
Kennedy, Charles A. 2014. "When Little Cairo Met Main Street." In *Music and Culture in America, 1861–1918*, edited by Michael Saffle, 271–97. New York: Routledge.
Lim, Eng-Beng. 2013. *Brown Boys and Rice Queens*. New York: New York University Press.
McClintock, Anne. 1995. *Imperial Leather: Race, Gender and Sexuality in the Colonial Contest*. New York: Routledge.
Muñoz, José Esteban. 1999. *Disidentifications: Queers of Color and the Performance of Politics*. Minneapolis: University of Minnesota Press.
---. 2006. "Feeling Brown, Feeling Down: Latina Affect, the Performativity of Race, and the Depressive Position." *Signs* 31 (3): 675–88.
---. 2020. *The Sense of Brown*. Edited by Tavia Nyong'o and Joshua Chambers-Letson. Durham: Duke University Press.
New York Journal. 1896. "He Danced for the Jury," August 8, 1896, 5.
New York Times. 1893. "Miniature World's Fair," December 1, 1893, 5.

———. 1894. "New York Has a Midway," March 6, 1894, 5.
———. 1896. "Vachris Danced in Court: An Oriental Exhibition by the Coney Island Policeman," August 8, 1896, 9.
Pellegrini, Ann. 2007. "'Signaling through the Flames': Hell House Performance and Structures of Religious Feeling." *American Quarterly* 59 (3): 911–35.
Raibmon, Paige. 2005. *Authentic Indians: Episodes of Encounter from the Late-Nineteenth-Century Northwest Coast*. Durham: Duke University Press.
Rydell, Robert W. 1984. *All the World's a Fair: Visions of Empire at American International Expositions, 1876–1916*. Chicago: University of Chicago Press.
Said, Edward W. 1994. *Orientalism*. New York: Vintage.
Schaefer, Donovan O. 2019. *The Evolution of Affect Theory: The Humanities, the Sciences, and the Study of Power*. Cambridge, UK: Cambridge University Press.
Scott, Gertrude M. 1991. "Village Performance: Villages at the Chicago World's Columbian Exposition, 1893." PhD Diss., New York University.
Sieg, Katrin. 2009. *Ethnic Drag: Performing Race, Nation, Sexuality in West Germany*. Ann Arbor: University of Michigan Press.
Snorton, C. Riley. 2017. *Black on Both Sides*. Minneapolis: University of Minnesota Press.
The Sun [New York]. 1896. "Couchee Dance in Court," August 8, 1896, 7.
Wells, Ida B., ed. 1893. *The Reason Why the Colored American Is Not in the World's Columbian Exposition: The Afro-American's Contribution to Columbian Literature*. Chicago: Ida B. Wells.

Pris Nasrat is an independent scholar. Her research focus is on performance through affect theory and power with particular attention to race, gender, and sexuality.

9

Reverse, Rewrite, Reclaim Coloniality in Chicanx Flamenco at the Miss Indian World Pageant

ERICA ACEVEDO-ONTIVEROS

The performance at the Gathering of Nations Pow Wow Miss Indian World pageant begins with a soft and slow *cante* from Vicente Griego, singing cautiously, *libre*, the beginnings of a *sigiriya*, the first *palo* of flamenco.[1] The song comes out cautiously but with drive as the notes permeate the stillness and the simmering cante continues and hangs in midair, reminiscent of the source of sigiriya as the first moment one cries out to see if they are alone in the darkness. After about a minute, Griego is joined by Native American singers with their libre song and just the slight hint of a hand drum, and it is during this back and forth, less a call-and-response and more a dialogue, when the *toque* comes in and Griego's *grito* accompanies the toque, slowly at first.[2] The strings that are plucked on the guitar are performing their own *baile* with the cante and thus with the *cantaor*.[3] As Griego sings, his image is projected on a screen for the full-house audience to see. The image appears as his voice undulates and finds its *pareja* in the toque.[4] The relationship between the cante and the toque is like a spousal partnership—intimate, serious, and with lasting reverberations. As Griego develops this relationship onstage, the audience becomes more invested in the toque and the shifts in tonality with the cante that follows. Griego then extends his hand with an open palm, and the main traveler opens, and four *bailaores* (two female and two male) begin their *zapateo* and their *remate*.[5] Griego's cante rejoins the performers as the bailaores lift their arms in *floreo*.[6] There are two *tocaores* and one *palmera*.[7]

Onstage, there are Native American singers and two large tipis flanking stage right and left. As the bailaores continue their remate and their *palmas* and the rhythm and the toque speed up, a fancy dancer and a fancy shawl dancer come out as if called or beckoned by the palmas of the dancers, and everyone ends the remate together and on time.[8] Their ending reverberates

179

through the performance venue. But this is not the end. The Native American singers and hand drums enter with more insistence, and the palmera joins the group of dancers. She takes her place in the center of the circle of the four flamenco bailaores as they continue to dance with their *bulerias floreo* and *llamadas*; the fancy dancer and the fancy shawl dancer continue, and all the performers stop as the Native American singers end.[9] The Native American musicians and dancers transition into a round dance, and as the Native American fancy dancers create a circle, they take their time promenading around the stage.[10] The flamenco bailaores continue to dance their llamadas, and when the fancy dancers dance toward them, they pick up each bailaor, and they all join hands and participate in the round dance. The moment the bailaores join the round dance is when Griego sings with the Native American musicians. Griego's cante overlays on the singers as the performers dance together to large audience applause. The dancers dance hand in hand as they snake through and dance offstage. They move in unison, with the rhythm extending through their hands into each performer. The musicians of both groups end together long after the dancers have left the stage. The audience is left with the resonance of witnessing these groups share space, breath, and touch—each in their element, separate but together in their survivance, purposeful and active in their presence.

Albuquerque, New Mexico, commonly referred to as Burque by locals, is home to the Flamenco Festival Internacional de Albuquerque (FFI), the longest flamenco festival in the US, held annually in the summer (typically June) and produced by the National Institute of Flamenco (NIF) and the Gathering of Nations, the largest Pow Wow in North America, traditionally held annually in the spring (usually the fourth weekend in April). These two events never overlap, leaving each to exist in its own self-contained bubble. In 2018, the Gathering of Nations invited the NIF dancers to perform flamenco with shawl and fancy dancers at the culminating event of the Miss Indian World pageant (typically a two-day event), which takes place the day before Grand Entry and marks the official start of the Gathering of Nations Pow Wow. The performance united the musicians from each respective cultural form. Vicente Griego, a New Mexico–based flamenco cantaor and a professional Pow Wow drummer, performed for the groups' respective dancers and performed together.

These two performance styles do not come to mind in conversation with each other, but in New Mexico, specifically Albuquerque, this pairing is not unusual. In the unique setting of Northern New Mexico, these styles connect and complement each other. Using Vizenor's idea of survivance from

Manifest Manners: Narratives on Postindian Survivance, I explore how each dance form aids in reformatting the narrative of colonization on the bodies of the young performers and on the audience. I also introduce an intervention that I refer to as *no sé que*, a means to attempt to grapple with what to do with the ephemerality of dance as it colludes across cultures. Flamenco, fancy, and shawl dancers perform collaboratively in Indigenous cultural spaces opens an opportunity to reverse, rewrite, and reclaim the colonial script on the bodies of the performers and the audience.

Flamenco at the Gathering of Nations Pow Wow? Pow Wow dancers with flamenco performers? In New Mexico? Yes! The prestigious Miss Indian World annual competition has been in existence since 1984. Young women are selected based on their knowledge of their tribe traditions, culture, and history. The culminating presentation takes place the day before the Gathering of Nations Pow Wow begins. The Gathering is the world's largest Pow Wow in terms of attendance and has been in existence since 1983, always held in Albuquerque. New Mexico is widely known as Pueblo country, but in terms of population numbers the largest Indigenous group in the state is the Navajo Nation.[11] The Native American presence in Albuquerque and by extension New Mexico is significant. Albuquerque is surrounded by various pueblos, and the hour-long drive north to Santa Fe has the driver reading signs for at least four pueblos on Interstate 25. Not only has Albuquerque been home to the Gathering of Nations Pow Wow since its inception, but it is also the home of Southwestern Indian Polytechnic Institute (SIPI), which is a public tribal land-grant community college. The University of New Mexico (UNM) main campus in Albuquerque, the state's flagship university, leads the nation's Research One universities with the highest enrollment of Native American undergraduate students at a little over 5 percent.[12] Native Americans are about 10 percent of the New Mexico population.[13]

Conversely, the presence of flamenco in New Mexico is also significant. New Mexicans have the reputation among US Chicanx of referring to themselves as Hispanic and aligning culturally with a Spanish sensibility. Historically, in the larger US Chicanx community, this type of flamenco popularity would be explained as typical of New Mexico's wavering Chicanidad, which yearns to be connected to a Spanish colonial past rather than to its Indigenous Mexican roots. However, I believe the interpretation has a lot more friction. What makes New Mexican Chicanx different, I argue, from the larger US Chicanx community is that they utilize flamenco and its Gitano roots as a cultural example of their Chicanidad. In my dissertation, *Olé You Guys: Flamenco Influences of Chicanx Identity in New Mexico*, I initiated a conversation that places flamenco and the precarious identity of Chicanx, Gitanos, and Nuevomejicanos in dialogue through the body, the art form, and the cultural stylings of flamenco rooted in the FFI. I argue that the connection between Gitanos and Chicanx in Burque has a lot to do with the Gitano-centric flamenco curriculum based on mutual diasporic traditions. In this project, I extend that conversation into another realm of New Mexican cultural identity, the nexus of indigenous dance forms and flamenco.

The influence of flamenco is concentrated in Northern New Mexico. Flamenco has been taught at UNM since the 1980s and is now a formally established part of the dance curriculum, with students able to obtain undergraduate and graduate degrees in flamenco and flamenco choreography, respectively. The FFI has completed its thirty-seventh year. Albuquerque is home to multiple professional and preprofessional flamenco groups. There are many flamenco schools in northern New Mexico, in Taos, Santa Fe, and Albuquerque. Flamenco and Native American culture thrive in New Mexico. These two cultures attract tourists but rarely attract each other publicly.

New Mexico has the least illustrious reputation among Chicanx scholars since New Mexicans often refer to themselves as Hispanic, and there are many examples in the larger populous that choose to align culturally with a Spanish sensibility. I have witnessed the vocal dismissal of the New Mexican experience as an authentic Chicanx experience at conferences, from subtle microaggressions to more overt defiance, rolling of the eyes, loud sighing, and an insistence on recentering the New Mexican experience in a colonial metric that does not allow for New Mexicans to define their historiographic relationships for themselves.[14] As proof of New Mexico's Hispanicization, *gente* point to flamenco's popularity in New Mexico, especially among New Mexicans.[15] However, I believe the complexities of this relationship have not been examined with a lens toward the benefits for Chicanx identity. I will argue the unique contribution of New Mexican Chicanx is their utilization of flamenco and its Gitano roots as a manifestation of their Chicanidad.

Chicanx *Clima* en Nuevo Mexico

In *Occupied America*, Rodolfo F. Acuña defines Chicano as "an experience, a historical memory of growing up Mexican in the United States and experiencing racism.... [The term] Chicano acknowledges a history of oppression and a trajectory that has uplifted Mexican-origin people in the United States" (Acuña 2007, 325). Chicanos became Chicanos after the Treaty of Guadalupe Hidalgo in 1848 marked the end of the Mexican-American War. Chicanos became landed in the United States Southwest, where they first attempted to live their lives under a government that did not speak their language, know their customs, or care about their well-being. As the Southwest was divided into territories then states by the US, the fate of the majority Mexican population was in jeopardy as they attempted to adapt to the laws imposed by the US government. The gross flouting of the stipulations in the Treaty of Guadalupe Hidalgo—namely, maintaining the cultural integrity of Mexicans living in the United States—contributed to the inferior status Mexicans experienced in the newly annexed lands of the Southwest. As territories moved into statehood, New Mexico found itself in a precarious position.

New Mexicans have had a storied relationship with how they refer to themselves. Some New Mexico Hispanics claim direct patronage with Spain. Juan de Oñate's exploits feature prominently in New Mexico's historical narratives sponsored by the state's self-described Hispanic population (Acuña 2007, 27).[16] When I moved from California to New Mexico in the fall of 2000, I was struck by how frequently the New Mexican population referred to themselves as Hispanic. In California, my heavy involvement in protests in favor of affirmative action and bilingual education informed my understanding of the word *Hispanic* as a term reserved for use during direct engagements with the federal government.[17] However, in New Mexico the term *Hispanic* seemed to be used widely, both on television and at the university, while the term *Chicano* seemed to be used more sparingly. One area where the term *Chicano* is used as a self-descriptor is in flamenco culture.

Flamenco in New Mexico has largely been the generational project of the Enciñias family, currently led by the matriarch Eva Enciñias. Eva and her children politically identify as Chicanos.[18] The gross inconsistencies of power within the political structures in New Mexico had favored old-money Anglo and Hispanic families with long lineages of settlement in New Mexico and fueled the phenomenon of looking back toward a previous age, akin to the romanticization that can occur when migrants look back to their home countries, even Chicanos looking back toward Mexico. This was not an uncommon phenomenon during the Chicano movement in the 1960s, especially in the Southwest. The political climate in New Mexico encouraged Chicano activism as it was also brewing around La Raza Unida Party in Texas and the student walkouts in California (Acuña 2007, 263). According to Acuña in *Occupied America*, "Simply said, New Mexicans lacked education, a key factor in the new labor market. Illiteracy was 16.6 percent for Mexicans compared with 3.1 percent for others. . . . In 1965, New Mexico had the highest percentage of draftees failing the intelligence exam of any southwestern state—25.4 percent" (Acuña 2007, 231). Acuña's representation of New Mexico displays a population wanting in basic skills of education. Advancement in the political climate in New Mexico favored cultivated individuals, typically from established land-grant families. Eva Enciñias's family did not fit the mold of a politically successful family, and her disenfranchisement led her toward political activism.[19] The base of much of the Chicano political activism in the Southwest in the 1960s surrounded grassroots movements that inspired a renewal of heritage cultures (Broyles-González 1994, 3). Although the Chicano movement is known for promoting a renewal of Mexican identity, demonstrated in El Teatro Campesino and in the popularization of Ballet Folklórico groups, the New Mexican sensibility pursued a Spanish history. Eva's mother, Clarita, taught flamenco out of a studio in her home in Albuquerque.[20] Eva soon continued the work of Clarita, the initiator of a four-generation legacy of flamenco in New Mexico. The impetus as to why Clarita taught flamenco could be traced to the history of Spanish colonization in New Mexico. Inquiring with New Mexicans as to why Spanish culture is important elicits a typical response placing Spanish culture at the center of what makes New Mexico unique from the rest of the Southwest. "The racial attitudes of New Mexicans are deeply rooted in the Spanish conquest and colonization" (Acuña 2007, 77). New Mexico highly regards the influence of colonization, which Spain oversaw by the self-proclaiming Hispanic population. In short, New Mexicans claim Spain as the source of their cultural heritage, not Mexico. The power of this affiliation between New Mexico and Spain colors how New Mexicans perceive Spanish culture and perhaps is a reason for New Mexicans' specific zeal for flamenco culture. Pero lo que es seguro es que ahí hay algo. There is something there.

The Gathering of Nations Pow Wow is a huge event that has approximately seventy thousand attendees over the course of four days at the UNM basketball arena known as the Pit. It is nearly impossible to live in Albuquerque and not know that the Pow Wow is happening. The influx of people at popular Albuquerque restaurants, the increased traffic, and the billboards around town make the event difficult to ignore. The FFI is a large event that happens over the course of a week in June but does not have anywhere close the attendance or the city footprint that the Gathering of Nations does. In their first collaboration, it was significant that it would take place at the Gathering of Nations Pow Wow, the event with the largest city impact.

Although New Mexico has a reputation among California and Texas Chicanx as being Spanish, the focus of the flamenco programs in New Mexico do not align with that belief. In New Mexico, there is an alignment with Gitanos, with the underrepresented, that forms the basis of the flamenco culture. It is an alliance between one underrepresented group, Gitanos, and another underrepresented group, Chicanx.[21] It is a message that has been in the making for decades, and the collaboration between NIF and the Gathering of Nations Pow Wow is evidence that the message has permeated beyond NIF's curriculum. The Flamenco Dance program at UNM follows the pedagogy of the NIF program very closely, sharing many instructors and fitting within a strict academic structure in terms of the coursework available, including technique courses in the contemporary dance model of beginning, intermediate, and advanced. However, the Flamenco program also exists outside of this ideology in its approach to how it situates Flamenco culture. Presenting a Gitano-centered Flamenco experience brings what has been traditionally marginalized into the center.

Flamenco and the presentation of a Gitano-centered curriculum in Albuquerque, New Mexico, backed up by an international festival that invites and succeeds in bringing many Gitano performers to meet, mingle, and perform in Albuquerque inspires a radical representation of Chicanidad. By training in flamenco from a Gitano historical perspective, the UNM and NIF dance curricula alter how students approach their self-identity expressions. This is possible not only due to the deep history of flamenco in the region of New Mexico but also because of the international teaching of Gitanos as the originators of flamenco.

An example of this Gitano-centered curriculum is how Gitano experiences are central to the teachings of flamenco history—not just in flamenco history class but also in the technique classes at both UNM and NIF. Students are taught to embody the different gestures in the baile, hand expressions, and the remates with a Gitano aesthetic. A common refrain in flamenco classes is if you want to learn more about flamenco, you need to watch live professional flamenco from Spain. An implicit but important part of the curriculum is the way Gitano *músicos* are highlighted and consistently praised in class and included on playlists students are encouraged to listen to as warm-up music and to enhance their flamenco education.[22] Also, there are the headlining stars from the festival and the consistent conversation on the cultural differences and accommodations of Gitano performers for the festival.[23] These reasons contribute to how flamenco students in Albuquerque are offered the message that Gitano culture is central to flamenco.

The translation of a Gitano-centered curriculum produces students who possess a desire for inquiry toward the cultural ramifications involved in learning an art form, which has persevered through an imposed diaspora. The complexities of power and the body as a vessel of power struggles offer a rare opportunity for dance exploration, one that has not been historically addressed in the contemporary dance curriculum. At UNM, the curriculum appears to be an organized and technically advanced offering of Flamenco technique, but enmeshed in it is ideology, as it is enmeshed in all curricula.

Manifest Manners: Narratives on Postindian Survivance by Gerald Vizenor defines survivance as "an active sense of presence, the continuance of native stories, not a mere reaction, or a survivable name" (Vizenor 1994, vii). This open-ended definition serves to encompass the application of a broad term to the unique cultural exchange that transpired between NIF and the Gathering of Nations Pow Wow performers because of the colonial passivity that New Mexicans have historically been associated with. The performance of two groups actively surviving by leaning into each other and having a performance on their terms disrupts that reading.

This encounter with Chicanx flamenco is in conversation with indigeneity. There has been a sharing of flamenco with Native American dancers, but the Miss Indian World pageant at the Gathering of Nations Pow Wow in 2018 was one of the first times they worked collaboratively. In Homi K. Bhabha's *The Location of Culture*, he discusses institutional location and geopolitical locale: "What is the theoretically innovative, and politically crucial, is the need to think beyond narratives of originary and initial subjectivities and to focus on those moments or processes that are produced in the articulation of cultural differences. These 'in-between' spaces provide the terrain for elaborating strategies of selfhood—singular or communal—that initiate new signs of identity, and innovative sites of collaboration, and contestation, in the act of defining the idea of society itself" (Bhabha 1994, 2). NIF and the Gathering of Nations Pow Wow offer a confluence of cultural expressions through their active presence, which is rooted in cultural expressions that decolonialize the performance and also "initiate new signs of identity," like Bhabha suggests. In order to better understand the application of these examples, I propose new frameworks. I call them *órale, quihúbole*, and *no sé qué*.

Órale, Quihúbole, y No Sé Qué

Órale is the affirmation expressed when we enter into a communal gathering and that decision is embraced eagerly.[24] According to urbandictionary.com, órale is a Chicano word that means "hell yeah" or "right on" but has many meanings, including to indicate surprise. For example:

"Are you staying for dinner? We bought Blake's."[25]
Response: "Órale! [Hell yeah!]"
Or:
"I just figured out Alfonso Losa's llamada and I can do it in *compás*![26]
Response: "Órale! [Right on]."

It is an affirmation of shared knowledge that, through positive communal support, has the possibility of personal and social transformation. We performed at the Gathering of Nations Pow Wow with Pow Wow dancers. Órale! (Surprise!) In the NIF and Gathering of Nations performance, the órale was the elation and recognition the crowd felt when the fancy dancers came out and ratcheted up the intensity and the focus of both the spectators and the performers. It is both "we see you" and "right on!"

Órale! Yjastros, the American Flamenco Repertory company, is a professional dance company from NIF based in Albuquerque. Artistic director Joaquín Enciñias performed their show Xicano Power at Festival de Jerez, one of the most prestigious flamenco festivals in Spain, on February 28, 2023. They are the first US flamenco group to ever be invited to perform in the history of the twenty-seven-year-old Spanish flamenco festival. Órale! (Right on, and they see us!)

Quihúbole is "what's up? How are you doing? How is this relationship we have now embraced working out? What is the situation?" According to urbandictionary.com (where the word is spelled quiobole or quiovole[27]), it means "hey, what's up?" or simply "what's up?"[28] Studying flamenco in Albuquerque and being immersed with so many flamencos in classes at the university as well as at NIF, there is a sense of driving and moving forward. Do I have the step? What do I look like? Do I look like I know what I'm doing? "Quihúbole cómo están? Quihúbole, qué pasó?"[29]—said with less concern and more a need to assert a calm and collected identity and establish a rapport of sly confidence. Quihúbole . . . what do you think? It's an inquiry into the reification of the actions as we perform and reperform them for each other. I would argue that the quihúbole happens when the round dance begins and the fancy dancers silently invite the bailaores to participate with them. Their invitation is silent, but their bodies call to their fellow dancers as they move in unison. Sharing a quihúbole lays the groundwork for how we can begin to be vulnerable with each other, and this will hopefully lead to being able to be with each other with intention when we are in various states of unknowing.

Sharing a quihúbole intention is where the Festival de Jerez Xicano Power audience intersected. In Xicano Power, there is a reading of the 1967 poem "I AM Joaquín" by Rodolfo "Corky" Gonzales. The poem sits at the intersection of the Chicano movement of the 1960s and the unification of the artistic and the political. Joaquín Enciñias, born in the shadow of the Chicano movement to Chicano conscious parents, has a twin sister named Marisol. He utilized the poem to anchor and situate the show not just in a flamenco aesthetic movement but also with the word of political agitation, asserting his identity with a sly sense of confidence. Quihúbole! Xicano Power had "I Am Joaquín" in it along with a large number of New Mexicans who attended the show in Jerez, Spain (about fifty), all of who leaned into their shared recognition of language and movement.[30]

The no sé qué is the mystery. The "I don't even know."[31] According to SpanishDict.com, the phrase *no sé qué* is used to express doubt—"I don't know what," or something you cannot label; "a certain something." The definition I use is more closely aligned to the latter one. I witnessed Manuela Carrasco performing, acting as the conduit/interpreter between flamenco music and the audience;[32] she performed her famous Soleá, the one she has danced her whole life, and because she has danced the same Soleá her entire life she and her músicos are in perfect synergy.[33] But I cannot describe her performance. I can describe what I felt, how I remember it, but I am hard-pressed to offer details about specific body movements. The only proof I have is that the others in the theater and I witnessed it together—we all breathed in the resolve at the end of the remate together. We agree that it happened because we were all witnesses to it. The no sé qué between NIF and the Gathering of Nations performers came in fits and spurts. There was the tingle when you first heard Griego find tono in his libre.[34] There was the magic of seeing the fancy dancers and the flamencos end simultaneously at the conclusion of a strong musical cue. Then there was the subtle (and not so subtle) magic of seeing these two dance groups that have been depicted in dominant culture as being in conflict in terms of their shared colonial legacies. The dancers went offstage hand in hand, leaving the audience with a sense of hope, like something had been permanently changed and we could no longer go back. Not only were they dancing together, sharing space and musicians, but they also touched each other in this space and ended together, holding hands. The musicians from each group ended together, toque and hand drums and their singing in unison, not in competition and with neither group dominating, offering a small peep into a world without hierarchies. A new world where the strain of colonialism has dissipated and the practice of what reality would look like has an opportunity to breathe and take up space.

The no sé qué in the Yjastros performance of Xicano Power in Jerez . . . pues no sé qué . . . I don't even know. Perhaps the magic of what happened was not on the stage but what happened before, during, and after. There were approximately fifty people affiliated with NIF (either alums like myself or avid supporters) who attended the performance, most on their own dime, just to bear witness. Joaquín Enciñias spoke about a Jerez flamenco aficionado coming up to him and saying the Yjastros show was incredible and that she could not believe what she had seen. This mimicked my own experience with another flamenco aficionado I sat next to during the Yjastros show. After the show, she told me as she walked away with her Xicano Power program in her hand that

I should be very proud of Yjastros, that they had performed well, and that she was impressed with this US flamenco group. The no sé qué was Xicano Power setting the groundwork for something else. Now that a US-based flamenco group had been formally invited to Spain, that opened up the possibility of other groups being invited. But there will never be another first time, like the first time that Yjastros crossed the stage in Jerez de la Frontera en Andalucía, the heart of flamenco. No sé qué pero algo pasó, and I am left with words that do not accurately describe the impact that Nuevomejicano flamenco Chicanx had on Jerez and the audience, rewriting coloniality into a space that has never before existed. Here, no sé qué means something has shifted, changed, moved, and it cannot move back.

Nuevomejicanos identities and their relationship to flamenco and the Gathering of Nations Pow Wow are complex, multilayered, and multifaceted.[35] They are not just the remnants of colonialism. Nuevomejicanos have been active participants in shaping their cultural expressions and how they interact, share, and build with other cultures. They are not passive; they are not what California and Texas Chicanx who have dominated the conversation around Chicanidad assume of them. In many ways, this project has felt like defining magic, describing something you feel in your gut and know is true, but you are hard-pressed to locate evidence that you can point to. In other ways, it feels like vocalizing and writing down the importance that NIF flamencos have in the dialogue with Gathering of Nations Pow Wow performers. How do these two groups actively survive in a society designed for them to be marginalized and to not be in community with each other?

Vizenor's idea of survivance helps open a door to understanding how to approach the collusion of fancy shawl and flamenco dancers at the Gathering of Nations Pow Wow in Albuquerque, New Mexico. By considering the cultural context of Nuevomexicano Chicanidad and its unique relationship with flamenco, the stage is set to use no sé qué to reformat the narrative of colonization on the bodies of the performers along with the ephemerality of dance as it shifts and slips across dance cultures.

The no sé qué is the place where we sit in visceral uncomfortableness and indecipherability. It exemplifies the limit of language where we do not know how to describe what we are witnessing. We are literally without words. No sé qué allows us to not know but still be on the precipice of full engagement. Just because we do not know does not mean we do not care. It means we currently do not have language for it. But give me a minute, and I can dance it for you, or make up a nickname for it, or a fun pun. As survivance morphs and changes, the cartography it has on the body may inspire revolutionary alliances between Chicanx flamenco cultures and Native American populations.

Notes

1. The meanings of many of these terms, although they are in Spanish, are from a flamenco perspective. *Cante* means song. *Libre* means free. *Sigiriya* is a twelve-count flamenco rhythm pattern. *Palo* literally means stick, but in flamenco *palo* refers to any flamenco rhythm pattern.

2. *Toque* means flamenco guitar. *Grito* means yell; in flamenco it typically marks the beginning of a song, calling the listeners to the singer.

3. *Cantaor* means singer.

4. *Pareja* means couple.

5. *Bailaores* means flamenco dancers. *Zapateo* means footwork. *Remate* is how you punctuate the end of a rhythmic phrase, typically with stronger footwork and/or a definitive hand gesture.

6. *Floreo* means circular hand movements.

7. *Tocaores* means flamenco guitarists. *Palmera* refers to a musician who provides percussive accompaniment through hand clapping.

8. *Palmas* refers to rhythmic hand clapping. The fancy dancer is Larry Yazzie, and the fancy shawl dancer is Josy Bird. Fancy dancers are typically known for their costumes, flash, and athleticism. To be *on time* is a common phrase in flamenco; it means to be on beat with the music and with the other dancers. In this instance, it means dancers and musicians ending with the music simultaneously.

9. A twelve-count flamenco rhythm pattern that starts on twelve and ends on ten. A series of movements by the dancer that signals to the flamenco cantaor (singer) that you are ready for another *letra* (lyric), also known as calling for the letra.

10. The round dance is a friendship dance that has a simple beat, typically 1–2.

11. The Pueblos in New Mexico are: Acoma, Cochiti, Jemez, Isleta, Kewa, Laguna, Nambe, Ohkay Owingeh, Picuris, Pojoaque, San Felipe, San Ildefonso, Sandia, Santa Ana, Santa Clara, Taos, Tesuque, Zia, and Zuni. There are also Hopi in Arizona and Ysleta del Sur in Texas.

12. These statistics are from UNM 2018.

13. Compared to 3 percent Native Americans in Arizona, the numbers in New Mexico are high even for the US Southwest.

14. Primarily at the National Association for Chicano/Chicana Studies (NACCS).

15. *Gente* translates to people. However, I am referring to those who say things with a weight in their voice and a knowing gleam in their eye. All social groups are made up of gente; they could be elders, charismatic leaders, professors, scholars, *curanderos*, or cults of personality whose words carry weight in the community.

16. Juan de Oñate was an explorer and governor of the province of New Mexico. He is a contentious figure in the state's history. He was exiled from New Mexico by Spain for excessive cruelty toward the Acoma people. How-

ever, statues are still erected of him by the Hispanic majority, though he is publicly decried by the Native American population, particularly the Pueblo people, for his cruelty and harsh behavior toward the Native peoples of New Mexico. For more information on the Native American viewpoint of Oñate, please see Michael L. Trujillo's (2008) article "Oñate's Foot: Remembering and Dismembering in Northern New Mexico."

17. I was in college in California when Propositions 187, 209, and 227 were passed. Proposition 187 in 1994 sought to prevent illegal immigrants from using nonemergency public services like education and preventative health care. Proposition 209 in 1996 repealed affirmative action in public education, contracting, and employment. Proposition 227 in 1998 effectively repealed bilingual education for non-English speakers in public education, imposing an "English only" curriculum. The rhetoric on college campuses was that these propositions were backed by conservative Hispanic groups. True or not, it made the gap between Hispanics and Chicanos and immigrants wider.

18. I took class with Eva for two years at UNM and spent a lot of time with her during the Flamenco Festival. I also took a class with Eva's twin children Marisol and Joaquín, for two years and three years respectively, and consistently would hear mention from all three, typically in light banter, that they were Chicanos. My memories are backed up by Nevarez "Navy" Enciñias, Joaquín's eldest son.

19. These are my words and my reading of Eva's family's history. I impose a political agenda on dance and performance. A strong case is made for the reading of political acts on Mexican/Chicano bodies through their dances and performances in the book *Dancing across Borders: Danzas y Bailes Mexicanos*, edited by Olga Nájera-Ramírez, Norma E. Cantú, and Brenda M. Romero. Full disclosure: photographic images of me appear in this book in Nájera-Ramírez's chapter 16, "Staging Authenticity: Theorizing the Development of Mexican Folklórico Dance."

20. For further information on Eva's mother and the Enciñias family's legacy in Albuquerque, please see the documentary *Flamenco School* (2010), directed by Brent Morris and Reinhard Lorenz.

21. My dissertation addresses this topic in depth.

22. For example, the singers, *cantaores* Montse Cortés, Emilio Florida, and José Angel Carmona, and musicians, *tocaores* Jesús del Rosario y Tomatito.

23. This came to the forefront during FFI 25, when the festival appeared to have a cloud of bad luck. One of the Gitano singers fell and busted his lip open during rehearsal and broke someone else's guitar in the process. Later on, it was said this bad luck appeared because Fuensanta la Moneta, a *Paya bailaora*, was performing a *Petenera*, a taboo palo that is not supposed to be performed or bad luck will follow. Due to her cantaor being in the emergency room and out for the rest of the festival, Fuensanta took the *Petenera* out of her set that evening. Gitanos came up to me and made it a point to tell me that they did

not believe in the superstition but had to admit they were spooked by the degree of bad luck that seemed to have befallen the festival.

24. Órale also has roots in Chicanx cholo culture.

25. Blake's Lottaburger is a local chain restaurant in Albuquerque, famous for their Lottaburger, which is basically a green chile cheeseburger. There is one Blake's in Tucson.

26. Alfonso Losa is a popular flamenco bailaor known for complicated footwork. Compás is how all flamenco rhythms are measured according to their specific time signatures.

27. Although this is the spelling on urbandictionary.com, I maintain the quihúbole spelling. It is the spelling that I have found to be the most common.

28. In Mexican slang, the shortened version is Q'vo. For now, I think that the full word better encapsulates what I am trying to convey.

29. Mariachi singer Beatriz Adriana has a song called "El Quihúbole" from her album *Ora Pues*, which offers many more examples of how Quihúbole is used.

30. Eva Enciñias, in her YouTube clip about Jerez, states there were approximately fifty New Mexicans who attended the show in Jerez, Spain.

31. Said in the thickest LA Chicano you can muster.

32. She is a famous flamenco performer who is viewed as one of the grandes of flamenco.

33. A flamenco rhythm pattern that is slow and reserved for older and more experienced performers.

34. *Tono* means musical tone.

35. *Nuevomejicanos* refers to New Mexicans.

Bibliography

Acuña, Rodolfo. 2007. *Occupied America: A History of Chicanos*. 6th ed. New York: Pearson Longman.

Adriana, Beatriz. "El Quihúbole." Track 13 on *Ora Pues!* Peerless, originally released on vinyl in 1983. Released on CD in 1988 (version used).

Bhabha, Homi K. 1994. *The Location of Culture*. London: Routledge.

Broyles-González, Yolanda. 1994. *El Teatro Campesino: Theater in the Chicano Movement*. Austin: University of Texas Press.

Enciñias, Eva. 2023. "Eva Encinias Tells Us All about Jerez, and What's Next for Yjastros and NIF." National Institute of Flamenco, March 15, 2023. YouTube video. https://www.youtube.com/watch?v=LMyPkry5-Mg.

Enciñias, Joaquín. 2023a. "Joaquin Encinias Recaps Yjastros' Performance in Jerez." National Institute of Flamenco, March 6, 2023. YouTube video. https://www.youtube.com/watch?v=T5nwnV-EIxA.

———. 2023b. "Joaquin Talks 'Xicano Power.'" National Institute of Flamenco, March 6, 2023. YouTube video. https://www.youtube.com/watch?v=jHv8X1p3168.

Morris, Brent, and Reinhard Lorenz, directors. 2010. *Flamenco School*. Albuquerque, NM: Indieproduction.

Nájera-Ramírez, Olga, Norma E. Cantú, and Brenda M. Romero, eds. 2009. *Dancing across Borders: Danzas y Bailes Mexicanos*. Urbana: University of Illinois Press.

National Institute of Flamenco. 2018. "2018 Gathering of Nations Collaboration." July 10, 2018. YouTube video. https://www.youtube.com/watch?v=oryiHhW-2mM.

Trujillo, Michael L. 2008. "Oñate's Foot: Remembering and Dismembering in Northern New Mexico." *Aztlan: A Journal of Chicano Studies* 33, no. 2 (Fall): 91–119.

Vizenor, Gerald. 1994. *Manifest Matters: Narratives on Postindian Survivance*. Lincoln: University of Nebraska Press.

Erica Acevedo-Ontiveros has a PhD in Theatre Performance of the Americas from Arizona State University. She teaches, acts, directs, stage manages, dramaturgs, choreographs, dances, and examines Azteca, Flamenco, and Mexican Folklórico dance and how they relate to expressions of Mexican and Chicanx identity. She teaches at Benedictine University and Chandler-Gilbert Community College.

10

Queerly Beloved
Reflecting on Embodiments and Explorations of Gender and Pleasure through Tango Queer

CELIA MEREDITH

The thrumming bass pulls you in first, summons you, sinks its hook into your bones, and brings you to the edge of the dance floor. The whistling cry of the violin—or perhaps the timbre of the bandoneón, the shimmering piano—pulls you into a world of "charming men dancing with women in high heels, tables ordered around a dimly-lit dance floor, wine bottles over here, candles over there."[1] The music aches and begs you to pull someone close—to dance cheek to cheek and let time melt away. The ghosts of tangos past, present, and future haunt the movements of every sole that has made its way into a milonga with the promise of a dance that has always existed, has never existed, and is always being built and rebuilt.

For many, tango represents a melancholy and dramatic sensuality, an over-the-top and attention-grabbing performance on a theater stage. There are as many tangos as there are dancers, but a particular sort of magic exists in the more intimate spaces of social tango—one that requires its own vocabulary through the joining of bodies in (often) small and dark spaces.[2]

For every dancer, there is another possible story about tango: the Argentine dance has been mythologized, exported out of and imported back to Argentina, and blended with dance styles all over the world.[3] More than a dance, tango generates a space[4] and culture.[5] Discussing the kind of tango danced in milongas,[6] Mariana Docampo, the founder of the Milonga Tango Queer emphasizes that tango isn't just music and movement. "Tiene que ver con la comunicación entre dos personas. Es un lenguaje que se establece entre dos cuerpos, y a través del cual fluye la sensualidad. Durante los pocos minutos que dura la canción, se instauran entre quienes bailan emociones profundas."[7] Thus, there are myriad ways to approach tango: through music,[8] choreography,[9] material culture, and what interests me most: embodied communication.

Dancers, along with those who attend milongas as social participants, often engage with an imagined history of Buenos Aires, regardless of where they are. The iconography of tango music, for example, relies on the invocation of "old" Buenos Aires through its use of specific imagery and of lyrics in lunfardo.[10] This narrative is constructed along distinct aesthetic, cultural, and political lines, particularly to uphold ideals of embodiment and intimacy within dance spaces. The world of tango queer confronts these ideals to define new spaces where the potential for queer seductions can blossom and where individuals can reestablish new and different relationships to their own bodies and the bodies of others.

Methodology and Language

This chapter is a work of cultural critique that engages in interdisciplinary modes of discourse and analysis. It is deeply influenced by José Esteban Muñoz's writings on queerness and utopia, which resonate with my own experience as a dancer. His approach to "hope as a critical methodology . . . as a backward glance that enacts a future vision"[11] speaks to my interest in the history of tango and the formation of alternative spaces that are critical of the harms inflicted on vulnerable individuals who also seek connection and pleasure. As a dancer-scholar, I look to Mariana Docampo's description of tango as an opening door: "si bien la frecuencia con que milongueamos puede ser fluctuante, si bien podemos dejar de bailar tango por un tiempo, o incluso podemos decidir no bailar nunca más, sabemos que hay un lugar al que podemos volver cuando lo decidamos."[12] The milonga, and the dances within it, are spaces of performances grand and small that illuminate the political and emotional possibilities of embodied and performed queerness. The "theories I bring into my analysis have been practices in performance; experienced, learned, and felt on my own body."[13] Tango queer, in my experience, allows for a situated form of knowledge that subverts historical imaginaries of tango and births queer futurity.

By privileging the body, particularly my own queer body, I hope to illuminate the interplay of gender and pleasure within tango to broaden the conversation around these themes to include the experiences of those who play with gender beyond the milonga. How do we formulate gender in the milonga, and how does gender factor into the pleasure experienced or lost at the milonga? What do the possibilities of loosening and subverting gender norms represent to individuals who are not shedding gender fluidity at the edge of the dance floor?

Because I am focusing on a dance that has its roots in Buenos Aires and the Rio Plata region, I have chosen to preserve quotes in Spanish that were originally written in Spanish. This decision to maintain whole quotes as well as individual terms in Spanish, as Arielle A. Concilio theorizes, is not "to insist on the impossibility or limits of translation, but, on the contrary, to enable the reception of translation both as a pedagogical tool and a form of resistance against Anglocentrism."[14] It is particularly important to emphasize the contributions of Argentine writers and dancers writing about tango while acknowledging the complexities of translation that occur in a culturally specific performance, as well as the complexities that arise from translating a particularly gendered dance form/history from a language that has linguistic gender to one that does not. For these reasons, English and Spanish both appear in regular typeset.

Further, with the exception of direct quotes, I default to gender-neutral Spanish to refer to groups of mixed gender. For example, instead of referring to tangueros and amigos, I will use tangueres (or tanguerxs) and amigues (or amigxs).[15] The fluidity between English and Spanish, as well as the use of gender-neutral language, should be viewed as an invitation to search for playful, pleasurable, linguistic representation. This invitation extends into the format of this chapter as well; following in the footsteps of Ana-Maurine Lara, the endnotes in this text are "symbolic doorways, placeholders and landing points signaling where the reader might need to go to know more, to contemplate, to connect—not just with what lies behind the note but with our own physical and emotional experiences of the text."[16] Endnotes may lead you to translations or sources, "sometimes, just to an ancestor, an embodied presence, a question."[17]

Defining Tango Queer

I have been dancing tango for nearly ten years now, and among the many dances I have danced and the milongas I have visited,[18] the tango nearest and dearest to my heart is tango queer. As a queer person who has always loved dance, learning that there was space to explore queer imaginaries of a particularly romanticized dance engaged my own imaginative and romantic soul. Mercedes Liska says that "the queer tango is a practice that lends itself to an analysis of how identity and the subject are being redefined in contemporary life."[19] Docampo, in answering the question ¿por qué? writes that

> la gente 'queer' baile tango de la manera que siente es un gesto de apropiación de una danza que excluye la diversidad desde su misma estructura y que refleja y promueve relaciones de poder entre los sexos. Desde esta apropiación, se propone una dinámica distinta para todo el mundo, que tenga que ver con una más igualitaria comunicación entre las personas.[20]

These definitions demonstrate a departure from a "traditional" tango by highlighting differences beyond social identification. The political and aesthetic attributes of tango queer offer a practice that opens new avenues for the consideration of culture, gender, and power. Resituating tango among queer dancers raises questions about the function and embodiment of gender in the milonga; it invites critical examination of machismo in lyrical expressions of tango[21] as well as the dynamics of power through expressions of gender and class.[22]

Many tango queer interventions have come from cisgender women, and many academic analyses have come from straight women.[23] As a genderqueer person, as much as I have been drawn to tango—especially queer and open tango spaces—I have struggled to find space in these communities because of my shifting relationship with my own gender and body. While Mercedes Liska (2017), Mariana Docampo (2018), and others include chapters in their books about queer tango, or when writing exclusively about queer tango, focus on an exchange of roles and fluidity of gender that is available to dancers on the dance floor, the experiences of transgender and nonbinary individuals are missing: What do the possibilities of loosening and subverting gender norms represent to individuals who are not shedding gender fluidity and nonnormative practices and embodiments at the edge of the dance floor?

* * *

Not everyone who attends a queer milonga or dances tango queer is themself queer. There are those who view "tango queer" as a merely social identification[24]—one that does not imply an aesthetic framework or political orientation beyond the idea that any dancer can occupy either role, regardless of gender.[25] This (mis)understanding is an aspect of the transnationalism of tango, by the complex web of tango migrations outside of Buenos Aires, where it is common to understand a queer milonga as interchangeable with open role or alternative milongas.[26] The milonga in Buenos Aires has long served as a community gathering place and has, at least to some extent, been cognizant of tango's political history. International and transnational dance spaces, however, have historically characterized tango as a sexual/sensual partner dance and focused on either its health or social benefits.[27]

As much as tango has "become" an international dance,[28] explicitly gay and lesbian milongas existed in Buenos Aires in the late 90s and early 2000s, and queer milongas were emerging in Europe and Argentina on parallel timelines.[29] Dance scholars have written about the ways in which tango and some ballroom dances were important to LGBT expressions in the early twentieth century, and while this context may be described as anticipating tango queer,[30] I want to emphasize that tango argentino should not be instantly categorized with ballroom dance particularly in the international context, as ballroom tango is an entirely different dance from Argentine Tango, and thus tango queer as well.[31] The work scholars like Docampo have done in situating tango queer in the Argentine context invite us to place tango queer within that broader LGBT history while emphasizing its non-European roots. Milongas with an explicit queer theory framework may have been articulated in German tango spaces in the early 2000s, but they have functioned and evolved differently to how tango is culturally situated in Argentina.

Some milongueres and scholar-critics take issue with the point that that "queer" is not a Spanish word: they claim that tango queer is an entirely foreign intervention and not considered "real tango." Such claims ignore (1) political organizing around queer identities in Spanish[32] that is currently happening throughout Latin America; (2) the transnational dynamic of tango over time[33] that has greatly influenced its history and vitality; and (3) the transphobic and normative implications in drawing such stark lines around the "authenticity" of different forms of tango, particularly ones that are engaging in active discourse about power, gender, and sexuality. Scholars have explored the homosocial histories of tango,[34] but regardless of historical "proof" of existing queerness within the dance form, the act of declaiming some forms of tango as "not tango" is, as Docampo writes, "la manera nostálgica y muy tanguera de ver en la transformación un movimiento que aleja la danza de su esencia, de su 'núcleo de verdad.'"[35] Resistance to shifts in gender and sexual dynamics is not unique to tango but does demonstrate the transformative possibilities of tango queer histories and actualities.

Tango queer in Buenos Aires has largely been characterized by its political roots. As Liska explains, organizers "published documents and held workshops on tango and gender relations with an eye toward transforming the deeply rooted heteronormative culture in Argentina" while in contrast, in other cities, "the stated purpose of queer tango spaces could be summed up in a single demand: the right to dance with whomever one chose."[36] While many dancers will use the labels "open role milonga" and "queer milonga" interchangeably, there is a fundamental difference in the structures and performances felt by queer dancers. I believe these analyses could also be applied to current political-social movements surrounding tango in Buenos Aires, such as the Movimiento Feminista del Tango (MFT), which has been organizing against the machismo and violence present in tango communities, both in physical spaces and through cultural artifacts such as music.[37]

Tango queer, as well as movements such as MFT, interrogates the histories and modern iterations of tango to arrive at two themes that have enticed me since I started dancing tango: gender and pleasure. How do we formulate gender in the milonga, and how does gender factor into the pleasure experienced or lost at the milonga? Gender and pleasure in the milonga and through tango are especially complicated for those with complex relationships to gender and the body because of (individual, societal, spatial) trauma. Docampo connects the history and aesthetic of tango queer by first inviting us to think of the dance "no como una materia abstracta de pasos y técnica, sino como una danza que expresa en cada cuerpo que la baila la variedad de elementos culturales y humanos que forman su identidad."[38] Tango is not just the means to learn certain moves but "un canal de transmisión de una experiencia única."[39] When we express ourself with bodies that have lived a life different from our own, "estas experiencias pueden abrir zonas nuevas en la percepción de la danza, la relación entre los cuerpos, la música, inspirar espacios, o su transformación."[40]

Other writers and dancers have focused on the aesthetic vocabulary of tango queer as in between different styles of tango, resonating with Docampo's description of abriendo zonas nuevas. Mercedes Liska noted that the style of queer milonga regulars was "closer to everyday gesturally and moderate movements, and more subtle adornments with the feet closer to the ground," incorporating elements from both salón and milonguero styles.[41] The abrazo, or frame of dancing, "is intermediate: less close than in the *milonguero* style and farther apart than in the new tango style."[42] The stylistic in-between space builds a practice that allows dancers to redefine their relationships to their bodies as well as those they touch. Docampo references this space not only in the contact between bodies that have lived different lives but as a key aspect of tango as a dance that "se alimenta del contacto con 'lo otro,' que abre por un lado un horizonte de expectativas, y a la vez propone transformaciones."[43] Additionally, I would argue that this stylistic fluidity reflects pedagogical lineage: my first tango professor used teaching about the abrazo as a way to begin conversations about consent in college spaces. Framing the distance within the abrazo as an embodied discussion of consent allowed students to talk both explicitly and implicitly about sexuality and comfort within the body. Thus, this in-between space introduces room for conversation about boundaries and consent that I identify as an important signal of a certain political attribute of queer spaces and queer community building.[44]

Pasos, choreography, should be considered a resource used by dancers to enact, intentionally and on intuition, certain embodied knowledges and gestural explorations of identity. Dancers are taught moves in workshops by watching other couples on the dance floor, by dancing in prácticas, and by dancing in milongas. I've yet to meet a dancer who doesn't have a favorite move—some paso that they tend to repeat to a certain beat of music, after a certain point of the night. These pasos, quirks of the abrazo, of making way onto and through the dance floor are gestures that "transmit ephemeral knowledge of lost queer histories and possibilities"[45] while also offering the specific memory and experience of the other dance.

Ramón Rivera-Servera suggests that "past performance histories ... need not always be explicitly acknowledged or valued by participants, both performers and audiences, in order for their enactments to offer significant pleasures and effects in the very moment they unravel."[46] History has weight, even when not acknowledged by dancers, because of the ways it is signaled through action. We consider not only the political and social history of tango branching over decades and centuries but also certain moves and choreographies that are passed along from dancer to dancer within a lineage and present as a deeply embodied and social experience that is invested in the present.

Gender and Pleasure

How does gender function within the worlds that tango creates? My introduction to tango was technically not in queer tango spaces, but I did start learning how to lead and follow from day one.[47] The pedagogical approaches in tango vary,[48] but my first teacher emphasized how learning both roles can make you a stronger dancer: you learn how the different pieces fit together.[49] Even with this encouragement to slip between each part, there was a reinforcement of a strict binary reflecting the world off the dance floor: that of the masculine leader, and that of the feminine follower.

While tango queer invites dancers to imagine alternative combinations, many of the people who are writing and talking about these gendered performances do so with the suggestion that the performance may be shrugged off at the end of the night.[50] Women may lead and be either masculine or feminine, but they will ultimately return to being women when they step off the dance floor. The dancers and scholars writing about the possibilities of tango queer point out that the performances available within the tango are flexible, but only to a certain extent without "breaking" the dance.[51] I must wonder, then, how is gender played with and explored by those who bring fluid identities with them?[52]

During my time dancing tango, my relationship to my own gender and body has shifted greatly. I lost seasons of dance due to feeling forced to perform a particular embodiment of femininity to have access to milongas and lacked both the verbal and physical vocabularies to create a gendered expression that was externally legible while remaining internally comfortable. As I write this, I am more settled in my body and gender and am in a much smaller tango community: one of the benefits of being known as a "good dancer" who can lead and follow is further flexibility for nonnormative gendered performances.

Unfortunately for me, my body and role as a leader are read still as feminine, causing issues that every woman leader (even those simply read as woman) has experienced: if you are not a man, and you lead, you must be twice as good as the men to be able to dance unharrassed.[53]

Still, I practice certain exercises when I stand at the oven, while I'm brushing my teeth.[54] I experience great pleasure in being present in my body when I dance. Through tango, I find fully in-body experiences that help me embody a gender I feel euphoric in. I would argue that tango as a social dance trains our imaginations and bodies and serves as a method of inscribing knowledge of alternative euphoric futures *on* and *through* the body. The pedagogy of tango embodies this training in part through the abrazo: it is through a focus on the abrazo and the tactile relationship between dancers that one learns to move through the world(s) of tango queer.

The abrazo is the thing I recall most quickly about other dancers: Do they hold a light frame? Do they tend to emphasize certain pasos with a heavy hand? The abrazo has extended into my everyday life by reshaping my posture as I walk down the street, appearing in my dreams of milongas past and future. If, in the words of José Esteban Muñoz, utopia "renders potential blueprints of a world not quite here . . . a moment when the here and the now is transcended by a then and a there that could be and indeed should be,"[55] performances serve as utopic experiences. Bringing aspects of that performance into everyday life helps us to manifest that blueprint into our everyday reality. The difference between performance and everyday reality is not the difference between "unreal" and "real" worlds: the worlds or universes created on the dance floor *are* real, even if they exist parallel to the world we usually occupy. It is far more interesting to ask how we can shape the world around us by bringing the creations from dance into quotidian life than it is to section it off into an untouchable realm.

Manifesting Gender

I am interested in the ways that dancers code, signal, and feel their gender(s), and how performances on the dance floor may echo, contradict, or complicate such performances on the periphery and outside of the dance floor. In considering the style of dancers, particularly of women leaders at queer milongas, Liska noted that women who wore more "masculine" clothing and lower heels would often be shunned or ignored in more traditional settings and described such "bodily strategies for making evident different feminine erotics in the queer context. How you dressed was the starting point for recognition."[56] For dancers who wish to embody both leader and follower throughout the night, there is a tension in deciding how to adorn their bodies. Wearing a skirt often means you are not taken as seriously as a leader while wearing trousers that do not evoke the silhouette and movement of a dress means you are taken less seriously as a follower. Footwear also functions as a coded signal to other dancers regarding which role you will take. Although it is possible to lead in heels and easy to follow in flats, a dancer who wears the "wrong" shoes for a role is marked as distinctly nonnormative and, unless they are already known, assumed to be a novice. It takes a skillful leader to lead in heels, but there are certain moves that are abandoned to maintain the stability of the abrazo—certain pasos rely on the counterbalance of the leader to safely conduct their follower's mass, and pulling off such feats in two- or three-inch heels is difficult.

These physical manifestations work in at least two directions: they are read by other dancers, and they are felt by the one embodying the gender. How is this internalized and felt by dancers moving in and out of different gendered performances? At times, I am not aware of my gender until I make a misstep that suddenly makes me more aware of the *process* of queerness. These missteps often involve a feedback loop of observation and perception: becoming aware of how adornment or gesture is being read on my body and finding that my own perception is out of sync with how I am being observed. As Rivera-Servera says, "Being queer is never a completed journey but a continuous process of becoming queer that requires queer acts. These strategies may range from a queer approach to everyday practices such as dress, speech, gesture, and, of course, sex, to more formal presentations of self in public contexts such as the theater or the dance club."[57] The continuous process of becoming queer in public relies on external and internal forces: an audience to read certain acts and practices in ways that engage and often reject cisheteronormative readings of the body. Additionally, as Docampo points out, tango is a necessarily observed dance and "esta conciencia de 'estar siendo observados' es inseparable del tango, y posibilita la composición de una imagen que es a la vez íntima y pública."[58] Thus, even if a dancer settles on a gendered embodiment that is internally apt, there are certain movements that are often abandoned not only to negotiate the adornment chosen for the night but also to negotiate how the body is read in movement.

These practices of seeing myself and constructing an expression that can be read as queer both to those "in the know" and others in milongas feel like a mix of magic and science. There is a ritual that begins beyond the milonga to decide how I will signal my gender for the night, from footwear to clothing to other adornments. This ritual began the moment I started learning my first pasos. It is a process that begins again in preparation for each milonga because of how my gender shifts each day, but also in reflection of how previous genders succeeded or failed in previous milongas. "Success" can be reflected by: How many leaders asked me to dance? How many followers accepted my offers to dance? How stable did I feel on my feet throughout the night? How long did it take me to settle in to each abrazo? This process involves explicit reflection as well as an intuitive reach toward certain adornments and a hopefulness of what sorts of dance(r)s I may encounter that night.

How does this process offer possibilities of pleasure? Muñoz writes that "queer dance is hard to catch—and it is meant to be hard to act. . . . But it matters and takes on a vast material weight for those of us who perform and draw important sustenance from performance. Rather than dematerialize, dance rematerializes."[59] I can often tell which dancers have been dancing together longest, or if they have shared a teacher, because they have signature moves or vocabularies that pop up within the dance or to certain songs or with certain orchestras. These gestures are "vast storehouses of queer history and futurity"[60] that link movement to memory. A process of adornment that intimately shapes and reshapes the possibility of movement within the milonga offers a space of playfulness from night to night. Every step I take is rewriting the tangos I have danced, to reify certain embodiments while rejecting others. I remember greater playfulness when the gesture I borrow is from a friend, male, embodying the femme fatale; when another friend, sleek and coquettish, becomes the strongest and softest leader. This embodiment destabilizes and complicates the interplay between gender and sexuality to allow dancers to explore pleasure in a multifaceted way.

Articulating Pleasure

My tango is defined by pleasure—sometimes a spark of recognition, sometimes warmth in a soft abrazo, sometimes the exhaled chuckle as a boleo is executed and momentum grows as we whip across the dance floor. This pleasure is the exact opposite of an out-of-body experience: it is the sensation of being intimately aware of the muscles wrapping around your ankles, anchoring you to the ground; the muscles in your thigh alert and eager for the next sweeping takeoff; every point of connection in the abrazo from the curve of the arm to the kiss of palms, to the brush of cheek to cheek or cheek to chest or chin or forehead. Beyond this sense of pleasure, my relationship to tango has always been underpinned by a sense of playfulness: my first tango teacher would always remind us that "if you can drive, if you can push a shopping cart in the store, you can lead." This served both as a reminder that the leader's role first and foremost is to ensure that their follower makes it around the dance floor without running into someone—or something—else, but the warmth and goofiness (a smile and wink) also remind us that we are there to have *fun*.

My experiences at milongas over the years, however, have demonstrated that some dancers view each tanda, each turn of dancing, as having higher stakes, or perhaps a kind of pleasure illegible to me: the almost-disgust with which a man chided me for daring to cabecear him, his reminder that "soy el hombre, soy el líder, vamos cuando *yo* quiero y vos me sigás."[61] The seemingly endless wait to be asked to dance at the cliquey milongas in my hometown, and failing to click with certain dancers because they were more preoccupied with looking good from the outside than with reinforcing a sense of connection with me.[62] Tango queer has offered a specific kind of pleasure in its visibilization of alternative representations of identity and its opening of new *expectations* of aesthetic representation.[63]

There is something about the abrazo that allows the world to fall away. In that space, I know where I am from the top of my head to the tips of my toes; I am intimately familiar with the extension of my arms, can feel every bit of my body relax into place. I am able to let gender melt away: I feel the strength of my thighs, aching to push off into the next step; the breadth of my shoulders as I lead, full of grace and quiet surety; the brush of stubble against my cheek, the caress of perfumed hair. I am nothing but a body, I am two bodies, my "self" is the entire dance floor and the suspension of one note. In this tango, I am allowed, encouraged, begged, to fall in love for a tanda. For twelve minutes, I am connected beyond words with another body, and I am simultaneously aware of the beats ticking down our time and entirely unaware of the universe around me. I have described this as falling in love knowing that it will end, that there is a chance that we will never meet on the dance floor again. On other nights, during other songs, a dance can mean nothing more than movement: there is power in letting a dance mean only as much as you want, only as much as you can bear. Connection between partners and between bodies is central to my understanding of tango queer.

This pleasurable connection is emphasized by its temporal and improvisational aspects. Because of the códigos of the milonga, dances (particularly with strangers) are emphasized by the promise of an impending loss—the dance is *going* to end and thus creates a space where a utopian performance "emerge[s] out of moments where the aesthetic event becomes, temporarily, a felt materiality that instantiates the imaginable into the possible."[64] These dances are one of a kind—even the same moves to the same song with the same partner create a different space because of the necessarily improvisational aspects of dance and the realities of sharing a dance floor with other couples. While dances can be cataloged and sensations articulated, the pleasure of dance resides in the body/ies of those dancing; an "ephemeral, temporary happening in which singular beings crash into each other for a time to become a singular plural. But then the dawn breaks, the performance ends, the party comes undone, and they slip away from each other, falling back into the void."[65] The song ends, the tanda too, and the dancers separate. Perhaps the dance is written, indelibly into memory and body, or perhaps it sinks, forgotten, into the night.

Outro

I long to return to the milonga and to the abrazos I have experienced in my dreams. To the genders I constructed that lie folded at the back of my closet. There are ways of expressing myself that can be done only in movement, can be understood only while the bandoneón flirts and the violin wails into the night. Docampo writes that "si el tango 'te toma,' lo hace con exclusividad, y para siempre."[66] No matter how long it has been since I've last danced tango, part of me is ready to step immediately back onto the dance floor. It is the part of me that remembers every abrazo I've held. Every dance I have ever danced lives in my body, as a leader, as a follower, as both simultaneously, switching, playfully in the seconds between each step. A palimpsest of the dances I have loved and the dances I have forgotten—they add to the existing language within my body that reminds me of where I am. I am here, I have been here, and I will be here again.

Rather than being a space where I shrug different genders on or off at the edge of the dance floor, tango queer has allowed me an articulation of the pleasure found through playing with gender throughout an evening. It creates a space in the embrace of another, the embrace of the dance floor, to fully embody myself in a way that only other dancers can understand.[67]

Notes

1. Relmucao, Juan. 2020. "In Buenos Aires, Queer Tango Takes a Revolutionary Dance Back to Its Roots." *Atlas Obscura*, February 12, 2020. http://www.atlasobscura.com/articles/queer-tango-in-buenos-aires.

2. Many of these spaces are not as small nor as dark as they once were, but part of the allure is the illusion.

3. Forms like tango nuevo and blues-tango fusion, among others, play with the forms and traditions of tango music and movement. Each path to the dance floor offers a different perspective.

4. See, for example, Karush, Matthew B. 2012. *Culture of Class: Radio and Cinema in the Making of a Divided Argentina, 1920–1946*. Durham, NC: Duke University Press; Varela, Gustavo. 2016. *Tango y Política: sexo, moral burguesa y revolución en Argentina*. Buenos Aires: Ariel Argentina.

5. Arguably spaces and cultures, given the aforementioned mixing and multiplicity of possible experiences of both the dance and the milonga.

6. The event where tango is danced, but the word may also refer to the venue where a milonga is held, a sub-genre of tango music, or the dance that is danced to that music. Here, tango milonguero is referenced to distinguish it from stage or salón tango.

7. Docampo, Mariana. 2018. *Buenos Aires: Tango Queer.* Buenos Aires: Madreselva, 117.

8. Liska, Mercedes. 2017. *Argentine Queer Tango: Dance and Sexuality Politics in Buenos Aires.* Translated by Westwell and Vila. Lanham: Lexington; Savigliano, Marta. 1995. *Tango and the Political Economy of Passion.* Boulder, CO: Westview.

9. Varela (2016); Saikin, Magali. 2004. *Tango y Género: identidades y roles sexuales en el Tango Argentina.* Córdoba, Spain: Abrazos.

10. Savigliano discusses the use of lunfardo, an argot or slang developed in the late nineteenth and twentieth centuries in Buenos Aires, in re-creating a tango experience in Japan in *Tango and the Political Economy of Passion*; Mariana Docampo, cited throughout this chapter, also references this in discussions of pedagogy throughout *Buenos Aires Tango Queer.*

11. Muñoz, José Esteban. 2019. *Cruising Utopia: The Then and There of Queer Futurity.* Revised ed. New York: New York University, 4.

12. Docampo (2018, 19).

13. Ramón Rivera-Servera articulates his approach to ethnography of performance in this way to capture his experience as a co-witness and co-performer, dancing "both in the literal sense of partnering on the dance floor and in the sense of being attuned bodily and emotionally to those around" him. Rivera-Servera, Ramón. 2012. *Performing Queer Latinidad: Dance, Sexuality, Politics.* Ann Arbor: University of Michigan Press, 19.

14. Concilio, Arielle A. 2016. "Pedro Lemebel and the Translatxrsation: On a Genderqueer Translation Praxis." *TSQ: Transgender Studies Quarterly* 3, no. 3–4 (November): 462–84, 470. Concilio's work locates translation as a site of possible political engagement, a genderqueer praxis that engages the multiplicity and multivocality of gender of writers and translators.

15. For further discussion of gender-neutral Spanish en español and in English, see the following: Maldonado, Lorena G. 2017. "La lengua no tiene sexo: 'Elle está cansade.'" *El Español*, June 18, 2017. https://www.elespanol.com/cultura/20170617/224478043_0.html; Papadopoulos et al. "Global Spanish." Gender in Language Project. https://www.genderinlanguage.com/spanish.

16. Lara, Ana-Maurine. 2020. *Queer Freedom: Black Sovereignty.* New York: SUNY Press, 1 n.1.

17. Ibid.

18. To date: Western Massachusetts, Chicago, DC, Houston, Portland, Seattle, Reykjavik, Buenos Aires, Valparaíso (Chile), Indianapolis and Bloomington (IN), Champaign (IL), Montreal, Boston, New York.

19. Liska (2017, 44).
20. Docampo (2018, 117).
21. See Peña (2019); Julie Taylor about violence within the códigos of the milonga more broadly as well. See Taylor, J. 2013. "Death Dressed as a Dancer: The Grotesque, Violence, and the Argentine Tango." *TDR* 57 (3): 117–31.
22. See e.g, Guillén, Marissa E. 2008. "The Performance of Tango: Gender, Power, and Role Playing." MA Thesis, Ohio University.
23. This is based both on personal experience with various organizers and teachers, as well as what is available via individuals' bios on their webpages or books. Notably, Docampo is emphatic in centering the lesbian experience in articulating alternative tango histories. Her approach is still via a non-trans specific lens.
24. Liska (2017, 132).
25. But see Docampo (2018); Groshek, Lou. 2019. "Avocation and Vocation: So You Want To 'Help' Queers Learn Tango . . ." https://lougroshek.com/posts/2019-06-12-help-queers-learn-tango/.
26. Some dancers may differ, but my definitions are as follows: an open role milonga is one wherein dancers are allowed/not discouraged from dancing the "opposite" role. An alternative milonga is one often focused on tango fusions, such that the traditional códigos are relaxed.
27. Liska cites heavily to Savigliano and Varela for histories of the rhetoric surrounding the regulation of tango and dance as exercise.
28. Tango was declared intangible cultural heritage in 2009. UNESCO noted that beyond the Rio Plata region, the dance spreads "the spirit of its community across the globe even as it adapts to new environments and changing time." United Nations Educational, Scientific and Cultural Organization. "Intangible Cultural Heritage: Tango." Accessed August 9, 2024. https://ich.unesco.org/en/lists.
29. Relmucao (2020) and Havmoeller, Birthe, Ray Batchelor, and Olaya Aramo (2018). *The Queer Tango Book: Ideas, Images and Inspiration in the 21st Century*. Queertangobook.org identify the first Queer Tango Festival as one organized in Hamburg by German dancers in 2001, Docampo emphasizes that only in Buenos Aires was "la potencia que podía hacer de la movida del tango queer un fenómeno que irradiara hacia todas partes y transformara incluso el circuito tanguero tradicional con fuego modernizador" (81).
30. Scholars such as Batchelor, however, caution that homosocial/sexual readings are not the only possibility available in of same-sex tango imagery. Batchelor, Ray. 2016. "Queer Tango's 'Image Problem': Men, Intimacy and Pictures from the Past." Delivered at Pomona College, SDHS + CORD Conference, November 3–6, 2016. https://www.academia.edu/30995057/Queer_Tangos_Image_Problem_Men_Intimacy_and_Pictures_from_the_Past.
31. Tango queer is stylistically closer to tango milonguero. For a comparison of American or International tango and Argentine tango, see Lee, Szewai. 2015. "What Is Tango? What Are the Differences between Argentine and American

Tango?" Duetdancestudio.com, July 3, 2015. https://duetdancestudio.com/blog-dance-lessons-chicago/what-is-tango-what-are-the-differences-between-american-and-argentine-tango.

32. Theorists like Sayak Valencia have differentiated between "queer" and "cuir," identifying related but distinct political valences and epistemological roots, where cuir "invokes a space of decolonialized enunciation, at once playful and critical." This, as well as other conversations around gender-neutral pronouns and inclusive and politicized language to describe non-cis-hetero identities in Spanish directly combat assertions of the foreign nature of queer explorations of cultural forms. See also Trujillo, Valentina. 2019. "Cuir: pistas para la construcción de una historia transfeminista en América Latina." *HJCK* (blog), January 8, 2019. https://hjck.com/reportajes/transfeminismoencolombia/.

33. While tango has its *roots* in Argentina, it has been travelled widely; its history is mythologized and romanticized, and the old guard is always upset about the "real tango." Transnational relationships have helped tango survive, particularly during times of great censorship during the military dictatorship that suppressed tango communities. Zapata, Mariana. 2016. "Rock 'n' Roll and Military Dictatorships Almost Destroyed Argentine Tango." *Atlas Obscura*, December 7, 2016. http://www.atlasobscura.com/articles/rock-n-roll-and-military-dictatorships-almost-destroyed-argentine-tango; Karush (2012).

34. E.g, Tobin, Jeffrey. 1998. "Tango and the Scandal of Homosocial Desire." In *The Passion of Music and Dance: Body, Gender and Sexuality*, edited by William Washabaugh, 79–102. New York: Berg Publishing; Goldhill, Olivia. 2016. "The History of the Tango Is Actually Kind of Gay." *Quartz*, August 13, 2016. https://qz.com/757223/the-history-of-the-tango-is-actually-kind-of-gay/. See de Robertis, Carolina. *Gods of Tango*. New York: Knopf, 2016 for a fictionalized historical possibility.

35. Docampo (2018, 101).

36. Liska (2017, 99).

37. MFT started organizing at least in part in response to Ni Una Menos protests and organizing around legal abortion. These movements around bodily autonomy though often framed in the context of cisgender women's bodies are intimately interrelated with the rights of other LGBTI individuals. See Peña, Milciades. 2019. "Tango sin violencia machista." *Megafón*, August 20, 2019. https://www.megafonunla.com.ar/notas/2019-08-20_tango-sin-violencia-machista; and Peña, Milciades. 2019. "Milongas sin machismo." *Megafón*, June 25, 2019. https://megafonunla.com.ar/notas/2019-06-25_milongas-sin-machismo.

38. Docampo (2018, 89).

39. Ibid.

40. Ibid.

41. Liska (2017, 133).

42. Liska (2017, 63).

43. Docampo (2018, 86).
44. One of the conversations I frequently have with followers, especially women, is about discomfort in the abrazo of certain (almost always) male leaders. These discussions echo many of the conversations that I led as a peer sex educator in college, as well as the conversations arising in queer kinky communities.
45. Muñoz (2019, 67).
46. Rivera-Servera (2012, 8).
47. Influenced by the fact that I attended a historically women's college, where than 90 percent of the class were women. In the words of my teacher, "If you want to dance, you have to learn both parts!"
48. It would be fascinating to trace the ways that language shapes pedagogy: what techniques are available through the vagaries in English that are not available in Spanish due to linguistic gender?
49. That being said, many leaders have told me this isn't true and is a surefire way to "ruin" a follower because then "she won't do either well."
50. There is often a stark difference in the expectations of gender between show tango versus other varieties, but here I am specifically referencing analyses of open role milongas, queer milongas, and tango milonguero.
51. Groups like MFT *are* questioning the rigidity of gender at milongas and within tango more generally. They have some of the more trans-inclusive rhetoric that I have encountered in digital tango spaces, but it is unclear if trans and GNC voices are being centered in any of these conversations.
52. In an ideal world, I would have conversations with dozens of trans and nonbinary dancers, and we would dream our queerest, loveliest milonga. Unfortunately, COVID-19 has largely disrupted social dance communities. Even before the pandemic, and now that milongas are starting to come back, there seems to be a severe dearth of trans and nonbinary dancers that could be explained in part by (1) a lack of disposable income for those who may otherwise have an interest in learning and (2) the cisheteronormative frameworks of many intro-level tango classes.
53. Dance teachers have emphasized this over the years: if you are not what people expect as a leader, you must be able to prove that you are that much better to even be considered capable.
54. meredith, celia. 2021. *Soñad-/despiert- contigo:: day(dreaming) of you*. Performance in Bloomington, IN, 2021.
55. Muñoz (2019, 97).
56. Liska (2017, 136).
57. Rivera-Servera (2012, 27).
58. Docampo (2018, 22).
59. Muñoz (2019, 81).
60. Ibid.
61. This happened in January 2015 at a milonga I attended at the behest of a roommate. Needless to say, I never returned to that milonga.

62. This connection can be at the physical level, like comfort in the abrazo and a sense of balance, but can also continue along an emotional spectrum.

63. See Docampo (2018, 22).

64. Rivera-Servera (2012, 35), citing Jill Dolan.

65. Chambers-Letson, Joshua. 2018. *After the Party: A Manifesto for Queer of Color Life*. New York: New York University Press, xxi.

66. Docampo (2018, 19).

67. "There's no other place where I can feel what I feel when I dance here. It is like being myself, but being it in such a beautiful way. . . . Tango is a passion you could only understand when dancing, and dancing it in full freedom is a way of reaching the best expression of myself." Relmucao (2020).

celia meredith (they/elle) holds a JD/MA from Indiana University Bloomington. They are a graduate of Smith College, where they studied Latin American Studies and Sociology.

IV
PERFORMING COMMUNITY, SITUATING DISSENT

11

Performing Together
Rethinking Definitions of Performance as Participatory Practice

KATHERINE BORLAND

In this essay, I explore the emergent dimensions of performance through a review of foundational texts in engaged theater and dance. By way of Richard Schechner's early theorizing, I center the contributions of Augusto Boal, Liz Lerman, their fellow travelers, and their successors. Practice-based insights offer a way to address the operations of social inequality in performance, which has been undertheorized in folklore scholarship. Approaching performance as behavior rather than as a way of speaking, I identify a challenge to the centrality of traditional mastery and heightened self-consciousness in current folkloristic definitions of performance by taking embodied, participatory group practices as my emblematic forms. I place my own adventures in collaborative dance and theater-making in dialogue with the contributions of artists and teachers who have developed a powerful set of techniques to train ordinary people in alternative world making. Engaged artists offer a compelling lens for understanding emergence as arising from a responsive thinking body operating outside of ingrained habit. How might folklorists draw on these insights to produce ethnographies of sensory responsiveness that attend to relations of power?

The foundational text for considerations of performance in folklore studies is, of course, Richard Bauman's (1977) synthesizing essay, "Verbal Art as Performance." As he emphasized in his introduction, Bauman restricted his focus to spoken art in a field that encompasses a vast array of verbal and nonverbal forms. Subsequently, Bauman suggested that theories of verbal art might be applied successfully to other expressive domains of interest to folklorists. Indeed, he enlarged the scope of performance analysis to include three spheres of communication: the face-to-face, public display events, and mediated forms, applying his language-based understanding to these spheres (1989). As Abrahams

(1981), Stoeltje and Bauman (1988), and others explored large-scale display events, for instance, they described them in verbal terms as either shouting matches among groups organized by their difference or collective statements of a group's values (see also Turner 1986). Retrospectively, Bauman regarded his focus on the performance event as a weakness in his theorization because it bracketed out "larger social formations of power and authority" (2002, 95). Nevertheless, he continued to assert that a focus on the performer's interactional power was a necessary corrective to an anthropological and folkloristic tendency to disregard the individual's active role in shaping tradition. This approach bracketed out unequal access to interactional authority within the traditions folklorists study, as Sawin (2002), focusing on gender, and Noyes (1995), focusing on ethnicity and gender, have described.

Subsequent folkloristic theorizations of performance have expanded the notion of performance to include the somatic, kinesthetic, and sensual elements that accompany "ways of speaking," pointing to affective as well as linguistic forms of persuasion (Kapchan 1995). They have pointed out that performers manage their own attention—toward their aesthetic practice, toward their bodies, toward co-performers, toward their audience, toward other unrelated thoughts and emotions—according to specific ideologies of attention given by the genre within which they are working (Berger and del Negro, 2002). Together, these statements demonstrate a trajectory that, beginning with a consideration of situated speech, has increasingly engaged with embodied forms of cultural expression. What remains constant in these definitions is the distinctive roles of performers and audience, the performer's heightened self-consciousness as a central marker of performance, a focus on individual virtuosity, and a tendency, even when acknowledging intersubjective dynamics, to view the singular performer as having the power as well as the responsibility to define the situation as performance and not some other kind of communicative interaction.

Meanwhile, theater scholar Richard Schechner (2004) was developing a broad-spectrum approach to performance studies in order to expand the Eurocentric, text-based orientation prevalent in theater studies of the 1970s to include a global diversity of practices that anthropologists such as Victor Turner were already documenting.[1] Schechner recognized performance as a mode of behavior that ranged from the most routine and quotidian to the most elaborated and institutionally sanctioned. As someone who had been director of the Performance Group, an avant-garde theater company in New York, he brought a practitioner's sensibility to his theorizing. In his wide-ranging essay "Restoration of Behavior," Schechner introduced the idea that performances of many kinds—rituals, dramas, gestures, dances—are made up of strips of behavior removed from their originating context and rearranged through a process of rehearsal to produce something new. For Schechner, performance entails a movement from the world as we encounter it to a world of possibility, from the indicative to the subjunctive mood (1985b). He offers an alternative way to understand the vast array of performance forms that folklorists label customary practices as primarily modes of behavior rather than ways of speaking.

Moreover, Schechner's practice-based, comparative approach recognizes a sequence of cross-culturally identifiable stages, including training, workshops, rehearsals, warm-ups, the performance, the cooldown, and post-performance routines, all of which constitute a particular performance complex (1985a, 99). In contrast to the theory of performance based on verbal art, Schechner recognizes emergence more as a feature of the process-oriented, liminal pre-performance stages of the complex than of the performance itself (1986, 8). Recognizing the somewhat chaotic aspects of rehearsal, he says, "The process of collecting and discarding, of selecting, organizing, and showing are what rehearsals are all about. And it's not such a rational, logical-linear process as writing about it makes it seem. It's not so much a thought-out system of trial and error as it is a playing around with themes, actions, gestures, fantasies, words: whatever's being worked on" (1985a, 120). For Schechner, then, trying things out seems more a doing than a thinking-through. I will return to this distinction later. Moreover, in his cross-cultural explorations, Schechner emphasizes the ways that many non-Western theater traditions rely on long periods of physical training in order to transmit a performance text across generations. Almost offhandedly, he remarks that training with a group is easier both mentally and physically than training directly with a master (1985a, 229). Taken together, these observations point to the importance of embodied group practices both to the emergent aspects of performance and to building expressive competence in a cultural form.

Although the spontaneous coming together of unique circumstances among performers and audiences in the moment of performance may constitute an opportunity for emergence, I argue with Schechner that rehearsals offer greater flexibility for trying things out and thinking, feeling, and acting in a subjunctive mood. Moreover, understanding performance as part of a larger complex rather than a singular breakthrough allows for the development of tools that can democratize access to performing for groups whose speech/expression has been traditionally circumscribed. Schechner's theory is relevant to staged cultural performances—plays in the Western context, rituals and theatrical forms across Asia—as well as to participatory forms, such as workshops, jams, pickup games, protests, and countless other ad hoc gatherings.

In 1989, Schechner invited Brazilian-born theater activist Augusto Boal to conduct a series of workshops in New York. Early in his career, Boal had moved away from stage- and text-based traditions, in which the playwright and director control and contain the dramatic action, toward shared authority with an audience to stimulate social and personal transformation. Adapting his countryman Paolo Freire's ([1967] 1970) popular education model, Boal's "theatre of the oppressed" ([1974] 1993) blurs the lines between trained artists and community members, creating spaces for ordinary individuals to explore and then act on their creative problem-solving potential. Moreover, Boal regards the theatrical frame as a rehearsal for action in the world (1995, 44). In Paris, where Boal established himself in exile, he provided flexible principles and exercises not only for a growing number of socially and politically engaged theater projects and programs (see Cohen-Cruz 1990, 2010; Schutzman 1990) but also for theater training more generally. Over the past half century, Boal's methods have been folded into a rich and varied constellation of devised or collaborative theater-making that extends well beyond the specific methods of theater of the oppressed (Heddon and Milling 2006).

Practice-based understandings of performance push against the idea that verbal expression provides the template for other kinds of performances. As Solimar Otero (2022) notes of Latinx queer and women's theories of performance, dance and ritual enactments are modes of rematerializing what has heretofore been understood as ephemeral in a persistent remaking of community. And as Regina Bendix has suggested (2000), the focus on textualizing spoken language that folklore inherited from the ethnography of speaking paradoxically erases the expressive force that initially attracted researchers/documenters to a given performance, privileging verbal content over the multifaceted sensory experience of expressive activity. Bendix's call for an ethnography of listening turns attention away from the performer to consider the responsive audience.

Theorizing from practice similarly moves our focus away from individual virtuosity toward ensemble processes, play, and internal kinesthetic, body-centered ways of knowing. It encourages a rethinking of the performer-audience relationship as well as our understanding of when and how emergence occurs. Dance scholar Susan Leigh Foster recognizes a range of possible thought/action relations governing emergent performances: "Improvisation involves moments where one thinks in advance of what one is going to do, other moments where actions seem to move faster than they can be registered in full analytic consciousness of them, and still other moments where one thinks the idea of what is to come at exactly the same moment that one performs that idea" (2003, 7). In this way, Foster asserts the possibility of bodily as well as cognitive intention, which is not the same thing as losing oneself in experience. In what follows, I combine a survey of a small portion of the voluminous literature in community theater and dance studies with my own experiments in practice in Columbus, Ohio, to explore what we learn about expressive culture from those who teach improvisation to ordinary people. Thinking through movement, as one recent anthology claims, forces us to rethink our traditional assumptions about knowledge and meaning (Bunker, Pakes, and Rowell 2013). Moreover, thinking about how those who lack both virtuosity and social standing might successfully improvise affecting performances may help shift entrenched hierarchies among performers and between performers and their audiences within any given performance tradition.

Self-Consciousness

Definitions of performance deriving from the ethnography of speaking reiterate the performer's self-conscious, reflexive stance. If we turn our attention from the highly skilled to the inexpert, however, we find that self-consciousness is a barrier to rather than a sign of expressive accomplishment. Indeed, Boal and his many adapters recognize the importance of deactivating self-consciousness through a series of ensemble-building exercises. In his early work with socially marginalized communities in Brazil and Argentina, Boal developed a flexible format that starts with the body rather than language as the primary means of expression. A physical warm-up allows people to sink into their bodies. Games establish a sense of play and informality, encourage cooperation, build trust, and reduce inhibitions, all of which provide the foundation for the creation of an ensemble. Boal's Image Theatre challenges the ensemble to build visual metaphors with their bodies, playing with stillness and motion, sometimes adding sound. Forum Theatre and Invisible Theatre return to language, offering skits of everyday forms of oppression and inviting audience members to stop the action, intervene, and change the course of events.

In his writing and interviews, Boal credits the forms of theatrical devising that he has popularized globally to his own interchanges with spect-actors, audience members who have shown him the way from theatrically dictating toward a more engaged, dialogic, and inclusive process.[2] Yet he takes the power of theater a step further by asserting, "If the oppressed-artist is able to create an autonomous world of images of his own reality, and to enact his liberation in the reality of these images, he will then extrapolate into his own life all that he has accomplished in the fiction. The scene, the stage, becomes the rehearsal space for real life" (1995, 44). By introducing the idea of oppression, Boal introduces an imperative for change to the status quo. He asserts, "Every oppressed person is a subjugated subversive" (1995, 42). In Boal's terminology, his submission is his Cop in the Head; the objectives of theater of the oppressed are to make submission disappear and to cultivate the subversive quality of the spect-actor instead. This self-liberation extends beyond the individual, Boal argues, because, when an oppressed person becomes an artist and produces images of real life, those images become extrapersonalized symbols of larger social issues. And in this way, the artist belongs both to the world of her experience and to the world of her creation (Boal and Epstein 1990a).

Critics respond that theater of the oppressed techniques do not necessarily result in critical awareness of injustice and a commitment to fight oppression among ordinary participants. Boal himself reports on a case of Invisible Theatre gone awry, when actors used the form to create division and violate the trust of the ensemble (Boal and Epstein 1990b). Reporting on a Chinese experiment in community theater, Shen Liang (2014) notes her rural spect-actors preferred constructing fantasies to critiques. On the other hand, Mady Schutzman (1990) argues that measuring the efficacy of Boal's methods by the quantity of political activism they generate misses the point. In a first-world context they have been adapted to many purposes, not least of which is the recognition of one's experiences of oppression and privilege regardless of the social category to which the actor belongs. She concludes, "Boal insists that theatre of the oppressed does not open any doors. Its techniques are weapons requiring subjects to implement them, to extrapolate them for real life, whether one defines real life in therapeutic or political terms" (82). Turning to the evidence of experience, I offer an account of moderate successes in cultivating improvisational, emergent practices among ordinary people in Columbus.

Devising in Columbus, Ohio

For three spring terms between 2018 and 2020, Be the Street,[3] an engaged community devising project at Ohio State University, developed diverse performance ensembles in the economically distressed Hilltop neighborhood of Columbus, Ohio. With the help of visiting theater directors, our faculty trained students in methods of community devising and recruited community groups for them to work with.[4] Community devising is a mode of making performance with nonprofessional actors and movers, drawing on the ideas, experiences, and capabilities of the group. With roots in oppositional politics, state-funded "community improvement" schemes, and university outreach efforts, and sometimes involving professional theater companies, the approach prioritizes participation as a means of building community and often emphasizes process over product (Heddon and Milling 2006, 130–56). For Be the Street, students and community participants built performances around personal and neighborhood experiences until the COVID-19 pandemic forced us to abandon in-person gatherings.[5]

Of the five groups we organized during the first year of the project, I worked most closely with graduate students Katherine Moore (dance) and Tessa Jacobs (folklore), who offered twelve creative movement workshops to seniors at the Hilltop YMCA. My role was that of an enthusiastic participant. Many of the seniors I met in Tessa and Katherine's class—Debbie and George, Liz and Dennis, Patty—continued to participate in the third iteration of Be the Street's Still Moving ensemble with student devisers Michaela Nield and Hannah Griswold in 2020. That year, they were joined by Judy and Nel. A handful of others joined and left the group. One early participant, Annette, passed away.

In the 2018 iteration of Still Moving, Katherine led a twenty-minute warm-up to popular music from the 1960s of arms, legs, head, fingers, and trunk, all performed seated in chairs so that no one was disadvantaged.[6] Then Tessa asked each participant to introduce themselves by stating their name and offering a personal gesture that described how they were feeling in that moment. The whole group repeated the name and gesture before the next person introduced themselves. Next the group stood to play a theater game where a participant introduces an imaginary object, explores it, and then passes it along to the next person, who is free to transform it, making it grow or shrink, grow heavy or light, or change its shape entirely before passing it on to the next person.[7] This game mitigates the kind of debilitating self-consciousness that blocks exploration by displacing the focus of attention to the (non)object. Each session of Still Moving built gradually in this way, using short, low-risk exercises to establish a shared repertoire and to create an atmosphere conducive to exploration and experimentation.

To interrupt the tendency for participants to default to verbally describing and explaining their intentions, facilitators offered representational puzzles or challenges. In this way, they privileged showing over telling, demonstration over explanation, doing over describing. In the 2020 workshops, for example, Michaela and Hannah asked each member of their group to depict an adjective as they walked across the room. Dennis, a tall, square-shouldered eighty-year-old, received the word *frozen*. He began walking with his hands hugging his chest, shivering, but in the middle of his journey he changed his strategy entirely. Stretching arms out and down to their full length, he teetered on unbending legs in a stiff triangular shape. Nel, somewhat younger and more agile, followed with a lively invocation of *purple*. Arms, legs, and torso akimbo, her body prickled as she hopped gingerly along an irregular path. In both these cases, the participants abandoned an imitative representational strategy to create a novel movement sequence. Those observing appreciated how surprising and surprisingly effective they were in our postexercise debriefing conversation.

Contrasting with these visually and emotionally striking improvisations were moments of frustration, when novice devisers found themselves unable to move participants toward greater experimentation and risk taking. For instance, several weeks into the 2020 workshop, Michaela and Hannah introduced an exercise based on creating an alternative alphabet of random sounds—a slap, a wheeze, a laugh, a sigh—for letters. After our group generated twenty-six sounds, we had five minutes to spell our names using our new alphabet. Participants worked at the exercise for about a minute and then fell silent. Hannah let us know we had four more minutes of rehearsal time left to try things out. She suggested that if someone had two of the same letter in their name, they might vary the sound they were using. George picked up on this suggestion, varying his dog bark for G. Dennis remained silent, waiting for the sharing. As an enthusiastic participant, I began to feel tired. I realized I'd fallen into repeating my first effort, as my two immediate neighbors, Nel and Liz, were doing. When the sharing finally arrived, everyone's offering provoked hearty laughter. A success from the perspective of group enjoyment, the session underscored participants' tendency to do the first thing that came into their heads and stop. As the weeks progressed, facilitators confronted these limitations, and they were inspired by flashes of improvisational beauty. From this material, they built a set of improvisatory activities for the culminating performance. That performance, while somewhat more choreographed than the workshops, offered a review of the participants' weeks of improvisatory work woven into a set of audience-participation exercises.

Admittedly, most of the repertoire our groups developed lacked overt attempts to overcome specific forms of oppression and thus would not support Boal's claim that the theatrical production is a rehearsal for revolution. As Mady Schutzman (1990) explains, the politically repressive Latin American context within which Boal developed his techniques resulted in a strong connection between theater and revolutionary action that does not translate to the neoliberal first world settings within which many subsequent devisers work. Indeed, the effects on participants of interventionist devising are not always obvious. Heddon and Milling remark, "It can be difficult to assess sometimes whether this change leads the community or individual to resist the status quo or conform more effectively to mainstream demands" (2006, 137).[8] In the case of our Hilltop engagement, within the context of a declining neighborhood, which is often represented in the news as crime- and drug-ridden, our participants constructed an alternate portrait of the people living on the Hilltop. Whereas the older group I primarily worked with were nostalgic in their approach, a group of teenagers tackled themes of bullying and everyday violence, and our Spanish-speaking group explored the complex meanings of home for recently arrived immigrants. Moreover, when the groups came together to share their work in a culminating event, they recognized and acknowledged the sharing as a rare opportunity to convene across differences of age and language that otherwise kept them apart.

In her thoughtful survey, which introduces a variety of models—Brecht, Boal, Kushner, Appalshop, Animating Democracy Initiative, and others—Jan Cohen-Cruz dubs US engaged theater a practice of call-and-response (2010). She states, "By whatever language, engaged art is characterized by a high level of participation, whether in early phases of researching and building the artwork, in the presentation phase, or in activities following, and often in all three. For people frequently get more out of making art than seeing the fruits of other people's creativity" (175). This focus on process over product fits well with the work that the Be the Street team was able to accomplish during our limited community engagement with a shifting group of faculty and student devisers.

Movement Training

A similar exploratory dynamic prevails at the Perennial Movement Group classes, where participants over fifty have been gathering up to three times a week since 2015 to study contemporary dance with Sarah Ramey and Chloe Napoletano.[9] However, in the dance studio, older dancers must negotiate a primary source of self-consciousness: the mirror. Their bodies don't meet the long, lean, and flexible dancer ideal; their range and speed of motion are restricted to varying degrees. After a particularly challenging class, Ken, Kathy, and Mark jointly expressed their frustration at not being able to learn the sequence of movements their twentysomething teacher, Chloe, had been modeling. Part of the problem, they recognized, was a physical disorientation they experienced during the multiple directional shifts the sequence required. Another part involved memory, as the sequence was longer than usual. This mutually felt frustration allowed us to consider the focus of attention in the class. Although different dancers expressed different tendencies in this regard, we learned that we all avoided looking at ourselves in the mirror. Kathy said she looked at other people "to see if someone else is figuring it out. . . . And I also see that other people are not getting it, so I'm not the only one. And that's really helpful. And then we can laugh at ourselves."[10] Interestingly, she looks to her cohort for both guidance and reassurance. Mark admitted he had been looking at me. Surprised, I said, "I didn't know what I was doing." Kathy said, "You seemed to be a lot freer." What is important to underscore here is that even when a participant (me, in this example) is in the throes of a disorienting experience of lack of mastery, others may recognize some measure of skillfulness.[11] In other words, in group practices such as these, what the audience perceives and appreciates is sometimes hidden from the performer's perception.

Building on Sara Ahmed's (2006) observation that occasional disorientation offers an opportunity to question stable identities and principles, dance scholar Ann Cooper Albright identifies physical, emotional, and psychic disorientation as "opportunities to rethink our habitual ways of being in the world" (2019, 50). Engaging in forms of spatial disorientation requires "the willingness to feel awkward and lost without undue anxiety" (66). This, in turn, Albright contends, builds psychic resilience for subjects confronting an increasingly unstable world. Getting comfortable with disorientation, then, helps us engage in emergent processes.

Returning to our studio discussion, Ken shared that he was mostly internally focused. Echoing Kathy, he explained, "If I look in the mirror, I'm not looking at myself, but I'm looking to see how other people are making that particular move." As someone who has extensive dance training and has watched a lot of dance, then eighty-year-old Ken considers himself to have a discriminating eye. He confides, "I'm kind of picky about sort of admiring people that do things that look just great, and I see flares of that in everybody in our class. Certain moves. I don't know, just seeing that is really satisfying to me." These comments eloquently demonstrate two interacting principles of participatory performance. First, performers in these settings simultaneously adopt an audience perspective, evaluating those around them. Second, as participating spectators, they discover moments of beauty in other people's movements. Experiencing those moments is one reason they return to the class week after week, year after year. This feature of participatory performance blurs the distinction between performer and audience, leader and follower, as well as experience (the internal somatic sensation of movement) and representation (what others see/interpret in the dancers' movements).[12] As such, it requires a rethinking of our theoretical models of performance, at least in the case of participatory group behavior, toward more dialogic, harmonizing, call-and-response models of communicative activity.

Sarah and Chloe's instructional practice intentionally broadens the idea of who counts as a dancer, an inclusive notion derived from Liz Lerman's pioneering dance classes for residents of DC-area retirement communities in the 1970s (1984). Lerman recognized that dance offered a great deal more than physical conditioning to her elderly students. It improved brain function as well as balance, and it provided a respite from social isolation (see also Cooper and Thomas 2002). Over time, though, Lerman recognized an expressive force in the older dancers rooted in their life experience that younger, more virtuosic dancers lacked.[13] She made it her mission to teach audiences to see and appreciate the range of human expressivity in movement by forming a generationally integrated company, Liz Lerman Dance Exchange. Years later, reflecting on her life's work, Lerman (2014) introduced the concept of hiking the horizontal, of viewing art making as a spectrum of practices, from the most socially embedded to the most abstract and detached, and regarding none as more valuable or important than another. This perspective challenges the commonly accepted notion that high social impact means low artistic value and high artistic achievement means low social relevance.[14]

Sarah, who had danced in Lerman's company from 2007 to 2013, brought those ideas to Columbus. Initially, she marketed Perennial Movement Group to her sponsors as a holistic health intervention for seniors, an hour-long modern dance class followed by a half hour of socializing twice a week. She subsequently recruited Chloe in 2017 through a service-learning class she was teaching at Ohio State. They are the instructors of record, but after the initial grant ran out, they continued as volunteers until an invitation to relocate to BalletMet offered a modicum of financial stability. Much of our interview revolved around the way the dance group had changed as a result of different funding models. Whereas Sarah and Chloe were, in 2019, happy to be working as paid employees of Columbus BalletMet and recognized additional advantages to being part of this institution, they regretted the fact that their Perennial Movement Group dancers were less diverse in terms of economic status, physical ability, and racial background. The absence of transportation, which had been provided in the early days of the program, when it met at a neighborhood church, meant that only the more affluent and mobile seniors could continue attending.

The COVID-19 epidemic shut down in-person arts programs and forced Chloe and Sarah to return to voluntary, donation-based instruction, which they provided over YouTube, over Zoom, and, weather permitting, at a local park.[15] Although it is important for Chloe and Sarah to be able to make a living, they recognize that working with the Perennial Movement Group has a special quality. The half hour of socializing after class is an unusual feature that has led to strong social bonding among participants. Sarah points out that this coffee klatch right out in the lobby also suggests to the younger dancers hurrying past that dancing can be a lifelong pursuit, and in that way it shifts the prevailing narrative around dance training as a practice for limber, youthful, fit bodies. But Sarah and Chloe simultaneously regard the classes as a space for their creative experimentation. Chloe explains, "How do I bring my interests into the room? If it's only for the people you're teaching, I find that's exhaustive, and not sustainable for like a career. So what are my interests? And how am I getting—it's a collaboration. How do I stay true to my values and needs and interests while staying, while listening really deeply to what the class needs and interests are? How do they intersect or diverge? I know about body alignment, compositional tools, but I'm teaching people who have three times as much life as me." Chloe's investment in her own creative process as well as her recognition that her students are sources of knowledge make the classes something more than an instructional delivery system.

Then seventy-six-year-old Maureen tears up when she attempts to describe why she returns year after year to the classes. During her childhood, Maureen had had several years of classical ballet training, but she'd had to let it go when her then fifteen-year-old body failed to develop into that required of a ballerina. Over her lifetime, she intermittently participated in several kinds of community dance—square dancing, Israeli and Greek dancing, European folk dancing, free-form improv—all of which she enjoyed. The Perennial Movement Group offers a kind of mental and physical stretching that she finds addictive. She says, "It gives me as much, just plain joy. All you have to do is show up and be open. That's all you have to do. And they, Sarah and Chloe and the rest of the students, just do the rest." Resonating with other participants' observations, Maureen's response recognizes the group as both a support and an inspiration for exploratory improvisation. Although Chloe and Sarah are the movement experts, they rarely extract themselves from the practice to observe what their students are doing, as is common in formal dance pedagogy. Sarah and Chloe describe this as an accommodation to older dancers' great difficulty with remembering sequences, but that decision heightens the participatory nature of the class, of doing things together.

Maureen still feels she should be able to draw on her early dance training more, and she frets about losing her physical ability to, for instance, participate in floorwork. Nevertheless, she constantly circles back to the heightened expressive experience the classes provide: "And I think that's unusual at this point, you know. It's not your average senior center. It's not classified. I don't even think about my age really, especially when our teacher is in her twenties. You don't think about anything. I get sort of transformed or transfixed into some other, you know, maybe it's a meditative state. I do. And that doesn't happen in that many places. It's just pure, it's just pure joy [tears up again]." In summing up her experience, Maureen strongly asserts the possibility that the nonexpert dancer enters something akin to flow (Nakamura and Csíkszentmihályi 2002) by taking up a kinesthetic challenge that requires intense mental and physical focus on the one hand and witnessing/borrowing other participants' movements on the other.

Perennial Movement Group had one formal performance in 2019, which both participants and facilitators remember fondly. However, when I interviewed them in fall 2019 and winter 2020, many commented that the work of rehearsing for that performance had been quite rigorous, and they were happy to continue with classes without any expectation of developing a performance to share with a public. Sarah and Chloe concurred. Their lives had become busier, so they were less inclined to put in the extra time to develop a formal performance that would showcase their dancers. Nevertheless, the group's longevity has prompted Chloe to expand their reach. She devised a second performance score with her dancers that included both movement and storytelling in 2021–22 that they performed at senior living facilities in and around Columbus and at local dance reviews.[16]

Disrupting Habitual Patterns

In participatory models of community theater and dance, disorientation and doing things together provide potent opportunities to break habitual patterns and improvise toward performances that have expressive force. The students who facilitated Be the Street represented a mix of artists and scholars, most of whom had no prior community-based devising experience. In order to jumpstart their process, our semester began with an intensive weekend training, provided in 2020 by members of Teatro Travieso (Jimmy Noriega, director; Aviva Neff and Janna Haywood, company members). Our trainers followed Boal's format of playing games to warm up, building ensemble and strengthening trust, using movement to collaboratively build compelling metaphors, and ultimately trying things out and telling stories. On the final day, our facilitators asked us to reconvene in groups of five with a set of five objects and a thematic focus. My group chose travel. We were given several parameters: we had to "quote" a performance that had already emerged during the weekend: a phrase, a movement, an exercise. We had to perform squats. We needed three monologues. We had to use our objects. The facilitators barked out other stipulations, too many to keep in our heads.

The five of us convened with our random collection of props. We had many ideas, many directions to head in. But the clock was ticking. We had one hour to create a five-minute performance. After fifteen minutes of talking without deciding, nervous about our time, we jumped into trying things out. Initiative moved fluidly among the group. We started with one idea and worked in an additive fashion. We circled back, revised, went in a different direction. We lined up. We tried a sequence. We modified. Someone came in and told us we had fifteen minutes left. We had our story. We had some interesting choreography. We hadn't constructed our monologues, but we didn't have time, so we picked three people. "You, come up with something to say here." And then it was time. The final performance? Maybe we didn't have quite five minutes of material; maybe we hadn't addressed all the requirements. We were strong on plot and symbol, weak on dialogue. But we had a unified vision and some interesting formations. In short, five people with very different initial ideas had managed to make something that hung together in interesting ways.

If I were to analyze how we had accomplished our goal, I would begin with the idea that the time pressure disrupted the tendency to solidify a social structure within the group and allowed for the possibility of nonhierarchical interactions and shared authority. The impossible task format of the exercise—too many stipulations and not enough time—provoked the kind of productive frustration/disorientation necessary for thinking and acting outside of our habitual patterns. It also forced us to abandon planning as a verbal exchange of ideas in favor of an embodied cocreation or doing things together. As in the Still Moving and Perennial Movement Group classes, we became observant participants, each offering our ideas while simultaneously watching for moments of beauty, insight, and surprise in what others offered. Recognizing what worked, we borrowed from our neighbors, as Chloe admonishes her dancers to do.

Taken together, these vignettes of improvisational practice in workshops and classes reveal a set of practical tools for making performance among differently abled, differently trained individuals. After creating the conditions for a group process by building ensemble, they disrupt ordinary patterns of behavior and interaction in order to activate an embodied, collaborative sensing/thinking. The group is both the performer of and audience for its own creative process. Schechner identifies the psychic state of performing as an awareness of being simultaneously not me (an other) and not not me (the self) (1985b, 110). Participatory practices share in this enhanced sense of identity by combining the *I* and *we* experience. To be clear, the *I* does not dissolve into a *we*; participants inhabit both identifications simultaneously. This double awareness may produce a heightened sense of efficacy even for nonexperts.

Returning to consider the definition of participatory practice as performance, we can highlight several features that contrast with Bauman's [1977] 1984 definition of performance as verbal art. First, particularly when working with untrained participants, the goal of participatory practice is to disable self-consciousness in order to facilitate the play of embodied ideas. Second, the practice dissolves the boundary between performer and audience as participants work to cultivate responsiveness to the thought-actions of others. Rather than locating virtuosity in a singular performer, spect-actors recognize expressive power as distributed across the participating ensemble. Finally, while the work can be harnessed toward external audiences and purposes, it retains a strong intrinsic value—provoking laughter, wonder, appreciation, even joy—among the bungling, disorienting, at times frustrating, and half-baked qualities that are equally part of the experience.

Conclusion

In this review of practice-informed theory, I have worked to decenter verbal art as emblematic of performance in general. In doing so, I challenge a long-standing scholarly elevation of language over other forms of meaning making. Following Schechner, I expand the folklorist's object of analysis to include all aspects of a performance complex, particularly the participatory, doing-things-together rehearsal stage. Indeed, my ethnographic examples are gathered from the rehearsal-like spaces of workshops and classes that participants, including myself, find intrinsically valuable, even when they don't result in full-blown displays of virtuosity. Drawing on the work of Boal, Lerman, and others, I have argued for greater consideration of embodied practices as a place to intervene in and democratize the creative process. Because folklorists have generally taken a diversity of creative expression among ordinary people as a given, the barriers to performance inherent in historical and existing gender hierarchies and other deeply embedded forms of social inequality have remained undertheorized. One might argue that Boal and others embrace a deficit model when they identify a category of person as a nonactor. Yet by recognizing barriers to self-expression, they have developed a set of improvisational tools that have been taken up and productively used in multiple social spheres, from factories, refugee camps, and community centers to theater schools and companies. In the correlative field of contemporary dance, Liz Lerman has built an intergenerational company and in the process instructed audiences in new ways of perceiving bodily expressiveness.

Even the most utopian spaces for cultivating improvisation can reflect and sustain embedded hierarchies, if they remain unexamined. Wherever we find ourselves—at the university, in the community recreation center, or in the workshop studio—we must cultivate an ethnography not only of listening (Bendix 2000) but of heightened sensory responsiveness to performance occasions of all kinds, while at the same time remaining mindful of which individuals or groups in a given circumstance are licensed to perform their truth, which are hindered from doing so, and why. In her survey of engaged performance in the United States, Jan Cohen-Cruz (2010, 111–28) described a theater initiative, proposed by Richard Schechner, called Home-New Orleans to address post-Katrina gentrification. Given New Orleans's celebrated tradition of parades, Schechner initially wanted to bring in an outside artist of spectacle to lead the project. Cohen-Cruz, on the other hand, embraced a community consultation approach that ultimately led to the construction of a sustained local network of artists and community organizers. The results were perhaps less attention-grabbing, but the approach relied on local conditions and affordances to shape the work. Initiatives such as these can offer models to folklorists for how to move beyond documenting and analyzing the cultural traditions of ordinary people, whether from mainstream or marginalized communities, toward increasing those groups' creative worldmaking potential while at the same time broadening participation within and among groups. Responsiveness in this sense is not simply an analytic orientation toward performance practices but a commitment and obligation to extend opportunities for creative expression, whether or not these become a rehearsal for revolution.

Notes

1. For an account of Turner's early engagement with the performance frame, see his *From Ritual to Theatre* (1982). See also his posthumous collection, *The Anthropology of Performance* (1986).

2. One place to find these anecdotes is Taussig, Schechner, and Boal (1990, 56–57).

3. The name of our project was suggested by our principal investigator, Ana Puga. It references a charge that Bertolt Brecht made to Danish working-class actors in the mid-1930s: "Be the street, the underground, the shops. You should observe all the people there, strangers as if they were acquaintances, but acquaintances as if they were strangers to you." This project was generously supported by two Global Arts and Humanities Discovery Theme grants from the Ohio State University.

4. The faculty team included Ana Puga (Theatre and Spanish and Portuguese), Harmony Bench (Dance), Katherine Borland (Comparative Studies/Folklore), Elena Foulis (Spanish and Portuguese), Paloma Martínez-Cruz (Spanish and Portuguese), and Shilarna Stokes (Theatre). Dr. Stokes acted as instructor and artistic director in 2018. In 2019–21, Postdoctoral Scholar Moriah Flagler took over that role. In the first two years of the project, David Feiner, Maggie Popadiak, Stephanie Paul, and four students from the Albany Park Theatre Project, Carlos De Santiago, Maidenwena Alba, Ashlie Hankins, and Dayana Soto, facilitated the orientation workshops. In year three, members

of Teatro Travieso, Jimmy Noriega, Aviva Neff, and Janna Haywood, ran the orientation workshops.

5. For more on Be the Street and to watch group performances, visit our website: https://u.osu.edu/bethestreet.

6. For more on this approach to working with older adults, see Lerman (1984).

7. For more ideas on exercises for community theater ensembles, see Kerrigan (2001), Cohen-Cruz (2010), and Boal ([1992] 2002).

8. For a particularly complicated example of this difficulty, see Alicia J. Rouverol's (2005) report on incarcerated adults' life history dramatizations that are designed to instruct youth on the dangers of becoming involved in criminal activity. Although Rouverol describes the intervention as a success, the repressive context within which this work was accomplished (the prison) required that incarcerated individuals take personal responsibility for their actions without considering larger structural conditions that influenced their choices.

9. Perennial Movement Group began as In Motion, a grant-funded university engagement project in 2015, but it has become a much more rooted community of practice than Be the Street. As of this writing, a core group of older dancers continues to assemble twice a week for classes, and perform work at senior living centers.

10. All interviews of members of the Perennial Movement Group (formerly In Motion) were conducted in 2019–20 by the author for Be the Street at Ohio State University.

11. Theorizing from practice involves including oneself as part of the research, perhaps more than is customary in ethnography. In this work, I have endeavored to temper the impulse to posit my own experience as generalizable to the ensemble by listening carefully to what others say about what they are doing, experiencing, feeling, and reversing—in a sense, Diedre Sklar's (2000) imperative to engage kinesthetically in order to describe embodied practices. In the Perennial Movement Group, I was somewhat younger than the dancers who regularly attended the class, who were mostly well into retirement. This may account for their perception that I seemed "freer."

12. For an extended description of the different perspectives of experience and representation, and their relevance for raced, sexed, and differently abled dancers, see Albright (1997).

13. Certain forms of Japanese dance reverse the age prejudice in the Western tradition (Watanabe 2017). See also Schechner (1985a).

14. In addition to her choreographic interventions into the hierarchies of professional dance, Lerman developed an approach to offering feedback to dancers (or any other creator) that replaces critique with a method that centers the needs of the artist. This approach recognizes and seeks to ameliorate the emotional distress that being evaluated by others entails (Lerman and Borstel 2003).

15. In contrast, Be the Street was intermittent (spring term only) and was working with more transient communities (students, new immigrants, teens). After the COVID-19 shutdown, artistic director Moriah Flagler successfully translated our devising workshops to a Zoom format, but rather than reassembling our Hilltop ensembles online, these workshops were directed toward new audiences. By 2021, the engagement with communities had ended.

16. The group received a small grant from Be the Street to support this work. Having received a grant from the Columbus Arts Council in 2023, Sarah Ramey, Chloe Napoletano, John Giffin, and Crystal Michelle Perkings engaged in a yearlong cocreative process with an intergenerational group of dancers and performed "Glad You're Here" at the Columbus Performing Arts Center on May 03, 2024.

Interviews

All interviews were conducted by Katherine Borland, principal investigator, Be the Street. Contact the researcher for access/transcriptions: borland.19@osu.edu.

Interviewees

Kathy, Ken Vale, and Mark Metcalf (BalletMet postclass discussion)
In Motion_20200116kb_kathy_vale, ken_metcalf, mark.wav
Chloe Napoletano and Sarah Ramey (Preliminary discussion Cup-O-Joe, 2990
   N. High St., Columbus, OH 43214)
In Motion_20191123kb_napoletano, chloe_ramey, sarah.wav
Maureen Clark
In Motion_20191210kb_clark, maureen.wav

Bibliography

Abrahams, Roger. 1981. "Shouting Match at the Border: The Folklore of Display Events." In *"And Other Neighborly Names": Social Process and Cultural Image in Texas Folklore*, edited by Richard Bauman and Roger D. Abrahams, 303–22. Austin: University of Texas Press.
Ahmed, Sara. 2006. *Queer Phenomenology*. Durham, NC: Duke University Press.
Albright, Ann Cooper. 1997. *Choreographing Difference: The Body and Identity in Contemporary Dance*. Middletown, CT: Wesleyan University Press.
———. 2019. *How to Land: Finding Ground in an Unstable World*. New York: Oxford University Press.

Bauman, Richard. (1977) 1984. *Verbal Art as Performance*. Prospect Heights, IL: Waveland.
———. 1989. "American Folklore Studies and Social Transformation: A Performance-Centered Perspective." *Text and Performance Quarterly* 9 (3): 175–84.
———. 2002. "Disciplinarity, Reflexivity, and Power in Verbal Art as Performance: A Response." *Journal of American Folklore* 115 (455): 92–98.
Bendix, Regina. 2000. "The Pleasures of the Ear: Toward an Ethnography of Listening." *Cultural Analysis* 1:33–50.
Berger, Harris M., and Giovanna P. del Negro. 2002. "Bauman's Verbal Art and the Social Organization of Attention: The Role of Reflexivity in the Aesthetics of Performance." *Journal of American Folklore* 115 (455): 62–91.
Boal, Augusto. (1974) 1993. *Theatre of the Oppressed*. New York: Theatre Communications Group.
———. (1992) 2002. *Games for Actors and Nonactors*. Translated by Adrian Jackson. New York: Routledge.
———. 1995. *The Rainbow of Desire: The Boal Method of Theatre and Therapy*. Translated by Adrian Jackson. New York: Routledge.
Boal, Augusto, and Susana Epstein. 1990a. "The Cop in the Head: Three Hypotheses." *TDR/The Drama Review* 34 (3): 35–42.
———. 1990b. "Invisible Theatre: Liege, Belgium, 1978." *TDR/The Drama Review* 34 (3): 24–34.
Bunker, Jenny, Anna Pakes, and Bonnie Rowell, eds. 2013. *Thinking through Dance: The Philosophy of Dance Performance and Practices*. Binstead, Hampshire, UK: Dance Books.
Cohen-Cruz, Jan. 1990. "Boal at NYU: A Workshop and Its Aftermath." *TDR/The Drama Review* 34 (3): 43–49.
———. 2010. *Engaging Performance: Theatre as Call and Response*. New York: Routledge.
Cooper, Lesley, and Helen Thomas. 2002. "Growing Old Gracefully: Social Dance in the Third Age." *Ageing and Society* 22:689–708.
Foster, Susan Leigh. 2003. "Improvisation in Dance and Mind." In *Taken by Surprise: A Dance Improvisation Reader*, edited by Ann Cooper Albright and David Gere, 3–12. Middletown, CT: Wesleyan University Press.
Freire, Paolo. (1967) 1970. *Pedagogy of the Oppressed*. Translated by Myra Bergman Ramos. New York: Herder and Herder.
Heddon, Deirdre, and Jane Milling. 2006. *Devising Performance: A Critical History*. New York: Palgrave.
Kapchan, Deborah. 1995. "Performance." *Journal of American Folklore* 108 (430): 479–508.
Kerrigan, Sheila. 2001. *The Performer's Guide to the Collaborative Process*. Portsmouth, NH: Heinemann.

Lerman, Liz. 1984. *Teaching Dance to Senior Adults*. Ann Arbor: University of Michigan Press.

———. 2014. *Hiking the Horizontal: Field Notes from a Choreographer*. Middletown, CT: Wesleyan University Press.

Lerman, Liz, and John Borstel. 2003. *Liz Lerman's Critical Response Process: A Method for Getting Useful Feedback on Anything You Make from Dance to Dessert*. Washington, DC: Liz Lerman Dance Exchange.

Liang, Shen. 2014. "Performing Dream or Reality: The Dilemma of Chinese Community Based Theatre." *TDR* 58 (1): 16–23.

Nakamura, Jeanne, and Mihaly Csíkszentmihályi. 2002. "The Concept of Flow." In *Handbook of Positive Psychology*, edited by C. R. Snyder and S. J. Lopez, 89–105. Oxford, UK: Oxford University Press.

Noyes, Dorothy. 1995. "Group." *Journal of American Folklore* 108 (430): 449–78.

Otero, Solimar. 2022. "Rekeying Latinx Performance: Gesture, Ancestors, and Community." *Journal of American Folklore* 135 (536): 230–38.

Rouverol, Alicia J. 2005. "Trying to Be Good: Lessons in Oral History and Performance." In *Remembering: Oral History Performance*, edited by Della Pollock, 19–44. New York: Palgrave MacMillan.

Sawin, Patricia. 2002. "Performance at the Nexus of Gender, Power, and Desire: Reconsidering Bauman's Verbal Art from the Perspective of Gendered Subjectivity as Performance." *Journal of American Folklore* 115 (455): 28–61.

Schechner, Richard. 1985a. *Between Theatre and Anthropology*. Philadelphia: University of Pennsylvania Press.

———. 1985b. "Restoration of Behavior." In *Between Theatre and Anthropology*, edited by Richard Schechner and Victor Turner, 35–116. Philadelphia: University of Pennsylvania Press.

———. 1986. "Victor Turner's Last Adventure." In *The Anthropology of Performance*, edited by Victor Turner, 7–20. New York: PAJ.

———. 2004. "Performance Studies: The Broad Spectrum Approach." In *The Performance Studies Reader*, edited by Henry Bial, 7–9. New York: Routledge.

Schutzman, Mady. 1990. "Activism, Therapy, or Nostalgia? Theatre of the Oppressed in NYC." *TDR/The Drama Review* 34 (3): 77–83.

Sklar, Diedre. 2000. "Reprise: On Dance Ethnography." *Dance Research Journal* 32 (1): 70–77.

Stoeltje, Beverly J., and Richard Bauman. 1988. "Community Festival and the Enactment of Modernity." In *The Old Traditional Way of Life: Essays in Honor of Warren G. Roberts*, edited by Robert Walls and George Schoemaker, 159–71. Bloomington, IN: Trickster.

Taussig, Michael, Richard Schechner, and Augusto Boal. "Boal in Brazil, France, the USA: An Interview with Augusto Boal." *TDR/The Drama Review* 34 (3): 50–65.

Turner, Victor. 1982. *From Ritual to Theatre: The Human Seriousness of Play*. New York: PAJPublications.

———. 1986. *The Anthropology of Performance*. New York: PAJ Publications.
Watanabe, Tamotsu. 2017. "The Flower of Old Age." Translated by Nikolas Scheuer. In *The Aging Body in Dance: A Cross-Cultural Perspective*, edited by Nanako Nakajima and Gabriele Brandstetter, 51–60. Oxfordshire, UK: Taylor and Francis.

Katherine Borland is Professor of Comparative Studies in the Humanities at the Ohio State University. She is a folklorist who has written on topics such as dance, narrative, collaborative ethnography, international volunteering, environmentalisms, and festival.

12

A Framework for Analyzing Power and Performance
Music, Activism, and a Veterans' Anti-war Coffeehouse

LISA GILMAN

This essay offers a framework for studying power and performance that critically examines the simultaneous performances and performativity that occur within a given context and as they interface with a range of different manifestations of power. Analyzing how different types of power operate across the spectrum of performances in a complex event produces nuanced understandings of agency, creativity, competing interests, oppression, and social hierarchies within inequitable power structures.

Performance Studies is a broad field that is at once disciplinary, interdisciplinary, and transdisciplinary, complicating the positioning of folklorists and folklore scholarship in relationship to the intertangled methods and theories associated with the term (Kirshenblatt-Gimblett [2004] 2007). Richard Schechner posits that performance "must be construed as a 'broad spectrum' or 'continuum' of human actions ranging from ritual, play, sports, popular entertainments, the performing arts (theater, dance, music), and everyday life performances to the enactment of social, professional, gender, race, and class roles, and on to healing (from shamanism to surgery), the media, and the internet" ([2002] 2006, 2). Scholars from different disciplinary leanings or interested in particular lines of inquiry tend to focus on specific types of human behavior within this spectrum, often producing productive yet limited analyses. The variants of performance studies that inform contemporary folkloristics include the study of heightened events recognized as Performance (big P) inasmuch as the study of performance in everyday life (little p) in addition to textual analyses. Their foci are often on certain dimensions or genres to the exclusion of others within a single event. Examining power in performance is also challenging because in any social interaction, multiple forms of performance occur simultaneously, as do numerous manifestations of power. Power manifests in tangled webs, from institutional, authoritative Power (Power with a capital *P*) to the unofficial and subversive acts of resistance (power with a little *p*) (see Scott 1985), making it challenging to unravel all the different ways that it is operating at any given time. Take a simple greeting between two individuals. The utterance itself is a performance, as is each person's stance, dress, and hairstyle. Greetings typically occur within culturally appropriate constructs, as manifestations of authoritative Power, and the relationship between the two people is governed by each person's identity vis-à-vis existing social hierarchies and their relationship to one another: power.

In order to disentangle the complexities of power operant in any given event, Beverly Stoeltje (1993) offers an effective framework for analyzing ritual that considers both what happens at an event itself as well as how the form has developed over time, the organizational dimensions of its production, and the discourse related to it. Influenced by and building on Stoeltje's important contribution, the framework offered here provides a strategy to break down and analyze the components of performance, further examining different types of power that are operating within the layers of performances and performativity within complex events. The framework is situated within folklore studies in that it offers a mechanism for analyzing the cultural behaviors that tend to interest folklorists at the same time as it is transdisciplinary because it builds on performance theorists across multiple disciplinary spaces. The final section offers an example of the framework's potential by briefly analyzing a punk show that occurred on July 4, 2009, at Coffee Strong, a veteran-owned coffee shop and activist space in Lakewood, Washington.

Definitions and Concepts

Performance versus performance: Definitions and Approaches

Pinning down a definition of *performance* in Performance studies is difficult given the broad range of human behavior studied under the umbrella term. Here, I provide an overview to make visible the potential of integrating different approaches into a single analysis. Folklorists have often focused on performance, what Richard Bauman defined as an "aesthetically marked and heightened mode of communication, framed in a special way and put on display for an audience" (1992, 41). Folklorists' approach recognizes Performance as both heightened events that are explicitly framed as Performance (e.g., a holiday celebration, musical performance, or community festival) as well as those that manifest in everyday life. Each of these events is "a specially marked mode of action, one that sets up or represents a special interpretive frame within which the act of communication is to be understood" (Bauman 1992, 44). They are marked culturally as being opportunities for people to participate in artistic and expressive behavior, often with explicit recognition of a distinction between performers and audience members. Performances (capital *P*) tend to be scheduled and temporally and spatially bounded, and feature a series of programmed activities (46).

Folklorists also pay attention to performances that take place in everyday life. These performances may not be planned and are usually not framed as cultural events; yet, they are still marked as heightened moments when attention is drawn to a display of aesthetic expression, or "cultural behavior for which a person assumes responsibility to an audience" (Hymes 1981, 84). As with more explicitly designated activities, these Performances are "characterized by a higher than usual degree of reflexivity, whether calling attention to the rules of their own enactment (metapragmatics) or talking about the performance event (metadiscourse)" (Kapchan 1995, 479). These types of communicative events are recognized emically as standing out from the everyday; the moment is heightened because attention is focused on the performer(s). When the moment ends, people recognize that something has transpired as they transition back into everyday mundane activity. For the purposes of this essay, I am using Performance for both culturally designated artistic events and these less explicitly framed activities.

Another strand of performance studies considers people's participation in everyday life through a dramaturgical lens. The ongoing embodiments of self in interaction with one another produce ever-emergent social realities, categories, and institutions. Erving Goffman famously recognized that people play/act out social roles and constitute the social environment through their everyday activities, physical comportment, dress, use of space, and interactions with one another (1959). Building on Goffman, Butler was inspired by J. L. Austin's examination of utterances that *do* something—what he calls performatives through the simple fact of being said (marriage being official after "I do" is uttered in a wedding ceremony) (Austin [1962] 2004). Judith Butler argues that gender and sexuality are constituted through people's everyday performance of normative behavior associated with socially prescribed identities. Butler's theorizing about how discourse and embodied practices produce social categories on a day-by-day basis has been transformative for understanding how norms and social hierarchies are continuously generated—for example, in association with gender, race, ethnicity, sexuality, class, and disability. Characteristic of the reiterative process that produces norms are gaps and fissures within which nonnormative performativity can occur. These gaps and fissures echo Gloria Anzaldúa's *nepantla*, the "'liminal (threshold) spaces between worlds' where transformations occur" (Anzaldúa 2002, 1). Not conforming in subtle or more significant ways to social norms can eventually change them. Writing about relationships between race, exoticism, and sexuality, bell hooks, for example, argues that "when black women relate to our bodies, our sexuality, in ways that place erotic recognition, desire, pleasure, and fulfillment at the center of our efforts to create radical black female subjectivity, we can make new and different representations of ourselves as sexual subjects" (hooks 1997, 128). Butler's theory of performativity thus explains both how norms are sustained and the potential for transgression and ultimately transformation.

The performance shift in the late 1970s and 1980s in folklore studies made it relevant to consider the Goffman and Butler approaches to performance simultaneous to examining the kinds of Performance that typically are the focus of folklore scholarship. The move from more text-centered to processual and contextual approaches required considering far more than what happens on "stage" or during the time of a Performance (Paredes and Bauman 1972). Thus, to understand the significance of a storytelling or musical event, it is productive to examine the Performance as well as the larger context in which the performance occurs. Bauman writes, "All performance, like all communication, is situated, enacted, and rendered meaningful within socially defined situational contexts" (Bauman 1992, 46). Activities and discourse leading to the performance, to the process of producing an event, and the discourse about the event are critical for understanding the social significance of any folklore activity (Stoeltje 1993).

Though folklorists (academic and public) often structure their projects on certain types or genres of Performance, such as dances, jokes, festivals, or memes, performativity in everyday life happens simultaneous to any Performance. When someone tells a joke, they are producing a Performance (sharing an aesthetic narrative to an audience) while simultaneously performatively reproducing and/or contesting social categories in everyday life through what they wear, how they sit, their intonation, whom they select to tell their jokes to, and so forth (e.g., Pena 2006; Lyman 1987). The same goes for people attending a Chilimika dance competition in Malawi. A focus on Performance would typically attend to such things as dancers' costumes, their formation, rhythms, melodies, song lyrics, and relationships between performers and the audience (Gilman 2019). Attention to performance would recognize such things as the gender performativity in everyday life, who in the audience sits versus stands, what types of verbal and nonverbal interaction occur between people inside and outside the Performance, who is buying beverages for whom, and so on. It would also recognize the performativity in the Performance itself; thus the dancers are performing both chilimika *as well as* their gender, class, ethnic affiliation, and social values.

Power versus power: Definitions and Approaches

As with *performance*, pinning down *power* is challenging given the different ways the word is used but also because power emerges and operates in highly complex ways, some of which are far more visible and identifiable than others. Distinguishing power into two categories is overly simplistic, though it's useful for analytical purposes. Keeping with the big *P*s and little *p*'s, Power is associated with authoritative institutional or cultural structures versus power that exists outside of, but in relationship to, such structures. In this conceptualization, Power (authoritative power) refers to people, institutions, or physical structures that are recognized culturally as having *the authority* to wield power.

Power is vested within official institutional entities—for example, government structures, security systems, or people who hold authoritative positions within institutions (elected officials in government, doctors in hospitals, teachers in classrooms, CEOs of companies, or religious leaders) (Foucault 1982; Kertzer 1988). It is also associated with less formalized structures and thus part of hegemonic and systemic power structures—for example, men in a patriarchal system, white people in a white supremacist one, people with wealth in a capitalist society, heterosexual people in a heteronormative setting, or "able-bodied" people in an ableist environment (see Du Bois 1920; Applebaum 2010; Frankenberg 1993; Nario-Redmond 2019; Varela, Dhawan, and Engel 2011). While the authority is less explicit in the second category, it still falls within how I'm using Power. Within social hierarchies that are widely accepted, the exercise of greater power is expected and accepted more so for some categories of people/institutions/businesses than for others. Note that this demarcation is complex and often ambiguous; for example, someone who is a subordinate at work and may not have a great deal of power within the work hierarchy may have authoritative power in other spaces, such as being a parent or a leader in a church (see Pena 2006; Coles 2009).

Individuals exist within fluid, complicated matrices of power and authority, determined by social positioning, context, relationships with others, personality, wealth, and identities. Kimberlé Crenshaw offered the concept of intersectionality to articulate "the various ways in which race and gender intersect in shaping structural, political, and representational aspects of violence against women of color" (1991, 1244). This concept has been widely applied beyond race and gender to recognize the intersecting vectors of subordination or marginalization related to many different types of identities and social positionings. Individuals located within multiple categories of subordination experience greater oppression than those in a single category. A white woman might experience gender oppression while enjoying the privilege of being white in the US while a Black woman's experience will be shaped by the ways that gender and racial oppression intersect in US society to produce greater disadvantage (Frankenberg 1993). Adding such things as formal education level, wealth, sexual orientation, ability/disability, religion, and other categories adds further webs of disadvantage or privilege (e.g., Dance 2015; Manderson and Peake 2008).

Intersectionality is just as valuable for understanding how power becomes centered in individuals who belong to multiple categories of *privilege* or *dominance*. The intersectionality of someone in the US who is white, male, educated, able-bodied, cisgender, heterosexual, and Protestant yields power across familial/social/cultural/economic/political spaces in a way that would be different from a white man who did not belong to all the categories of dominance (Connell and Messerschmidt 2005). Thus, inasmuch as oppression and prejudice are intensified for people who exist within multiple vectors of oppression, so too is power intensified for those who exist within multiple vectors of privilege (Kendall 1997).

Power with a little *p* refers to the far more complex recognition of how power manifests within the world. Michel Foucault posits that "something called Power, with or without a capital letter, which is assumed to exist universally in a concentrated or diffused form, does not exist. Power exists only when it is put into action, even if, of course, it is integrated into a disparate field of possibilities brought to bear upon permanent structures" (1982, 788). Thus, an analysis of Power has to recognize both the institutional structures and *how* and *whether* institutional power manifests. Inasmuch as power is centered within certain individuals, locales, and institutions based on both institutional and cultural structures, power is not unidirectional (Foucault [1978] 1990, 92–94).

Take as an example the January 6, 2021, riot that took place at the United States Capitol to disrupt Congress's confirmation that Joseph Biden had won the presidential election and that Donald Trump had lost. The Capitol represents the helm of institutional state power in the US. On this day, then President Trump paradoxically represented both institutional Power as the president **and** oppositional power because he rejected the outcome of the official election. One power wielder (Trump) tangled in contradictory power streams attempted to dominate state power by encouraging his supporters (over whom he had p/Power/influence) to disrupt the event. His supporters, not high-level official power wielders, nevertheless dominated Congress (authoritative Power) through their presence in large numbers, being physically overbearing through aggressive behavior, wielding weapons, and, very significantly, defying the social norms for demonstrations at the Capitol; protesters typically defer to the Capitol Police officers' authority and respect that they cannot enter the building. Through a combination of breaking these norms and using physical force, the protesters ultimately dominated the institutional Power structures for a short duration when they entered the Capitol. Now, at the time of writing in April 2022, fifteen months later, the most egregious offenders are being tried in a court of law and thus subjugated within the state institutional Power system (Dreisbach 2022).

In most scenarios, people have the capacity to assert agency and exercise power in many different ways. Stoeltje writes that "studies of power as domination and subordination often fail to recognize that power also resides in the capacity to create, transform, or otherwise make things happen" (1993, 140). Most everyone has some agency and the capacity to exercise some power within the realms in which they exist, even when the intersectional positioning is particularly disadvantageous. Scholars interested in power (little *p*) include those who consider ways in which people in subordinate positions take advantage of the resources available to them to express themselves or do things that grant them greater access to resources than their position officially allows.

The exercise of power in these nonauthoritative ways is typically multivalent and multimodal. People can exercise power through dress, hairstyle, posture, stance, gestures, actions, inaction, words, silence, use of symbols, or the dissemination of memes (Muñoz 1999; Taylor 2020; Greene 2016). This exercise of power can be visible and recognized—for example, in overt transgressive acts such as someone refusing to follow a social expectation or command—or it can be less obvious, as in the example of someone singing a song with criticism that would not be accepted through other communicative channels (Abu-Lughod 1986; Timpunza Mvula 1985) or wearing a code that only some people recognize (Johnson 2006; Goodwin 1989; Radner and Lanser 1993; Gilman 2023). The p/Power manifesting in Performances can be particularly complex because of the multiple actors involved, different communicative genres operating simultaneously, social license afforded some artistic communication, and liminality (see Turner 1986). In her analysis of a Texas beauty pageant, Stoeltje argues that such rituals symbolically enact contemporary issues and serve to "legitimate the dominant social relations within the group that enacts it" (1996, 14). Yet, such rituals simultaneously provide opportunities for contesting the status quo in that the individuals involved may be strategically participating for their personal gain at the same time that they reinforce the status quo. And, individual participants can overtly or covertly contest the power dynamics while simultaneously reinforcing them (see Gilman 2009).

For example, Patrick Johnson analyzes the Black arts movement of the 1960s and more recent Black stand-up art routines and theater productions that treat oppression as a "static category," often "privileging race as the single most important identity marker" while denigrating "members of the black community who were also female, lesbian, gay, transgendered, or middle class" (2006, 459).

Scholarly attention has tended to focus on how those with less authoritative power creatively navigate the opportunities to subvert the power wielders or otherwise maximize their power. Yet, those with authoritative Power are just as likely to use power and thus increase their influence even more (e.g., Lyman 1987). To take a cliché scenario, in "Burning Dinners: Feminist Subversions of Domesticity," Susan S. Lanser offers examples from fictional and real-life heteronormative households that adhere to conventional gender roles in which women are expected to do all the domestic work. She argues that women sometimes feign incompetence, for example, by burning dinners or the ironing as a strategy to avoid doing unwanted work or to reject in small part their subordination (1993). Less often addressed is that in this type of household, men are just as likely to use similar strategies to reinforce their dominance.[1] Middle-class men left to iron their own clothing may feign incompetence and consistently burn their clothing or walk out the door to go to their white-collar jobs looking wrinkled as a way to "win" so that their wife relents and agrees to iron. In these passive-aggressive negotiations, because it is socially expected that the woman takes charge of these tasks, the implicit or explicit shaming of the woman for not doing her job may be louder than the man's more tentative silent declaration that he is not willing to budge.

P/power and P/performance: A Framework for Analysis

Having established that performance is always happening during Performance and that both power and Power always manifest in complicated ways in any setting, this framework distills the theories and methods of scholars working across performance studies in order to stimulate the robust examination of the critical roles performance plays in social and political situations across the world. The framework is based on the following propositions: (1) performance always operates in Performance; (2) p/Power are simultaneously operating through the multiple forms of p/Performance in any given Performance event; (3) the same p/Performance can operate in the interest of competing actors simultaneously; (4) in any given Performance, there are multiple dominants, as in people whose authority lies in different social roles; and (5) the same person is often simultaneously dominant and subordinate, even within a single event, dependent on the point of reference.

For analytical purposes, the first step is to demarcate the Performance under scrutiny. Performances happen as part and parcel of the ongoing activities of the world. For the purposes of analysis, one has to be explicit and deliberate about the framing of what one is interpreting. In an example of a musical Performance in a bar, the focus could be what happens onstage, the whole bar, the parking lot, the surrounding neighborhood, the social media about the event, or some combination of the above (see Messer 2010; Rivera-Servera 2012). In other words, what is considered to be the "performance" is mobile and relational in that it usually has more to do with the researcher's goals than it does with any definitive emic demarcation.

The second step is to analyze the Performance as it relates to Power by identifying what types of Power are evident and performed in relationship to the Performance. Informed by Stoeltje's call to attend to the organization of production and the discourse about it, what is the political environment? What is the economic context? Are there financial restrictions to participation in various capacities? What organizational or control mechanisms structure the event? Is it physically removed? Who has access, and in what capacities can different types of people participate? Who controls discourse in various communicative spaces (consider official newspaper stories and advertisements, signage, discourse about the event after)? In considering each of these questions, take into account intersectionality in terms of control and participation and restrictions. For example, if the event is organized by those with official power within the community, are the people dominating other dimensions of the performance from these same social categories or different ones?

The third step is to consider the mechanisms for the informal power that manifests through, during, and around the Performance. What to consider depends on the event and research questions. Such things as social role, gender, race, ethnicity, ability, citizenship, nationality, wealth, and physical size as well as who has access to instruments, movement, space, microphones, or weapons could be aspects to consider. Determining this step is complicated because these types of power are often not explicit. An event where payment is required for admission clearly stipulates financial Power for admission. The gatekeeper who stands at the entry and determines who can enter represents Power, the institutional structures that determined that the event would occur behind a gate and require payment. However, the analysis becomes more complicated if the gatekeeper is a lower paid BIPOC (Black, Indigenous, or person of color) person at an event in the United States dominated by wealthy white people. While the gatekeeper wields Power at the gate, they are subordinate within the socioeconomic structures producing the event.

After completing the analysis of Performance, the next step is to identify the most salient forms of performance relevant to the analytical questions one is pursuing. Consider such things as the performativity associated with gender, race, ethnicity, age, religion, class, citizenship, and ability, and intersections of all of the above. Deciding what to analyze can be overwhelming, especially for more complex performance events because so much is going on. The nature of the performativity will vary from event to event. Some possibilities would be: clothing, hairstyle, movement, space usage, facial expressions, gesture, physical location, spatial relations, who's buying things from or for whom, who is interacting with whom, what is being said, through what genres it is being said, who moves and has access to which spaces, who stands behind counters versus in front of them, what symbols are displayed and where, and so on.

Then begin to analyze Power and power as they relate to the performative elements identified. Note that the manifestations of Power will be explicit and overt while others will be vague, ambiguous, multivalent, or even contradictory. Moreover, p/Power usually exists simultaneously. Consider as an example the dress and/or costumes of people present. Performers and audience members wearing gender-conforming clothes within a patriarchal and binary gender system reinforce both authoritative Power (e.g., patriarchy) and power, the hegemony associated with male dominance even in a culture that purports to be egalitarian. At the same time, a woman wearing gender-normative clothing deemed sexually attractive by men may be reiterative of patriarchal power simultaneous to being an exercise of power to gain something from the men who are in the dominant position.

Applying the Framework: Analyzing a Coffee Strong Punk Show

I will now apply the framework to analyze a punk show that took place at Coffee Strong on July 4, 2009, on US Independence Day. Elaine Vradenburg and I attended and videotaped this event when we were making *Grounds for Resistance: Stories of War, Sacrifice, and Good Coffee* (Gilman 2011). The café, Coffee Strong, was a project of GI Voice, a nonprofit organization owned and run by US combat veterans located in Lakewood, Washington. It was down the street and across the highway from two military bases: the US Army Joint-Base Lewis McCord (JBLM) and Camp Murray, home of the Washington Air National Guard and the Washington Army National Guard. Young combat veterans from different military branches who were in their twenties and students at the Evergreen State College in Olympia, Washington, started Coffee Strong on November 4, 2008, the day that Barack Obama was elected president and at the height of the US wars in Iraq and Afghanistan. Though each has their own story, the founders and activists involved with the coffee shop returned from war deeply troubled by what they had seen and done. They started the nonprofit to provide support and services for other active duty military personnel and combat veterans and to participate in the anti-war movement. The Vietnam-era veteran anti-war movement and the activist coffee shops that were situated outside military bases during the Vietnam War inspired them to start Coffee Strong.[2]

From 2009 to 2011, I spent a great deal of time at Coffee Strong doing ethnographic research and participating in activism while I produced the documentary and did research for writing projects (Gilman 2016, 2012).[3] The café was a typical coffee shop that sold tea, coffee, cold drinks, and snacks. It offered seating where one could sit for hours, reading, working on a laptop, or chatting with others. As a nonprofit, it was part of the anti-war activist movement to support active duty and veterans of the US Armed Forces and to protest the two wars.

Though this event happened fourteen years ago, I selected it to illustrate the framework because the different types of power operating were especially vivid and complex. The event was explicitly an act of resistance against the US wars and the treatment of US troops; it was particularly salient because it was members of the military who were involved. Analyzing the multiple dimensions of power and performance sheds light on how the power manifesting at this event included the dyad of troop and US military/government in addition to the simultaneous enactment and reconstitution of inequitable power structures within the US more broadly. Bringing attention to this event is also important because the anti-war activism of US military veterans during these wars remains mostly invisible; yet, it is vital for understanding these wars, US history and politics, and the impact of the effects of US foreign policy on the young people who are typically on-the-ground actors in US conflicts.[4]

This event was radical. There is a culture in the US military that once you are in the military, you remain connected and loyal for life. Furthermore, the US wars in Iraq and Afghanistan were polarized. The discourse of "you are either with us or against us" dominated US politics after the September 11, 2001, attacks on the World Trade Center and US Pentagon. The job of US troops is to be "with us" and carry US foreign policy—in this case to be the people on the ground fighting the wars and not questioning their commanders or the country's decision-makers. By standing up against the government and the wars within view of the military bases, the Coffee Strong activists were actively demonstrating "against us," which was especially poignant given that they were also perceived as being against their fellow troops in the military with whom loyalty to the military is especially emphasized. Combat veterans performing their opposition to the military and US government outside of two military bases on Independence Day was an explicit affront to what was expected of them during a particularly polarized time in US politics.

For the purposes of this short analysis, I am designating the Performance to be the musical presentations by bands that were invited to perform. The drum kit and sound system were positioned to the side of the parking lot nearest the entrance to Coffee Strong, which offered a clearly demarcated space that set the musicians apart from the spectators. When the music was happening, the bands were the focal point of people's attention, given the logic of a punk show. This was a small event, with only thirty to forty attendees. Many in attendance were musicians in bands that also performed. Musicians thus switched from audience member to performer when it was their turn to enter the designated performance space, take up the instruments, and control the microphone. The relationship of performer to audience was thus fluid, and power associated with people in different roles was diffuse.

The context for this Performance was the coffee shop sponsoring the event, whose space for this day encompassed the interior of the café and the parking lot outside. Most of the analysis will focus on these spaces. However, the larger context of the adjoining Subway sandwich shop, the street full of businesses aimed at military personnel, and the nearby bases comprise the larger context. The setting beyond Lakewood, Washington, though providing contextual information, will not be considered due to length limitations.

The manifestation of Power occurred through multiple, at times competing, mechanisms. On the same day as the punk show, there was a big celebration happening on the nearby JBLM base that transpired dialogically to the event hosted by Coffee Strong. The Power structure from the base was visceral because of the many US flags flying up and down the street. The fencing around the base was omnipresent physically in that it was visible across the highway, but, more significantly, everyone present was explicitly aware of the significance of the location of the anti-war coffee shop within sight of the base and waving flags.

Other dimensions of official Power were that Coffee Strong was located in Lakewood, which had its own city laws and restrictions that shaped what the organizers could do. They could not take their party beyond the parking lot, nor could they fill the streets with moshing bodies. The show was thus restricted to the space for which they paid rent and were allowed to occupy. Nevertheless, the use of the parking lot was an affront to the city Power structure in that typically they would not be able to hold a concert outside; they usually held them indoors because of noise issues and because the parking lot was shared with their neighbor. On this holiday, all the nearby stores and restaurants, including the adjoining Subway, were closed, allowing for more flexibility in sonic and space usage. By being outside, the event was transgressive; however, the organizers were aware that at any time police officers, representing Power, could shut their event down or force them inside.

The Power structures within the event itself were completely different from those outlined for the larger context. Coffee Strong was a nonprofit run by veterans for veterans. The veterans who ran it therefore wielded the Power at the event. Among them, Josh, a musician himself, was the coordinator of the show. He had invited the performers, determined where they would play, and scheduled the lineup and was busy throughout making sure that everything ran according to plan. Two other veterans, Andrew and Joseph, set up the interior, worked as baristas selling coffee drinks, and otherwise took care of the business side of things. Though the event was informal and people sat in the coffee shop, stood outside, or skateboarded around, the business structure of the shop nevertheless determined the nature of people's participation and created parameters for acceptable behavior.

Now, for the less obvious types of Power—the socially prescribed authoritative rather than institutional Power. For the most part, hegemonic social hierarchies related to gender, sexuality, class, religion, race/ethnicity, ability, and gender were at play despite the social justice ethos of the individuals present and the movement that they were part of. Here, I will consider briefly some intersections between gender, class, race, and ability. This was a fairly egalitarian event as far as gender. Coffee Strong had women members, veteran and civilian, and made efforts at inclusivity. However, the founders were male, and the majority of active veterans in the organization were "able-bodied" cisgender men, a dynamic related to the male dominance, sexism, and widespread sexual abuse within the military.[5] Furthermore, while there were some women musicians, most of the band members were men, reinforcing the dominance of men as musicians in the punk scene specifically and popular music in the US more generally.[6]

The Coffee Strong community across veterans, active duty, and civilians included BIPOC, however the majority were white, including all of the founders and core leadership at the time of this event. Most people present were also white, which aligned with the demographics of the Pacific Northwest region, the punk scene, and the anti-war movement in Washington state at the time. While the veterans themselves came from a combination of middle-class and working-class backgrounds, most of the people in attendance were young college-age white students who likely came from middle- to upper-middle-class families. While gender, race, and class are relevant for thinking about power with a little *p*, I put it in the Power section in recognition that those with identities tied to hegemonic dominance enjoy privilege in the form of often silent authoritative Power.

Intertangled with manifestations of Power were the multiple ways that power also operated. This event, and the coffee shop more generally, was radical because it was run by combat veterans who were involved in the anti-war movement. That the event took place at all, or that the coffee shop existed, was an assertion of power. In the US at the time, troops were generally expected to be pro-military and pro-US foreign policy. There was little public recognition of the diverse political views among military personnel, the feelings of troops who were severely troubled by their experiences at war, or military anti-war activism. Holding a public event on the Fourth of July outside the base was thus an assertion of power for this marginalized group that was in opposition to the Power of the military and the US government.

The parking lot sat across the fence from the train tracks that ran alongside Interstate 5, the major highway that runs north–south from the border of Canada to the border with Mexico. It was a relatively small, somewhat dirty lot that provided parking to Coffee Strong and Subway customers. On this day, it was transformed into a festive space. The cars belonging to attendees, some with their trunks open and full of coolers, food, and instruments, created the frame or physical boundary around the event. The people standing around, skateboarding, chatting, bobbing their heads, or aggressively dancing and occasionally shoving one another defined the space as a heightened and liminal event in which the everyday activity of the parking lot was transformed from a place to walk through from car to business into one for dancing and socializing (Turner 1986).

Other assertions of power within the Performance were the choice of genre: straight edge hardcore punk rock. Straight edgers enjoy the "raw energy, aggressive style, and do-it-yourself attitude" of the punk scene but reject the nihilistic tendencies associated with drug and alcohol abuse, casual sex, violence, and other "self-destructive 'live fast, die young' attitudes" (Haenfler 2006, 8). The straight edge subculture is grounded in strong morals associated with "clean living" and social justice.

The genre was significant because of its political associations. Veteran Josh was active in the regional straight edge hardcore scene as a musician and producer of events; for him, the musical scene aligned with his politics and anti-war activism. Putting on a counterculture punk show at Coffee Strong was radical given the mainstream dominant politics of Lakewood. Nearby Olympia, Washington, home of Evergreen College, was known for its radical politics and alternative music scene, and these types of shows were commonplace. In

Lakewood, it was intended to counter the politics of the military base and the surrounding community.

Punk is aggressive, loud, heavily amplified, and distorted, with driving beats and singers screaming into the microphone. The sonic power at this event was juxtaposed to both the patriotism in the heavily militarized space and to the sonic Power associated with the military and war: jet engines, tanks, gunfire, and exploding bombs. Though war sounds were not present at the event, they nevertheless were part of the sonic imagination within this militaristic space (Daughtry 2015). Had the event been inside and just as loud, this dialogic sonic symbolism would have been muted.

The choice of genre was also limited in terms of the organizers' objectives. Hardcore is an esoteric genre that was not appreciated by the majority of military personnel the Coffee Strong organizers hoped to attract. The mission of Coffee Strong was to provide a place for active duty troops and their families to come, relax, talk about their experiences at war openly, and access important resources associated with trauma, military sexual violence, and political ambivalence. In a short interview before the Fourth of July show, Josh said that he hoped the events he organized would attract soldiers to come for the music and then ultimately learn about the nonprofit's goals. However, Josh realized that few soldiers listened to this type of music. He realized that the show could be counterproductive if it deterred soldiers from coming in even for coffee. Someone hoping for a cappuccino could be dissuaded from maneuvering through the driving beats and head-bobbing young, tattooed people filling the parking lot. Furthermore, hardcore fans tend to support, and some engage in, anti-racist and inclusive activism. However, that the scene is majority white and that the artists performing at this event were mostly white could communicate to BIPOC troops that Coffee Strong was not a place for them, regardless of the intentions or feelings of the event organizers or attendees.

That this event was held on the Fourth of July was important symbolically but not practically. All of the businesses around Coffee Strong were closed for the holiday, and the streets were empty. On a typical day, soldiers came in and out of the adjacent Subway. They parked in the same parking lot, saw the postered windows of the coffee shop that included a sign saying that coffee was free for troops, and could wander in for a cup of coffee, which was a big part of the nonprofit's passive outreach. Because the city was closed down for the holiday, the only people who came that day were those coming for the show. The only veterans present were a few of the volunteers already active in the organization. Joseph shared that he was disappointed because the show was not attracting active duty military personnel, and thus "we're not accomplishing the goals that I had hoped to be able to accomplish right now." The oppositional symbolism of the event was loud, though the audience was limited to those already sold on the message, thus tempering its success as an activist endeavor.

Coffee Strong asserted its own dominant messaging on a daily basis that was in opposition to its surrounding environment through numerous forms of performances that were salient at this event. Within the coffee shop hung a huge camouflage banner with "Support War Resistors" on top, a cartoon image of a soldier in the center, and "Iraq Veterans Against the War IVAW" on the bottom.[7] A spoof of the famous Uncle Sam poster read "I want out" instead of "I want you." The bulletin board with pamphlets about filing for conscientious objector status, sexual trauma resources, and mental health along with the free library full of political books further contributed to the atmosphere. These messages were reinforced by the self-presentation of the veterans running the event. The young fit men with short hairstyles resonated with what is required of troops; yet the T-shirts, tattoos, and other elements of their corporal presentation countered their military performativity, a performance of their oppositional positioning as being both of the military and against it (see Hebdige 1991). Josh, his arms covered with tattoos, wore cut-off camouflage pants with a black T-shirt on which was written "Iraq Veterans Against the War." Andrew similarly wore cut-off camouflage shorts. Joseph, on this day, wore no obvious military references. Joseph's muscled body and short hair indexed his veteran status while the stars tattooed on each of his triceps strategically referenced his identity as a socialist, which interacted dialogically with the military referents that aligned with US capitalism (Gilman 2012).

By contrast, veteran Alan, who was present for part of the show, performed a very different identity. As with Josh, Joseph, and Andrew, Alan was a young white male veteran. He had served in the Marines, suffered from a severe brain injury, and struggled with mental illness at the time of this event. Unlike the others whose fit bodies and short hair referenced physical ability, military strength, and hypermasculinity, Alan supported his frail body with a cane, and his curly hair was long and straggly. For those who didn't know Alan, he was just another person present. For those who knew him, his presence represented the enormous impact of these wars on the young people fighting them.[8]

Military uniforms are costumes that are performative in the Austin sense of utterances that *do* something through the simple fact of being said ([1962] 2004). Join the military, don its costume, and become immediately dominant. Think of the respect and/or fear that is granted one for simply wearing a military (or other law enforcement) uniform, even if one knows nothing else about the uniformed person.[9] The symbols associated with military branches, ranks, awards, and names that adorn uniforms further perform an individual's positioning within a variety of hierarchies within and outside the military. Context is everything. Uniformed officers coming from one of the nearby bases to Coffee Strong to buy a cappuccino would often draw the attention of activists who wondered how an officer would respond to the anti-war surroundings. The same officers entering the Subway right next door might draw little attention from the sandwich makers, who would be most concerned about whether they wanted turkey or ham. Within the military base, they would command respect and discipline from their subordinates. Among other officers, they would be expected to demonstrate respect to their superiors. In the streets of Iraq or Afghanistan during the wars, they might evoke fear or hatred.

The dress of the attendees at the punk show contrasted with the military uniforms that characterized the common sartorial culture on the base and in Lakewood. Their sartorial choices were also costumes in the Goffman sense, but ones with less performative power. They expressed symbolic opposition to the military norms that dominated their surroundings. Attendees, most of whom had no direct affiliation with the military, performed their identities as mostly white young college students. While individual dress varied, everyone more or less fit a general dress code/costume of cut-off or torn jean shorts and T-shirts (with some clothing items being visibly dirty or stained), and flip-flops and Vans or other sneakers as the preferred footwear. Women's hair was mostly long and not styled, and men's heads were mostly shaved.

Through their dress, the attendees performed intersectional identities, including the straight edge hardcore scene but also white middle classness. Clothing is often used to denote criminality in our country, especially with BIPOC people (e.g., De Casanova and Webb 2017). Correspondingly, torn and worn clothing in some settings index poverty. In this setting, however, it indicated privilege related to whiteness in the US. White people are assumed to be financially stable and dominant, and thus in many settings they do not have to perform wealth through dress. These young, mostly white people could wear torn and stained clothes and worn out shoes and have straggly hair, all while conforming to acceptable middle-class white mainstream society. In other words, wearing torn clothing as a symbol of antiestablishment punk rock ironically is most acceptable for those who most benefit from the structural racism/white supremacy of the establishment. Their sartorial performances were iterative of white middle classness and thus reproduced those norms.

By contrast, the majority of young people who were enlisted in the military during this time were from lower socioeconomic levels within the country, and they represented the full range of US race and ethnic identities (Lutz 2008). Many selected to enlist in the military because they perceived it to be one of only a few viable opportunities for employment or a pathway to funding for higher education (Faris 1981; Dempsey 2010, 46; Lutz 2008, 184). Though no active duty military personnel were visible at this event, their presence in Lakewood is a constant, and thus the symbolism existed even in their absence. The young, ragged punk college students performed dialogically with the young soldiers who regularly came in and out of the Subway wearing their full army uniforms, with clean haircuts and perfectly polished shoes. While the soldiers performed the Power of the military, they also largely represented a lower social class. The contrast between the young, enlisted people wearing their disciplined uniforms on base and the antiestablishment dress of the hardcore fans articulated the social hierarchies tied to class and race/ethnicity that produce a US military of poorer people who fight the wars for those who are wealthier.

The Coffee Strong veterans' incorporation of bits and pieces of military symbolism was significant because they were themselves veterans and wore elements from their own uniforms. Yet, they defied the strict discipline that governed their dress as they would have worn it during their service. Dick Hebdige (1991) writes about the transgressive placing of symbols in ways that transform their meanings to produce social commentary or, sometimes, the very opposite of what the symbols were intended to create. Josh's cut-off camouflage shorts interacted with his tattoos and Iraq Veterans Against the War T-shirt, thus transforming the symbolism of the camouflage from being about militarism generally, or the US Army more specifically, to a social critique of war. The symbolism of his shorts was even more complex because of the person wearing them and the location of the event. The Coffee Strong vets strategically performed their military identity through their dress, hair, and folk speech as a way to actively *align* themselves in relationship to their service. Their activism was centered in their veteran identity, and they selected to position their nonprofit right next to the base. They performed their identity as veterans and thus proclaimed their legitimate right to speak firsthand about their perspectives on these wars. Yet, as in Hebdige's theorizing about symbols, they simultaneously expressed their distance from the military by wearing the clothing improperly and juxtaposing military elements to items that expressed the very oppositive of what was intended by the military symbols (see Gilman 2012).

Conclusion

In a lecture to the American Folklore Society membership in 2021, Anand Prahlad criticized folklorists' approach to theory and scholarship because of what he perceived to be a lack of adequate engagement with real social critique: "The great tragedy here is that folklorists are in many obvious ways better equipped to bring insight to such aspects of American society than those in any other field. But the intellectual and methodological parameters of our field do not facilitate the engagement with larger social ideas as the core material of research, but insist instead on a constant deference to and reverence for genres and intellectual tools that are not suited to radical thinking or political engagement" (2021, 263). Unlike Prahlad, I do think that many folklorists have participated in critically important theorizing and analyses that are radical and politically engaged. However, I do agree that we have done too little and that the socially engaged work that folklorists have done about inequality and oppression has often not received the same visibility or been as influential as some of the more conventional work that Prahlad characterizes as heavy with "a reverence for nostalgia, the notion of folk groups as small, the insistence on a materialist methodology, a preoccupation with genres, an isolationist perspective and rejection of outside theoretical models, and the study of exclusively 'beautiful' things" (262).

Folklorists study the mundane, that which most people take for granted but that nevertheless shapes the power structures and social identities in which people live. As such, folklorists are especially well "equipped to bring insight to such aspects of American society than those in any other field" (Prahlad 2021, 263). The interpretive framework offered here provides a multilayered strategy for analyzing p/Power in a variety of performances, enabling the untangling of how social hierarchies are created and maintained and thus also shedding light on how they are resisted and can be deconstructed. Though short and incomplete, the analysis of the Coffee Strong punk show elucidates just how complex and contradictory power manifests. An activist event that effectively confronts war and the US military-industrial complex nevertheless reinforces social hierarchies and inequities in ways that are both explicit and implicit. I hope it will inspire readers to apply the model to produce nuanced analyses that will offer radical socially engaged scholarship. Following Prahlad's call, the framework is part of "revising our accepted notions that underlie all that we do, for example, questioning what it means to be human; and (8) a movement toward imagining folklore as a hub, an intellectual center where other disciplines can gain tools for understanding and navigating the complexities of cultural tensions" (Prahlad 2021, 264).

Notes

1. Lanser notes that "male and female incompetence are often inversely defined, so that men may demonstrate their manhood when they boast of incompetence at precisely those behaviors that signal female capability" (1993, 39).

2. The documentary *Sir! No Sir!* provides a detailed history of the coffee shop movement during the Vietnam-era war resistance (Zeiger 2005). The film inspired the founders of Coffee Strong to open the café.

3. For more information about Grounds for Resistance and information on accessing the documentary, go to https://groundsforresistance.com.

4. In the years since this event, GI Voice continued operating though the original founders went their separate ways due to completing educational training, diverse professional and personal trajectories, and interpersonal conflicts. Eventually, the organization shut down the café but continued their nonprofit work. As the wars diminished, so did the activism of civilian and veteran anti-war activists, and the organization eventually dissolved.

5. Many of the women involved in the organization were nonveterans, mostly students from the Evergreen State College and activists living in Olympia. The nonprofit worked to support active-duty and veteran women and regularly strategized about how to make the organization more inclusive and inviting to women. These efforts were not very successful for many reasons that are beyond the scope of this essay. *Grounds for Resistance* touches on these issues.

6. The Pacific Northwest is known for its women-driven punk scene fueled by the riot grrls in the 1990s. Correspondingly, the performers and attendees at this event considered themselves to be gender-inclusive. Yet, as with many popular music scenes in the country, it's not unusual to have bands made up of mostly male musicians.

7. Iraq Veterans Against the War (IVAW) is an organization that was founded by US veterans of the Iraq War in 2004 to "give voice to the large number of active duty service people and veterans who are against this war, but are under various pressures to remain silent." Their membership was restricted to recent veterans and active-duty personnel (thus mostly those who were involved in the wars in Iraq and/or Afghanistan), and their efforts were aimed at ending the wars and providing support for troops who fought them. Their website is archived at https://www.ivaw.org. The local chapter of IVAW at the time of this event met at Coffee Strong, and the founders, leaders, and other veteran participants of Coffee Strong were active members.

8. The mental health impact of these wars has been astronomical for those who fought them. The psychological struggle of all who participated in the film project was palpable; at least four veterans involved in the project attempted suicide just during the two years that we were making the film. Alan's physical and mental struggles were particularly acute. He reached out to me a few years ago to let me know that he was doing much better. However, many others continue to struggle, and the suicide rate for veterans of these wars has been staggering (Friedman 2014).

9. See Civile and Obhi (2017) for a troubling study with university students at a Canadian university. Students who wore police uniforms were more likely to be racist and biased in their judgments of people than those who did not.

Bibliography

Abu-Lughod, Lila. 1986. *Veiled Sentiments: Honour and Poetry in a Bedouin Society*. Berkeley: University of California Press.

Anzaldúa, Gloria. 2002. "Preface: (Un)natural Bridges, (Unsafe Spaces)." In *This Bridge We Call Home: Radical Visions for Transformation*, edited by Gloria Anzaldúa and AnaLouise Keating, 1–5. New York: Routledge.

Applebaum, Barbara. 2010. *Being White, Being Good: White Complicity, White Moral Responsibility, and Social Justice Pedagogy*. Blue Ridge Summit, PA: Lexington Books/Fortress Academic.

Austin, J. L. (1962) 2004. "Lecture II." In *The Performance Studies Reader*, 2nd ed., edited by Henry Bial, 177–83. New York: Routledge.

Bauman, Richard. 1992. "Performance." In *Folklore, Cultural Performances, and Popular Entertainments: A Communications-Centered Handbook*, edited by Richard Bauman, 41–49. Oxford: Oxford University Press.

Butler, Judith. 1993. *Bodies That Matter: On the Discursive Limits of "Sex."* New York: Routledge.

Civile, Ciro, and Sukhvinder S. Obhi. 2017. "Students Wearing Police Uniforms Exhibit Biased Attention toward Individuals Wearing Hoodies." *Frontiers in Psychology* 8:62.

Coles, Tony. 2009. "Negotiating the Field of Masculinity: The Production and Reproduction of Multiple Dominant Masculinities." *Men and Masculinities* 12 (1): 30–44.

Connell, R. W., and James W. Messerschmidt. 2005. "Hegemonic Masculinity: Rethinking the Concept." *Gender & Society* 19 (6): 829–85.

Crenshaw, Kimberlé. 1991. "Mapping the Margins: Intersectionality, Identity, and Violence against Women of Color." *Stanford Law Review* 43 (6): 1241–1300.

Dance, Daryl Cumber. 2015. "Can Trayvon Get a Witness? African American Folklore Elucidates the Trayvon Martin Case." *CLA Journal* 58 (3/4): 147–53.

Daughtry, J. Martin. 2015. *Listening to War: Sound, Music, Trauma, and Survival in Wartime Iraq*. New York: Oxford University Press.

De Casanova, Erynn Masi, and Curtis L. Webb. 2017. "A Tale of Two Hoodies." *Men and Masculinities* 20 (1): 117–22.

Dempsey, Jason K. 2010. *Our Army: Soldiers, Politics, and American Civil-Military Relations*. Princeton, NJ: Princeton University Press.

Dreisbach, Tom. 2022. "In a D.C. Jail, Jan. 6 Defendants Awaiting Trial Are Forming Bitter Factions." National Public Radio, April 14, 2022. https://www.npr.org/2022/04/14/1092580753/capitol-riot-january-6-insurrection-defendants.

Du Bois, W. E. B. 1920. *The Souls of White Folk*. New York: Harcourt, Brace, and Company.

Faris, John H. 1981. "The All-Volunteer Force—Recruitment from Military Families." *Armed Forces and Society* 7 (4): 545–59.

Foucault, Michel. [1978] 1990. *The History of Sexuality. Vol. 1, An Introduction.* New York: Vintage.

———. 1982. "The Subject and Power." *Critical Inquiry* 8 (4): 777–95.

Frankenberg, Ruth. 1993. *White Women, Race Matters: The Social Construction of Whiteness.* Minneapolis: University of Minnesota Press.

Friedman, Matthew J. 2014. "Suicide Risk among Soldiers: Early Findings from Army Study to Assess Risk and Resilience in Service members (Army STARRS)." *JAMA Psychiatry* 71 (5): 487–89.

Gilman, Lisa. 2009. "Complex Genres, Intertextuality, and the Analysis of Performance." *Journal of American Folklore* 12 (485): 335–62.

———. 2011. *Grounds for Resistance: Stories of War, Sacrifice, and Good Coffee.* Done Did Productions. Distributed by Films Media Group. https://www.films.com/ecTitleDetail.aspx?TitleID=25096&r=SR.

———. 2012. "Oppositional Positioning: The Military Identification of Young Anti-War Veterans." In *Warrior Ways: Explorations in Modern Military Folklore*, edited by Tad Tuleja and Eric Eliason, 181–201. Logan: Utah State University Press.

———. 2016. *My Music, My War: The Listening Habits of U.S. Troops in Iraq and Afghanistan.* Middleton, CT: Wesleyan University Press.

———. 2019. "*Chilimika*: Dancing in the New Year in the Nkhata Bay District of Malawi." In *Africa Every Day: Fun, Leisure, and Expressive Culture on the Continent*, edited by Kemi Balogun, Lisa Gilman, Melissa Graboyes, and Habib Iddrisu, 219–27. Athens: Ohio University Press.

———. 2023. "Cake Is Better than Sex: Folklore and Asexuality. Special Issue Folklore and Queer Theory." *Journal of Folklore Research* 60 (2–3): 196–228.

Goffman, Erving. 1959. *The Presentation of Self in Everyday Life.* New York: Doubleday.

Goodwin, Joseph. 1989. *More Man than You'll Ever Be: Gay Folklore and Acculturation in Middle America.* Bloomington: Indiana University Press.

Greene, Shane. 2016. *Punk and Revolution: Seven More Interpretations of Peruvian Reality.* Durham, NC: Duke University Press.

Haenfler, Ross. 2006. *Straight Edge: Clean-Living Youth, Hardcore Punk, and Social Change.* New Brunswick, NJ: Rutgers University Press.

Hebdige, Dick. 1991. *Subculture: The Meaning of Style.* London: Routledge.

hooks, bell. 1997. "Selling Hot Pussy: Representations of Black Female Sexuality in the Cultural Marketplace." In *Writing on the Body: Female Embodiment and Feminist Theory*, edited by Katie Conboy, Nadia Mediana, and Sarah Stanbury, 113–54. New York: Columbia University Press.

Hymes, Dell. 1981. *"In Vain I Tried to Tell You": Essays in Native American Ethnopoetics.* Philadelphia: University of Pennsylvania Press.

Johnson, E. Patrick. 2006. "Black Performance Studies: Genealogies, Politics, Futures." In *The Sage Handbook of Performance Studies*, edited by D. Soyini Madison and Judith A. Hamera, 446–63. Thousand Oaks, CA: Sage.

Kapchan, Deborah A. 1995. "Performance." *Journal of American Folklore* 108 (430): 479–508.
Kendall, Diana Elizabeth. 1997. *Race, Class, and Gender in a Diverse Society: A Text-Reader*. Boston: Allyn and Bacon.
Kertzer, David I. 1988. *Ritual, Politics, and Power*. New Haven, CT: Yale University Press.
Kirshenblatt-Gimblett, Barbara. (2004) 2007. "Performance Studies." In *The Performance Studies Reader*, 2nd ed., edited by Henry Bial, 43–55. New York: Routledge.
Lanser, Susan S. 1993. "Burning Dinners: Feminist Subversions of Domesticity." In *Feminist Messages: Coding in Women's Folk Culture*, edited by Joan Newlon Radner, 36–53. Urbana: University of Illinois Press.
Lutz, Amy. 2008. "Who Joins the Military? A Look at Race, Class, and Immigration Status." *Journal of Political and Military Sociology* 36 (2): 167–88.
Lyman, Peter. 1987. "The Fraternal Bond as a Joking Relationship: A Case Study of the Role of Sexist Jokes in Male Group Bonding." In *Changing Men: New Directions in Research on Men and Masculinity*, edited by Michael S. Kimmel, 148–63. Newbury Park, CA: Sage.
Manderson, Lenore, and Susan Peake. 2008. "Men in Motion: Disability and the Performance of Masculinity." In *Bodies in Commotion: Disability and Performance*, edited by Carrie Sandahl and Philip Auslander, 230–42. Ann Arbor: University of Michigan Press.
Messer, Lucas. 2010. "Queer Migrant Culture: Undocumented Queer Latinos and Queer Clubs in Phoenix." PhD diss., Arizona State University.
Muñoz, José E. 1999. *Disidentifications: Queers of Color and the Performance of Politics*. Minneapolis: University of Minnesota Press.
Nario-Redmond, Michelle R. 2019. *Ableism*. Newark, NJ: John Wiley & Sons.
Paredes, Américo, and Richard Bauman. 1972. *Toward New Perspectives in Folklore*. Austin: University of Texas Press.
Pena, Manuel. 2006. "Folklore, Machismo and Everyday Practice." *Western Folklore* 65 (1–2): 137–66.
Prahlad, Anand. 2021. "Tearing Down Monuments: Missed Opportunities, Silences, and Absences—A Radical Look at Race in American Folklore Studies." *Journal of American Folklore* 134 (533): 258–64.
Radner, Joan N., and Susan S. Lanser. 1993. "Strategies of Coding in Women's Cultures." In *Feminist Messages: Coding in Women's Folk Culture*, edited by Joan Newlon Radner, 1–30. Urbana: University of Illinois Press.
Rivera-Servera, Ramón H. 2012. *Performing Queer Latinidad: Dance, Sexuality, Politics*. Ann Arbor: University of Michigan Press.
Schechner, Richard. (2002) 2006. *Performance Studies: An Introduction*. 2nd ed. New York: Routledge.
Scott, James. 1985. *Weapons of the Weak: Everyday Forms of Peasant Resistance*. New Haven, CT: Yale University Press.

Stoeltje, Beverly. 1993. "Power and the Ritual Genres: American Rodeo." *Western Folklore* 52 (2/4): 135–56.

———. 1996. "The Snake Charmer Queen: Ritual, Competition, and Signification in American Festival." In *Beauty Queens on the Global Stage: Gender, Contests, and Power*, edited by Colleen Ballerino Cohen, Beverly Stoeltje, and Richard Wilk, 13–29. New York: Routledge.

Taylor, Diana. 2020. *¡Presente!: The Politics of Presence*. Durham, NC: Duke University Press.

Timpunza Mvula, Enoch. 1985. "Tumbuka Pounding Songs in the Management of Family Conflicts." *Cross Rhythms, Occasional Papers in African Folklore/Music* 2:93–113.

Turner, Victor. 1986. *The Anthropology of Performance*. New York: PAJ.

Varela, María do Mar Castro, Nikita Dhawan, and Antke Engel. 2011. *Hegemony and Heteronormativity: Revisiting "The Political" in Queer Politics*. London: Routledge.

Zeiger, David. 2005. *Sir! No Sir!* Displaced Films. https://www.displacedfilms.com/films/sir-no-sir/.

Lisa Gilman is Professor of Folklore at George Mason University and Editor-in-Chief of *Journal of American Folklore*. She is author most recently of *My Music, My War: The Listening Habits of U.S. Troops in Iraq and Afghanistan* and (with John Fenn) of *Handbook for Folklore and Ethnomusicology Fieldwork* (IUP, 2019). She is editor (with Michael Dylan Foster) of *UNESCO on the Ground: Local Perspectives on Intangible Cultural Heritage* (IUP, 2015). She produced the documentary *Grounds for Resistance* and the Dzaleka Art Project (www.dzalekaartproject.com).

13

Spectacular Dissent

SABRA J. WEBBER

Oh my God honey did you see this? Apparently, the police have been beating up Negros like hotcakes! It's in the May issue [of Newsweek].

Dave Chappelle (2000)

Fifteen years after stand-up comedian Chappelle's viciously hilarious police brutality routine, "Killin' Them Softly," journalist Matthew Love observed that the well-known routine had become "even more painfully prescient" (Love et al. 2015). By that time, the Black Lives Matter movement was three years old and growing quickly as incidences of police brutality and vigilante "justice" against Black citizens continued. And on September 1, 2016, in support of BLM, 49ers quarterback Colin Rand Kaepernick took a knee before seventy thousand spectators exuberantly awaiting the start of a preseason game against the San Diego Chargers. Instead of standing under the American flag, hand over heart, Kaepernick knelt to the earth beneath the flag as the national anthem was sung. News of his small folk tableau, a performative call to action against police brutality toward Black citizens, sparked a contentious conversation that has resonated globally.[1] At the time of this writing, individuals in sports as disparate as fencing and hammer throw can be found taking a knee. In reaction, some spectators still boo, yell anti-Black insults, and hurl food and drink from the stands.

Despite long struggles on the streets and in courtrooms, achieving social justice for all Americans, in law or in practice, is failing. During the twentieth century, individual elite athletes have protested this status quo at times, but aside from the famous winners' podium resistance tableau designed by runners John Carlos and Tommie Smith at the 1968 Mexico City Olympics, such game day displays have sparked little pushback or progress in race relations—until Kaepernick's kneel following the very visible police murders of Black Americans in the 2010s and the rise of Black Lives Matter.

Big money game days are meticulously scripted by community leaders under the guidance of professional event planners in the big money sport business (Ziakas and Costa 2010). The Black Power salute and the kneel and its subsequent folk performances make visible marginalized citizens and thus are hyper contrastive to these professionally designed "politics-free" festivities that have been considered de rigueur for decades. As we will see, woven through other popular reasons given for visceral expostulation against such affect-imbued protests as the kneel were owners' fears that such protests would be bad for businesses private and public and would turn away fans (Biderman 2017). The flag and anthem heavily mark big money sports game days with patriotism and often, since 1999, with militarism (McCain and Flake 2018). Kaepernick's and Carlos and Smith's tableaux challenged viewers to resee a comfortable American sports-day ritual, a metanarrative of pride and unity, flag, and anthem. Their simple thus powerful tableaux flipped the script offering two *petits récits*—modest, localized, and, in contrast to game day hubbub, silent and still narratives of reproach.[2] Insights of scholars in folkloristics and performance studies have proven fruitful for me in explicating the effectiveness of such small performances. Their research provides resources to explain the roles of actors and reactors (audiences) by drawing on multiple modalities and layers of context in shaping "who gets heard, how, why, and by whom" (Otero 2022, 231), and to what effect.[3] Their work led to deeper insights into the performative power of elite athletes on game days.

Performance studies founder Richard Schechner invites attention to performance aesthetics within professional sports.[4] Theater, dance, music, ritual, play, games, and sports all share, Schechner notes, basic qualities: a special ordering of time and space, special value attached to objects, nonproductivity in terms of goods, and a set of rules that govern the performers' behavior.[5]

Performance studies scholar Tracy Stephenson Shaffer further marks the originating essence of her field as "conspicuous aesthetic performance" that is "distinct, rehearsed, and staged." Performances of elite sports figures both on and off the playing field or court are often just such performances. The question arises whether performances expect a text, for in both performance studies and folkloristics verbal art has been focal. However, as David Rubin (2009) observes, "One can have coherent narratives in mime, in silent film . . . [in] a single painting or picture without . . . any words." He adds tellingly, "In addition . . . emotions would be needed . . . reactions that depend . . . on your experiences up to that time." The athlete-bricoleur's silent and stationary dissent enactments usefully engage with a panoply of modalities including the vision of the waving flag, the sounds of the anthem, and the commotion of game day. The quiet and stationary BLM tableaux have proved highly affecting when bracketed within top-down choreographed, hyper multisensory game days.

Athletes' styling of these game day folk performances draws on the insights of colleagues who share cultural and aesthetic values. Importantly, this collaborative, mutually recognizable assemblage with its folk elements is also relevant to many players' performances during games. As Cochran (1976) described for basketball, players perform on their hometown courts from a young age with panache, humor, and complex and innovative athleticism that can transcend interest in the score. A bricoleur player who can rapidly suss out possible moves or plays in the heat of the moment with what or who is at hand is a performative skill admired early.

But performative opportunities, while central to sport (as game), necessarily trouble the big money sports model. When young players' artful improvisations are displayed in the context of big money competitions, players risk bans, fines, and endless media debates.[6] Top-down management become ruffled by loss of control when players step outside the status quo on or off the field, court, or track on game day. Certainly, artful improvisation talents translated well to Carlos and Smith's as well as Kaepernick's disruptions of top-down designed game day ceremonies. The redesigning and redefining by Carlos and Smith of medal awards and by Kaepernick of the flag and anthem ritual led to a "who's in charge?" moment of outrage for owners, managers, and spectators heavily invested (financially or emotionally) in the status quo—sidelined by athletes.

Folklore's originating essence is what Martha Beckwith (1931) described as the "poetizing touch in folklore" (2) as well as William Thoms's "customs and feelings" (Webber 2015, 55). And long before Alan Dundes determined that "we are all the folk" (1980, 19), Beckwith observed that all groups, "even the most advanced in learning retain this folk tradition" (5). These states of mind are then shared artfully, performatively, by us folk with the "people who come from where [we] come from" (Hickey 1977 quoting Waylon Jennings 146). Drawing on local traditions and local bricoleurs, stages for folk performances might be improvised—a truck bed or someone's front porch or, for the athletes as children, performances in pickup games on the street, a field, or a school playground, often with a bit of material bricolage: a piece of cardboard for first base, an improvised ball, or contrived lighting for a night game, neighbors parking cars, lights on, around a temporary ball field. Local communities draw on communal conventional wisdom to piece together game rules that meet the physical and social requirements for the games—intangible folk heritage.[7] It follows in the case of the Olympic salute or Kaepernick's kneel that similar bricolage led to a temporarily repurposed space within stadiums—a patch of earth or an Olympic podium transformed into a stage for the duration of the anthem.[8]

The performances discussed here are fashioned from resources at hand: communally defined grassroots, the performers and supporters together planning the "script," adjusting and drawing on, as folk performances do, recognizable referential elements from past performances as well as elements, tangible, or intangible, already at hand, or emergent in the moment. Folk communities are born among elite players as they recognize cohorts from similar formative locals who also have shared relatable experiences through their sports culture journeys. Even before the twenty-first century-onslaught of new media, we can think of places (in terms of people who come from where you come from) "as a heavily trafficked intersection, a port of call and exchange, instead of [or, I suggest, in addition to] circumscribed territory" (Conquergood 2002, 145).

Performance studies scholar Elizabeth Bell intertwines performance and folklore studies by drawing on Richard Bauman's insights into expressive culture forms. These highlighted nuggets of social exchange, the athletes' tableaux, for example, draw special attention to a particular cultural experience, thus commenting on it and triggering feedback. A successful tableau results in contemplation and evaluation by stadium audiences of thousands as well as millions in coffee shops, sports bars, homes, and other watch party venues and subsequent discussions in various genres of social media.

To appreciate performance of a particular cultural experience, it must be recognized that its signifying practices[9] are "simultaneously anchored in their situational contexts of use and transcendent of them linked by . . . ties to other situations, other acts, other utterances" (Bauman 2004, 2). Such insights gained from attention to verbal art studies are centrally important for accessing and complexly understanding these quiet, stationary performances that are particularly dependent on a range of heightened senses on and off the field or court. For example, the sports practice of taking a knee with its various folk variants is already familiar. Often, when an athlete is seriously injured during play, players remove their headgear and take a prayer-like knee (Mayer 2016). But the same kneel feels disconcertingly out of place in its new iteration even while (or because) it offers sundry recognizable affordances for BLM performers to take advantage of—racism also leading to injury, even death.

Smith and Carlos: Olympics 10/16/1968

Effective grassroots performances live on in legend, marking their performers as folk heroes, "spokespersons" for the vulnerable "othered."[10] Two of these local heroes are Tommie Smith and John Carlos.

The year leading up to the '68 Olympics had been fraught for Black communities. Muhammad Ali was banned from boxing for three years for refusing military conscription, apartheid nations continued to be allowed to participate in the Olympics, and the dunk (then Black players' specialty) was banned in college basketball as "showboating."[11] Tragically, that spring the Reverend Martin Luther King Jr. was murdered. And days before the Olympics began, Mexican students protesting their government's choice to fund the Olympics rather than fund social programs were surrounded by the army and fired on. Over two hundred students were killed, and hundreds were injured.

In that pre-Olympics atmosphere, Smith and Carlos, student track sensations at San Jose State in California, had discussed with other Black athletes and the Black community on and off campus the idea of boycotting the Olympics over admittance of apartheid nations' athletes and the murders of Mexican students.[12] Instead, they decided to compete and have a say should they win medals. Smith won gold, and Carlos won bronze in the 200-meter. Smith, Carlos, and a white Australian, Peter Norman, who won silver, stepped up on the trilevel winners' podium. While the American flag was raised and the anthem began, the young Americans had their say. Rather than seeming human props to celebrate American excellence, they stood with heads bowed, shoeless, silently raising a black-gloved hand in the Black Power salute. All three men wore the Olympics Project for Human Rights (OPHR) badge, accepted as a compromise to outright banning of competitors from apartheid-practicing countries.

They did not model for the world America's metanarrative of unity. As their anthem rose, they reversed the message of flag and song, podium, and athletes from celebratory to accusatory. Through slight adjustments to proper podium stance and dress, the familiar was made strange.[13] Commonplace referents of the Olympics' celebratory ritual were passed unexpectedly through limonoid space to emerge repurposed via the mise-en-scène of Smith and Carlos. The traditional ritual flipped the script by its new associations—flag and song instantly recurated from emblems of unity to disunity and reminders of American freedom and justice for all promised, not delivered. The young men artistically used "stocks of shared cultural knowledge to explore, negotiate, comment on, or transform the culture itself" (Berger and Del Negro 2002, 64). Not all modalities affect audiences instantaneously, but when well performed the stationary, silent tableau is powerful. The scene instantly hits spectators and lingers, understood as a reminder of worldly realities. That narrative in its context is a shock, yet for Black American communities at the least, surely it was quickly read as a narrative variant, one always already recognized.

Smith and Carlos had found a means to emotively share their message within the cacophonous moments of the Olympic games. Their recourse to the noise was to perform a visual story that was strikingly contrastive in mode and message to the expected game day celebration. As Smith observed, "We had to be seen because we couldn't be heard." Expressivity on and off the field or court, before, during, or after games, necessarily depends on visual cues, but Tommie's comment was triply meaningful. They had to be seen because they couldn't be heard—in the stadium on the podium, in their resistance to apartheid, or back home, where justice for all was not working for Black or working-class citizens.

I was in the Peace Corps in North Africa in 1968 and watched the men's performance proudly from afar, assuming that there would be no consequences for the two Americans' act of civil disobedience. However, unbeknownst to me until we received the next edition of *Newsweek*, as the mise-en-scène commenced, the stadium had hushed in shock, followed by a hysterical reaction: spectators hurled food and drink and spewed racist epithets at the two college students who had just won for America.[14] The men were ejected from the stadium and suspended from the team for transforming the ceremony into a political statement.[15] An unintended consequence was that Peter Norman was never again allowed to compete internationally for Australia. The Australian government apologized to him in 2012, long after his early death.

What had Smith and Carlos pitted themselves against? Long gone are the days when elements in a festive feast day creatively challenged the status quo.[16] Big money game day pageants disallow the disruptive but productive behavior historically emblematic of festival days with their "tolerated margin of mess" (Babcock 1975) in which human trickster interventions might challenge injustices. Planners of sports pageantry have come to assume that such a scene as Smith and Carlos enacted was a disagreeable rupture in the fun of American combative games. And perhaps their win and other Black American citizens' successes on the world stage were especially important to Americans wishing to counter global awareness of US civil rights failures, agitation against apartheid, anti-Vietnam upheavals, Black Power politics of the mid- to late 1960s, and Alcindor's well-known boycott. The outrage and rigid response of the IOC to the men's actions helped ensure that their "distinct, rehearsed, and staged" tableau would become legendary. It was not matched in affect or effect for over fifty years until the kneel, post-2018, found a place in international venues, including in Olympic settings. Although Smith and Carlos's ties to Black culture issues and concerns would be recognizable today, their Olympic venue started with a different challenge from today's post–social media kneel both in how their tableau was staged and in their "situation" in an international sports village.

Offended viewers in that international context became very important to the tableau's power, as they would later with the kneel. Literally disquieted spectators rather amusingly seemed to be trying to unsee the tableau by flooding it with their outcries.[17] Despite other politically inflected game day resistance since the '68 Olympics, none until Kaepernick took a knee would make a similarly powerful impact on American culture.[18]

Kaepernick Era, BLM, 2016

In the mid-2010s, with the burgeoning of social media and police body cameras, visual evidence of murders, often unredressed, of Black citizens by police or by self-appointed vigilantes became more common. The BLM movement gained traction with protests in the streets in late 2014, when grand jury verdicts ruled out trials for the white police killers of Eric Garner (New York City) and Michael Brown (Ferguson, Missouri). College and professional athletes stepped up on the courts on game days with designed, affect-inflected protests that were immediately reported in the press and circulated on social media. On December 13, 2014, the Notre Dame women's basketball team wore pregame warm-up T-shirts emblazoned with "I can't breathe," echoing Garner's dying gasps. The same year, professional basketball players, including LeBron James, also wore warm-up shirts inscribed "I can't breathe" before their Cleveland Cavaliers games.

The summer of 2016 brought widespread witnessing on video of the murder by police of Black citizens Philando Castile (*New York Times* 2017) in the Minneapolis-Saint Paul area and Alton Sterling in Baton Rouge. On their next game day, July 9, 2016, the WNBA Minnesota Lynx donned warm-up shirts with the two men's names printed on the back and "change starts with us—justice and accountability" displayed on the front (Krawczynski 2020). Their sponsor fined the team for altering the shirts. After Kaepernick took a knee two months later, the Lynx and other WNBA teams and later some high school girls basketball teams began taking a knee side by side during the anthem.

Kaepernick was born on November 3, 1987. At Turlock High School in California, he was all state in baseball, basketball, and football. He chose to play football at the University of Nevada. He finished college having passed for over 10,000 yards (5.7 miles) and rushed for over 4,000 yards—a feat that has not been duplicated in his division. He maintained a 4.0 GPA. He then played for six seasons with the 49ers. In four of those seasons, he set one or more records. In his last season, 2016, coming back after three surgeries, he joined only four other NFL players in history to record at least 3 passing touchdowns and 100 yards rushing in a game. However, since the kneel controversy, he has not been hired by another team—blackballed, many players and fans assert, by the NFL (Bois 2017; Samaha 2023).

Kaepernick's kneel, like the Black Power salute, threw off an American sports game plan organized to be innocent of recognition of political or social tensions that would contradict the ideal grand narrative of communitas. American big money sports by design evoke innocent days of yore.[19] Memories of youth in sports—of sitting with one's family looking out over green fields, an ice rink, tennis courts, or basketball courts, eating hot dogs or Cracker Jack or ice cream and experiencing the excitement of the day—are tied to introducing a new generation to weekend escapes into a semipublic venue of innocence and purity, an almost hallowed time-out in which to eat, drink, cheer, and relax.[20]

But we are warned by Miriam Ticktin about celebrating spaces of innocence. She lays out the human consequences of erasing recognition of poverty, class, religious hypocrisy, racism, or sexism within a communal venue. When game day professional planners achieve an innocent space, "unsullied," she writes, "by knowledge or politics," it "institutes a pathetic, docile figure at the heart of this space." She adds, "The centrality of innocence to the political imagination . . . renders invisible the structural and historical causes of inequality. We need . . . to open up political, moral, and *affective* [my emphasis] grammars beyond innocence" (Ticktin 2017, 578). In the context of big money American sports, this observation recalls Biaett's (2017) critique of passive spectatorship quoted in note 18 of this chapter. It also dictates the necessity for a physical or metaphorical space within a space for civil disorder (Babcock 1975, Thoreau 1903). Writes Mary Douglas, "Purity is the enemy of change, or ambiguity and compromise" (1966, 200). When spectacular dissent performances abruptly break through the imposed silence on politics using performed silence in a noisy stadium, some spectators' complacency is jolted by the disagreeable reminder of American failures to ensure justice for all. The subaltern on game day is not only speaking out on racism, but it is doing so taking center stage before thousands of spectators, often with the approval of the most elite players.

The understanding of silence as power is a tactic not limited, of course, to game day displays, nor is silence as resistance limited to folklore and performance studies. Law professor Dorothy Roberts notes that silence can be deployed by dominant or subordinated groups. She posits that dominant groups "misinterpret the silences of subordinated people" (Roberts 927). I suggest that in the case of the resistances discussed here, where silence lends power in a space where noise typically reigns, certain dominant groups who cannot look away *conveniently* misinterpret performers' intent—unable to or refusing to engage with the complexities of the small performances or the severity of the BLM crisis.[21]

Roberts continues, "Silence is not just the absence of voice; silence is 'an interactive process' that responds to the conduct of other human beings" (927). In fact, some spectators' hysterical verbal and physical responses served in marked contrast to the disciplined podium and kneel tableaux.[22] Berger and Del Negro, in their discussion of the role of reflexivity in performance aesthetics, underscore the slippery slope between spectator and participant whereby some spectators, by choice or chance, become actors.

Roguish Utterances

Growing numbers of athletes taking a knee to hysterical verbal displays was especially striking from fall 2016 through winter 2018 and kept the kneel alive. Three typical negative outcries that made headlines during that time seemed to be seeking help or approval from an audience yet were oddly off topic. They were typical in not addressing kneelers' explications for why they were supporting Black Lives Matter or, in fact, in not mentioning BLM at all.

First, three weeks after Kaepernick started taking a knee, Donald Trump wielded his presidential rant—widely televised and circulated in print and social media:

> Wouldn't you love to see one of these NFL owners, when somebody disrespects our flag, to say, "Get that son of a bitch off the field right now, out, he's fired. He's fired." You know, some owner is going to do that. He's going to say, "That guy that disrespects our flag, he's fired." . . . If a player wants the privilege of making millions of dollars . . . he should not be allowed to disrespect . . . our Great American Flag (or Country) and should stand for the National Anthem. If not, YOU'RE FIRED. Find something else to do![23]

The next day, the NFL protests became more widespread when over two hundred players sat or kneeled silently in response to Trump's call for owners to fire the protesting players. Kaepernick's mother summed up the effect of Trump's rant, observing that with his statement he ignited one tiny ember into a forest fire.

A month later, as the kneel and approbation of it grew among players, NFL owners, concerned about fan ire and fearful of losing sponsors, met to try to decide how to stop players from taking a knee. The then Houston Texans owner Bob McNair tellingly said, "We can't have the inmates running the prison." Troy Vincent, a Black former player and head of football operations, overheard, stood, and remarked that as a player he'd been called everything in the book including the N word, but not "inmate." McNair apologized (Belson 2017). Seahawks player Richard Sherman said that McNair should not apologize as this "allows ppl to see you for who you really are" (Henderson 2017).

Third, in early 2018, Fox television commentator Laura Ingraham reacted to a CNN interview with basketball elites LeBron James and Kevin Durant in which LeBron defended Kaepernick and criticized Donald Trump. Her icy comment to LeBron James, Akron's hometown folk hero and basketball great, concluded, "It's always unwise to seek political advice from someone who gets paid $100 million a year to bounce a ball." And she added, "Keep the political comments to yourselves . . . shut up and dribble."

Referring to the trio's responses and other backlashes to athlete protest performances, I borrow and adapt Erving Goffman's consideration of "emotive cries (1978, 787)."[24] In the abstract to his article on response cries, he writes of them as "some roguish utterances that appear to violate [interactional] interdependence, entering the stream of behavior at peculiar and unnatural places, producing communicative effects but no dialog." Roguish utterances, he says, are all moments in which a speaker flounders around in reaction to heightened emotion triggered by an unexpected or out-of-control situation. Although the response cries that I tender in this paper are longer than those from which Goffman draws (and are politically marked), they are, like his, used for moments when one has lost guiding control of their world. It strikes me that they fall into his label of "wails to the world" (800), rituals to repair a self-other alignment when "a piece of the world has gotten loose" (802). Response cries or exclamatory interjections, like "shut up" or "son of a bitch," are flung out to anyone who happens to be around or even to certain imaginary kindred spirits whom the speaker hopes will get it. I add to the self-talk category Goffman's term "recipient design," emotions refelt and reenacted when emoters continue to feel out of control of the situation.[25] By this he suggests that what appears to be blurted out at the spur of the moment is not necessarily so uncontrolled, the pretend blurter even being prepared, if challenged, to reel back the blurt with an excuse or claim to have been misunderstood. So McNair later claimed that he was not referring to the players as prisoners. Such exclamatory imprecations may be impossible to reel in successfully.[26]

Folks feeling entitled might feel less obligated to watch their words and be bolder about deploying unsavory sentiments in chosen public contexts—expecting their rant to be "an understandable reaction to an understood event" (Goffman 1978, 797–98) by their (imagined) audience. In the case of Ingraham, that audience would not be LeBron, who was ostensibly the person she was addressing.[27] Rather, her attack would be, initially, directed to a Fox television audience among whom, it appears, she hoped that her cutesy phrase "shut up and dribble," adapted from her book *Shut Up and Sing* (2003), might catch on.

Considering the three media-enabled outcries above as well as the Norman, Oklahoma, announcer's more overtly racist example below (p. 269), each speaker raises the curtain in one way or another to reveal through emotion-inflected comments the "othering" or devaluing of the actors (as Black or as athletes) through what Goffman labeled "moments of non-person treatment" (1978, 807).

All three examples are spoken by people considered consequential enough to be widely heard, and each throws out a catchy phrase designed to cleverly and performatively, explain why Black professional athletes are unqualified to occupy game day center stage in support of marginalized citizens and, further, are somehow unqualified to interpret their own actions. An NFL team owner, a television commentator, and the now former president of the United States further revealed frustration that they found themselves sidelined vis-à-vis the kneelers—dependent on these lesser mortals to be in on an athlete-led conversation.

In each of these response cries there is frustration that the Black athletes under the flag are harshly revealing social hierarchies more conveniently swept under the rug. McNair tellingly misquoted the old folk saying "inmates running the asylum" as "running the prison." Trump evoked his former television show to try to fire kneeling athletes, and Ingraham wanted only people with higher degrees and good grammar to share political opinions. To them, these athletes represented cultural disorder, "matter out of place" to borrow Mary Douglas's term. Metaphorically and in fact, the athletes invaded center stage, the place where the three commenters clearly considered they belonged. Douglas continues, "Though we seek to create order, we do not simply condemn disorder. It symbolises both danger and power in its ability to overthrow existing power centres" ([1966] 1978, 117).

In riposte to diversionary strategies that were shifting focus from the purpose of the kneel, other elite athletes' silent performances have subsequently refocused on social justice conversations.[28] Japanese tennis star Naomi Osaka, raised in the United States by a Japanese mother and a Haitian American father, and Malcolm Jenkins, at the time a Philadelphia Eagles safety, doubled down in their performances to remind people about police brutality, other BLM social justice issues, or athletes' work on solutions.

Jenkins's short performance for reporters on June 13, 2018, was designed after the Eagles had chosen not to celebrate their NFL championship at the White House, a visit that until the Trump presidency had been customary. The press was fascinated, quite diverted from BLM issues. Jenkins's act pushed back. One by one he held up black on white handwritten signs indicating systemic disparities and inequities disproportionately hurting communities of color. He also noted athlete-activists' donations of time and money to support relevant, often hometown projects. These signs were punctuated by a "You're

Not Listening" sign as, for an excruciating two minutes and forty-seven seconds, confused reporters continued to fixate on the non–White House visit (Chippin 2018). In a similar riposte to diversionary tactics, Osaka played seven matches at the 2020 US Open tennis tournament and, in the spirit of "say their names" (the movement to remember the uniqueness of each person killed), wore a mask before each of her matches inscribed with the name of a murdered Black citizen (Schild 2020). Such additions to game day acts are among hopeful signs that the popularity of the kneel might avoid becoming perceived as simply a "mode of performative appeasement intended to placate protesters while preserving the status quo," a trap that, of course, is always set (Brooks 2021a).

Since fall 2016, the influence of the kneel has spread beyond the States, with the Jaguars and Ravens NFL teams kneeling during a road game in London (BBCNEWS 2017), and to other players of color, white players, often gay or lesbian players, and entire teams along with some coaches and referees. Many soccer teams now take a knee when occupying their own playing fields, both teams together creating a colorful design. In June 2020, when the Premier League teams returned to play after the hundred-day pandemic hiatus, teams and officials knelt but also replaced their names on the shirts with "Black Lives Matter," another move to, in the flesh, reject social media diversionary tactics that claim the players who kneel are communists, fascists, or failed players choosing another means of gaining attention (Bois 2017).

Younger players tend to learn about the kneel through social media. A champion girls' high school team from Norman, Oklahoma, began taking a knee together before each game. In a 2021 state tournament quarterfinals game, a response cry rang out when an announcer, unaware that his mic was on, noticed the girls kneel and launched into a racist diatribe (Bray 2021). He later apologized and blamed his emote on his diabetes.

That same year, just before the 2021 Summer Olympics in Tokyo (delayed from 2020 due to the coronavirus), the International Olympic Committee prohibited its members and the Tokyo Organizing Committee from sharing photos of Olympic athletes taking a knee (Zucker 2021). At the last minute, the IOC backed off on enforcing Rule 50 against demonstrations or political, religious, or racial propaganda in any Olympic venues since "sport is neutral." Leading from behind, the IOC permitted athletes to engage in protests like taking a knee or raising a fist within certain parameters that were immediately breached by players without repercussions (Chappelle 2021). The British women's soccer team took a knee as did the Chileans, the New Zealanders, and the Japanese.

The men's English Premier League teams took a knee as they had done since the death of George Floyd (Bushnell 2021).[29] In spring 2022, Hungarian spectators, mostly children as Hungarian adults had been sanctioned earlier for similar behavior, booed English players as they took a knee (BBC Sport with Phil McNulty 2022). These negative outbursts to witnessing a kneel on game days are a measure of the success of the tableaux and continue to expose racist emotions that are other times kept hidden and under control. At the commencement of the 2023–24 season, Premier League team captains affirmed that a knee would be taken before the opening and final matches of the season, and matches would be dedicated to No Room for Racism in October and April as well as Boxing Day matches. Like Kap's kneel, the League's kneel affirmed a resistance to racism and support for diversity. Sadly, new cold-blooded murders of Black citizens have kept the kneel relevant and Kaepernick off the playing field since January 1, 2017.[30]

Conclusion: "Kaepernick Fooled . . . Everybody!"

Announcer Calling a Kaepernick Touchdown NFL 2016, 00:1.23

American game day spectacular dissent has received global attention and growing approbation for, and frequently adoption of, Kaepernick's kneel both in and outside the sports world.[31] In the era of social media, as we witness "right before [our] eyes" astonishing numbers of cold-blooded and even enthusiastic murders of Black citizens, Kaepernick's kneel resonates.[32] Public intellectuals are frustrated with the failure of rationalism to overcome refusal by too many to attend to researchers' data documenting the devaluing of Black American lives. Hence the importance of performative resistance in and outside stadiums to the trampling of liberty and justice for all. Consider Biaett's call for the physical, emotional, and creative rather than what he calls passive spectatorship (see note 18), Babcock's discussion of trickster figures' talent for performatively shaking up social hierarchies, or Mary Douglas's support of matter out of place toward the same objectives. Pertinent as well is John Brook's appreciation of métis, the tricky literary flourishes that former slave-become-statesman Frederick Douglass employed to artistically awaken nineteenth-century white readership used to "the more familiar and objective logic of Western rationalism" to new perspectives on race, slavery, and slaves.[33] As we have seen, taking a knee has many tricky qualities and thus, trickster-like, confuses and troubles hyperscripted game day expectations. On the field, Kaepernick was celebrated as a great scrambler, a master bricoleur. As quarterback, when a planned play was sussed out by the opposition, he could immediately assess the field to try a new way to advance the ball, captivating spectators and players alike, "fooling everybody." Such a quality came in handy as well to "fool everybody" by game day deployment of affecting, signifying strategies to challenge racial metanarratives that cover up the devaluing of Black citizens.

Kaepernick is no Brer Rabbit, who tricked Brer Fox into throwing him right where he wanted to be—in that tasty briar patch, for it seems Kap is not going to land back on the football field he loved. However, what we learn from the little rabbit about overturning expectations is relatable to Kaepernick's breaking of rules in that shady land where lies the duty to perform civil disobedience as it is popularly understood.

To sum, in this essay, I have studied aspects of elite athletes' American big money game day dissent—foregrounding the legendary 1968 Black Power salute of Smith and Carlos and Kaepernick's 2016 kneel, a practice now recognized and enacted far from America. I consider situational context—both immediate game day contexts and pre- and post–game day reactions as conveyed via various media. I examined three specific well-known negative reactions to the kneel and trace some variations in game day dissent performances since 2016 as the conversation responds to social changes and cultural moods.

Although performance and folklore studies are heavily invested in speech, I have found that broadening theoretical and methodological work with artful speech to study game day performative behavior across the senses has yielded rich insights. The saga of American sports figures addressing social issues creatively is not surprising. Space permits only a hint in this short piece at how players apply their rich toolboxes of performative talents on playing fields to build sideline resistance performances. In considering the complexities of the Kaepernick age, folk elements that players deploy to address issues of hierarchy within the sports world itself, for example, are visible as players artfully "artlessly" use their player platform and body language to remind a vast and varied audience within a venue where play is supposed to cancel all thought of festering national concerns, of injustice issues reaching far beyond the sports world. Players' spectacular dissents open cracks in the metanarrative of what a player, sport, and game might be and what America represents in the experiences of various "othered" socioeconomic, linguistic, gender, racial, or ethnic communities. In this context, embodied expressivity flips the script so viscerally that it immediately jolts spectators. They witness the quiet, still sorrow of kneelers enacting the vulnerable within a stadium replete with jubilancy and self-congratulation.

Colin Kaepernick recognizes the sacrifice and even danger that he might be facing as a very visible Black man. And, as long as he cannot play ball, the image of his kneel is more powerfully indexical of social injustice. That elite athletes and others in many corners of the globe could read the tableau and apply its restorative urgency to their own small places inspires cautious hope that fewer in our global treasury of lives will die unfulfilled.

Notes

Acknowledgments. My thinking about folk elements in nonfolk games was triggered by Robert Cochran's paper "Folk Elements in a Non-Folk Game," read at the 1974 American Folklore Society annual meeting in Portland, Oregon. Many thanks to Suzanne Enzerink for my title and to James Dorsey for his early essays on the complex relationship between politics and soccer culture in the Middle East/North Africa. Thank you, Katey Borland, Simon Bronner, John Brooks, Robert Cochran, Steve Hall, Marge Lynd, Linda Sims, Timothy D. Taylor, and Alex McDougal-Webber for pointing me in helpful directions or offering thought-provoking insights while I was thinking, speaking, and writing about spectacular resistance.

1. A tableau (vivant) is a static scene of one or more silent, stationary actors posed carefully, often costumed, with props or scenery. It combines elements of theater and the visual arts.

2. See Webber and Mullen (2011, 214–15) for the interplay between grand narratives and *petits récits*.

3. "Semiotic modes other than language are . . . fully capable of serving for representation and communication. Indeed, language . . . as speech or as text, may now often be seen as ancillary to other semiotic modes" (Kress and van Leeuwen 2001, 46).

4. Begging the question of why sport, infused with performative moments, is less attended to in terms of aesthetics or affective resistance than are these elements in other performing arts—a complex issue that needs more study.

5. "Conceptualization of space is resolved through human practice with respect to it" (Harvey 2006, 125–26).

6. Consider knee-jerk reactions over excessive celebration or balletic leaps over approaching tacklers in football, or similar kerfuffle in basketball over dunks as showboating, or bat flipping in baseball.

7. I suggest that the space between an individual's communally shared emotions and the resultant artful folk expressivity, including material culture, might fruitfully be considered in the context of Raymond Williams's "Structures of Feeling" (1977, 128–135).

8. It would be interesting to unpack why no one rushed to remove the actors from their tableaux.

9. That is, signifying practices across modalities.

10. Folk heroes are local although they may become incorporated into popular culture—for example, John Henry. Cf. Roberts (1989) throughout.

11. Critics called the dunk ban the "Alcindor rule" and called it racist as the move had been refined primarily among young Black players during their days

playing street basketball. With that fearful weapon, Lew Alcindor, later to be Kareem Abdul Jabbar, was unbeatable.

12. While teaching at San Jose State in 1968, Professor Harry Edwards instigated the Olympics Project for Human Rights (OPHR).

13. *Ostranenie* as described in Hawkes (1977, 62).

14. Mise-en-scène is the arrangement of props or scenery on the stage of a theatrical production.

15. Olympics competitions have, in fact, seen cancellations, bans, and boycotts due to geopolitical issues.

16. Biaett (2017, 189–91), a festival and events consultant, laments that festivity is no longer "a time of physical, emotional, and creative expression" and is now "passive spectatorship," a form of social engineering imposed by local, national, and international political powers as "economic engines."

17. See discussion of "spontaneous narrative" (Kaivola-Bregenhoj 1966, 52).

18. In 1972, another podium protest was reckoned either a failed performance or not a performance at all (Wikipedia 2023).

19. Perhaps this secular sacrosanct approach to game days explains why folklorist Alan Dundes, in publishing *Into the Endzone for a Touchdown* (1978), earned death threats for his homoerotic approach to football.

20. The conflict over how American sport, including big money sports, should fashion or reflect American social values is also a point of contention when designing the stadiums themselves. The conclusion of Lisle's work, *Modern Coliseum*, gently excoriates the over-the-top-ness of today's sports stadiums. "We could demand that stadiums be affordable. . . . The stadium could again live up to its image as a democratic space where we experience our whole communities. We can have a society . . . in which citizenship isn't measured in income but engagement . . . a crowd that makes its own noise, not one pulverized by the Jumbotron. Professional stadiums once were great public spaces, and they can be again." He sums up that sports can and should cut across economic, ethnic, and racial boundaries, should reflect how society ought to work, and concludes, "Sport *can* do these things, and so too could our stadiums" (Lisle 2017, 266).

21. In a recorded lecture a year after the first kneel, Michael Butterworth noted the seemingly disingenuous claim to confusion about the tableau's purpose, though the point had been very clearly articulated as state-sponsored violence against unarmed Black men.

22. And the kneel tableau is powerfully contrastive aesthetically and emotively to the explosive physicality of the same bodies performing on the field, track, or court.

23. Here, Trump invokes his business mogul television persona by referencing "You're fired" four times.

24. "These emotive cries . . . have the sort of open aside which adults are especially prone to employ in exasperated response to children, servants,

foreigners, and other grades who easily qualify for moments of non-person treatment" (Goffman 1978, 807).

25. Goffman gives credit to Harvey Sacks for this term.

26. The purposeful misreading of the tableaux and similar performances seems a fruitful topic for further investigation into how and why avoidances are triggered and how they are responded to.

27. These behavioral examples relate closely to Goffman's understanding of Piaget's and Vygotsky's descriptions of children's egocentricity.

28. See Bronner for a discussion of taking a knee in the context of the practice of folklore (2019, 24–27) and for early examples of players modifying the tableau (24–25) to refocus spectators' appreciation of its core intent—protest against state-sponsored, allowed, tolerated, ignored, or justified violence against unarmed Black citizens.

29. Rekeying of BLM dissent displays continues: On June 8, 2022, the NBA wore orange warm-up T-shirts reading "end gun violence" as a response to the Uvalde, Texas, massacre of children—a recognizable nod in content and context from BLM to a related issue.

30. Kaepernick has garnered attention and approval in and outside the sports world. Some of the awards he has won include: the 2017 *Sports Illustrated* Muhammad Ali Legacy Award; the 2017 ACLU Eason Monroe Courageous Advocate Award; the 2017 Puffin/Nation Prize for Creative Citizenship; the 2018 Amnesty International Ambassador of Conscience Award; the 2018 Harvard University W. E. B. Du Bois Medal; and the 2020 Ripple of Hope Award from the Robert F. Kennedy Center for Justice and Human Rights.

31. A 2018 Nike commercial narrated by Kaepernick affectingly echoes a push for sports to be inclusive.

32. Kris Kristofferson, "Don't Let the Bastards Get You Down" (country music recording).

33. Term derived from the name of an ancient Greek goddess. Her name originally connoted "magical cunning." She possessed trickster qualities highly prized by Athenians. By one account, Zeus was worried enough about her as a rival that he swallowed her, thus incorporating trickster abilities into his power repertoire.

Bibliography

Babcock, Barbara. 1975. "'A Tolerated Margin of Mess:' The Trickster and His Tale Reconsidered." *Journal of the Folklore Institute* 11, no. 3 (March): 147–86.

Bauman, Richard. 2004. *A World of Others' Words: Cross-Cultural Perspectives on Intertextuality*. Malden, MA: Blackwell.

———. 2011. "Commentary: Foundations in Performance." *Journal of Sociolinguistics* 15, no. 5 (November): 707–20.

BBC News. 2017. "NFL Protests: Why Did Players Kneel or Link Arms?" September 25, 2017. https://www.bbc.com/news/world-us-canada-41392433.

BBC Sport with Phil McNulty. 2022. "English Players Jeered for Taking a Knee in Hungary by Crowd Made Up Largely of Children." https://www.bbc.com/sport/football/61692552.

Beckwith, Martha. 1931. *Folklore in America: Its Scope and Method*. Poughkeepsie, NY: Vassar College, the Folklore Foundation.

Bell, Elizabeth. 2008. *Theories of Performance*. Thousand Oaks, CA: Sage.

Belson, Ken. 2017. "Texans Owner Bob McNair Apologizes for 'Inmates' Remark." *New York Times*, October 27, 2017. https://www.nytimes.com/2017/10/27/sports/football/bob-mcnair-texans.html.

Berger, Harris M., and Giovanna P. Del Negro. 2002. "Bauman's Verbal Art and the Social Organization of Attention: The Role of Reflexivity in the Aesthetics of Performance." *Journal of American Folklore* 115, no. 455 (Winter): 62–91. https://doi.org/10.2307/542079.

Biaett, Vernon. 2017. "Festivity, Play, Well-Being . . . Historical and Rhetorical Relationships: Implications for Communities." In *Handbook of Community Well-Being Research*, edited by Rhonda Phillips and Cecilia Wong, 189–98. New York: Springer.

Biderman, Chris 2017. "Why Giants Owner John Mara's Statement on Colin Kaepernick Is Dangerous." Niners Wire, May 29, 2017. https://ninerswire.usatoday.com/2017/05/29/why-giants-owner-john-maras-statement-on-colin-kaepernick-is-dangerous.

Bois, Jon. 2017. "Let's Talk about Colin Kaepernick." Chart Party. https://www.youtube.com/watch?v=1IocUTXwr-k&ab_channel=SecretBase.

Bray, Dwayne. 2021. "The Story behind the High School Basketball Team That Took a Knee in Oklahoma." Andscape.com Social Justice, April 12, 2021. https://andscape.com/features/the-story-behind-the-high-school-basketball-team-that-took-a-knee-in-oklahoma.

Bronner, Simon. 2019. The Practice of Folklore: Essays toward a Theory of Tradition. Jackson: University Press of Mississippi.

Brooks, John. 2021a. "Monumental Fugitivity: The Aesthetics of #BlackLivesMatter Defacement." *Critical Inquiry Blog*, July 14, 2021.

———. 2021b. "Sandy's Root, Douglass's *Métis*: 'Black Art' and the Craft of Resistance in the Slave Narratives of Frederick Douglass." *Journal of Nineteenth-Century Americanists* 9 (1): 185–205. https://doi.org/10.1353/jnc.2021.0019.

Bushnell, Henry. 2021. "USWNT, Other Soccer Teams Kneel before Olympic Openers to Protest Racism." *Yahoo!Sports*, July 21, 2021. https://sports.yahoo.com/olympics-soccer-players-kneel-uswnt-090330888.html.

Butterworth, Michael L 2017. *Athletes and Activism: Mediating the Politics of the NFL*. The University of Texas, Austin: Moody College of Communication. https://utexas.box.com/s/hf8mbpvcga6hcmcjqy8i5zi417w6ztdf.

Chappelle, Bill. 2021 "NPR Olympians Take a Knee against Racism, under New Policy Allowing Protests." July 21, 2021. https://www.npr.org/sections/tokyo-olympics-live-updates/2021/07/21/1018811516/players-take-a-knee-at-tokyo-olympics-as-the-first-competitions-kick-off.

Chappelle, Dave. 2000. *Killin' Them Softly*. Live stand-up comedic performance. Washington, DC: Lincoln Theater. Duration 1:05.35. https://www.youtube.com/watch?v=FclScfPoKes&ab_channel=Jordan.

Chippin, Alex. 2018. "Eagles' Jenkins Responds to White House, Critics with Signs on Social Injustice." theScore.com, June 16, 2018. https://www.thescore.com/nfl/news/1554635.

Cochran, Robert. 1976. "Folk Elements in a Non-Folk Game: The Example of Basketball." *Journal of Popular Culture* X, no. 2 (Fall): 398–403.

Conquergood, Dwight. 2002. "Performance Studies: Interventions and Radical Research." *Drama Review* 46 (2): 145–56.

Douglas, Mary. (1966) 1978. *Purity and Danger: An Analysis of Concepts of Pollution and Taboo*. London: Routledge and Kegan Paul.

Dundes, Alan. 1978. "Into the Endzone for a Touchdown: A Psychoanalytic Consideration of American Football." *Western Folklore* 7 (2): 75–88.

———. 1980. *Interpreting Folklore*. Bloomington: Indiana University Press.

Goffman, Erving. 1978. "Response Cries." *Language* 54, no. 4 (December): 787–815.

Harvey, D. 2006. *Spaces of Global Capitalism: Towards a Theory of Uneven Geographical Development*. London: Verso.

Hawkes, Terence. 1977. *Structuralism and Semiotics*. London: Routledge.

Henderson, Brady. 2017. "Richard Sherman Denounces Texans Owner Bob McNair's Comments." ESPN, October 27, 2017. https://www.espn.com/nfl/story/_/id/21187946/richard-sherman-seattle-seahawks-says-houston-texans-owner-bob-mcnair-showed-true-self.

Hickey, Dave, ed. 1977. "Romancing the Looky-Loos." In *Air Guitar: Essays on Art and Democracy*, 146–54. Los Angeles: Art Issues Press.

hooks, bell, ed. (1990) 2019. "Chapter 5: Homeplace: A Site of Resistance." In *Yearning: Race, Gender, and Cultural Politics*, 41–49. New York: Routledge.

Kaivola-Bregenhoj, Annikki. 1996. *Narrative and Narrating: Variation in Juho Oksanen's Storytelling*. Helsinki: FF Communications 261.

Krawczynski, Jon. 2020. "How Four Days in 2016 Shaped Lynx and Wolves' Reaction to George Floyd's Death." *The Athletic*, June 15, 2020. https://theathletic.com/1863580/2020/06/15/how-four-days-in-2016-shaped-lynx-and-wolves-reaction-to-george-floyds-death.

Kress, G., and T. van Leeuwen. 2001. *Multimodal Discourse: The Modes and Media of Contemporary Communication*. London: Arnold.

Lisle, Benjamin D. 2017. *Modern Coliseum: Stadiums and American Culture*. Philadelphia: University of Pennsylvania Press.

Love, Matthew. 2015. "6. 'Dave Chappelle: Killin' Them Softly'(2000)." In Steve Ciabattoni, David Fear, Tim Grierson, Matthew Love, Noel Murray, and Scott Tobias. "Divine Comedy: 25 Best Stand-Up Specials and Movies." 2015. *Rolling Stone*, July 29, 2015. https://www.rollingstone.com/culture/culture-lists/divine-comedy-25-best-stand-up-specials-and-movies-70696/mitch-hedberg-comedy-central-presents-1998-228975.

Lutterbie, John. 1999. "Performance in the Proximity of Silence." *Performance Research* 4 (3): 12–16. https://doi.org/10.1080/13528165.1999.10871686.

McCain, John, and Jeff Flake. 2018. "Tackling Paid Patriotism: A Joint Oversight Report." October 1, 2018. https://s3.documentcloud.org/documents/2506099/tackling-paid-patriotism-oversight-report.pdf.

Mayer, Steven. (2014) 2016. "Taking a Knee: Is It Required Etiquette on the Field?" *Bakersfield Californian*, September 7, 2016. https://www.bakersfield.com/archives/taking-a-knee-is-it-required-etiquette-on-the-field/article_ca906840-2165-5059-88f3-3ba18d5539f6.html.

New York Times. 2017. "Dash Camera Shows Moment Philando Castile Is Shot." June 20, 2017. https://www.nytimes.com/video/us/100000005176538/dash-camera-shows-moment-philando-castile-is-killed.html.

NFL. 2016. "Colin Kaepernick Shreds the Packers." YouTube video, 00:1:16. https://www.youtube.com/watch?v=6rHWeDOJYDM&ab_channel=NFL.

Nike. 2018. "Colin Kaepernick Nike Commercial." YouTube video, 00:2:05. September 7, 2018. https://www.youtube.com/watch?v=lomlpJREDzw&ab_channel=NDJ.

Otero, Solimar. 2022. "Rekeying Latinx Performance: Gesture, Ancestors, and Community." *Journal of American Folklore* 135, no. 536 (Spring): 230–38, 264.

Phelan, Peggy. 1993. *Unmarked: The Politics of Performance*. London: Routledge.

Roberts, Dorothy E. 2000. "The Paradox of Silence: Some Questions about Silence as Resistance." *University of Michigan Journal of Law Reform* 33 (3): 927–41. https://repository.law.umich.edu/mjlr/vol33/iss3/6.

Roberts, John. 1989. *From Trickster to Badman: The Black Folk Hero in Slavery and Freedom*. Philadelphia: University of Pennsylvania Press.

Rubin, David C. 2009. "Oral Traditions as Collective Memories: Implications for a General Theory of Individual and Collective Memory." In *Memory in Mind and Culture*, edited by Pascal Boyer and James V. Wertsch, 273–87. Cambridge, UK: Cambridge University Press.

Samaha, Albert. 2023. "The NFL Has Done the Bare Minimum and Salvaged Its Reputation." *Buzz Feed News*, February 10, 2023, 927–31. https://www.buzzfeednews.com/article/albertsamaha/nfl-super-bowl-rihanna-racism-kaepernick-pr-savvy.

Schechner, Richard. 2006. *Performance Studies, an Introduction*. 2nd ed. New York: Routledge.

Schild, Darcy. 2020. "US Open Champion Naomi Osaka Wore 7 Different Face Masks at the Tournament to Honor Police Brutality Victims." *Business Insider*, September 16, 2020. https://www.insider.com/naomi-osaka-tennis-us-open-face-masks-pictures-2020-9.

Shaffer, Tracy Stephenson. 2002. "The Place of Performance in Performance Studies." *Text and Performance Quarterly* 40 (1): 49–71. https://doi.org/10.1080/10462937.2020.1709742.

Slyomovics, Susan. 2005. *The Performance of Human Rights in Morocco*. Philadelphia: University of Pennsylvania Press.

Taylor, Timothy D. n.d. Accessed February 2, 2023. https://www.timothydtaylor.com.

Ticktin, Miriam. 2017. "World without Innocence." *American Ethnologist* 44, no. 4 (November): 577–90.

Thoreau, Henry David. (1849) 1903. *On the Duty of Civil Disobedience*. London: Simple Life Press.

Webber, Sabra J. 2015. *Folklore Unbound: A Concise Introduction*. Long Grove, IL: Waveland Press.

Webber, Sabra J., and Patrick B. Mullen. 2011. "Breakthrough into Comparison: Stories, Local History, and the Narrative Turn." *Journal of Folklore Research* 48 (3): 213–47.

Wikipedia. 2023. "1972 Olympics Black Power Salute." Last edited January 8, 2023. https://en.wikipedia.org/wiki/1972_Olympics_Black_Power_Salute.

Williams, Raymond. 1977. *Marxism and Literature*. Oxford, UK: Oxford University Press.

Ziakas, Vassilios, and Carla Costa. 2010. "'Between Theatre and Sport' in a Rural Event: Evolving Unity and Community Development from the Inside-Out." *Journal of Sport & Tourism* 15:7–26. https://doi.org/10.1080/14775081003770892.

Zucker, Joseph. 2021. "Report: Olympic Social Media Teams Banned from Posting Pictures of Athletes Kneeling." Bleacher Report, July 21, 2021. https://bleacherreport.com/articles/10008310-report-olympic-social-media-teams-banned-from-posting-pictures-of-athletes-kneeling.

Sabra J. Webber is Professor Emerita and a member of The Ohio State University Emeritus Academy. She is the author of *Romancing the Real: Folklore and Ethnographic Representation in North Africa* and *Folklore Unbound: A Concise Introduction*.

14

Performative Landscapes
An Exploration

LISA GABBERT

The concept of performance gained traction in folklore studies in the 1970s and was the dominant paradigm for over thirty years. Drawing on a variety of overlapping veins of thought, performance was variously conceived as a means of reorienting the discipline away from more textual, referential, and static approaches and toward understanding folklore as a kind of social process. The history of performance studies in folklore is well known and does not need to be rehashed here (see, for example, Bauman 2012). Scholars such as Roger Abrahams, Barbara Kirshenblatt-Gimblett, Richard Bauman, Charles Briggs, Dell Hymes, Deborah Kapchan, and many others thought about and experimented with various ways in which to reconceptualize folklore. The landmark book *Toward New Perspectives in Folklore* (Paredes and Bauman 1972), for example, which, along with Robert Georges's 1969 article "Toward an Understanding of Storytelling Events," institutionalized the word *toward* in innumerable subsequent titles in folklore scholarship, explored folklore as a situated performance by investigating interactions between tellers and listeners; notions of competence and appropriateness; the role of audience; the role of style; and the overall multifunctionality of language, including how poetic and formal features convey nonreferential meaning. And, of course, ideas about performance spanned far beyond folkloristics to include such examples as the interdisciplinary Department of Communication at Northwestern with scholars of communication studies, theater, and performance, and the well-known performance studies program at New York University's Tisch School of the Arts, with such noted scholars as Richard Schechner, Diana Taylor, José Esteban Muñoz, Fred Moten, and folklore studies' own Barbara Kirshenblatt-Gimblett.

Performance orientations have been more commonly applied to the verbal and ritual genres (e.g., Turner 1986; Bell 1992), although scholars have successfully applied performance to material culture and other emerging forms. Drawing on J. L. Austin's (1962) notion of performative utterances, for example, Jack Santino (2006) applied the term *performative commemoratives* to certain kinds of temporary public memorials such as roadside crosses, sites of terrorist bombings, and the public memorials that occurred after the death of Princess Diana. These commemorative sites often emerge after an untimely death, and they seek to both commemorate the actual person and draw attention to the conditions of the death. They therefore also are forms of political protest and hence performative in Santino's view, in that they attempt to enact change. Robert Dobler similarly applied this concept to ghost bike memorials (2011), writing that ghost bikes both remember the person who died and comment on bike safety. The integration of the internet into daily life further expanded ideas about performance as scholars identified social media activities such as tweets and Facebook posts as bids for attention and user comments and "likes" as new forms of audience response and evaluation (Buccitelli 2012).

In this article, I apply performance orientations to concepts of landscape and place to develop the idea of a performative landscape and suggest some preliminary types. The term *performance* in relation to landscape has been used among cultural geographers since the mid-1990s, but the concept is somewhat different there. Here, I want to think about landscapes and places that have qualities of performance based on folkloristic understandings of that term. In doing so, I use the terms *landscape* and *place* somewhat interchangeably and note from the outset that the types outlined below are not meant to be comprehensive. This is simply a hopefully fruitful initial attempt at thinking about how landscapes and places might be considered as having performative qualities from a folkloristic perspective.

The term *landscape* in geography studies has a long and complex history. It has been closely linked with rurality and representations in art, and it is characteristically thought to be a way of seeing associated with an authoritative, usually colonialist gaze that relied on perspectives like panoramas and vistas in which the (male) viewer was located both outside of the landscape and above it in a moment of conquest (Bacchilega 2007). During the midtwentieth century, geographers such as J. B. Jackson moved away from traditional emphases on rurality to include urban vernacular environments in definitions of landscape while also emphasizing the idea that landscapes signify. This emphasis on signification generally held sway throughout the midtwentieth century and into the twenty-first.

The term *performance* appeared in the mid-90s and increased in use throughout the 2000s (as an example, see Crouch 2012). In a move that paralleled folklore studies, cultural geography's uses of performance moved away from the idea that landscapes were texts to be read. One prominent use aligns with Judith Butler's use of *performativity*, which argues that subjects are produced through performances. When applied to geography, the idea is that places and locations are produced through performance rather than preexisting in a prior state to them. Landscape also came to be used as a verb: actions tied to the environment such as walking, boating, hiking, and so forth could be considered as discursive regimes and tied to larger ideologies. Other approaches embraced phenomenology, examining how landscapes are embodied and practiced. The most prominent performance-oriented variations are found in nonrepresentational theory, which refers to approaches that seek to go beyond discourse or representation, such as affect. They focus on presentation rather than representation and place an emphasis on practice, creativity, and playfulness. This work draws on folklorists, anthropologists, and others who have long looked at space and place (Low and Lawrence-Zúñiga 2003). Arjun Appadurai (1996), for example, noted that much of the anthropological record consists of ways in which localities are not only created but also maintained, sustained, and contested while Cashman notes that place-making practices are often folkloristic in nature and have real-world consequences (2019).

One very important work that draws together anthropology, cultural geography, and performance studies is *Choreographies of Landscape: Signs of Performance in Yosemite National Park* by the anthropologist dance scholar Sally Ann Ness (2016). Ness uses the term *landscape performance* to identify and analyze micromovements that would not normally be considered performance in conventional terms but that emerge in activities such as bouldering, climbing, and hiking. Ness notes that the term *landscape performance* may be used in two ways. The first is in a relatively straightforward manner in which landscape is the primary subject matter. In the second, more vexing way, she writes, "Landscape performance identifies landscape *itself* as something that is a kind of performance, something that is itself capable of performing" (6).

It is this second meaning of Ness's definition that I am suggesting when thinking about performative landscapes from the point of folkloristics. I start with suggestions made in earlier articles that places are constructed in performance and emergent (Gabbert 2007, Gabbert and Jordan-Smith 2007). In an early move that gestured toward performance orientations, Robert Georges (1969) suggested that storytelling should be reconceptualized as a kind of "communicative event" during a period of scholarship when folklore was largely conceived as an aggregation of texts. Edward Casey (1997) famously suggested that places "happen" in that they gather together memories, histories, narratives, peoples, and actions within a single location. As the result of networks of human and nonhuman actions, landscape is beyond the control of any single individual, and so we might think of a landscape as greater than the sum of its parts.

Richard Bauman notes that performance approaches start with the idea that performance is a special mode of communicative display, generally consisting of formal features, special modes of delivery, and particular participant structures that differ from ordinary modes of communication; this special mode of delivery calls attention to itself as a special mode and is subject to an evaluation by an audience (2012, 95). Breaking this statement down into its component parts, performance calls attention to itself through a variety of means and, because it purposefully calls attention to itself, is therefore subject to evaluation by an audience. Formal features, modes of delivery, and different participant structures all mark performance as performance, although how such features manifest, what counts as markers, and to what degree vary.

The role of audience typically has been a lynchpin in conceptions of performance, as scholars came to realize that they played a crucial role, in many cases actively helping construct and even participate in performance, rather than simply acting as passive receivers. As essentially coauthors (Duranti 1986), audience members may respond to utterances or exclamations to spur or encourage the performer; Daniel Crowley's (1990) examination of the Bahamian phrase *Bunday!* is a classic example. Audience response also indicates evaluation, and/or the audience may even extend the initial performance frame in time and space with performances of their own. In thinking about landscape as performance, I start with the audience, which immediately leads to thinking about tourists or visitors, people who, to one degree or another, are cast (or cast themselves) as audience by traveling to a particular location and then evaluating it according to certain criteria. The more a place is shaped by an audience and subject to its evaluation, the more overtly it seems to be a performance.

Another important indicator is the degree to which a performance is framed or marked off from more ordinary surroundings. In verbal performances, this occurs largely through formal features and generic markers such as "once upon a time" or "I heard this crazy story from a friend the other day" or perhaps a shift in register, where speech becomes more formalized and stylized through word choice, tone, or pitch. These features function reflexively and metapragmatically, heightening the poetic, emotive, and other nonreferential functions of language and in so doing call attention to the performance as a performance. Performances like rituals and festivals may be marked off from ordinariness through the stylized marking of time and space while objects may be framed, put on display, or otherwise lifted out of their ordinary surroundings to somehow mark them as "special" and therefore differentiated from ordinary objects. Similarly, performative landscapes may be marked off by way of gates, bridges, or other objects; they may also be marked off by discourse alone, with no overtly visible sign that one has left an ordinary landscape and is now entering another special kind of place. Locations that become sites for legend trips, discussed below, are an example. The marking off vis-à-vis the heightening of aesthetic and poetic aspects also may occur through the more embodied senses rather than the merely visual. Scents, sounds, or perhaps even temperature might play a role in performance since all can produce forms of affect in the visitor, the awareness of and response to which is contingent on the subjectivity of the individual. Again, the more such features call attention to the landscape as somehow special, the more we might say that we are closer to performance.

Finally, the existence of a script is important. A script can be thought of as a preexisting template that forms the basis of each iteration of performance. A script may consist of specific words or sequences of actions or objects, or a script may be more vague and general and simply exist out in the world, such as a social script upon which ideas about something like, say, gender are based. The repetition of scripts gives performances coherence and a sense of continuity over time so that one performance can be seen as an instantiation of another, making the performances seem "the same" or "traditional" in the commonsense use of that term, even if they clearly are not. Further, the ways in which audience orients to the script varies, as the experience, interpretation, and evaluation of scripts by an audience are shaped by factors of race, gender, class, and other identity features. Performative landscapes have scripts, but like other kinds of scripts they are experienced in different ways by different kinds of people.

The nature of scripts, and the attitudes toward them, also vary. Some scripts are seen as more authoritative, and such scripts are seen as not easily changed, nor is it understood as desirable to do so. Rituals are an example in which participants typically hew as closely as possible to a script to attain performative efficacy. Other scripts are more flexible, open, and subject to change (Bauman and Ritch 1994). But all scripts leak, even authoritative ones, meaning that they are subject to disruption or being toyed with. Performance can unsettle by going "off script" for various purposes, including calling attention to the existence of the script itself or to the nature of the directions it provides—such interference is the basis of performance art as well as some kinds of folklore. Some performative landscapes have a more authoritative script while others have a script that is more flexible and contingent. The degree to which the script is curated and by whom appears in part to determine the landscape type; an open, more flexible script suggests a more vernacular performance landscape.

The types of performance landscapes outlined below are tourist destination resorts, intersectional landscapes, interactional landscapes, and commemorative landscapes. Again, they are not meant to be hard and fast categories but rather an initial attempt to explore different kinds of places that have different kinds of performative qualities.

Tourist Destinations: Full Performance

The most identifiable type of performance-oriented landscapes are full-scale tourist attractions, perhaps the place-based equivalent of full cultural performances. Full cultural performances are formal and bounded in time and space; the roles of performer/s and audience are clearly delineated; and adherence to an authoritative, preexisting script is quite close. Examples of place-based equivalents in this category would be Disneyland/Disney World or other kinds of all-inclusive resorts in which the landscape or built environment is itself the attraction.

Tourist destination resorts are clearly marked off from their more ordinary surroundings; in Barbara Kirshenblatt-Gimblett's (1998) words, this marking helps transform a location into a destination. Entrances and exits into and out of destination landscapes may be framed by a large gate, a change in vegetation and architectural style, or a stylized entryway; they also may be heavily guarded. Or one may pass through a series of doorways. Just getting from one's car into Disneyland, for example, is a journey through a series of liminal spaces from the parking lots to a shuttle, to a walkway, through checkpoints, and into the Magic Kingdom. And of course, Disneyland is subdivided into kingdoms or lands, each set apart from the others by prominent, heavily stylized visual and aural markers.

All-inclusive destination tourist resorts function in a similar manner. Miriam Kahn (2011) clearly outlines the journey a visitor might take to get to Tahiti. Once there, visitors enter what she calls the "tourist bubble," a landscape designed to keep tourists (and more specifically their money) within the resort complex so that they don't wander around anywhere else, particularly the more "ordinary" parts of Tahiti that don't match resort promises.

Aesthetic features and formal qualities are heightened in such places, acting as attention-getting devices to signal that the location is on display. There are no ordinary fences. Disney flags not only mark property boundary lines but call attention to the nature of the property. In Tahitian resorts, the white sand in the iconic beaches is imported, clearly marking off tourist resorts from other parts of Tahiti, which apparently have none. The heightening of these specific aspects of the location function similarly to the metapragmatic features of discourse.

Heightened aesthetics include not only visual features but other sensorial realms, affectively embodying landscape in visitors. The olfactory realm, as Aisha M. Beliso-De Jesús (2015) explains, is particularly powerful. For example, certain tropical scents might perform Tahiti for visitors inhabiting certain bodies while for the Tahitians themselves, foreignness itself might give off a range of smells (Beliso-De Jesús 2015, 149–51). In the aural realm, particular music may be played (Disney musicals, anyone?), or in the haptic realm the feel of humidity or dryness may constitute a heightening of aesthetic experience for some people and therefore be part of a place performance. Yet while the embodiment of the landscape occurs, interpretation/experience of that embodiment will vary according to a multitude of factors so that again, everyone does not experience the landscape in the same way.

The relationship between script, audience, and audience evaluation in tourist destinations is closely linked. The script is inexorably interconnected to capitalism and consumerism, as such places exist solely to attract an audience for economic purposes. They entice people to pay high fees by claiming competence for the production of a particular script. Disney's script promises nonstop family-friendly fun and entertainment while Tahiti promises relaxation, beautiful scenery, and the allure of the exotic. Their very existence depends on successful performance. If audience evaluations are poor, perhaps in the form of bad Google and Yelp reviews, people will not return. If others are influenced by the evaluations and decide not to go, the resort closes up shop.

This heavy dependence on audience evaluation means that the script tends toward the authoritative end of the spectrum. All aspects of the landscape are tightly organized and controlled to produce a predetermined outcome. I think of this type of landscape as somewhat similar to Erving Goffman's (1961) "total institution," which refers to institutions such as prisons, hospitals, schools, and monasteries where the experience of residents is highly regimented and organized for purposes of control. Such "total landscapes" obviously do not discipline their guests to the degree that prisons do, but control over visitor experience is important. The result is that visitors usually get what is promised, but those promises are fulfilled in a narrow, tightly controlled way. Variation exists, but anything that veers completely off script is considered detrimental.

Even the most controlled and scripted locations, however, are not airtight, as people, things, and events contradict the overarching narrative. Goffman notes this fact in his chapter called "Underlife of a Public Institution," in which he discusses how inmates subvert institutional norms. Disneyland seeks nearly total control over its script. Utah State University master's student David Giles (2017), however, collected contemporary legends about Disney's Haunted Mansion attraction for his thesis. According to this legend, people love the Haunted Mansion so much that after they die, their relatives spread their ashes inside the ride. Part of the legend is that it is a secret job of custodians to go in and vacuum up the mounds of human remains deposited there. How family friendly can you get? Folklore, which often is used to prop up scripts, is also an excellent tool of subversion.

National parks and nature preserves, designated wilderness areas, and other sites of ecotourism provide another interesting set of examples in this category. Many US national parks are marked off just as obviously as destination resorts, as the distinction between "park" and "not park" is obvious due to the rough transition between the sprawling development of hotels, water slides, T-shirt shops, and restaurants outside the park and the park itself, where allegedly no such development is allowed (although national parks obviously have quite a bit of "approved" development). West Yellowstone, Montana, outside of Yellowstone National Park, and Gatlinburg, Tennessee, outside of Smokey Mountains National Park come to mind as examples.

Certainly heightened sensorial and affective realms play an important role in the performance of ecotourism, as the visitor inhales air and scents associated with mountains or deserts or bodies of water that have been put on display, processes that essentially emplace the body. Sally Ann Ness (2016) examines these kinds of embodied realms in her work on performance and Yosemite National Park. Utilizing her training as a dance scholar, she focuses on involuntary or semivoluntary micromovements such as a slip during a climb or a scream during bouldering. She frames these movements as landscape performances in which the body is integrated with immediate factors of the environment such as rock, temperature, and gravity that are largely prediscursive.

Ness also illustrates that such performances can immediately reshape the overdetermined nationalist and patriotic symbology associated with Yosemite. By focusing on the process of meaning-in-the-making vis-à-vis the body, she demonstrates that landscapes are not (or not only) discursive formations and that the script can be flipped even with something as simple as a word or involuntary movement. In addition, I would add that the relationship between script, audience, and audience evaluation in cases of ecotourism is more complex than resort destinations described above. The script remains connected to capitalism and consumerism (and often nationalism) as visitors consume ecologically oriented landscapes as much as ones filled with Disney paraphernalia, but because the landscape on display also is framed as natural or wild, the mere existence of the audience constitutes an interruption of it, since the script entails the promise of few or no people.[1] Wilderness scripts also imply a lack of control or even absence of a script altogether. In other words, due to the landscape's proclaimed status as "natural" rather than "human-made," the script suggests that the script itself is beyond human interference. Yet anyone who has been to a national park likely has encountered crowds, signs of civilization, extensive development, and a plethora of rules and regulations designed to keep the park "natural"—all examples of how this type of script leaks by its very existence. Perhaps such places are less dependent on audience evaluation, however, because unlike destination resorts, poor audience evaluations, which might presumably lead to people not coming, may ultimately prop up the script rather than detract from it.

Intersectional Landscapes: In and Out of Performance

The use of the term *intersectionality* in this context refers to places that have multidimensional identities and aspects, some of which might be of interest and available to various audiences and some of which may not be of interest and/or inaccessible. All locations are, of course, inherently intersectional, as all have a multiplexity of interests, perspectives, and identities and exist within broad global networks of relations from which they are constituted. Here, however, I am thinking of places in which tourists and visitors play an important role as audience yet are only one dimension of the location rather than the primary one. These are places in which some aspects are more or less heightened, aestheticized, and put on display, yet that aspect is one of an array of dimensions that constitute the location. Others are not necessarily purposefully displayed for audiences.

Examples might include places famous for an urban identity, such as Chicago, Los Angeles, Boston, New Orleans, and New York with their well-known buildings, distinctive neighborhoods and boroughs, museums, local color and speech styles, restaurants, and skylines (or, in the case of LA, lack of skyline); another example is perhaps a more broadly invented regional identity such as "the South" or "the West." There are a multitude of practices and discourses that constitute the overall framing of the location, yet certain aspects are selectively highlighted for audiences who seek them out.[2] Examples might be the so-called ethnic enclaves found in large cities such as Little Havana in

Miami, Little India in New York, or the various Chinatowns scattered across the country. Anthony Buccitelli (2016), for example, studied Boston neighborhoods, documenting how ethnic identity can become connected to particular areas through various processes of social remembering, which then might become sites for visiting.

These places are not always as clearly marked off from their surroundings by formal features as the tourist destination resorts described above. Distinctive neighborhoods gradually separate themselves from more ordinary ones through architectural styles; there may be a gradual increase across several blocks of particular kinds of stores and restaurants that mark the location, such as an increase in the number of expensive, high fashion shops along Rodeo Drive in LA or an increase in the number of businesses catering to LGBTQIA+ communities as an indicator of a queer neighborhood, like South Beach in Miami. A famous marker such as the statue of the girl facing the bull on Wall Street in the middle of New York's global financial district may not be well marked at all, and visitors may have to wander around if they wish to see it. Other spots may be very well marked and quite self-conscious. Little Italy in New York distinguishes itself from other neighborhoods by flying outdoor flags, sidewalk dining with tables sporting red-and-white checkered tablecloths signaling family style, or more upscale dining featuring white linen. Vendors stand outside stores and restaurants to entice visitors inside with promises of authentic performance. Other markers of New York may be entirely unhighlighted: a conversation in the street using local terminology; a style of dress; or a thrift store hidden down a narrow street, all of which may still fulfill (or not) the expectations of an audience.

People visit such places in hopes of having a particular kind of experience, but unlike at tourist destination resorts, they are not guaranteed to get it. They may not know where to look, or their own expectations may not match reality. The location may not intentionally display itself or claim competence and so is not responsible to the audience, or, alternatively, there may be a disconnect between ideas about audience expectations and what those expectations actually are. This is because the script in intersectional landscapes is more fluid, flexible, and emergent. There may be a loose set of preexisting ideas, narratives, and expectations about a place, but what specifically constitutes those ideas and expectations is not guaranteed and varies. The audience evaluation is still important since identity is a relational construction (if everyone thought Rodeo Dr. was cheesy instead of posh, it would be a different kind of place), but unlike the full performances of tourist resorts, intersectional landscapes are not as closely tied to consumerism and so don't live or die according to audience evaluations; audience is only one aspect of existence.

Interactional Landscapes: Folk Performance

Interactional landscapes are landscapes in which the audience interacts with and shapes the script in a much more profound way than in the previous examples. I have written about this type of place previously, although I did not identify it as interactional but rather more generally as performative (Gabbert 2015). The example here is the location of legend-tripping activities in Logan Canyon, Utah, known as St. Ann's Retreat and colloquially as "the nunnery." It is a compound of now dilapidated but historically significant cabins and other structures located on Forest Service land. It was owned during the midtwentieth century by the Catholic Diocese of Salt Lake City and used as a weekend spiritual retreat for various orders of nuns throughout the state, although it was never actually a nunnery. It is located in a predominantly LDS area (Church of Jesus Christ of Latter-day Saints), and after the site was purchased by the Salt Lake Diocese in the 1950s, supernatural horror legends about the nuns began to circulate among the local population. For decades these stories prompted local teens to go legend tripping to the site in order to explore and confront the supernatural. Legend tripping often is based on othering, which in this case is the othering of celibate, unmarried Catholic women (Thomas 1991). Other examples include legend tripping based on disability (Torrez [2016] 2022) and racism (Gencarella 2022). Teen legend tripping contributed to the deterioration of the site, which eventually was sold by the diocese in the early '90s and today is abandoned.

The entrance to the site itself is not particularly well marked and easy to miss. There is a dirt road with a locked gate, an attempt by the property owners to keep out unwanted visitors. However, the dirt road and gate look like many other such entrances to cabins and properties that exist along this stretch of highway and so do not stand out in any particular way. What does mark the property as slightly more special than its neighbors are the predominance of "no trespassing" and warning signs saying that unwanted visitors will be recorded on surveillance cameras hidden throughout the property and then prosecuted. Such "visible language" is part of the linguistic landscape that shapes perception and apperception (Kallen 2023). There are also sections cordoned off by razor wire. The reason is that property damage from legend-tripping teens has been a significant problem over the years, leading to some heightening in the way this property is visually marked off from its surroundings.

The clearest marking off the site occurs in the linguistic realm, as people exchange stories of ghosts and supernatural horrors that allegedly occurred at St. Ann's. These stories make up a lurid script consisting of murderous nuns, rape, illegitimate births, shame, infanticide, witches, and hounds of hell. In other words, the site is primarily marked out as something special in narrative by local people themselves; visual markers followed after the fact. Landscapes in this category often are not clearly visually marked or delineated from their immediate surroundings. There may be markers, but often it is up to the visitors themselves to find them.

The script in interactional landscapes is created entirely by visitors. In this case, the landscape is transgressive or, in Yi-Fu Tuan's words, "a landscape of fear" (1979) consisting of supernatural legends, an admixture of history and folklore associated with the location, and people's memorates and personal experience narratives of their own visits.[3] This folk-generated script is quite powerful; it commands attention and compels people to visit and determine for themselves whether the narrative is true. As I previously argued, legend trippers enter the landscape and *inhabit* the script by becoming characters in an ongoing event that they themselves create. This is a slightly different perspective from the more common understanding of ostension, which suggests that legend trippers imitate, copy, or reenact the legend. I argue that by visiting the landscape of a legend (legend tripping), participants literally insert themselves into the script and in doing so ritually transform themselves into story. Interactional landscapes are therefore most actively and fully embodied in/by visitors who become part of the script. Visitors engage with the script by reaffirming existing aspects, playing roles, creating new parts, and discarding others as it relates to their own emerging experiences and inclinations. These experiences, stories, and memorates then feed back into the overarching narrative, so while a preexisting script exists, it is flexible and contingent. The audience creates, inhabits, and shapes it according to collective will.

The location makes no promises of competence of performance, although legend trippers do evaluate whether St. Ann's lived up to its supernatural reputation by talking about their experiences after the fact. These memorates feed back into the script and, whether positive or negative, invoke curiosity in other people about the location. A legend-tripping teen who experiences something spooky lends credence to the overall narrative, but even stories that evaluate the location as uneventful—"nothing happened" or "it was boring, just a normal place"—motivates others to visit and form their own impressions. This is the reason that interactional landscapes like St. Ann's are more than the sum of their parts. No one controls the script, and the landscape takes on a life of its own.

Commemorative Landscapes: Ritual Performance

Commemorative landscapes are places where an important event occurred and is subsequently recognized and remembered. These landscapes may be sacred or secular and encompass more official commemorative sites such as war memorials, battlefields, and holy places as well as more informal folk sites of commemoration such as those examined by Jack Santino (2006), Holly Everett (2002), and others. The landscape plays an important role because it "holds" the memory of an event in place. Audience and remembered event coexist within the same location, spatially collapsing past and present.

Official commemorative landscapes are clearly marked off from their surroundings and are more self-conscious about the way in which they set themselves apart from their surroundings. The markers call attention to the site and cast an audience, and they therefore are similar to other kinds of tourist destinations. A site like Gettysburg Battlefield, for example, is well marked by maps and interpretive signage, directions, and, in some cases, an entry fee. The script is fairly official and inflexible, having been authorized by professional historians, governments or officials, and culture brokers. Such sites are subject to the evaluation of an audience because they promise something: a connection to national history, an educational experience, additive information and value to knowledge, or simply feelings such as awe, inspiration, patriotism, or a deeper sense of history.

The script, however, may be actively contested as other points of view lay competing claims to interpretations of events and hence to power (cf. Norkunas 1993). One example of a commemorative landscape with contesting official scripts is the Bear River Massacre Heritage site, located along the Utah-Idaho border near Preston, Idaho. This site commemorates the 1863 massacre by the 3rd Regiment California Volunteer Infantry, which attacked a band of Northwestern Shoshone living near the Bear River as they slept in their village. It was apparently the worst massacre during the so-called western "Indian Wars" of the nineteenth century, with over four hundred native people killed (Parry 2019).

The site is marked with commemorative markers, although not particularly well or accurately, which have undergone multiple revisions over time. An early interpretive monument was erected in 1932 by the Daughters of Utah Pioneers and the Boy Scouts of America along a highway pullout on land owned by the Daughters of Utah Pioneers. The monument frames the massacre as a "battle" and glorifies the soldiers as heroes who led a successful campaign against hostile Indians. In gallant tones, the marker explains that 250 to 300 tribal people were killed and 70 lodges burned while only 14 soldiers lost their lives. A second marker on the monument, erected in 1952 also by the Daughters of Utah Pioneers, continues the heroic interpretation and emphasizes the courageous and caring role of pioneer women. "Scores of wounded and frozen soldiers were taken from the battlefield to the Latter-day Saint community of

Franklin. Here pioneer women, trained through trials and necessity of frontier living, accepted the responsibility for caring for the wounded until they could be removed to Camp Douglas, Utah. Two Indian women and three children found alive after the encounter were given homes in Franklin." In contrast, there is also a large "memory tree" located off to one side of the markers that stands as a counterstatement to these narratives. The tree is decorated with feathers, drawings, dream catchers, and other Native American indicators, objects presumably put there by Shoshone people who live in the area. The tree visually contradicts these official commemorative scripts and historically has stood as a reminder of alternate perspectives on the event.

Over time, Indigenous understandings and memories of the massacre have become more prominent in official narratives. A third historical marker, erected sometime in the 1980s by the State of Idaho on the edge of the property and next to the memory tree, reframes the event from a battle to a massacre. The first sentence reads, "Bear River Massacre—very few Indians survived an attack here when P. E. Connor's California Volunteers trapped and destroyed a band of Northwestern Shoshoni." Then, in the early 2000s, the state of Idaho constructed a small memorial park above the land owned by the Daughters of Utah Pioneers. The rest stop includes seven additional historical markers, all written by the Northwestern Band of Shoshone, which tells the story of the massacre from their own perspective and in their own words. The last sign begins with the words "The Earth Will Remember" and "we cry for the loss and sacrifice of those who did not survive and we honor the strength of those who lived."

Interestingly, however, *none* of these markers are located on the actual site of the massacre. The signs described above cluster along the pullout of Idaho State Highway 91. The actual location of the massacre is two miles away, along a dirt road with no identifiers. This land was purchased by the Northwestern Shoshone in 2008. It is undeveloped, but, led by former tribal chairman Darren Parry (2019), the tribe is raising money to construct a preserve and interpretive center on a bluff that overlooks the Boa Ogoi River (Bear River) and the killing field. This tribal space is, at the time of this writing, not intended for outside audiences; it is known only to local people but is essential in the construction of history.

The killing field along the Boa Ogoi River is similar to sites described by Henry Glassie (1982) in his work on Ballymenone in which the main class of historical stories are battles. He points out that while local historians could be somewhat imprecise in dating important historical events in time, they were quite precise in locating those events in space. This is, he notes, because land "obliterates chronology," connecting people in the present to people of the past (1982, 111). His theory of emic history in Ballymenone is that history is spatial and categorical because landscape joins events together in place that are disparate in time: there were two battles on this very bridge; this is the river that connects the story of St. Febor to Black Francis (1982, 200). Richard Bauman (1986) distinguishes between the "narrated event," which is the story being told, and the "narrative event," which is the situation in which the story is told. Commemorative sites (and interactional sites) collapse these dimensions spatially. People are part of history because they occupy the same space across time, and in commemorative landscapes, the audience is witness to memory.

This collapse of script, audience, and location means that commemorative landscapes have a ritualized dimension to them. People enter the landscape and return having been transformed in some way by being there/here where that happened. Commemorative landscapes are similar to interactional landscapes in this sense except that the audience is witness to the remembered event rather than a participant in it, and so inhabits and shapes the script to a lesser degree.

Conclusion: Vibrant Matter, Vibrant Landscapes

In applying performance in the service of identifying types of performative landscapes, I have thought about landscape in relation to audience, to framing, to scripts, and to the ways in which they are heightened aesthetically and put on display. It is fruitful to think about landscapes in relation to performance because performance largely has been relegated to the human realm, and in particular to human words and actions. But landscapes, places, and localities are larger-than-human phenomena. Landscapes are partly created by humans, but a large portion of them are not, as they also include animals, rocks, trees, plants, soil, microbes, and many other nonhuman elements, including supernatural or spiritual ones.[4] Landscapes are assemblages par excellence of the living and nonliving, human and nonhuman realms and, as an assemblage, have a life of their own.

Thinking about landscapes and places as performative gives landscapes and places agency and power that sometimes has not been attributed to them historically. Often in folklore studies, landscapes and places are treated merely as background scenery for folkloristic action and processes, rather than being examined as something more primary. Jane Bennett argues for a new materialist perspective in her book *Vibrant Matter* (2010). She coins the term "thing-power," which she defines as "the curious ability of inanimate things to animate, to act, to produce effects dramatic and subtle" (2010, 6). "My goal," she writes, "is to theorize a materiality that is as much force as entity, as much energy as matter" (20). She argues that materials can be "lively and self-organizing," meaning that all forms of matter, down to the molecular and atomic levels, can be actants. Part of her project is to decenter the individualism latent in notions of agency that privilege human actors, and in doing so she suggests a "congregational" or "distributive" notion of agency in which material actants never actually act alone: "A lot happens to the concept of agency once nonhuman things are figured less as social constructions and more as actors" (21). Landscapes and places are arenas in which multiple actants from the animal, mineral, human, and nonhuman realms gather together and in which a notion of congregational or distributive agency can be fruitfully applied. It is a perspective that dovetails nicely with the notion of performative landscapes, which, while inexorably tied to humans and networks of human relations, are better understood as living assemblages of vibrant, congregationally agent actants that sometime break through into performance.

Notes

1. A landscape that is framed as somehow natural or wild is obviously every bit as constructed as other kinds of landscapes. This construction of "naturalness" occurs through legislation, regulation, wilderness management, and heavy governmental regulations.
2. The very idea of performance means that some aspects of reality are always selectively highlighted while others are ignored. In the case of intersectional landscapes, the point is that only a few aspects are selected out of a much larger whole.
3. Kenneth Foote (1997) describes a somewhat similar type of landscape, which are those that are abandoned and unused after horrific crimes or tragedies occurred. He identifies such places as "obliterated."
4. I am grateful to the audience member in our American Folklore Society panel of October 2022 who pointed this out.

Bibliography

Appadurai, Arjun. 1996. *Modernity at Large: Cultural Dimensions of Globalization*. Minneapolis: University of Minnesota Press.
Austin, J. L. 1962. *How to Do Things with Words*. Cambridge, MA: Harvard University Press.
Bacchilega, Cristina. 2007. *Legendary Hawai'i and the Politics of Place: Tradition, Translation, and Tourism*. Philadelphia: University of Pennsylvania Press.
Bauman, Richard. 1986. *Story, Performance and Event: Contextual Studies of Oral Narrative*. Cambridge, UK: Cambridge University Press.

———. 2012. "Performance." In *A Companion to Folklore*, edited by Regina F. Bendix and Galit Hasan-Rokem, 94–118. West Sussex, UK: Blackwell Publishing, Ltd.

Bauman, Richard, and Pamela Ritch. 1994. "Informing Performance: Producing the *Coloquio* in Tierra Blanca." *Oral Tradition* 9 (2): 255–80.

Beliso-De Jesús, Aisha M. 2015. *Electric Santería: Racial and Sexual Assemblages of Transnational Religion*. New York: Columbia University Press.

Bell, Katherine. 1992. *Ritual Theory, Ritual Practice*. New York: Oxford University Press.

Bennett, Jane. 2010. *Vibrant Matter: A Political Ecology of Things*. Durham: Duke University Press.

Buccitelli, Anthony Bak. 2012. "Performance 2.0: Observations Toward a Theory of the Digital Performance of Folklore." In *Folk Culture in the Digital Age: The Emergent Dynamics of Human Interaction*, edited by Trevor J. Blank, 60–84. Logan: Utah State University Press.

———. 2016. *City of Neighborhoods: Memory, Folklore, and Ethnic Place in Boston*. Madison: University of Wisconsin Press.

Cashman, Ray. 2019. "Folklore, Politics, and Place-Making in Northern Ireland." In *The Routledge Handbook of Memory and Place*, edited by Sarah De Nardi, Hilary Orange, Steven High, and Koskinen-Koivisto Eerika, 291–304. New York: Routledge.

Casey, Edward. 1997. "How to Get from Space to Place in a Fairly Short Stretch of Time: Phenomenological Prolegomena." In *Senses of Place*, edited by Steven Feld and Keith H. Basso, 13–52. Santa Fe, NM: School of American Research Press.

Crouch, David. 2012. "Landscape, Land and Identity: A Performative Consideration." In *Land & Identity: Theory, Memory, and Practice*, edited by Cristine Berberich, Neil Campbell, and Robert Hudson, 43–54. Amsterdam, Netherlands: Rodopi.

Crowley, Daniel J. 1990. "Bahamian Narrative as Art and as Communication." *Western Folklore* 49 (4): 349–69.

Dobler, Robert. 2011. "Ghost Bikes: Memorialization and Protest on City Streets." In *Grassroots Memorials: The Politics of Memorializing Traumatic Death*, edited by Peter Jan Margry and Cristina Sánchez-Carretero, 169–87. New York: Berghahn Books.

Duranti, Alessandro. 1986. "The Audience as Co-Author: An Introduction." *Text* 6 (3): 239–247.

Everett, Holly. 2002. *Roadside Crosses in Contemporary Memorial Culture*. Denton: University of North Texas Press.

Foote, Kenneth E. 1997. *Shadowed Ground: America's Landscapes of Violence and Tragedy*. Austin: University of Texas Press.

Gabbert, Lisa. 2007. "Distanciation and the Recontextualization of Space: Finding One's Way in a Small Western Community." *Journal of American Folklore* 120 (476): 178–203.

———. 2015. "Legend Quests and the Curious Case of St. Ann's Retreat: Performative Landscapes." In *Putting the Supernatural in Its Place: Folklore, the Hypermodern and the Ethereal*, edited by Jeannie Thomas, 146–69. Salt Lake City: University of Utah Press.

Gabbert, Lisa, and Paul Jordan-Smith. 2007. "Introduction: Space, Place, Emergence." A special issue of *Western Folklore* 66 (3&4):217–32.

Gencarella, Stephen Olbrys. 2022. "Soft Racism in the Contemporary Legend of Anawan Rock: A Critique." *Journal of Folklore Research* 59 (1): 59–100. https://doi.org/10.2979/jfolkrese.59.1.03.

Georges, Robert A. 1969. "Toward an Understanding of Storytelling Events." *Journal of American Folklore* 82 (326): 313–28.

Giles, David. 2017. "The Magic of the Magic Kingdom: Folklore and Fan Culture in Disneyland." MA thesis, Utah State University.

Glassie, Henry. 1982. *Passing the Time in Ballymenone*. Philadelphia: University of Pennsylvania Press.

Goffman, Erving. 1961. *Asylums: Essays on the Social Situation of Mental Patients and Other Inmates*. New York: Anchor Books.

Kahn, Miriam. 2011. *Tahiti beyond the Postcard: Power, Place, and Everyday Life*. Seattle: University of Washington Press.

Kallen, Jeffrey L. 2023. *Linguistic Landscapes: A Sociolinguistic Approach*. Cambridge, UK: Cambridge University Press.

Kirshenblatt-Gimblett, Barbara. 1998. *Destination Culture: Tourism, Museums, and Heritage*. Berkeley: University of California Press.

Low, Setha M., and Denise Lawrence-Zúñiga, eds. 2003. *The Anthropology of Space and Place: Locating Culture*. Malden, MA: Blackwell Publishing.

Ness, Sally Ann. 2016. *Choreographies of Landscape: Signs of Performance in Yosemite National Park*. New York and Oxford: Berghahn Books.

Norkunas, Martha. 1993. *The Politics of Public Memory: Tourism, History, and Ethnicity in Monterey, California*. New York: SUNY Press.

Paredes, Américo, and Richard Bauman, eds. 1972. *Toward New Perspectives in Folklore*. Austin: University of Texas Press.

Parry, Darren. 2019. *The Bear River Massacre: A Shoshone History*. Salt Lake City, UT: Common Consent Press.

Santino, Jack. 2006. "Performative Commemoratives: Spontaneous Shrines and the Public Memorialization of Death." In *Spontaneous Shrines and the Public Memorialization of Death*, edited by Jack Santino, 5–15. New York: Palgrave Macmillan.

Thomas, Jeannie. 1991. "Hecate in Habit: Gender, Religion, and Legend." *Northwest Folklore* 9:14–27.

Torrez, Mercedes Elaina. (2016) 2022. "Evoking the Shadow Beast: Disability and Chicano Advocacy in San Antonio's Donkey Lady Legend." Reprinted in *North American Monsters: A Contemporary Legend Casebook*, edited by David J. Puglia, 216–32. Logan: Utah State University Press.

Tuan, Yi-Fu. 1979. *Landscapes of Fear*. Minneapolis: University of Minnesota Press.
Turner, Victor. 1986. *The Anthropology of Performance*. New York: PAJ Publications.

Lisa Gabbert is Professor of Folklore Studies in the Department of English at Utah State University. She is author of *The Medical Carnivalesque: Folklore among Physicians* (IUP, 2024); with Keiko Wells, *An Introduction to Vernacular Culture in America* (Maruzen, Tokyo 2017); and *Winter Carnival in a Western Town: Identity, Change, and the Good of the Community* (USU Press 2011). Her research interests include place and landscape, festivity and play, and folklore in medical contexts.

INDEX

Page numbers in italics indicate illustrations.

Abakuá spirits, 43, 50, 51
Abegunde, Maria Hamilton, 8, 116, 127–30, 131
Abrahams, Roger, 3, 79
abrazos (frames of dancing), 199, 201, 202, 209n44
Abu-Lughod, Lila, 62
Académie française, 48
acculturation, 6, 40
Acevedo-Ontiveros, Erica, xvi, 10, 179–89, 193
Acuña, Rodolfo F., 182–84
aesthetics, 81, 89; Afrofuturist, 124; of excess, 162; performance, 259; social, 24
affective dimensions, 162, 170, 172, 173, 174; of repetition, 19–20, 24–28
"affective economies" (Ahmed), 162
"affective grammars" (Ticktin), 265
Afghanistan war, xiv, 244, 250
Afro-Atlantic creolization, 125
Afro-Cuban cultures, 40, 44–45, 119, 125, 126
Afro-Diasporic performances, 116, 130
Afrolatinidad, 131; Espiritismo and, 116–19; queerness and, 99, 103, 105, 109, 113
Afrolatinx spirituality, 99, 103, 105, 109, 113
Ahmed, Sara, 24, 64, 71, 222
Alagemma, the Chameleon, 110
Albright, Ann Cooper, 222
Albuquerque, NM, 180, 182
Ali, Muhammad, 261–62
Allen, Jafari S., 63
Allen, Robert, 164, 173

American Flamenco Repertory (Yjastros), 187, 188–89
American Folklife Center, 81
ancestoring, xv–xvi, 8–9, 116–31
Animating Democracy Initiative, 220–21
anthropology, 62; as entertainment, 168; fieldwork in, 60–64, 65; linguistic, 140. *See also* ethnography
antisemitism, 150, 151
Anzaldúa, Gloria, 236
apartheid, 262
Appadurai, Arjun, 281
Arrizón, Alicia, 41
Asian Caribbean rituals, 119, 133n35
athlete-bricoleur, 259–61, 270
audience participation, 133n36
Auslander, Philip, 20–21, 23
Austin, J. L., xiii, 3, 22, 236, 249, 280
authoritative power, 238, 247

Babcock, Barbara, 270
Bachmann-Medick, Doris, 1, 4
Bakhtin, Mikhail, x, xiv, 47–48; Benítez-Rojo and, 56n6; on carnivalesque, 172–73; on dialogism, 48–49; Goffman and, 6, 37, 38, 45, 55; Ortiz and, 49; on performance, 38, 48–49, 55
ballads, 29–30, 78, 79
Ballet Folklórico de México, 184
Bancroft, Hubert Howe, 163
Barad, Karen, 101

299

Barkley, Christine, 32n8
Bartók, Béla, 144
Batchelor, Ray, 207n30
Bateson, Gregory, 22; Goffman and, 3
Bauman, Richard, ix–x, 37, 261, 282; Bakhtin and, 49; Burke and, xv, 80; on entextualization, xiii; on "folklore as event," 140; on genre, 31n3, 48; Gilman on, 235–36, 237; Goffman and, 22; on narrated/narrative events, 293; on performance, 63, 68, 92, 141, 214, 226–27; Sawin on, 5; "Verbal Art as Performance," 213, 215
Bear River Massacre Heritage site (Idaho), 291–92
beauty pageants, 240. *See also* Miss Indian World pageant
Beauvoir, Simon de, 62
Beckwith, Martha, 260
Beethoven, Ludwig van, 142
Behar, Ruth, 69
Beisswenger, Drew, 84
Beliso–De Jesus, Aisha Mahina, 62, 65–66, 105–6, 285
Bell, Elizabeth, 261
belly dancing. See *danse du ventre*
Bembé de Sao, 43, 50
Ben-Amos, Dan, 3, 5
Bendix, Regina, 216
Benítez-Rojo, Antonio, 56n6
Benjamin, Walter, 31n2
Bennett, Jane, 293–94
Berger, Harris, 28, 30, 262, 266
Berlioz, Hector, 151
Bersani, Leo, 67
Be the Street collective (Ohio), 11, 218–21, 225, 230n15
Bhabha, Homi K., 186
Biaett, Vernon, 265, 270, 273n16
Biden, Joseph, 239–40
BIPOC (Black, Indigenous, and People of Color), 7, 63, 74; classical music and, 148; Espiritismo and, 117–19; Gilman on, 242, 248. *See also* race
Bizet, Georges, 50
Black arts movement, 241
Black Lives Matter (BLM), xiv, 11, 258–61, 264–72
Black Power salute, 11, 258–64, 271
Bloom, Sol, 163, 167, 170

bluegrass music, 83, 85
blue laws, 171
blues music, 78, 79
blues-tango, 205n3
Boal, Augusto, 11, 227; Invisible Theater of, 217; Schechner and, 213, 216; on self-consciousness, 217–18; Theater of the Oppressed of, 216–18, 220–21
Boas, Franz, 65
Bogatyrev, Petr, 21, 22, 31n2
Borges, Jorge Luis, 26
Borland, Katherine, xvi, 11, 213–28, 233
bóveda (spirits' table), 116–22, *118*, 130, 131
bozal (Afro-Cuban Spanish), 125
Brahms, Johannes, 149–52, *150*, 153, 154n14
Brecht, Bertolt, 221, 228n3
bricoleurs, 259–61, 270
Briggs, Charles L., ix–xix, 2; Bakhtin and, 49; on entextualization, xiii; on genre, 31n3, 37, 48; on response cry, 52–53
Bronner, Simon, 20–21, 29–30, 274n28
Brook, Peter, 49
Brooks, John, 269, 270
Brown, David H., 133n34
Brown, Jayna, 124, 174–75
Brown, Michael, 264
brown commons, 124–25, 175. *See also* BIPOC
Buccitelli, Anthony Bak, xv, 1–12, 15; on ethnic identity, 288; on performance, 140–41, 153; on repetition, 6, 19–31
Buerra, Ramiro, 44
Burke, Kenneth, xv, 7–8, 80–83, 87–93
Butler, Judith, xi, 237; Austin and, 236; Gordon and, xv; on performativity, 3, 281

cajón pa' los Muertos (ceremony), 132n14
Calvino, Italo, 26, 27
Caribbean ritual theater, 39, 43–45, 51, 55–56
Carlos, John, 11, 258–64, 271
carnivalesque, 172–73
Carrasco, Manuela, 188
Cashman, Ray, 281
Castañeda, Quetzil, 63, 64
Castile, Philando, 129, 264
Catholicism, 44; Espiritismo and, 119; Islamic elements in, 125
Cauthen, Joyce, 82–84
Chapelle, Dave, 258

Chapin, Harry, 81
Chicanx, 181–86, 189
Chicanx flamenco, xvi, 10, 179–89
Chilimika dance, 237
Chopin, Frédéric, 144–49, *146*, 151
Citron, Marcia, 151
classism, 47, 53–56. *See also* intertextuality
Cochran, Robert, 260
Coffee Strong punk show, 11, 235, 243–52
Cohen-Cruz, Jan, 220–21, 228
Colbert, Soyica Diggs, 19
colonialism, 10, 48–49, 61, 105; Fanon on, xii–xiii; settler, 163–64; traumas of, 41, 53–54
Columbian Exhibition (1893). *See* World's Columbian Exposition
comedy clubs, 140, 258
community theater, 213–28
Comstock, Anthony, 164, 168
Concilio, Arielle A., 196, 206n14
Coney Island exotic dancer trials, 9–10, 161, 168–76
La Conga Portuguesa (spirit), 125
"El Congo de Guinea" (song), 8, 116, 121–27, 132n13
Conjunto Folklórico Nacional (Cuba), 44
contextualism, 79
convivencia (coexistence), 50
coochee-coochee dancers, 9–10, 161, 168–76
copresences, 105–6
Costello, Adjie, 162, 171, 172, 173–76
country music, 83, 88
COVID-19 pandemic, 10, 104–5, 108, 209n52, 223
Crenshaw, Kimberlé, 238–39
Crowley, Daniel, 282
Cuban music, 43–45
Cuban Revolution (1959), 43, 44
"cuir," 208n32
Culin, Stewart, 163
Cumachela (Orisha), 51, 52
cyborgs, 99–100

dancing, 9–10, 166, 286; Chilimika, 237; coochee-coochee, 9–10, 161, 168–76; flamenco, xvi, 10, 179–89; folk, 164–65; Malawi, 237; rumba, 50, 124, 127; tango queer, xv, 10, 194–205
Danowski, Kit, xv, xvii, 8, 99–113, 115

danse du ventre (belly dancing), xvi, 9–10; in New York City, 161, 168–70; at World's Columbian Exposition, 161, 162–68, 169–71, 176
Dante Alighieri, 61
Davis, Tracy, 3
Dawkins, Richard, 142, 153n2
Dean, Tim, 165
"death drive" of social order (Edelman), 66
de Beauvoir, Simon, 62
de Certeau, Michel, 28–29, 149
decolonization, 55, 75
Dégh, Linda, 24
Deleuze, Giles, 31n4
Del Negro, Giovanna, 28.30, 262, 266
Denton, Dora, 174, 176
Dewey, John, 23, 32n4
dialogism, 48–49, 53, 56n6
diffraction theory, 101
disidentification, 111, 162, 175, 176
Disneyland, 284–86, 287
Disney World, 163, 284
distinctive-other tradition, 62–63, 65–66, 73
divination rituals, 43, 44, 133n34
Dobler, Robert, 280
Docampo, Mariana, 194–99, 202, 205, 207n29
Douglas, Mary, 265, 268, 270
Douglass, Frederick, 270
Dragún, Osvaldo, 44
drumming, 39, 51, 52; dance and, 10, 179–80; spirit possession and, 104
Dundes, Alan, 56n3, 260, 273n19
Durant, Kevin, 267

Eagleton, Terry, 24, 173
Edelman, Lee, 64, 66
Eleggua (trickster Orisha), 109–10, 112
Enciñias family, 183–84, 187–88, 191nn18–20
Enlightenment philosophy, 109, 111
entextualization, xiii, 49, 64, 80
Espiritismo, 8, 43–45, 101, 104–8; Afrolatinidad and, 117–19; Black spirits of, 119; Catholic elements in, 119; contiguous traditions of, 116; good works in, 122; spirit guides in, 121
Espiritismo cruzado, 127
Espírito Santo, Diana, 120, 130
ethnic identity, 287–88; "ethnic drag" and, 175; gender and, 214; performing of, 10, 175

ethnography, 7; auto-, 101; of dancing, 166–67; definitions of, 62; of listening, 216; of sensory responsiveness, 213. *See also* anthropology
ethnomusicology, 40, 43, 79–93
eugenics movement, 40–41
Everett, Holly, 291
everyday life, 30, 43–45, 234, 236, 237; de Certeau on, 28–29; genealogies of, 37–39, 54–55; Lefebvre on, 28; Mayer-García on, 7; norms of, 60; universalizing paradigms of, 45–50

Fanon, Frantz, xii–xv, 63, 132n8
Feintuch, Burt, 79
feminism. *See* gender issues
Fernandez, Alexander, *117*
fiddle tunes, xv, 7–8, 81–93
Flagler, Moriah, 230n15
flamenco, xvi, 10, 179–89
Flamenco Festival Internacional (FFI), 180, 182, 191n23
"Flop-Eared Mule" (fiddle tune), xv, 7–8, 81–93
folklore, 279, 294n2; Bauman on, 140; Beckwith on, 260; de Certeau on, 29; digital, 140–42; ethnomusicology and, 40, 43, 79–93; as genre, 22; Jakobson on, 21; literature versus, 21, 31n2; performance of, 2–3, 21, 79, 140; Tolkien on, 32n6
folkloresque, 25, 32n5, 165
folkloristics, 22, 153, 213, 274; lesbian, 75; social critique and, 251–52, 259
Foote, Kenneth, 294n2
Foster, Michael Dylan, 25, 27–28, 32n5, 165
Foster, Susan Leigh, 216
Foucault, Michel, 165–67, 239
Francisca (Congo spirit), 124, 126, 127
Freire, Paolo, 216
Freud, Sigmund, 89
Fuellda León, Gerardo, 44
futurism, 66, 71, 108

Gabbert, Lisa, xvi–xvii, 12, 279–94, 297
Garner, Eric, 264
Gates, Henry Louis, Jr., 103, 110, 112
Gathering of the Nations Pow Wow, xvi, 10, 179–81, 184–89
gaze, 40, 280; Orientalist, 173, 175–76; white, 162

gender issues, 3, 47, 53–56, 238–39; beauty contests and, 240; classical music and, 148; domestic chores as, 241; ethnicity and, 214; femicide as, 54; glitch feminism as, 102, 111; machismo and, 53, 54; nonbinary, 102, 108–13; race and, 169, 174; tango and, 195–205. *See also* intertextuality; LGBT
gender-neutral Spanish, 196, 208n32
genealogies of performance, 37–39, 43, 54–55
genre, 30, 83; Bauman on, 22, 48, 49; form and, 81; intertextuality of, 31n3, 48; transculturation and, 50
Georges, Robert, 3, 279, 281
ghost bike memorials, 280
Giddens, Anthony, 22
Giles, David, 286
Gilman, Lisa, xiv, 11, 234–52, 257
gitanos. *See* Rom people
GI Voice (organization), 243, 253n4
Glassie, Henry, 292–93
Glenn, John, 102
glitch art, 102, 111, 113
glitching, xvii, 8, 99–113; definitions of, 99, 102–3; history of, 102–3; spirit possession and, 100
Goffman, Erving, 45–47, 133n36; Bakhtin and, 6, 37, 38, 45, 55; Bateson and, 3; Bauman and, 22; on dramaturgical approach, 140; on response cries, 52–53, 63, 267, 268, 274n74; social interaction theory of, 39, 53, 236, 237; on "totalizing institutions," 285–86
Goldstein, Diane, 165
Gómez, Sara, 44
Gonzales, Rodolfo "Corky," 187
González, Tomás, 44
Gordon, Sarah M., xv, 7, 60–75, 77
gospel music, 78, 79
Gray, Mary L., 64
Griego, Vincente, 179–80, 188
Grotowski, Jerzy, 49
Grounds for Resistance (documentary), 243–44
Gualtieri, Sarah, 163–64, 175
gypsies. *See* Rom people

Haddon, A. C., 62
Hafler, Earl "Pop," 79
Halberstam, J. Jack, 62–63, 67, 68
Hamera, Judith, 1–2
Hansen, Gregory, xv, 7–8, 78–93, 96

Hawthorne, Julian, 163
Hebdige, Dick, 251
Heddon, Deirdre, 220
Heidegger, Martin, 33n9
Hernandez, Jillian, 162
Hernández, Luisa Josefina, 44
Hernández Espinosa, Eugenio, 39, 44, 50–54
heteroglossia, 48
heteronormativity, 60, 62, 66, 202; Gilman on, 238; Lanser on, 241
heterosexism, 50, 53, 64, 147, 173, 238–39. *See also* gender issues
Highmore, Ben, 24
Hispanics, 181–84, 189, 191n17
Hong Kong, 142
hooks, bell, 237
Hucks, Tracy, 132n11
Hughes, Langston, 65
Hurston, Zora Neale, 7, 56n2, 65
Hyltén-Cavallius, Sverker, xvi, 9, 157, 161–76
Hymes, Dell, ix, xv, 37, 80, 88

Ikú (Orisha of death), 51
image macros, 142
imperialism, 61
impostor syndrome, 69
improvisation, 216, 226
Indigenous peoples, xvi, 44, 181; Bear River Massacre of, 291–92; cosmologies of, 109; Espiritismo and, 119; Gathering of Nations Pow Wow of, xvi, 10, 179–81, 184–89; research paradigms of, 66–67; transculturation and, 42. *See also* BIPOC
Ingraham, Laura, 267–68
initiation ceremonies, 106, 107
intersectionality theory, 53, 55–56, 238–39, 246–47, 250
intersectional landscapes, 287–88, 294n2
intertextuality, 27; of genre, 31n3, 48; of memes, 143, 153n3
Iraq Veterans Against the War (IVAW), 249, 253n7
Iraq war, xiv, 244, 250
Islam, 126, 133n21; Catholic elements in, 125
Iwabuchi Koichi, 25

Jabbar, Kareem Abdul, 273n11
Jabbour, Alan, 78–82, 85–87, 91–92
Jabbour, Karen, 86

Jackson, J. B., 280
Jacobs, Tessa, 219
Jakobson, Roman, xv, 21, 22–24, 31n2
James, LeBron, 267
January 6th riot (2021), 239–40
Jarmakani, Amira, 164, 165
jazz music, 80, 82
Jenkins, Henry, 149
Jenkins, Malcolm, 268–69
Jeyifo, Biodun, 57n8
Johnson, Patrick, 241
joint memeing, 9, 139–41, 148–49
joint storytelling, 9, 140, 141, 152

Kaepernick, Colin, xiv, 11, 258–60, 264–72, 274n30
Kahn, Miriam, 284
Kapchan, Deborah, xvii, 236
Kardec, Alan, 104
Kasson, John E., 172
Kennedy, Charles A., 163
Kenny, Dennis, 73
Kierkegaard, Søren, 6, 19, 20, 23, 32n4
King, Martin Luther, Jr., 262
Kirshenblatt-Gimblett, Barbara, x, xvii, 38, 284
Kress, G., 272n3
Kristeva, Julia, xiii, xv
Kundera, Milan, 26–27

landscapes, 12, 279–94; commemorative, 290–93; interactional, 289–90, 293; intersectional, 287–88; wilderness, 286–87, 294n1
language academies, 48
langue/parole, 21, 47, 139
Lanser, Susan S., 241, 252n1
Lara, Ana Maurine, 124–25, 196
Latinx, 74, 99, 181–86, 189, 214
Lawless, Elaine, 68
Lawrence, David Todd, 68
Learman, Liz, 213
Lefebvre, Henri, 28
legend tripping, 289, 290
León, Argeliers, 44
Lerman, Liz, 11, 222–23, 227, 229n14
LGBT, 60–63, 75, 110, 113, 269; enclaves of, 288; memes and, 148; sports and, 269, 273n19; tango and, 197–98, 208n37. *See also* queer

Liang, Shen, 218
Lim, Eng-Beng, 174
Limón, José, x
Liska, Mercedes, 196, 197, 198, 199
Lisle, Benjamin D., 273n20
Liszt, Franz, 144–48, *146*, 151
Love, Matthew, 258
Lukumí religion, xiv, xvii, 101, 104, 106–13; cosmology of, 109; Martiatu on, 43, 45, 50, 51; Ocha ceremony of, 107–8; Palo practitioners and, 127; *patakins* of, 133n33
lunfardo (Buenos Aires argot), 195

Madison, D. Soyini, 1–2
Madre de Agua, 109
magical realism, 26
Malinowski, Bronislaw, 64
Manzor, Lilian, 41
María Antonia (Hernández Espinosa), 39, 50–54
Mariatu, Inés María, xiv, 7, 37–39, 43–45; on Hernández, 50–54; on transculturation, 49–50
Marschall, Sabine, 121
Martínez-Rivera, Mintzi, 63, 74
Mason, Charlotte Osgood, 65
Mason, Molly, 83
Matory, J. Lorand, 133n27
Mayer-García, Eric, xiv, 6–7, 37–56, 59
McClintock, Anne, 166
McGlotten, Shaka, 66
McNair, Bob, 266, 267, 268
mediums, 104, 116, 119; spirit dolls of, 121; spirit guides of, 107
Melberg, Arne, 23
memes, 240; of classical musicians, 9, 143–52, *146*, *150*; definition of, 139; as digital folklore, 140–43; formats of, 142, 144, 147–48, 154n10; joint, 9, 139–41, 148–49; meta-memes and, 146, 154n8; origin of, 139; performance of, 141, 152–53
Mercer, Nina Angela, 109
meredith, celia, xv, 10, 194–205, 210
metaphrasis, 88
Mexico City Olympics (1968), 11, 258–64, 271
Miller, Perry, 1
"minting money," 61, 75
misa, 104, 121, 132n13; Danowski on, 107–8; Otero on, xvii, 131

Miss Indian World pageant, xvi, 10, 179, 180, 181, 186
Miyazaki Hayao, 25, 32n5
Moore, Katherine, 219
Moore, Robin, 132n15
Morsy, Soheir, 62
Moser, Hans, 32n5
Moten, Fred, 120
mourning work, 131n3
movement training, 221–25
Movimiento Feminista del Tango (MFT), 198, 208n37, 209n51
Muñoz, José Esteban, xi, 2, 124; on disidentification, 111, 162, 175; Edelman and, 66; Gordon and, xv; on race, 162, 175; on sexuality, 66, 67, 69, 195, 201, 203; on transculturation, 41
Murdock, George, 62
Musser, Amber Jamilla, 63
Mustilier Garzón, Hilario, 119

Nakamura, Lisa, 147
Los Nani (musical group), 123, 132n13, 132n16
Napoletano, Chloe, 221–24, 226, 230n16
Narayan, Kirin, 64
Nasrat, Pris, xvi, 9–10
national affect, 162, 170, 172, 173, 174
National Institute of Flamenco (NIF), 180, 186; Gathering of Nations Pow Wow, 185, 189; Yjastros and, 187, 188
national parks, 286
Native Americans. *See* Indigenous peoples
Navajo Nation, 181
nerds, 150, 153
Ness, Sally Ann, 281, 286
New Orleans, 228, 287
Neyelle, Morris, 74
Ngai, Mae, 175
ngangas (cauldrons), 122, 127
Nietzsche, Friedrich, 24, 26–27, 33n9
nonbinary identity, 102, 108–13. *See also* gender issues
Noriega, Jimmy, 11, 225
Norman, Peter, 262, 263
no sé qué, 188, 189
Noyes, Dorothy, 214

Obama, Barack, 243–44
Ocha ceremony, 107–8, 112

Ochún, 130, 133n33
ojubona (godmother), 116, 131n1
Oludumare (Yoruba heaven), 123, 126, 133n33
Olympic Games: Mexico City (1968), 11, 258–64, 271; Tokyo (2021), 269
Olympics Project for Human Rights (OPHR), 262, 273n12
Oñate, Juan de, 183, 190n16
onomatopoeia, 91
opera, 50, 140
órale, 186–87
Orientalism, xvi, 47, 175–76; belly dancing and, 164–68, 170, 171, 173–75; sexuality and, 174
Orishas, 39, 51–53, 109, 110; possession by, 101, 104, 105; spiritualist mass for, 44, 45
Ortiz, Fernando, xiv, 37–39; *Contrapunteo cubano del tabaco y el azúcar*, 40; *Los negros brujos*, 39; on transculturation, 6, 39–43, 49–50
Osaka, Naomi, 268, 269
Oshún (Orisha), 51, 52, 53
Otero, Solimar, xiv, 1–12, 15; on Afrolatinx spirituality, 43–44, 113; on ancestoring, xv–xvi, 8–9, 116–31; *Archives of Conjure*, 107; on dance, 216; on Madre de Agua, 109; on *misa*, xvii, 131

Palo religion, xvii, 45, 50, 101, 104, 106–13; contiguous traditions of, 116; cosmology of, 108–9; Lukumí and, 127
paranoia, 67, 69
Paredes, Américo, 279
parole/langue, 21, 47, 139
Parry, Darren, 292
Parton, Dolly, 88
Peele, Jordan, 133n31
Pellegrini, Anne, 167
Pepe the Frog (meme), 142
Perennial Movement Group, 221–26, 229nn9–11
Pérez, Elizabeth, 133n32
performance, 1–2, 19, 30, 153; aesthetics of, 259; Bakhtin on, 38, 48–49, 55; Bauman on, 63, 68, 92, 141, 214, 226–27; Buccitelli on, 140–41, 153; communications-oriented, 22; definitions of, 235–36; of ethnicity, 10, 175; of folklore, 2–3, 21, 79, 140; of form, 78, 81, 92–93; foundational unit of, 4–5; genealogies of, 37–39, 43, 54–55; Goffman on, 38, 46–47, 55; Kirshenblatt-Gimblett on, 38; as participatory practice, 11, 213–28; power and, 234, 238–43; Schechner on, 22, 37, 140, 226; semiotics of, xvi; of stigma, 165; Taylor on, 22, 54–55
performance studies, 37–39, 234; aesthetic communication approach to, 38; Briggs on, ix, xvii–xviii; broad spectrum approach to, 38; Swain on, 4–5; Taylor on, 2, 54–55; transculturation of, 41–42
performance theories, 19, 140; Bronner on, 20–21; instrumental music and, 79–82; Martiatu on, 43–45; precursors to, 12n2
"performance turn," 1–4, 6–7, 20
"performative commemoratives" (Santino), 280
performative landscapes, 12, 279–94
performativity, 1, 3, 5–6, 237, 281
Petenera (palo ceremony), 191n23
Phelan, Peggy, 31n1, 42
Phillips, Rasheedah, 108
Phillips, Whitney, 147–48
Pocock, J. G. A., 22
police brutality. *See* Black Lives Matter
Poltergeist (film), 103
Pontara, Tobias, 154n5
"potential literature" (Calvino), 26
power, 234, 238–43, 247
pragmatics, 236
Prahlad, Anand, 251–52
prendas (intercessors), 107
Pueblo peoples, 181, 191n16
punk music, 247–48, 253n6

Quashie, Kevin, 130
queer, xv, 7, 60–75, 202; Afrolatinx spirituality and, 99, 103, 105, 109, 113; alienation and, 64; glitching and, 102; Orientalism and, 174; race and, 175, 176; utopia and, 195, 201. *See also* LGBT; tango queer
quihúbole (what's up?), 187–88, 192n27

race, xii–xiii, 19, 53–56, 119; Black Lives Matter and, xiv, 11, 258–61, 264–74; eugenics and, 40–41; Fanon on, 132n8; gender and, 169, 174; Goffman on, 47; hierarchies of, 41, 61; Ortiz on, 39; sexuality and, 175, 176; sports and, 11, 234, 258–272; white supremacists and, 162–64, 238–39. *See also* BIPOC; intertextuality

Raibmon, Paige, 163, 164
Raines law (blue laws), 171
Ramey, Sarah, 221–24, 230n16
La Raza Unida Party (Texas), 183
Reddit, 141, 143–53
Redfield, Robert, 6, 40
Reed, Henry, 81–82, 85–87, 90–92
reggae music, 88
Relmucao, Juan, 210n67
re-manifestation, 130–31
repetition, 283; affective dimensions of, 19–20, 24–28; Auslander on, 20–21, 23; Bronner on, 29–30; Buccitelli on, 6, 19–31; characterizations of, 20; de Certeau on, 29; Deleuze on, 31n4; Kierkegaard on, 6, 19, 20, 23; Melberg on, 23; Schechner on, xv; social networks and, 24; temporality of, 20–24; valuation of, 28–31
response cries, 52–53, 63, 267, 268, 274n74
Reynolds, Diamond, 129
riot grrls (music group), 253n6
ritual performance, 290–93
ritual studies, 3, 235, 282–83
ritual theater, 39, 43–45, 51, 55–56
Rivera-Servera, Ramón, 200, 202, 206n13
Roach, Joseph, 31n1, 42
Roberts, Dorothy, 265–66
Roberts, John W., 56n2
Rojas, Rafael, 39, 56n6
Rom people, 44, 119, 181–82, 184–85
"rootedness," 26
Rott, Hans, 152, 154n14
Rouverol, Alicia J., 229n8
Rubin, David, 259
Rudy, Jill Terry, 3–4
rumba, 50, 124, 127
Russell, Legacy, 102, 111–12
Russom, Gavilán Rayna, 113

sacred/profane, 43, 45, 51
Said, Edward, 165
"Salamale Malekunsala," 126, 133n21
Sandoval-Sánchez, Alberto, 41
Santería, 45, 50, 51, 106, 116
Santino, Jack, 280, 291
Saussure, Ferdinand de, 21
Savigliano, Marta, 206n10, 207n27
Sawin, Patricia, 4–5, 68, 214

Schechner, Richard, ix–xii, 1, 3; Boal and, 213, 216; Borland and, 11; broad-spectrum approach of, 141, 153, 214, 234; Martiatu and, 39, 49; on performance, 22, 37, 140, 226; on performance aesthetics, 259; on repetition, xv; "Restoration of Behavior," 214–15
Schumann, Clara, 151
Schumann, Robert, 150
Schutzman, Mady, 218, 220
Scott, Gertrude, 168–69
séance, 2, 116, 122, 124
Searle, John R., 3
Sedgwick, Eve, 67–69
Seizer, Susan, 7, 73, 75; "Paradoxes of Visibility in the Field," 60–64, 69
senior citizens' movement workshops, 219–27
September 11th attacks (2001), 244
Shabbar, Andie, 111
Shaffer, Tracy Stephenson, 259
Shaw, Caroline, 144
shawl dancers, 179–81
Sherman, Richard, 266
Shifman, Limor, 152
Shippey, T. A., 25, 32n7
Shoshone people, xvi
Shuman, Amy, 165
Sieg, Katrin, 175
Simpsons, The (TV show), 144–45, 153
Sir Gawain and the Green Knight, 25–26, 32n7
Sklar, Diedre, 229n11
Smith, Tommie, 11, 258–64, 271
soccer protests, 269–70
social Darwinism, 164
social interaction theory, 39, 53
social media, 143, 152, 269, 280
social networks, 24, 30
social reality, 46–47
Southwestern Indian Polytechnic Institute (SIPI), 181
spectacular dissent, 11–12, 258–72
spirit guides, 116, 121, 122, 124
spirit photography, 103
spirit possession, 8, 101, 104–8. *See also* Espiritismo
sports, 11, 234, 258–272
Sterling, Alton, 264
Sternbach, Nancy Saporta, 41
Stieler, Joseph Karl, 142
Still Moving ensemble, 219, 226

Stoeltje, Beverly, 11, 235, 240, 242
storytelling, 44; Benjamin on, 31n2; joint, 9, 140, 141, 152; Tolkien on, 25–26
Strathern, Marilyn, 62
surrogation theory, 42
survivance, 186, 189
symbolic interactionist sociology, 3

Tahiti, 284–85
Ta José (Congo spirit), 123, 126, 127, 133n23
tango nuevo, 205n3
tango queer, xv, 10, 194–205. *See also* dancing
Taylor, Diana, 2, 22, 31n1; on cultural memory, 42; on performance studies, 54–55; on transculturation, 42, 49
Teatro Campesino, 184
Teatro Travieso, 11, 225, 229n4
Thompson, Robert Farris, 107
Thoms, William, 260
Ticktin, Miriam, 265
Titon, Jeff Todd, 84
Tlatelolco massacre (1968), 262
Tokyo Olympics (2021), 269
Tolbert, Jeffrey A., 165
Tolkien, J. R. R., 25–26; on folklore, 32n6; writing style of, 32n8
Toshidon festival, 28
tourism, 12n1, 284–88
transculturation, xiv, 40; Mariatu on, 49–50; Ortiz on, 6, 39–43, 49–50; performance studies of, 41–42; Taylor on, 42, 49
transmigration of souls, 122
trans people, 110, 113, 198, 205n52. *See also* LGBT
trickster figure, 109, 112, 270, 274n33
Trump, Donald, 239–40, 266, 267, 268
Tsang, Martin, *117*, 133n35
Tuan, Yi-Fu, 290
Turner, Kay, 75, 140
Turner, Patricia, 56n2
Turner, Victor, ix–xii, 3, 37, 62, 214
Two-Spiritedness, 70

uncanny, 103
Ungar, Jay, 83

universalizing paradigms, 45–50
Urfé, Odilio, 44
usury, 61, 63, 75

Vachris, Anthony, 161, 169, 170, 171–73
Valencia, Sayak, 208n32
Van Gennep, Arnold, 3
van Leeuwen, T., 272n3
Vansina, Jan, 24
Vazsonyi, Andrew, 24
verbal art studies, 213, 215, 261
Vietnam veterans, 244, 252n2
Vincent, Troy, 266
Vizenor, Gerald, 10, 180–81, 186, 189
Vodún (voodoo), 43
von Bulow, Hans, 151
Vonnegut, Kurt, Jr., 27, 109
Vradenburg, Elaine, 243
Vrapanzano, Vincent, 62

Wagner, Cosima, 151
Wagner, Richard, 149–52, *150*, 153
Webber, Sabra, xiv, 11–12, 258–72, 278
Weiss, Margot, 66
Wells, Ida B., 164
white supremacists, 162–64, 238–39. *See also* race
Wiggins, Bradley E., 153n2
wilderness landscapes, 286–87, 294n1
Wilkins, Langston Collin, 63
Williams, Raymond, 272n7
Wilson, Shawn, 66–67, 74
Wirtz, Kristina, 125, 133n26
World's Columbian Exposition (Chicago 1893), 161, 162–68, 169–71, 176

Xicano Power (flamenco group), 187–88

Yao, Xine, 10
Yemayá, 52, 54, *117*
Yjastros (American Flamenco Repertory), 187, 188–89
Yoruba people, 43–44, 106, 109–10
Young, Harvey, 120
Young, Katharine, 9, 140, 141, 152

Solimar Otero is Professor of Folklore and Gender Studies at Indiana University. She is author of *Archives of Conjure: Stories of the Dead in Afrolatinx Cultures* and editor with Mintzi Auanda Martínez-Rivera of *Theorizing Folklore from the Margins: Critical and Ethical Approaches*.

Anthony Bak Buccitelli is Interim Assistant Dean for Graduate Programs, Associate Professor of American Studies and Communications, and Director of the Pennsylvania Center for Folklore at the Pennsylvania State University at Harrisburg—Capital College. He is author of *City of Neighborhoods: Memory, Folklore, and Ethnic Place in Boston* and editor of *Race and Ethnicity in Digital Culture: Our Changing Traditions, Impressions, and Expressions in a Mediated World, Volume One*.

For Indiana University Press

Sabrina Black, Editorial Assistant

Allison Chaplin, Acquisitions Editor

Anna Garnai, Editorial Assistant

Sophia Hebert, Assistant Acquisitions Editor

Samantha Heffner, Marketing and Publicity Manager

Katie Huggins, Production Manager

Darja Malcolm-Clarke, Project Manager/Editor

Dan Pyle, Online Publishing Manager

Michael Regoli, Director of Publishing Operations

Pamela Rude, Senior Artist and Book Designer

Stephen Williams, Assistant Director of Marketing